MW01035931

Critical Perspectives on the Denial of Caste in Educational Debate

This volume represents the first exploration of caste in the field of curriculum studies, challenging the ongoing silence around the issue of caste in education and curriculum theory. Presenting comprehensive critical examination of caste as a category of domination and oppression in the colonial power matrix, chapters confront Eurocentric educational epistemologies which deny the existence and influence of caste. The book examines the impact of such silence in educational policy, praxis, and curriculum, and draws from leading scholars to illustrate the fluidity of power and oppression in the caste system. By challenging historical, cultural, and institutional origins of caste and foregrounding perspectives from outside Western epistemological frameworks, the book pioneers a critical approach to integrating caste in educational debate to interrupt social and cognitive injustices. In so doing, the volume advocates for an alternative, non-derivative curriculum reason, through an itinerant curriculum theory as a path toward the emergence of a critical Dalit educational theory. As such, it makes a vital contribution for scholars and researchers looking to refine and enhance their knowledge of curriculum studies by highlighting the importance of theorizing caste in the role of education.

João M. Paraskeva is Professor at the University of Strathclyde, Scotland. Mozambican-born, he is an award-winning pedagogue and critical social theorist. The critique places him as 'undeniably one of the most acclaimed curriculum theorists in the world today.'

Routledge Studies in Education, Neoliberalism, and Marxism
Series editor Dave Hill
Anglia Ruskin University, Chelmsford and Cambridge, England

Social Haunting, Education, and the Working Class
A Critical Marxist Ethnography in a Former Mining Community
Kat Simpson

Artificial Intelligence in the Capitalist University
Academic Labour, Commodification, and Value
John Preston

Neoliberalism and Public Education Finance Policy in Canada
Reframing Educational Leadership as Entrepreneurship
Wendy Poole, Vicheth Sen, and Gerald Fallon

Progressive Neoliberalism in Education
Critical Perspectives on Manifestations and Resistance
Edited by Ajay Sharma, Mardi Schmeichel, and Elizabeth Wurzburg

State Schooling and the Reproduction of Social Inequalities
Contesting Lived Inequalities through Participatory Methods
Sharon Jones

Towards Rural Education for the Common Good
Resisting Capitalist and Neoliberal Priorities in Rural Schooling in the
United States
Jason Cervone

Critical Perspectives on the Denial of Caste in Educational Debate
Towards a Non-derivative Curriculum Reason
Edited by João M. Paraskeva

Critical Perspectives on the Denial of Caste in Educational Debate

Towards a Non-derivative
Curriculum Reason

Edited by João M. Paraskeva

Routledge
Taylor & Francis Group

NEW YORK AND LONDON

First published 2024
by Routledge
605 Third Avenue, New York, NY 10158

and by Routledge
4 Park Square, Milton Park, Abingdon, Oxon, OX14 4RN

Routledge is an imprint of the Taylor & Francis Group, an informa business

© 2024 selection and editorial matter, João M. Paraskeva; individual chapters, the contributors

Library of Congress Cataloging-in-Publication Data
Names: Paraskeva, João M., editor.
Title: Critical perspectives on the denial of caste in educational debate : towards a non-derivative Dalit curriculum reason / edited by João M. Paraskeva.
Description: New York, NY : Routledge, 2023. | Series: Routledge studies in education, neoliberalism, and Marxism | Includes bibliographical references and index.
Identifiers: LCCN 2023000143 (print) | LCCN 2023000144 (ebook) | ISBN 9780367725105 (hardback) | ISBN 9780367725112 (paperback) | ISBN 9781003155065 (ebook)
Subjects: LCSH: Dalits—Education—India. | Discrimination in education—India. | Caste-based discrimination—India. | Education—Social aspects—India.
Classification: LCC LC4097.I4 C75 2023 (print) | LCC LC4097.I4 (ebook) | DDC 371.826/940954—dc23/eng/20230221
LC record available at https://lccn.loc.gov/2023000143
LC ebook record available at https://lccn.loc.gov/2023000144

ISBN: 978-0-367-72510-5 (hbk)
ISBN: 978-0-367-72511-2 (pbk)
ISBN: 978-1-003-15506-5 (ebk)

DOI: 10.4324/9781003155065

Typeset in Sabon
by Apex CoVantage, LLC

To all of those who have perished under the brutality of the caste system

To Annand Teltumbde and to all of those who resiliently challenged such a 'chamber of horrors'

Contents

List of Contributors Bio   *ix*

A Brief Foreword: On Caste and Curriculum   *xiii*

1 On Caste: Towards Critical, Non-Derivative Caste
   Curriculum Studies   1
   JOÃO M. PARASKEVA

2 Caste: A Division of Labour and Labourers   82
   BHIMRAO RAMJI AMBEDKAR

3 The Caste Context   98
   ANAND TELTUMBDE

4 Archaeology of Untouchability   114
   GOPAL GURU

5 The Word and the World: Dalit Aesthetics as a Critique
   of Everyday Life   133
   ANUPAMA RAO

6 Casteocracy: A Millennium Standard of Merit and Tests   151
   SURAJ YENGDE

7 Reading Foucault's *History of Madness* to Obliterate
   Caste in Hindu-Majority Indian Society   169
   RAJESH SAMPATH

8 Epistemological Untouchability: The Deafening Silence
    of Indian Academics   188
    MURZBAN JAL

9 Critical and Caring Pedagogies: Habermas and
    Ambedkar at the Intersections of Caste and Gender   240
    KANCHANA MAHADEVAN

10 Contextualizing the Emergence of Dalit Studies
    in Indian Academia   272
    GAURAV J. PATHANIA AND K. KALYANI

11 Economic Reservation as Caste and Cultural Power:
    Posing Challenges to Representation, Equality and
    Diversity in Kerala, India   297
    K. V. SYAMPRASAD

    Index   *315*

Contributors Bio

Bhimrao Ramji Ambedkar was an Indian leading Dalit intellectual and political leader of the anti-caste struggle and arguably the most radical Indian thinker. He was the first highly educated, politically prominent Hindu 'untouchable' caste member. He had a leading role in the establishment of the state of India. He was chair of the committee that drafted the Indian Constitution, and Minister of Law and Justice in Jawaharlal Nehru's administration. He graduated from the London School of Economics in 1923 and Columbia University in 1927. While at Columbia, Ambedkar studied with prominent intellectuals such as Edward Seligman, James Shotwell, James Robison, and John Dewey. In fact, John Dewey was Ambedkar's mentor and quite influential in his rationale for social justice and equality. He had belligerent battles with Mahatma Gandhi and Congress. His book "Annihilation of Caste" is a must-read historical treatise for anyone who cares about a free, just, and equal world for all. In this volume, Ambedkar has been framed as a demiurge of the epistemologies from the South. He is also referred to by the nickname 'Babsaheb'—'respected father.'

Gopal Guru is a leading Indian political scientist and social activist. He is the editor of the iconic *Economy and Political Weekly*. Former Professor at Jawaharlal Nehru University and Visiting Professor at Columbia University, Oxford University, and the University of Philadelphia. With an enormous and diverse range of publications, Guru pioneered alternative ways to re-think Dalit reason and theory and advanced unique avenues and strategies in the anti-caste struggle. His chapter in this volume, "Archelogy of Caste," is one of the iconic masterpieces in the field of Caste Studies.

Murzban Jal is a senior fellow at the Indian Council of Social Science Research, New Delhi, India, and one of the most important contemporary Marxist-Freudian and Neo-Marxist theorists on caste. A very prolific intellectual and political scientist, Jal's reason articulates and re-articulates the caste phenomena out of the derivative and abyssal matrix of conventional counter-hegemonic platforms, and in so doing, it provides a powerful path to open the veins of a socially constructed beast that persists historically. With a sublime and refined provocative approach, Jal's "Seductions of Karl Marx, Zoroastrianism: From Antiquity to the Modern Period" *and* "The New Militants" echoes Ambedkar's call to 'educate, agitate and organize.'

K. Kalyani teaches at the Azim Premji University, Bangalore. She was awarded her doctorate degree in Sociology from the Jawaharlal Nehru University (JNU), New Delhi. She has served as a guest lecturer at Sri Venkateshwara College, Delhi University. She served as a core collaborator and resource person for the project *Just Futures Initiative*, Samata Foundation, Nepal. Her ethnographic research has explored different forms and practices of resistance in popular culture, particularly engaging with the question of caste, gender, culture through a subaltern discourse. Her work has been published in several academic journals.

Kanchana Mahadevan is a professor at the Department of Philosophy, University of Mumbai, India. Her areas of teaching and research include feminist philosophy, decolonization, critical theory, and political thought. Her book *Between Femininity and Feminism: Colonial and Postcolonial Perspectives on Care* (Indian Council of Philosophical Research and DK Printworld, New Delhi, 2014) examines the relevance of Western feminist philosophy in the Indian context. Her recent work attempts to situate the care theoretical perspective in the Indian context, with special reference to pedagogical philosophy and nursing practices. She is currently working on the significance of gender in debates on the secular and the post-secular.

João M. Paraskeva – Mozambican-born public intellectual, pedagogue, and critical social theorist. A former literacy, middle school, and high school teacher in Southern Africa. He is currently a full professor at the University of Strathclyde, Glasgow, UK. He was the founding chair of the Department of Educational Leadership and Graduate Program Director of the Doctoral Program in Educational Leadership and Policy Studies at the University of Massachusetts, Dartmouth. Paraskeva championed the post-abyssal turn in the field and the struggle against the epistemicides, advocating an itinerant curriculum approach as the future for the field's theory that needs to embrace the world's epistemological difference and diversity. Through his work, the field has been flooded with a new semantic: epistemicides, reversive epistemicides, radical-critical curriculum river, generation of utopia, curriculum involution, curriculum imparity, curriculum mechanotics, curriculum occidentosis, curriculum exfoliation, curriculum isonomy, curriculum ecology, momentism, curriculum disquiet, theorycide, curriculum abyssality, indigeneoustude, among others. His work has been translated for nations such as South Korea, China, Finland, Greece, Spain, Argentina, Chile, Mexico, Brazil, Angola, and Portugal. His publications include *Conflicts in Curriculum Theory; Curriculum Epistemicides; Towards a Just Curriculum Theory; Curriculum and the Generation of Utopia; Curriculum: A New Comprehensive Reader.* The critique places him as 'one of the most acclaimed curriculum theorists in the world today.'

Gaurav J. Pathania is an assistant professor of Sociology and Peacebuilding at the Center for Justice and Peacebuilding at the Eastern Mennonite University in Virginia. His first book, "The University as a Site of Resistance: Identity and Student Politics" (Oxford University Press, 2018) conceptualizes student resistance in higher education in India. His current research examines the socio-political activism of the South Asian diaspora in the United States. Dr. Pathania is an assistant editor to the *South Asia Research Journal* published by SOAS, University of London. He is also an anti-caste poet and writes poetry on social issues.

Syan Prasad, is a former visiting research fellow at the University of Winchester, where he concluded his Ph.D.—"Oppression, Marginalisation and Education in Kerala: In dialogue with Freire." He is currently Teacher of Foundation Learning at City College, Southampton. He also works as an assistant manager for Dimensions, supporting people with special educational and disability needs; under this capacity, he also mentors staff on principles of equality, diversity, and partnership. He is a reviewer of academic journals such as the *Journal of Critical Education Policy Studies,* with publications in various academic venues.

Anupama Rao is a professor of Middle Eastern, South Asian, and African History and Director of the Institute for Comparative Literature and Society at Columbia University. She has provided some of the sharpest theorizations of the caste system. Her volume "The Caste Question: Dalits and Politics in Modern India" provides crucial arguments to challenge the caste cannon unpacking it in genealogical and geographical epistemological terms. She is coediting "The Cambridge Companion to Ambedkar" with Shailaja Paik.

Rajesh Sampath is an associate professor of the Philosophy of Justice, Rights, and Social Change at the Heller School for Social Policy and Management at Brandeis University, USA, and an award-winning public intellectual. He studied under the French philosopher, Jacques Derrida, the founder of deconstruction. Originally trained in modern continental

European history and critical theory philosophies, he has spent the last few years engaged in comparative philosophical and ethical dialogues on rights, justice, and global sustainable development issues. He has been at the forefront of some of the most shrewd and innovative non-derivative poststructuralist phenomenological and deconstructionist approaches related to the Hindutva-caste system. Sampath's remarkable international scholarship focuses on comparisons of Western philosophy and various philosophical traditions in the Global South. His most recent research and published articles have been on comparative studies of caste and structural racism.

Anand Teltumbde is one of the most—if not the most—prominent contemporary Dalit intellectuals and a human rights leader of the global anti-caste struggle. He is a professor at the Goa Institute of Management, India. In 2020, he was arrested—at Taloja Central Jail, Navi Mumbai—charged with inciting caste-based violence through speeches triggering belligerent, violent clashes and dangerous connections with 'legally' banned, radicalized Maoist groups. He is a prolific intellectual and his volumes "The Republic of Caste" and "The Persistence of Caste" provide a unique and crucial examination of the Anti-caste struggle. According to the United States Commission of International Religion Freedom, Teltumbde 'suffers from various ailments and has reportedly not received adequate medical care.'[1]

Suraj Yengde is one of India's foremost scholars, a social activist, and an award-winning, eloquent public intellectual. He was considered one of the "25 Most Influential Young Indian" by GQ magazine and the "Most influential Young Dalit" by Zee. He is a Senior Fellow at the Harvard Kennedy School, a non-resident fellow at the Hutchins Center for African and African American Research, and was part of the founding team of Initiative for Institutional Anti-Racism and Accountability (IARA) at Harvard University, USA. His work has been translated into different languages. His volumes "Caste Matters" and "The Radical Ambedkar," edited with Anand Teltumbde, provided crucial examinations of what is considered a millenary 'chamber of horrors.'

Note

1. https://www.uscirf.gov/religious-prisoners-conscience/forb-victims-database/anand-teltumbde

A Brief Foreword
On Caste and Curriculum

David Hursh[1]

With the publication and enthusiastic reception in 2020 of Isabel Wilkerson's book *Castes and the Origins of our Discontent*, it is clear that the theory and practices of caste and caste systems still impact how we think about and organize societies today. The book has earned numerous awards and was on the New York Times bestseller lists for months. In addition, Wilkerson has been widely interviewed and featured in the mainstream media, such as Oprah Winfrey's book club, where Winfrey named the book 'her most important book club selection ever' (Apple News, 2020; also Winfrey, 2020). However, the contributors to this critical *oeuvre*—which is the first volume on Caste in the field of curriculum studies—assert that caste systems have never received the in-depth critical analysis it deserves, especially its role in reproducing inequality in education and society, and it has been misinterpreted frequently with race and class.

Therefore, in this foreword, I begin by suggesting that both race and caste systems have been used to produce and perpetuate inequality in society—to solidify an outcaste stratum—and that there are parallels in how caste and race function. Most significantly, both caste and race have been the basis for biological explanations for our unequal educational systems, curriculum frameworks, and society. Both caste and caste systems have a long history in both the eastern and western hemispheres. Caste and caste systems emerged as a theory and practice in ancient times—in fact, as this volume documents, it precedes colonial times—in the area that is now southern India (Ambedkar, Chapter 2; Telumbde, Chapter 3). Slavery began in 1619, though, in what would become the United States, when the first enslaved Africans were brought to the British colony of Jamestown (Hannah-Jones, 2021). However, as contributors of this volume insightfully argue, class, race, and caste are not the same, although they share a few close commonalities. Caste 'is inevitably about caste: class and race smell. However, caste smells differently' (Kapoor, 2021; Paraskeva, Chapter 1).

Both race and caste have provided biological explanations for social inequality, and because they were perceived as biological and as 'natural,' the ideology was not challenged. An example of how this occurred in society, schools, and curricula was the rise of the eugenics movement in the early 1900s, so well-examined in this volume (Paraskeva, Chapter 1). Eugenicists asserted that intelligence was largely inherited and, therefore, the intelligence of a population could be improved by selectively mating people who had similar, desirable hereditary traits—i.e., intelligence, while leaving behind those who were less intelligent (Galton, 1892; see also Paraskeva, Chapter 1).

In education—and in the curriculum field (Selden, 1999; Paraskeva, 2016, 2021, 2022b), eugenicists argued that students should be sorted into the appropriate academic and career tracks that reflected their 'probable destinies' based on their scores on intelligence, or IQ, tests. David Snedden (1921), a powerful Massachusetts commissioner of education, justified placing students in different ability tracks based on whether they were to be 'leaders' or 'followers.' (Paraskeva, 2022a) Thus, tracking perpetuated and exacerbated inequality. At the same time, progressive educators like John Dewey (1916) and others—some of them framed by Paraskeva (2021) as a radical, critical river within a generation of utopia—since then have continually pushed back against testing and sorting, arguing that schools needed to teach all students to develop their capabilities (Dabhoiwala, 2022) and 'flourish' in society (Ryan et al., 2023).

However, over the last century, race and racial differences (like ethnicity, gender, sexual orientation, and class) have been increasingly perceived not as biological but as ideological and socially constructed. Because these concepts are socially constructed, race and caste (and gender, ethnicity, sexual orientation, and class) can be deconstructed and dismantled. The contributors to this book—from diverse epistemological rivers from the South, as Santos (2018) would put it—have begun the process of dismantling the caste system—and its 'uniqueness'—and arguing for reforms in education and curriculum as well. As they argue—and rightly so—caste, race, and class, although intertwined, have an idiosyncratic relative autonomy.

Furthermore, some scholar-activists, such as Tolteka et al. (2019), argue that race should be replaced by ethnicity. Yet others, such as Gilroy (2000), argue that race should not be replaced but eliminated. In my own travels in 1999 to the post-apartheid Republic of South Africa, some of the government officials I met argued that their society was post-racial and, therefore, they desired to eliminate language, actions, and attitudes that highlighted race. When one member of a group with whom I was meeting asked for a photo that included only Black men, a diplomatic uproar ensued that required an official apology to the newly formed government (Hursh, 1999).

However, as I have argued, race—ideologically, historically, and materially—has been used to create our current inequalities. Not acknowledging the power and discourse about race within society will not make it go away (Hursh, 1999, 2000). Instead, to those who want to ban discourses about race, I have argued that we cannot avoid discussions about race. For others, such as Wilkerson (2020), reducing racial inequality is not that difficult. However, as this book teaches us, neither caste system can be reduced to racial problems, nor race dynamics are enough to lay bare the inequality that plagues humanity. Wilkerson simplistically reduces caste to race and asserts that those in the lowest castes can rise just by adopting the language, clothes, and mannerisms of the middle class (Gidla & Horn, 2021). She ignores the different ways in which structural and systemic casteism and racism constrain people in poverty. Boo (2014), in her book on underclass children growing up in Mumbai, describes how children of the 'untouchable' caste survive by sorting through rubbish piles, looking for aluminum foil, glass, and other 'valuables' to sell. We must start openly engaging in debates on caste as well. What Paraskeva's volume brilliantly documents is that, in certain parts of the world and in certain communities—what decolonial scholars call the Global South (Santos, 2014)—the basic category of discrimination is not race, but caste, a category that, despite showing some similarities with race, has very different roots and matrices.

Caste and race ignore the effects of structural racism and class, which leaves Wilkerson and others to blame racism on the attitudes of 'lower-class whites.' Similarly, Amartya Sen (2022), in his new autobiography, describes how, as a child growing up in one of the wealthiest families in India, he navigated schools, universities, and careers without having to worry about income (Dabhoiwala, 2022). Sen does not adequately acknowledge the advantages gained by his unearned privileges in a system of structural casteism and racism.

Paraskeva's *Critical Perspectives on the Denial of Caste in Educational Debate: Towards a Non-derivative Curriculum Reason* is a very timely and precious volume. The volume introduces Critical Caste Curriculum Theory (CCCT), a crucial, non-derivative itinerant river to what Paraskeva (2022a; 2022b) terms a 'just conversation' against the epistemicidal nature of the curriculum field. In his words 'CCCT is obsessed with "touchability," and places Dalit reason at the core of the anti-caste struggle through education and curriculum, provoking a co-habitus of both sides of the line.' Contributors of this volume challenge the 'eugenic' silence on caste in the field of education and curriculum and the erroneous impulses to reduce caste and the caste system to a racial category. The volume provides the beginning of a serious examination of the intersectionality of caste, race, gender, and class, unpacks their relative autonomy, and how inequality, poverty, and segregation continue to be produced and perpetuated. The volume helps to unpack how the anti-caste struggle in our field is also a struggle against epistemological untouchability.

Note

1. *University of Rochester, U.S.A.*

References

Apple News. (2020, August 4). Oprah Winfrey names Caste: The origins of our discontents her most important Book Club selection ever.

Boo, K. (2014). *Beyond the beautiful forevers: Life, death, and hope in a Mumbai undercity.* New York: Random House.

Dabhoiwala, F. (2022, December 8). Becoming Amartya Sen. *New York Review of Books.*

Dewey, J. (1916). *Democracy and education.* New York: Macmillan.

Galton, F. (1892). *Hereditary genius: An inquiry into laws and its effects.* London: Macmillan.

Gidla, S., & Horn, A. (2021). Caste, race, and class. *New Left Review, 131,* 9/10.

Gilroy, P. (2000). *Against race. Imagining political culture beyond that color line.* Cambridge, MA: Harvard University Press.

Hannah-Jones, N. (2021). *The 1619 project: The new origin project.* New York: One World.

Hursh, D. (1999). The struggle for democracy in South Africa: Race, history, and education, *Theory and Research in Social Education, 27*(1), 104–110.

Hursh, D. (2000). Rejoinder to Napie, Lebeter and Zungu. *Theory and Research in Social Education, 27*(1), 451–453.

Kapoor, S. (2021). The smell of caste: Leatherwork and scientific knowledge in colonial India. *South Asia: Journal of South Asian Studies, 44*(5), 983–999.

Paraskeva, J. M. (2016). *Curriculum epistemicide.* New York: Routledge.

Paraskeva, J. M. (2021). *Curriculum and the generation of Utopia.* New York: Routledge.

Paraskeva, J. M. (2022a). *Conflicts in curriculum theory* (2nd ed.). New York: Palgrave Macmillan.

Paraskeva, J. M. (2022b). *The curriculum. A new comprehensive reader.* New York: Peter Lang.

Ryan, R. M., Reeve, J., Kaplan, H., Matos, L., & Cheon, S. H. (2023). Education as flourishing: Self-determination theory in schools as they are, and as they might be. In R. M. Ryan (Ed.), *The Oxford handbook of self-determination theory.* Oxford: Oxford University Press.

Santos, B. S. (2014). *Epistemlogies from the South.* Boulder: Paradigm.

Santos, B. S. (2018). *The end of the cognitive empire.* Durham, NC: Duke University Press.

Selden, S. (1999). *Inherited shame.* New York: Teachers College Press.

Sen, A. (2022). *Home in the World. A Memoir.* New York: W. W. Norton & Company.

Snedden, D. (1921). *Sociological Determination of Objectives in Education.* Philadelphia: J. B. Lippincott Company.

Tolteka, C., Zavala, M. Sleeter, Ch. And Au, W. (2019). *Rethinking Ethnic Studies.* Milwaukee: Rethinking Schools.

Wilkerson, I. (2020). *Castes and the origins of our discontent.* New York: Random House.

Winfrey, Oprah. (2020). Oprah's Conversation with Isabel Wilkerson, author of "Caste". Retrieved www.facebook.com/OprahsBookClub/videos/oprahs-conversation-with-isabel-wilkerson-author-of-caste/2394599804178627/

1 On Caste

Towards Critical, Non-Derivative Caste Curriculum Studies

João M. Paraskeva[1]

> *Hindu society is like a multi-storeyed tower with no staircase and no entrance.*
> *Everybody dies in the storey in which they are born.*
> —*(Bhimrao Ramji Ambedkar, 2009)*

Caste is one of the most obnoxious absences within our field's solar system. A graphic example of *Freudian* hysterical blindness, as Murz-Ban Jal (Chapter 8) proclaims. Despite the field's eugenic nature—see, for example, the work of Steve Selden (1999, 2000) and Bill Watkins (1993, 2001)—and while challenged, at the turn of the nineteen century by, among others, intellectuals such as Frederic Douglass and William DuBois, the fact is that caste soon faded from the debates and became a non-issue, a non-existent reality, an egregious absence that was always passing unscathed through the raindrops of the many storms that shook the field. Even within Douglass and DuBois's rich *jouissance*, caste never assumed a substantive centrality—with its complex relative autonomy—as it was equated as class or race, a solid, inaccurate tendency noted in more contemporary approaches, among countless others, by Gunnar Myrdal (1944, 1967), Allison Davis *et al.* (1941),[2] Robert Havingusrt (1945),[3] W. Lloyd Warner (1936), W. Lloyd Warner and Allison Davis, (1939), Davis (1945) Nicholas Dirks (2002), Daniel Immerwahr (2007), Loïc Wacquant (2002, 2022), and Isabel Wilkerson (2020). Undeniably among the historical, hegemonic, and counter-hegemonic, fundamentally Eurocentric debates and struggles for the U.S. curriculum, the absenteeism of caste figures prominently (Paraskeva, 2011, 2021, 2022a). While, on the one hand, it is understandable why the dominant movements did not call on 'caste' as a primary category to be addressed in our field's theory and policy, on the other hand, it is odd that counter-hegemonic groups and movements either completely ignore caste as a substantive, segregated category or blended it with different categories, such as class and 'race, thus undermining caste. The absence of caste is a symptom of a blunt theoretical insufficiency of our field' (Paraskeva, 2021).

DOI: 10.4324/9781003155065-1

This is, arguably, the first book in the field to examine caste not subsumed in race or class but with relative autonomy like any other segregating
and socially constructed category. In doing so, contributors of this volume
provide powerful, non-derivative excavations (Santos, 2014; Walsh and
Mignolo, 2018) of its impact on the dynamics of ideological production
that frames our field and schools (McCarthy and Apple, 1988; McCarthy,
1998; Apple and Weis, 1983). As this work demonstrates, this egregious
and embarrassing silence related to caste in our field reflects much more
than our theoretical frailties; above all, it mirrors the eugenic nature of
a way of thinking and doing science imposed by Eurocentric modernity
that must be seen "as a form of violence trying to impose its order on
society" (Visvanathan, 1997, p. 21). The absence of caste speaks for itself
and constitutes a clear example of the epistemicidal nature of our field,
its history, theory, and research. (Paraskeva, 2011, 2016, 2018a, 2021).
Caste is a harmful institution (Ambedkar, 2016, 2018),[4] a structural pillar of 'segregation,' which I have framed comprehensively elsewhere (Paraskeva, 2022b) as our field's original sin. This sin is intimately related to
the nation's historical-cultural and political-economic master sin, eugenics. Caste, nonetheless, cannot be reduced to a 'pale,' eugenic matrix like
class, race, or gender. The caste system "doesn't embody the eugenics of
modern scientists" (Ambedkar, 2016, p. 241, 2018, p. 19). As this volume
documents, subsuming caste into a class and race category is an egregious
inaccuracy.

   Caste is just one powerful color of a divisive epistemological yarn. It
fosters curriculum epistemicidal sin. Let me now pencil briefly 'eugenics'
historically and its nexus within classed and racialized societies. In doing
so and following the contributors of this volume, I hope I will help clarify
why and how 'caste is caste.'

The Elimination of the Weakest

> *I have no patience with the hypothesis occasionally expressed and often implied,*
> *especially in tales written to teach children to be good, that babies are born*
> *pretty much alike, arid that the sole agencies in creating differences between boy*
> *and boy, and man and man, are steady application and moral effort.*
> —*(Francis Galton, 1892)*

Eugenics—in its multiple and complex metamorphoses—dates back to the
beginnings of human civilization. However, while 'eugenics' was already
overtly floating around since the dawn of Western civilization—specifically,
during the splendor of *Magna Graecia* through magistral oeuvres such as
Plato's (1968) *Republic*—it emerged aggressively in the nineteenth century

in England, coined by Francis Galton (1883).[5] Galton advocates 'pure' genetic and hereditary principles to improve the human race, triggering a "movement in favor of Eugenics scientifically recognized by the Academia and having the University of London as its hub" (Galton, 1883, p. vii; see also, Chitty, 2013).

Galton was profoundly influenced by his cousin's oeuvre, *The Origin of the Species*. Charles Darwin's theory, in Galton's terms, "should not be restricted to the breeding of domestic animals and cultivated plants. What was true for the breeding process in animals was equally true for the way human beings developed?" (Chitty, pp. 354–355; Forrest, 1974; MacKenzie, 1976). It was crucial "to produce a highly-gifted race of men by judicious marriages during several consecutive generations" (Galton, 1892, p. 1). According to him, the development of the human race couldn't ignore "that 'nature' not 'nurture' determined the amount of intelligence that any human being processed" (Chitty, 2013, p. 352). Genius, Galton (1892, p. 6) argues, is thus 'hereditary'—one of the great trump cards of the caste system, as we will see later—with no direct relation to education. Galton's hereditary cult and Cyril Burt's measurability theories blended dangerously. In Burt's thesis, the child's innate intelligence "could be measured with a remarkable degree of accuracy to age 11" (Chitty, 2013, p. 351). Burt and the intelligence movement worked "tirelessly to ensure that the idea of a fixed, innate intelligence entered the public domain" (Chitty, 2013, p. 356), a movement "that had an extraordinary influence on educational decisions and policymaking in the UK" (Chitty, 2013, p. 356)—and, I would add, beyond.

With Galton, one witnessed the emergence and consolidation of a worldwide middle- and upper-class eugenic ideology (MacKenzie, 1976) and assumed patriarchy movement (women were overtly absent from Galton's thesis of genius [Chitty, 2013, p. 355]). He was fundamentally concerned with the "problem of racial deterioration" (Lowe, 1980, p. 1, 1998), an ideology that unleashed all institutional apparatuses available to challenge "the malign propagation of the unfit and the feeble-minded" (Chitty, 2013, p. 355), an ideology that *Darwinistically* openly promoted "the survival of the fittest through the elimination of the weakest" (Chitty, 2013, p. 355)—both eugenic social constructions. This is a core feature of how eugenics emerged in the US and worldwide (see also Sofair, & Kaldjian, 2000).

Influenced by the eugenic tornado in the UK, the cult of "breeding and the uniqueness of white reason" took off in the US at the beginning of the twentieth century, championed by Charles Davenport, Harry Laughlin, Henry Osborne, and others. Osborne (1921, p. 312) argued in the US that "we are slowly waking to the consciousness that education and environment do not fundamentally alter racial values. In the matter of racial virtues, my opinion is that from biological principles, there is little promise in the melting-pot theory." Soon, the nation saw the emergence of an endless multitude of academic-based scientific societies deeply committed to the science of racial cleansing to 'whiten' humanity, a movement that showed close connections with the Nazi *Mendelian* 'final solution.' Race improvement implied race annihilation (Davenport, 1923; Davenport and Laughlin, 1915).

Deeply influenced by Francis Galton's claim of racial hygiene (Selden, 1999), and with substantial financial resources—Rockefeller Foundation, the Carnegie Institution of Washington (1939)—and solid political capital, scientists such as Charles Davenport, Harry Laughlin, Harry Crampton, Madison Grant, Henry Osborn, and Helen Dean King, to mention a few, were able to influence public policy fearlessly and openly at the federal and state levels. Naturally, such scientific momentum paved the way for racialized immigration policies (Selden, 1999), miscegenation was outlawed in states such as Virginia, sterilization became the law in 14 states, and the criminal wave of racial purity flooded the educational and curriculum field. It is "impossible to understand the history of educational and social policy without understanding the powerful effects of the popularization of Mendelian-inspired science" (Apple, 1999, p. 304).

Shockingly, the purpose of creating a superior, Nordic race, Edwin Black (2003, p. 15) argues, wiping out whole ethnic groups, "was fought not by the armies with guns nor by hate sects at the margins. Rather, this pernicious white-glove war was prosecuted by esteemed professors, elite universities, wealthy industrialists, and government officials colluding in a racist pseudoscientific movement called eugenics." To perpetuate such a saga, he (2003, p. 15) adds, "widespread academic fraud combined with almost unlimited corporate philanthropy to establish the biological rationales for persecution." With the blessing of academia, eugenic scientists employed "a hazy amalgam of guesswork, gossip, falsified information, and polysyllabic academic arrogance, and slowly constructed a national and juridical infrastructure to cleanse America from its 'unfit'" (Black, 233, p. 15). It was an era during which science and its multifarious fields—education and curriculum, inclusively—witnessed the flood of "specious intelligence tests, colloquially known as IQ tests, invented to justify the incarceration of a group labeled 'feebleminded'" (Black, 2003, p. 15). In eugenic, scientifically and legally rubber-stamped terms, so-called feebleminded individuals "were just shy, too good nature to be taken seriously, or simply spoke the wrong language, or were the wrong color" (Black, 2003, p. 15). Eugenicists looked upon sterilization as the scientific answer to interrupt, reverse, and correct such an 'erroneous' course of humanity. Education and curriculum saw the authentic epistemological colors of such malaise, acting dynamically within such new, needed commonsense.

As Steven Selden (1999) documents, the influence of this malady runs through the entire thought, work, and action of the demiurges in our field. He unpacks how leading educators and curriculum figures, such as Edward Ross, Stanley Hall, and Edward Thorndike, were strong supporters of eugenics. While the latter was "a conservative hereditarian who acknowledged the influence of Francis Galton's in his work and was a member of the American Breeders Association" (Selden, 1999, p. 73) and Stanley Hall was quite "supportive of a better society through breeding" (Selden, 1999, p. 72), Edward Ross "accepted the necessity of sterilization legislation" (Selden, 1999, p. 71).

Another important curriculum figure who openly endorsed the eugenic movement was Charles Eliot. He served "as Vice-President of the First International Congress of Eugenics in London (1912), the first such gathering of scientists, educators, and opinion leaders to explore the growing field" (Lombardo, 2014, p. 378). Moreover, Charles Eliot "sat on the central committee of the First National Conference on Race Betterment (1914), organized by the eugenically oriented Race Betterment Foundation" (Lombardo, 2014, p. 357). In Charles Eliot's reasoning, eugenics was the master tool to pave the road to prevent and cure human impurity, which caused "antisocial behaviors such as murder, robbery, forgery, and prostitution" (Lombardo, 2014, p. 378).

Notwithstanding our field's eugenic and epistemicidal nature, caste dynamics were never at the epicenter of the struggle for a more just and relevant curriculum. The emphasis in the battle for an appropriate curriculum was on class, race—posteriorly, ethnicity—and gender. Caste's historical and theoretical footprint is sharply different. Caste "prohibits persons belonging to different castes from intermarrying. It is not a positive method of selecting which two among a given caste should marry" (Ambedkar, 2016, p. 239, 2018, p. 17). It cannot be subsumed in other graded dynamics.

Challenging the Invincibility of the 'American Caste'

The void of economic freedom within the struggle for the emancipation of the slave would trigger a distinct labored segregated social construction, that of caste.
—*(William Edward Burghardt Dubois, 1911)*

Naturally, such a cult of racial purity faced resistance and setbacks. Once a solid financial fortress of the eugenic fever, the Carnegie Institution withdrew its support.

Also, Nobel-laureated Thomas Morgan (1925), once an open advocate of eugenics, ended up launching a violent attack on the movement, a movement that he saw working based on ill definitions and concepts, drawing on dangerous assumptions and false and gross perceptions, as well as producing extravagant interpretations of science and reality (Morgan, 1925).

Also, within the quarrels for US education and curriculum, voices were raised against the eugenic juggernaut. US state senator Charles Sumner and pedagogue William E. B. DuBois (1911) provided two good examples. The latter (1911) unequivocally placed caste at the core of slavery emancipation. The main question of freedom, he (1911, p. 303) argued, "was not legal but economic." However, slavery emancipation resulted in a "code of laws in nearly every southern State which granted the Negro nominal freedom but made economic freedom impossible, establishing a distinct laboring caste with restricted rights and privileges of all sorts and no prospect of any political rights at any future time" (DuBois, 1911, p. 305). The void of economic freedom within the struggle for the emancipation of the enslaved person would trigger "a distinct labored segregated social construction, that of caste" (Dubois's, 1911, p. 303).

DuBois's approach echoes the ancestral struggles fought by great black intellectuals who stood out in the battle against slavery, as was the case of Frederik Douglass, Sojourner Truth, and C. J. Walker, among many others. Challenging the "invincibility of the American caste," Frederik Douglass (1845; 1859) framed 'caste'—as a racialized category—at the core of abolitionist activism. Within the agenda of abolitionist leaders, the caste saga in the US, although paralleled with caste struggles in other nations—such as India, China, and Japan, to mention a few—was related to prejudice and bigotry based on skin color. The term 'caste,' in Frederick Douglass's and many abolitionists' words, "stands for the politics of 'race' " (Bressey, 2013, p. 39).

It was advocated that "the only drawback black prosperity is the caste which slavery has thrown in our mindset, and which is a chief minister is the continuance of slavery" (Smith, 1845, p. 29). If there was a site crucial in the struggle against eugenics in the US, such a site was/is public education. Questioned about "what was more important to the Black freedom struggle: the ballot or the book," Frederick Douglass (1845, p. 4) unequivocally stated books; he saw education as the 'tool' to dismantle the racialized, casteized system in the US—"there are 13,675 colored men above 21 years of age in the State of New York, while there are 15,778 colored children of school-going age. Contact on equal terms is the best means to abolish caste: it is abolished" (Burkholder, 2021, p. 13). US caste dynamics was (and still is)—eugenically—framed as only a class and racial matter.

The "1846 Report of the Minority of the Committee of the Primary School Board on the Caste Schools in the City of Boston" is another example of how racial struggles were defined in caste terms. The Committee addresses a "petition of sundry-colored citizens, praying for the abolition of the separate schools for colored children and their admission into the Common Schools" (Jackson, 2019). The Board "has decided that children of colored parents shall be excluded from the schools generally and shall be sent to separate or caste schools" (Jackson and Bowditch, 2019, p. 4). The committee, however, argues that "the principle of perfect equality is the vital principle of the system" (Jackson and Bowditch, 2019, p. 6), and advocates that "the colored man, as any other citizen, has the right to send his child to the nearest school [and] his race or color is an unlawful and inhuman reason for restraining his right of choice." (Jackson and Bowditch, 2019, p. 7). What is important to understand in this Minority Report—beyond the eugenic nature of the schooling system in the United States—is how the racial issue linked to the matrix of slavery is debated in terms of 'caste.' Erroneously, the words 'caste' and 'race' were used invariably and taken to be perfect synonyms.

US Senator Charles Sumner (1990b, p. 204) also stresses that "slavery itself revived in the spirit of Caste." He (1845, p. 161) argues that "the New Bedford Lyceum has undertaken within its jurisdiction to establish a distinction of *Caste* not recognized before." It was crucial, he stresses, to understand that, while it is essential to commit to an "utter and complete *extirpation* of Slavery from the soil of the Republic, that can only be accomplished only by the eradication of every inequality and caste, so that all shall be equal before the law" (Sumner, 1900b, p. 211).

Public education was viewed as a "sacred cause to help a distressed part of the population, an endowment for the equal benefit of all, without distinction of caste" (Sumner, 1900b, p. 318). Public education "must be open to all, without distinction of color. Should any persons be shut out from this right on the wretched apology of color, I trust they will make their indignation felt by the guilty authors of the outrage" (Sumner, 1990a, p. 269).

Education was the only "cure for such hurdles" (Holmes, 1939, p. 352). It is interesting to notice, though, that segregationists and abolitionists target education—particularly public education and curriculum—as the prime site of struggle. As we can see, caste has always been at the epicenter of abolitionist struggles; however, equated with race and class and, in many cases, replacing race and class, which is a manifest exaggeration and mystification—as this volume tries to deconstruct. Caste cannot be examined as a eugenic equation between whites and blacks. This is an error. A historical and theoretical absurdity. It deracializes the bloody, racialized US history and deforms and distorts theoretically and historically the caste system that is not just a eugenics issue.

Over a century went by, however, and as the historic developments during the past and present centuries throughout the world demonstrate, the perseverance of the eugenic cult is undeniable. It is in this context that one needs to situate publications such as Charles Murray and Richard Herrnstein's "The Bell Curve," the normalization of racialized brutality by the police against African Americans in the US, the rampant reemergence of Nazi impulses throughout the world, and, more recently, the ferocious attacks on Critical Race Theory in schools and curricula—within and beyond academia. Eugenics indeed pressed the reset button.

However, odd as it might be, despite such eugenic, aggressive resurgence pretty much around the world and from a multitude of angles, the problem of caste—as a crucial dynamic within the eugenic puzzle—keeps enjoying a monumental 'non-existence,' as Boaventura de Sousa Santos (2014) would put it, particularly in our field; such absence, I reiterate, defines the depth of the eugenic, epistemological nature of our field. That we have subscribed to this absence—in most cases, inadvertently, I admit—should stop us from thinking about endless other wants that we are producing in our theoretical incursions. These absences cause a silence so 'cacophonic' (Bal, Chapter 7) that it should embarrass us all. It is undeniably clear that the 'phenomenality of the phenomenon' of caste—as Jacques Derrida (1973, 1976) would phrase it—is radically different from other eugenic carburetors—such as class, race, or ethnicity—that structure the matrix of a particular form of humanity only conceivable through its sub-humanity (Paraskeva, 2016, 2021, 2022; Santos, 2018), a sub-humanity that precedes modern, Western Eurocentrism and dates back to ancient times. Caste metamorphosis different and diverse 'habitus and dispositions,' as Pierre Bourdieu (1980, 1984) would have argued. The caste system is the irrefutable evidence that there is no single form of domination and oppression (Santos, 1999)—an erroneous assumption through which too many critical and post-critical Eurocentric approaches structure and frame the struggle for US education and curriculum. It is thus a mistake to reduce caste to mere class and race dynamics; that is, to "de-historicized caste dialectically" (Teltumbde, 2010).

Caste cannot be 'exfoliated'—as José Gil (2018) would have certainly put it—only in Eurocentric epistemological terms. Anti-colonial and decolonial perspectives place caste as an egregious sociological absence—a decolonial and anti-colonial procedure that "unveils whatever social and political conditions, experiments, initiatives, conceptions have been either successfully suppressed or not allowed to exist" (Santos, 2001, p. 13). Caste, while a eugenic system before the Empire, isn't out of coloniality though, as it "intersects with capitalist modernity and its science" (Kapoor, 2021, p. 985). In fact, under coloniality's consulate, caste acquired an almost impassable armor, mercilessly continuing to slaughter millions of individuals. Under the current, neoliberal yoke, caste experienced a powerful blood transfusion (Teltumbde, 2010, 2018; Syamprasad, Chapter 11).

In our field, caste constitutes what I have called elsewhere (Paraskeva, 2018b) a double scandal. That is, it is either out of the table of the so-called commonsensical celebratory curriculum-complicated conversations—itself eugenic, as well as Dwayne Huebner (2021, 2022) insightfully denounced—or subalternized and subsumed in categories such as race and class—a blunt double-scandal; both scenarios constructed caste as a 'sociological absence' (Santos, 2014)—a refined eugenic spice. Such scandal echoes and escalates Eduardo Bonilla-Silva's (2003) pointing critique of '[casteism] without [cateists].' 'Casteism' without 'casteists' deracializes racism and declassizes classism.

Such double scandal speaks volumes to what I have termed theoretical atrophy framing our field, which fosters a curriculum involution and imparity (Paraskeva, 2021, 2022a, 2022b). In an era marked by the so-called internationalization of the field (Paraskeva, 2015), such absence and silence remain awkward. Like race, caste kills. It does, and today, in many nations, it kills more than the recent COVID-19 or the bloody 'military intervention' in Ukraine. Unquestionably suicide numbers among Dalit students are obscene (see, Senthilkumar Solidarity Committee, 2008); Suicide has become a form of struggle (Pathania and K. Kalyani, Chapter 10).

Whose Caste, Anyway!

> As long as caste in India does exist,
> Hindus will hardly intermarry or have any social intercourse with outsiders
> and if Hindus migrate to other regions on earth,
> Indian caste would become a world problem.
> —(Bhimrao Ramji Ambedkar, 1979)

Caste is inevitably about caste: class and race smell. However, caste smells differently (Kapoor, 2021). How "did caste originate in India? How did Hindu society originate?" When? Who did it? Why? From a traditional theoretical point of view, I argue that, for Hinduism, in the beginning— whatever it was—it was the Purusha Hymn of the Rig-Veda, 'thy' hymn that describes the creation of Castes,[6] a hymn that places the Brahmans within the perpetual bubble of purity. Indeed, in Book X, Hymn 90, verses 11–12, "an account is given to the creation of the four castes from the body of the great god Purusha" (Cox, 1959, p. 85). Conjeevaram Hayavadana Rao (1931) describes such a hymn:

> When they divide the Purusha into how many parts do they divide him? What was his mouth? What were his arms? What were his thighs and feet called? The Brahman was his mouth, of his arms, the Rajanya was made; the Vaisyas were his thighs; the Sudra sprang from his feet.
> (Rao, 1931, p. 53)

Traditionally, Rig-Veda designed, established, and consolidated a clear stratification between the Brahmans—an example of purity and superiority— and the Warriors or Agricultural—an instance of dirtiness (Rao, 1931; Cox, 1959; Dumont, 1970). Such a divine matrix "is as limited as that without elaboration, or further explanations it stands in stark finality, one of the most powerful bits in Hindu philosophy" (Cox, 1959, p. 86), conferring to the Brahmans s "superior privileges and inviolable condition" (Dumont, 1970, p. 24); a system of oppression constructed out of religious impulses and, since its beginning, that is at "the end of the seventeenth century the question of whether caste is, in essence, religious or simply 'social' has constantly arisen" (Dumont, 1970, p. 24).

Rig-Veda provided the spiritual legitimacy of a 'needed,' four-fold Varna system of Hinduism, one that "frames the Hindu system of inviolable political stability confining the individuals to occupations handed down immutability from father to son" (Senart, 1930, p. iii). Such 'inviolability' pushes the debate on caste to another level, quite different from class or race. The intolerant pride of the Brahman, Herbert Risley (1892, p. xiv) argues, "rests upon a foundation of fact, that it has shaped the intricate groupings of the caste system and has preserved the Aryan type in comparative purity throughout Northern India." Émile Senart (1930, p. 18) argues that the pivot of such hierarchy "is the recognized superiority of the Brahmanical caste and its numerous branches." Crafting from Célestin Bouglé's canvas (1908), Louis Dumont (1970) states:

> The caste system divides the whole society into a large number of hereditary groups, distinguished from one another and connected by three fundamental characteristics; separation in matters of marriage and contact, wheatear direct or indirect (food); division of labor, each group having, in theory, or by tradition, a profession from which their member can depart only within certain limits; and finally hierarchy, which ranks the groups as relatively superior or inferior to one another.
>
> (Dumont, 1970)

Such a hereditary division of labor—which, as we will see, Babasaheb Ambedkar (2016, 2018) complexifies as a division of laborers—is intimately related to its endemic hereditary and endogamy (Sinha, 1967, p. 94).

The caste system sustains its existence based on the divisive matrix of 'visibilities-invisibilities'—a key feature within all segregation systems that produced (and it was/is produced) irreversible, abyssal lines (see Santos, 2014) within and beyond the Varna system. To bring Guru (Chapter 4) to the debate caste is the abyssal line, a praxis that relates the 'impurity' and 'untouchability' of the Dalits with the 'purity' and 'touchability' of the Brahmins—a conceptual inseparable way of thinking and existing. The casted, Brahman-blessed protectorate not only graded society by drawing clear, abyssal lines between Brahmans, Rajanya, Vaisyas, and Sudras but also, in so doing, concomitantly established another unbeatable abyssal line between the four varnas and "whatever would be the rest." Such a non-monolithic 'rest,' the fifth varna (Pachamas), aka, Untouchables—(Asprushya and Achhuts), low born (Antyja), also referred to as Dalits, scheduled castes, and backward classes—socially tagged as dirty, polluted, smelly, cursed, hopeless, savage primates—constitutes a pluriverse plethora of maculate human beings, whose existence and visibility wasn't blessed and only doable out of the four varnas. Outside the graded bouquet of caste are the *Ati Shudras*, also known as 'Untouchables,' who are forced to perform the most 'polluted' and menial work (Ambedkar, 1989). More to the point, the caste system created an outcaste society. That is, the existence and visibility of the former are established by the non-existence and invisibility of the latter (see Santos, 2014). Leading Dalit intellectual Anand Teltumbde defines untouchability as

> a diverse but distinctive community in India, who are treated unequally in daily life because of the lowest status, according to them, the Hindu social order. At its worst victims, they characterized India's hierarchical caste society at its most essential. They were historically excluded from most social, cultural, religious, and economic situations for over two millennia. Although castes have undergone significant changes in their configuration as well as in their operation, for the majority of the Dalits at the bottom, they continued to be as oppressive as ever.
>
> (Teltumbde, 2018)

The outcasted fifth varna also breeds a divisive and graded matrix. Like the fourth varna, Anand Teltumbde (2018) argues, "it congregates not only castes and sub-castes but also class differences in it"—i.e., segregation. The caste-out-caste system "may be defined by a small number of persons characterized by endogamy, hereditary membership, and a specific style of life which sometimes includes the pursuit by a tradition of a particular occupation and is usually associated with a more or less distinct ritual status in a hierarchical system" (Béteille, 1965, p. 46). That is, castes "who are of different origins are also of different nature. One caste forbids the remarriage of widows; another permits it; one permits its members to accept food from certain outsiders; another forbids such acceptance from anybody but a caste fellow; in other parts of India, the same or similar castes are regarded as conveying pollution not only by touch but by mere proximity" (Blunt, 1969, p. 1).

Caste is an ancient Hindu institution whose origins go back to the second century BCE, when it was "legally codified in Manusmruti" (Thorat, 2020, p. ii); an institutionalized segregation matrix that tore apart society into five major castes—and endless sub-castes—a "system that laid down a legal and normative logic," as Walter Mignolo (2018, 2022) and other anti-colonial and decolonial intellectuals frame it—"to govern all aspects of the society, namely, cultural, economic, religious, spiritual, and political" (Thorat, 2020, p. ii). Such deplorable logic that "regenerates silently, secretly, and invisibly" (Sampath, Chapter 7) certified perpetually "a moral and legal framework that assigned—in a graded and unequal manner—the right to property, occupation, education and civil and religious right among the castes." Such eugenicist rights frameworks 'among the same' "were fixed in advance and made hereditary by birth and through endogamic lines" (Thorat, 2020, p. ii). At the top of the blessed hierarchy are the immaculate and pure Hindus, who enjoy most of the rights and privileges; and, at the bottom, one sees the "impure and polluting, thus 'untouchable' or unfit for any social interaction except among them" (Thorat, 2020, p. ii). While the former has assigned 'clean' duties in society, the latter was responsible for all "menial tasks of cleaning, scavenging, skinning carcasses, and so on—a stigma associated with them to this day" (Thorat, 2020, p. ii; see also Thorat & Joshi, 2015). Moreover, the 'Untouchables'

> had no right to property, education, or civic rights, except obligatory services to the four castes above them. Thus, the 'untouchables,' or atishudras in Sanskrit, suffer forced isolation and segregation in virtually all spheres of life. The denial of basic rights, fundamental for the social growth of human beings, has had a crippling effect on their psyche, from which they have not recovered for many centuries.
>
> (Thorat, 2020, p. x)

There is no existence out of caste. Thus, the task to open the veins of such a graded system, Bhimrao Ramji Ambedkar (2016, p. 199, 2018, p. xxi) argues, "was not to bring about inter-caste dinners and inter-caste marriages, but to destroy the religious notions on which Caste was founded." The eye of the socially constructed notion of such irreversibility was right at the core of religion in Babasaheb Ambedkar's (2016, 2018) terms. The brutality and slaughtering against the Untouchables "is as old as caste." (Teltumbde, 2018, p. 25)

Caste—like many other eugenic-based dynamics, such as racism, ethnicism, genderism, and classism—is a crime against humanity. Caste is a Republic (Teltumbde, 2018), a hate republic with a hate infrastructure (Teltumbde, 2018, p. 2), a 'neurotic and psychotic' Republic as defined by Murzban Jal (Chapter 8), a resilient eugenic system with no parallel in the written history of humanity—although "caste struggle cannot be seen in isolation from other injustices unleashed across the world" (Teltumbde, 2018, p. 28). Drawing on Freud, Jal (Chapter 8) frames caste a new form of mental illness

> that we call "neurosis-psychosis" (superseding Freud's old ideas of separation of neurosis and psychosis), where all forms of critical thinking

and the development of democratic culture are totally destroyed. For Freud, neurosis indicates the 'eternal return of the self-same trauma,' while, by psychosis, he meant the 'complete withdrawal from reality.' In the system of caste, the neurotic return (of caste) appears again and again, while in the psychotic dimension of caste, a complete detachment from reality is attained. Both the violence and silence that the caste system evokes suggest this neurosis-psychosis and the hysterical blindness emanating thereon, which leads to cultural and ideological hallucination and paralysis.

(Jal, Chapter 8)

As I have argued before, caste entails peculiar habitus—ways of interacting with each other and with the social environment—and dispositions— tendencies, inclinations, and propensities (Bourdieu, 1980); it also implies the embodiment of particular forms of eugenic habitus, which Pierre Bourdieu (1980) calls 'hexia'—gestures, ways of walking, looking, physical posture, stance (Syamprasad, Chapter 11). Oddly, despite being abolished by the Indian Constitution and its practice in any form made punishable under the law amid the cries of 'Mahatma Gandhi ki Jai,' the persistence of caste is irrefutable (Teltumbde, 2018).

Caste is the underlying logic[7] of a given system of domination that fosters a particular cultural and political economy. Cast dynamics crafted a graded social web "in which different forms of capital can be produced and exchanged in favor of the privileged castes" (Syamprasad, Chapter 11). The notion of caste, Arundathi Roy (2016, p. 17) argues, is "never encountered in a single school textbook." Caste is the logic subsumed to a particular—yet not local—system of dominance, a system whose roots go back around 1500/1600 BC and become uplifted and upgraded throughout history, constituting one of the carburetors of coloniality. It is the colossus of segregation. Caste is evil, a harmful institution, a monster that crosses the social sphere, one that blocks any political or economic reform. The task is to kill such a monster (Ambedkar, 2016, 2018). The caste system is perhaps the most complex phenomenon within the world's eugenics orbit. If caste "is the fundamental institution of Hinduism" (Weber, cited in Leach, 1960, p. 2), endogamy "is the only characteristic of caste that is peculiar to caste" (Ambedkar, 1979, p. 4). The caste system is a *Sanskritized* system; it fosters "Sanskritization allowing mobility only within the endogamic graded casted chain, blocking any Westernization which implies mobility outside the framework of caste" (Srinivas, 1962, p. 5). Undeniably, there is a religious spine within the caste system.

As one keeps exploring caste dynamics within the context of the South-Asian continent and from a Global South perspective and clarifies parallels that could eventually be established globally, many aspects immediately come to our attention. The first aspect relates to the appalling persistence (Teltumbde, 2010, 2017) of such divisive '(sub)conscious-surplus' logic. Caste shows remarkable historical adjustability to diverse power structures, incredible adaptability to play within the 'coercive and/or consent' matrix, jazzing creatively with dominance and power structures. While a malaise with medieval roots, caste remains an essential category within the power matrix of coloniality (Quijano, 1992, Mignolo, 2008). Its persistence—one of the defining features, one of the crucial feeders of coloniality—cannot be understood as a part of the *Gramscian* wrangle's hegemony/non-hegemony and 'coercion/consent' (Guha, 1997).

The second aspect that stands out is what I would call—drawing from Byung Chul Han (2018)—the 'cruelty of the identical.' That is, there is a dangerous tendency within particular progressive and counter-hegemonic, Eurocentric platforms to amalgamate class, race, and caste as 'identical'—which is a gross misreading of history—in its ancient and contemporary dynamics. While a division of laborers and not labors (Ambedkar, 2016, pp. 233–236, 2018, pp. 15–17), caste is caste and needs to be dwelled on as such. The way caste has been forcibly 'identicalized' as race and class by modern Western, Eurocentric platforms only reveals a blunt epistemological despotism that dares to create monolithic different oppressive categories and dynamics, regardless of its diverse historical and contemporary metamorphosis. As we will see later, caste is caste, eugenically articulating, re-articulating, and interpolating social relations differently. Intermingling caste with race and class extracts the victims from its factual matrix of oppression, a matrix pillared within specific caste dynamics—hereditary endogamy, for instance.

This monolithic impulse opens the door for another crucial aspect. The condescending nerve of a monocultural Prosperous reason (Henry, 2000) that frames the monumentality of modern, Western, Eurocentric reason that not only dares to determine, define, and label who is who regarding 'the other,' and frame such an 'other' as destitute of the accurate sage to define their deplorable existence, but also fosters egregious epistemological blindness that ignores that intermingling unidentical segregated categories, completely guts the oppressed form of its own peculiar identity and struggles and shows a eugenic reading of caste words and worlds from and within Eurocentric diopters. Moreover, such diopters are at the core of a divisive reading of the historicity of history, a twisted interpretation of crucial conflicts within the caste struggle, and the objective production of concrete 'invisibilities,' thus tainting the 'visibilities' (Santos, 2014). Coloniality—like its predecessors' systems of dominance—is a perpetual wrangle between 'monumentalist' existences/visibilities and 'monumentalist' non-existences/invisibilities.

The fourth aspect deals with the absence of caste in our educational and curriculum debates. As I have been able to flag previously, the 'non-existence' of caste within the struggle for the US curriculum is incomprehensible—a field that, since its inception, is eugenically welded. Quite a double scandal, I insist, after irrefutable, glorious battles for social justice, with caste not just being sidelined but explicitly produced as a 'non-issue.' In a field that saw the emergence and vitality of the robust, critical river of identity wrangles flooding its banks—thus shaking its very riverbed—such 'invisibility' is not a pleasant feeling—as Aijaz Ahmad (2008) would frame it.

Last but not least, it relates to what I call the South Asian doyens of the epistemologies of the South. The struggle against oppression in the Hindustan and in what constitutes the Indian nation today cannot be reduced to a single name and a simple movement. However, without underestimating the role played by a vast group of individuals and movements—namely, Ramchandra Babaji More, Jyotiba Phule, Periyar Ramasamy, Gopalbaba Valangkar, M. N. Srinivas, and others—and without falling into any reductionism or historical revisionism, there is consensus—even among its most bloodthirsty opponents—that history crafts Babasaheb Ambedkar in a prominent place in the fight against the caste system. He is among the most important of the essential, great demiurges of the caste struggle—and one of the most important makers of modern India (Malik-Goure, 2015; Banerjee-Dube, 2014; Sirswal, 2013; Omvedt, 1994; Basu, 2003; Jaffrelot, 2005; Teltumbde, 2010, 2018) and arguably one of the most important pioneers of the epistemologies from the Global South—as Boaventura de Sousa Santos would frame it. (Santos, 2014) Let me focus on the five issues I have highlighted—so crucial for our educational and curriculum debates, among countless others.

Pioneering the Epistemologies from the South

> *The South of the epistemology of the South is an ani-imperial epistemology.*
> —*(Boaventura de Sousa Santos, 2009)*

Bhimrao Ramji Ambedkar—aka, 'Babasaheb' Ambedkar ('respectful father')—was born on April 14, 1891, in Mhow—today, Madhya Pradesh—within a family of the Hindu Mahar case regarded as an Untouchable caste. His journey was not a fairy tale, and his existence could not be comprehended out of his caste. In 1912, he finished his BA in economics and political science. He did his graduate studies in political science at one of the Ivy League academic institutions in the US—Columbia University in New York. At Columbia, he worked closely with the most influential U.S. pedagogue, John Dewey, and established links with the African American struggle for emancipation (Stroud, 2023). His close relationship with John Dewey made him a sublime pragmatist (Teltumbde, 2016; see also Mahadevan Chapter 9), quite crucial to crafting what would be called 'Ambedkarism,' as an epistemology from the South (see Santos, 2014). In 1923, he was granted a PhD from the London School of Economics with a thesis, 'The Problem of the Rupee.'

The Untouchables had in Ambedkar their most outstanding son. Never in the past had an Untouchable reached such high levels—academically and socially. He was the father of the Indian constitution of India's first law Minister in 1947, resigning before his tenure ended in conflict with Jawaharlal Nehru. Babasaheb Ambedkar passed away in 1956.

Babasaheb Ambedkar—while not a Marxist—knew full well he could not ignite change 'under self-selected circumstances but under the existing circumstances, given and transmitted from the past.' He had a clear sense not just of the need to frame caste historically but also to place such miscreation as the logic undergirding the matrix of a very eugenic political economy, as he eloquently unveils in his famous 'Annihilation of Caste.' As he argues, the "caste system is not merely a division of labor. It is also a division of laborers." He deserves to be quoted at length. As a form of division of labor, he (2016) adds, the caste system "suffers from another serious defect. The division of labor brought about by the Caste System is not a division based on choice. Individual sentiment and individual preference have no place in it. It is based on the dogma of predestination." Odd as it might be, caste counters notable market flags—such as 'meritocracy, efficiency'—as it detaches both the hearts and the minds of the workers from their work. Caste is, therefore "a harmful institution, since it involves the subordination of man's natural powers and inclinations to the exigencies of social rules" (Ambedkar, 2016, p. 236, 2018, p. 17).

As the sublime logic underpinning the matrix of a eugenic political economy, one "can turn in any direction one likes, caste is the monster that crosses your path" (Ambedbar, 2016, p. 236, 2018, p 17). To such an end, political and economic reform and caste constitute mutually excluded realities. Addressing the socialist hemisphere, Bhimrao Ambedkar argued that political and economic reform implied opening up the veins of the caste system, a divisive eugenic system, a divisibility so endlessly abyssal, and dismantling it. Such constitutes a tough challenge to any revolutionary, transformative battle.

Socialists or any other revolutionary force, he argues, "will be compelled to take account of Caste after the revolution if they do not take account of it before the revolution." The future of India was undoubtedly out of caste; however, it could not avoid going through it to disassemble it. Such transformative logic—one that implies an epistemological revolution as well—is right at the core of the wrangle he led with Mahatma Gandhi—an issue we will examine briefly later. Babasaheb Ambedkar knew full well that it was erroneous to frame "society as a totality and that there was no single principle of social transformation" (see Santos, 1999, p. 201).

Babasaheb Ambedkar could well be placed among the pioneers of what Boaventura de Sousa Santos called the epistemologies from the South. In this regard, "the South is understood here as a metaphor for the human suffering systematically caused by colonialism and capitalism. It is a South that also exists in the global geographic North, the so-called third inner world of the hegemonic countries" (Santos, 2009, p. 12). That is, "the South of the epistemology of the South is an ani-imperial epistemology" (Santos, 2009, p. 12) drawn in the epistemological frameworks of the South. The struggle against the caste system, in the minds of Ramchandra Babaji More, Jyotirao Phule, Periyar Ramasamy, Gopalbaba Valangkar, Babasaheb Ambedkar, and others, was also a commitment against epistemological despotism, challenging a eugenic form of reason, a reason that obliterates 'about 13 million of the aboriginal population in India' (Ambedkar, 2016, 2018).

The caste struggle was also a struggle toward an ecology of knowledge (Santos, 2014), which would validate endless epistemological differences within the South, thus paving the way for a society based on liberty, equality, and fraternity (Ambedkar, 1979, 2016, 2018). Babasaheb Ambedkar's theory of minority rights is a graphic example of such an autochthonous approach that "went well beyond the terms of *Western* liberal constitutionalism" (Chatterjee, 2018, p. 107). In advocating to "abandon the British system" (Chatterjee, 2018, p. 124) and drafting a minority rights policy grounded within a "constitutional republicanism" (Chatterjee, 2018, p. 127), Babasaheb Ambedkar pillared his theory within autochthonous epistemological veins; a 'caste is caste theory' with three-fold foundational principles; that is "the abiding reliance on the collective autonomy and the will to self-representation of minority classes; a clear definition of what constitutes a minority within the Indian historical eugenic bio-cartography; and the acknowledgment that class exploitation is thoroughly intertwined with caste discrimination and that the elimination of the latter will necessarily involve a struggle against the former" (Chatterjee, 2018, pp. 128–129). While lessons could, should, and had to be learned from the struggles of other eugenic systems of dominance in other nations—case in point, the African American struggle against slavery in the US—in Babasaheb Ambedkar's terms, the legal, constitutional rights for the Untouchables, to be sustainable and successful, could not ignore autochthonous epistemological dynamics. That is, minority rights could not be achieved by ignoring or misreading the Indian idiosyncrasies, which are pretty crucial to edifying cultural and economic democracy. (Chatterjee, 2018). Gradually, 'Ambdekarism' became the dominant theory of Dalit liberation (Omvedt,

1994), an enzyme in the struggle against untouchability with clear prox-imities and distances from Marxism.

Crafting on Boaventura de Sousa Santos's (1999) rationale, I argue that, while Babasaheb Ambedkar, as well as Ramchandra Babaji More, Jyotirao Phule, Periyar Ramasamy, Gopalbaba Valangkar, and others should be considered within the leadership of an irreversible outrage against caste segregation, working from a non-Western epistemological platform open-ing the veins of the eugenic caste system and de-linking from the Euro-centric dominant and counter dominant perspectives, it was undeniably Bhimrao Ambedkar—the one who could well be defined as the demiurge of a well-structured theory of Dalit liberation and emancipation (Omvedt, 1994). While they were able to claim not only the legitimacy of southern epistemologies in the deconstruction of the monumentality of the caste as a system of segregation and power but also to demonstrate that the deconstruction and dismantling of such a system would never happen by silencing the historical legacy of non-Western reason, the truth is that Babasaheb Ambedkar—echoing the struggle triggered by Jyotirao Phule, Periyar Ramasamy, and others (Pathania and Kalyani, Chapter 10)—was able to craft a more systematized, autochthonous praxis of liberation, which became a major tour de force in India. (Omvedt, 1994). Ambed-karism and Ambedkarit "became the dominant markers of the Dalit uni-verse, reinforcing the identitarian orientation among Dalits" (Teltumbde and Yengde, 2018, p. xiii). By not ignoring the epistemological validity of some fundamentals that underlay Eurocentric analysis of caste and put-ting on the table all the non-Western epistemological artillery, leaders of the anti-caste movement promoted a decisive and irreversible ecology of saberes—an emancipatory translatability—thus "giving priority to specifi-cities and historical, sociological, cultural and epistemological innovations with which reality often surprise us when we conceive it from the assump-tions of southern epistemologies" (Santos, s/d, p. 40).

Contrary to his predecessors, Babasaheb Ambedkar did not believe edu-cation alone could trigger "Hindus to change their hearts" (Chatterjee, 2018, p. 108). According to Ambedkar (2016, 2018), the education of the masses would promote an emancipatory process of casteless nation-building; he adamantly urged for the end of untouchability by changing the system (Chatterjee, 2018). Hindutva, Natrajan (2022, p. 299) argues, "deploys its pedagogical mission effectively as a cultural, ideological pro-ject to make a new history and central to its mission is the cultural work of construction and negotiation of social identities." Equality policies applied in unequal social structures would only aggravate the deplorable condi-tions faced by the Dalits. Bhimrao Ambedkar knew full well that a suc-cessful "attack on the caste system implied an attack on Brahman and Hinduism. Such an attack needed to be carried at all levels elaborating a theory of history along with the re-interpretation of Indian mythology, and communicating it to the masses with polemic tracts, songs, plays, and organization-building" (Omvedt, 1994, p. 97)—such graphically grasps Babasaheb Ambedkar's powerful, autochthonous reason.

I reiterate that intellectuals such as Ramchandra Babaji More, Jyotirao Phule, Periyar Ramasamy, Gopalbaba Valangkar, and many others represent glaring examples of an alternative commitment to caste struggle—they fully understood that the struggle against caste was also epistemological, one that allowed reinventing the Dalit's social emancipation in its pluriverse forms and "evoke plural forms of emancipation not simply based on a Western understanding of the world" (Santos, 1999, p. 201). To this end, in some way, they were the demiurges of the epistemologies from the South, as their struggle against caste segregation was also a search "for knowledge and criteria of knowledge validation that gave visibility to the cognitive practices of classes, peoples, and social groups that have historically been exploited and oppressed by systems of dominion" (Santos, 2009, p. 12). However, it is undeniable that Babasaheb Ambedkar offered "an innovative diagnosis of the pathologies of caste and untouchability" (Ramesh, 2022, p. 728). He "set the Dalits on the path of an arduous emancipation" (Jaffrelot, 2005, p. 7), which triggered crucial ideological battles.

The Persistence of a Historical Chamber of Horrors

Caste bewilders the world by defying reason, contradicting any prophecy, and resisting any historical transformation from feudalism to today.

It has grown far more vicious, complex, and brutal
—(Anand Teltumbde, 2010)

A few approaches—Janet Abu Lughod (1989, 2001), Slavoj Žižek (cited in Dabashi, 2015), Sankar Muthu (2003), Kent Flannery and Joyce Marcus (2012), to mention a few—alert us to the dangers of 'Manicheistic' dogmatic approaches. They alert us to the existence of clear eugenic, non-Western structures of oppression that date back to the beginning of the first millennium. Pre-colonial epochs exhibited quite powerful, however unequal, cultural and economic dynamics intertwining power relations. Before the 'European game' (Fanon, 1963) "became one of the world economies in the twelfth century, when it joined the long-distance trade system that stretched through the Mediterranean into the Red Sea and the Persian Gulf and the Indian Ocean and through the Strait of Malacca to reach China, there were numerous preexistent world economies" (Abu-Lughod, 1989, p. 12) fostering a myriad of graded social systems. In other spaces, I have also alerted to avoid any form of 'indigenoustude' in our critique of Eurocentrism and Western modernity (Paraskeva, 2011, 2014, 2016, 2021, 2018a, 2022a, 2022b).

However, while inequality and segregation were critical features before the Empire, the truth is that, during colonial(ity) times, those dynamics became exacerbated to unthinkable barbaric plateaus. Caste is one of the ancient segregate dynamics and categories; for instance, the slavery traffic fluxes and constitutes a structural feature within the divisive epistemological colors of the colonial Empire—a persistent feature that crosses the so-called post-colonial momentum. Such dynamics—like race, class, and gender—constitute the segregated logic underpinning what decolonial and anti-colonial intellectuals call coloniality (Quijano, 1992; Mignolo, 2008; Santos, 2014; Dussel, 2013, 2000; Galeano, 1997; Walsh, 2018; Grosfoguel, 2011; Maldonado-Torres, 2008, 2012; Paraskeva, 2016, 2018a, 2018b, 2021, 2022a, 2022b).

Caste is a social system that precedes colonial occupation and persists within the contemporary yoke of coloniality (Quijano, 1992; Mignolo, 2008, 2018). It was, however, extending and multiplying its forms over the centuries, shaping successive frameworks of exploitation and power throughout history.

The caste system and caste-based discrimination are not, however, just confined to what is now geographically recognized as India, Pakistan, and Sri Lanka, among others. It is a grading system that operates historically in the culture of several countries of South Asia, especially Nepal, Siri Lanka, India, and Pakistan, but also in Europe—for example, in the UK and Spain (Pathania and Kalyani, Chapter 10; Mosse, 2020; Dhanda et al., 2014; Harney, 2015)—Japan, and Africa (Yengde, 2022; Gordon, 2017; Todd, 1977). The impact of caste globally "posits a geographical and ideological distinction" (Yengde, 2022, p. 343). It has also been framed as a crucial category in the sanguinary historical path of the United States. It also pervades the Roman (aka, gypsy) community across "vagrant tribes in Northern India, true nomads, living in temporary huts and wretched tents," as well as Western and Eastern European nations (Pathanoa and Kalyani, Chapter 10; Blunt, 1969, p. 148; also, Naumenko and Naumenko, 2018; Čvorović, 2007; Tamim, 2018; Swapnil, 2015). Coincidently the 'Roman Question' is out of the curriculum debates. Such divisive animosity isn't just based on color difference and diversity, and oddly, even pervades communist communities such as Kerala (Roy, 2016).

While not a system that invented the saga, the truth is that, under British domination, caste became a single term capable of naming and subsuming India's diverse forms of social identity and organization (Dirks, 2002). British colonialism not only "enabled caste to assume political functions" (Srinivas, 1962, p. 15) but also "saw education as highly instrumental"

(Guha, 1997, p. 81) to consolidating, normalizing, and perpetuating a graded theater of absurdity (Camus, 2005). Educational state apparatuses "become the guardian of habitus, reproducing the dominant caste and cultural power at the objectified state" (Syamprasad, Chapter 11). Education was a casteized apparatus "that systematically thwarted the ambitions of Dalits" (Pankaj, 2021, p. 934).

Such absurdity crosses ancient, colonial, and post-colonial times. Hindu's metaphysical cred struck the nation from its inception to our modern days (see Crooke, 1896). In fact, after the independence, "the provision of constitutional safeguards to the backward sections of the population, especially schedule Castes and Tribes, has given a new lease of life to caste. It is hardly necessary to add that this is at odds with the intentions to bring about a casteless society which most political parties, including the Indian National Congress, profess" (Srinivas, 1962, p. 15; see also Kumar, 1998). Colonialism—as well as post-colonialism—"and its ruling liberal ethos, rendered the Hindu establishment defensive about its ritual practices and traditions" (Teltumbde, 2010, p. 32). For most, it was a relic of Indian feudalism, which, it was thought, would disappear once capitalism was established. Capitalist production relations came to the villages and seemed to shake the caste structure to its roots—but caste survived, nonetheless (Teltumbde, 2010, p. 9; Syamprasad, Chapter 11).

Resistance to the caste system was nonetheless ferocious, as we have been able to examine previously. In fact, "if there was one Indian battle that Britain never won, it was the battle for the appropriation of the Indian past" (Guha, 1997, p. 1). Caste bewilders the world by defying reason, contradicting any prophecy, and resisting any historical transformation from feudalism to today. It has grown far more vicious, complex, and brutal (Teltumbde, 2010) under neoliberal globalization. The notion that neoliberal globalization "would create economic as well as cultural convergence, promote neoliberal values and thereby weaken caste" (Teltumbde, 2010, p. 11) becomes a nightmare. India has become the pristine eulogy of neoliberal globalization pillars, meritocracy, and the survival of the fittest ideology (Harvey, 2005; Hursh, 2015, Mclaren, 2022; Yendge, Chapter 6), upgrading the trivialization and 'thingification' of untouchability. This eugenic, epistemological matrix escalates caste segregation to another level. Like in feudal times, under neoliberal, global times (Hursh, 2015; Harvey, 2005), untouchability paved the way for a deplorable moral cleansing (Roy, 2016). Meritocracy and testocracy, as Yengde (Chapter 6) and Syamprasad (Chapter 11) argue, constitute crucial features within the neoliberal gaze, saturating our educational and curriculum institutions (Hursh, 2015); they constitute a "form of ethical violence desubjectifying Dalits and undermine their ability to become a speaking subject" (Vijay and Nair, 2019, p. 329). Merit, Syamprasad (Chapter 11) stresses, is determined by caste norms.

Caste is the face of the barbary of Hinduism, so well defined by Babasaheb Ambedkar (2009, p. 296) as "a veritable chamber of horrors." Caste
looks like a refined social chameleon, not just with the capacity to adapt
to different historical phases in the history of humanity but also to be
responsive to the diverse cultural and political graded needs and structures
of the various historical stages, placing resiliently "Dalit's aspirations as
a breach of peace" (Roy, 2016, p. 22). Under the neoliberal, global cult,
laissez-faire principles jazzed with the inheritance of karma that undergirds
the caste system. To such an end, the underpinning principles—however
different—of neoliberal globalization and caste rub against each other in a
not-negotiable metamorphosis, not just preserving what could well be the
irreconcilable hypothetical differences but also escalating and upgrading
each other's matrixes. The Hindutva eugenic, ideological impulses and the
economic logic underpinning neoliberal global forms are "not only recon-
cilable but also complementary" (Ahmad, 2008, p. 15).

As I argued elsewhere (Paraskeva, 2016, 2021, 2022a), neoliberal globalization needs to be contextualized within coloniality and its power
matrix (Quijano, 1992; Mignolo, 2008); neoliberal globalization is the
most contemporary 'ethos' of coloniality. Caste is one of the crucial
dynamics within such 'an ethos.' Caste and coloniality amalgamate, as Teltumbde (2017, p. 20) would have termed it. As a divisive reagent that cata-
lyzes the martyrdom of millions triturated historically through a matrix
whose existence depends on the bloodthirsty confrontation between the
oppressor and the oppressed, between the colonizer and the colonized, it
is not surprising, then, that caste persists over the centuries and finds itself
installed as a fundamental category in the social processes that structure
coloniality. Probably never has caste had such a perfect and manageable
nest as coloniality, the current "form of domination in the world today"'
(Quijano, 1992, 2008).

The aftermath of colonialism did not cease the "conditions nor the
modes of exploitation and domination between peoples" (Quijano, 1992,
2008). Contrary to colonialism,

coloniality accounts for the entangled, heterogeneous, and mutually
constitutive relations between the international division of labor, global
racial/ethnic hierarchy, and hegemonic Eurocentric epistemologies in
the modern/colonial/capitalist world system. Coloniality of the world
scale, with the United States as the undisputed hegemony over non-
European people, characterizes the globalization of the capitalist world
economy today: the old colonial hierarchies of the West/non-West
remain in place. They are entangled with the new so-called division of
labor. Herein lies the relevance of the distinction between colonialism
and coloniality. Coloniality refers to the continuity of colonial forms

of domination after the end of colonial administrations produced by colonial cultures and structures in the modern/colonial/capitalist world system.

(Grosfoguel, 2003, p. 4)

Colonialism and coloniality are two faces of the same eugenic currency—the epistemicide. Coloniality is the memory, the legacy of colonialism, yet it continues to be reborn through new, creative articulations and re-articulations around hegemonic battles. Caste is at the core of such conflicts. It upgrades particular forms of epistemicidal reason framed—and trivialized—in class, race, caste, ethnicity, and gender dynamics. Caste is intimately related to different metamorphoses within the coloniality process. It constitutes a trump card with the coloniality power matrix, conceived as a "matrix of knowledge, labor, power and being" (Maldonado-Torres, 2012, p. 2). Such a matrix paves the way for the coloniality/colonialities of caste.

The coloniality of the caste is related to a set of segregating axes; it constitutes a permanent "threat to cultural diversity" (Syamprasad, Chapter 11). Although many of them come from antiquity and the pre-coloniality periods, the truth is that, during the different historical processes of coloniality, they become more acute, taking on well-defined, diverse metamorphoses. The coloniality of caste speaks volumes to the plasticity and adaptability of caste as a segregating category, not precisely adapting to successive graded models of power but offering these models divisive dynamics that are important in structuring inequitable and segregating power relations. Let us now look briefly at some of these axes that structure the coloniality of caste and that so many erroneously predicted as its end with the natural advance of human society. For billions of people, it is impossible to perceive a divisive existence and way of thinking out of the coloniality of caste.

One of the most cynical characteristics of the coloniality of caste—which allows it to last throughout the centuries—is how it articulates and re-articulates with power and structures of domination. Its historical, lethal footprint reveals that we are in the presence of an apex predator—a predator without predators—that, unlike class, race, ethnicity, and gender, shows a remarkable malleability to intermingle within the dynamics of power without compromising its historical-divine eugenic matrix and 'bricolage' the wrangle 'coercive-consent' in creative terms. Appallingly, while, on the one hand, the structures of power and domination adjust to the predatory character of caste, on the other hand, caste presents itself as the needed divisive dynamic to act help welding—either coercively and/or consensually—antagonistic social constituencies under its yoke, regardless the matrix of power and domination.

Coloniality of caste is about "modifying and adapting feudal religious and tribal structures, but not dismantling them" (Teltumbde, 2010, p. 54). Casteized institutions—most of them from ancient times—"comfortably coexist within *coloniality*[8]" (Teltumbde, 2010, p. 54).

While, during colonial times, caste co-peppered an authoritarian, non-hegemonic state within the Global South, edified by the hallmark of Euro-centric democracy within the Global North, in post-colonial times, caste spiced the state differently—yet maintaining and upgrading its lethal impact (Guha, 1997). While on the former, Ranjit Guha (1997) argues, one faces a paradox of dominance without hegemony, as caste is a category within a form of domination based on coercion, in the latter, under the auspices of an imported—and imposed—a democratic state of power and dominance, caste did not fade away; quite conversely, it has been able to align, re-align, and 'coexist democratically,' exhibiting dubious plasticity within the wrangle 'consent and coercion.' Dominance remains doubly articu-lated—throughout colonial and post-colonial times—within a common denominator—the lack of hegemony (Guha, 1997, p. 100). Caste—and its Hindutva inner logic—defies/re-configures Antonio Gramsci's hegemony as a form of social control—an ideological praxis that needs to be placed within the yarn of 'state' and 'civil society.' Hindutva durability is related to its capacity to jazz "ethnonationalism and ultranationalism impulses assuming an authoritarian populist rage" (Natrajan, 2022, p. 303) so welcomed by the neoliberal consulate. Hindutva is a historical, social phenomenon "much deeper than its electoral victories or losses" (Natra-jan, 2022, p. 303). Hindutva reason is right at the core of the nexus of 'state-civil society' that it is crucial to situate the caste system, an endemic social construction whose persistence relies on its permanent capacity to de-construct and re-construct itself, addressing the cracks exhibited in any power structure—from pre-colonial and colonial times to the contempo-rary coloniality consulate—as Michel de Certeau (1988) would have put it. This issue deserves to be further explored and investigated.

A second, towering feature within the coloniality of caste is that caste dynamics framed an epistemicidal reason, "discriminating people and tar-geting communities" (Maldonado-Torres, 2008). Like other categories under such a matrix of power, the coloniality of caste is deeply implicated in the production and reproduction of a "hegemonic mind of eugenic dom-inance and control" (Paraskeva, 2016, p. 3), legitimizing particular forms of knowledge and existence while obliterating, criminalizing, and—if needed—slaughtering too many others. The coloniality—or colonialities—of caste is also about a divisive claim of the Hindutva's "epistemological perspective as unique and the only cognitive possibility, a cognitive fascism that fertilizes subjectivities" (Paraskeva, 2016, p. 3).

The caste system is also about the coloniality of the mind. This brutal, graded system continues to live in the minds of both 'Touchables' and

'Untouchables' throughout history, from feudalism until our current coloniality days. The coloniality of caste is about "intellectual sterility as the rule to perpetuate sub-humanity" (Diop, 1970, p. xv). Untouchability—as anti-colonial and decolonial intellectuals would put it, among others, Leopold Senghor (1970); Frantz Fanon (1963, 1967), Cheikh Anta Diop (1970), Ngugi Wa' Thiong'o (2005), Albert Memmi (1999, 2000), Aimé Césaire (2000) Kwame Nkrumah (1964), Achille Mbembe (2014; 2018), José Carlos Mariátegui (2011), Aníbal Quijano (1992) Eduardo Galeano (1997), Enrique Dussel (2000)—is about internalizing the brutality of a graded system.

Dalit reason—a street reason (Rao, Chapter 5)—blends with such anti-colonial and decolonial veins in the struggle for social emancipation. Like Mariátegui (2011), for example, the anti-caste struggle led by More, Phule, Ramasamy, Valangkar, Ambedkar, and others innovatively theorized the connections between identity and class, race, and caste but also respected the historical idiosyncrasies of class, race, and caste within—and as the output of—the different systems of domination and exploitation (Sirohi and Gupta, 2020). They provide a creative excavation of different 'indigenous questions' within a graded matrix of power. Caste and race are two deplorable categories of cleansing but related to different forms of indigeneity (see Harney, 2015). Along with Fanon, anti-caste intellectuals understand that "the past doesn't validate the politics of the present, and they reject the Dalit identity politics that is based only on the lived experiences of the Dalits and their histories of suffering" (Manoharan, 2017, p. 78). Anti-caste intellectuals are very aware of the dangers of anti-colonial movements, such as Negritude—and Babasaheb Ambedkar is a prominent example—as "privileging of an interiorized identity, its reification of the black skin will inevitably lead to compromise with the system of oppression" (Manoharan, 2017, p. 77).

Teltumbde (2018, p. 88) argues that Caste of mind is a "defining prowess of the caste system, that even its victim easily forgets their victimhood and assumes the oppressor's posture vis-à-vis others when the opportunities arise." In doing so, the victims of such a deplorable system forget how they actively and dynamically reproduced brutality and help normalize a pathology that commonsensically pervades the social sphere that upper castes have a justifiable privilege rubber-stamped sacredly on the basis "of their merit earned in the previous birth, or as it Is said nowadays, by dint of hard work, efficiency, talent, and so on" (Teltumbde, 2018, pp. 88–89). As Rao (Chapter 5) argues, "anti-caste activists contended that *jatibhed*[9] was not merely a social arrangement, but a mode of thought, indeed a *social abstraction.*" Such a caste of mind powerfully pervades India's social matrix, currently deepening the abyssal line between 'Touchables and Untouchables,' with the latter being officially referred to as Scheduled Castes (SC), Scheduled Tribes (ST), and Other Backward Classes (OBC).

For any human being, Arundhati Roy (2016, p. 20) argues, "to have to use terms like 'untouchable,' 'scheduled caste,' 'backward class,' and 'other backward classes' to describe fellow human beings, is like living in the chamber of horrors," a chamber that persists throughout the centuries and constitutes a defining characteristic of coloniality.

A third aspect is that the coloniality of caste upgrades the de-historicization of identities (Teltumbde, 2010, p. 34). Caste thus offers coloniality what coloniality most needs—graded stabilization of the commonsense required to fuel a segregated mode of production; caste is in sync with coloniality's segregated legacy; it constitutes one of its master pillars. It innovatively enhances the divisive dynamics underpinning *el patron colonial de poder* (Quijano, 1992; Mignolo, 2008). Through the web of caste dynamics, the coloniality of power, knowledge, and being implies not a coloniality of labor but of laborers—as Ambedkar (2016, 2018; also see Chapter 2) insightfully described—a key feature to understanding the idiosyncrasies of the caste system under coloniality. Caste dynamics is about the invisibility of outcast laborer (Rao, Chapter 5). Caste is about the coloniality of laborers that frames a matrix of divisive thinking and existence. The coloniality of caste is an abyssal reason. Boaventura de Sousa Santos (2007b, p. 45) helps a great deal here. Coloniality thinking, he (2007b) argues, "is an abyssal thinking." It consists

of a system of visible and invisible distinctions, the invisible ones being the foundation of the visible ones. The invisible distinctions are established through radical lines that divide social reality into two realms, the realm of "this side of the line" and the realm of "the other side of the line." The division is such that "the other side of the line" vanishes as reality, becomes nonexistent, and is indeed produced as nonexistent. Nonexistent means not existing in any relevant or comprehensible way of being. Whatever is produced as nonexistent is radically excluded because it lies beyond the realm of what the accepted conception of inclusion considers to be it's other. What most fundamentally characterizes abyssal thinking is thus the impossibility of the co-presence of the two sides of the line. To the extent that it prevails, this side of the line only wins by exhausting the field of relevant reality. Beyond it, there is only nonexistence, invisibility, and non-dialectical absence (Santos, 2007, p. 45).

The coloniality of caste is not just about the radical impossibility of co-presence of both sides of the line, however. It is also about the radical impossibility of the co-presence of 'Touchables' and 'Untouchables' on the other side of the line. The coloniality of caste is about the "continuous dividing of divisions in social space" (Sampath, Chapter 7) within and beyond "this side of the line." The Republic of caste (Teltumbde, 201) is a republic of divisive thinking. The sustainability of the coloniality of power, being, knowledge laborer, and gender relies on the commonsensical construction of categories as 'caste' on the realm of "the other side of the line" (Santos, 2007b, p. 45). Caste—in its visible invisibility—is instrumental in constructing, upgrading, and perpetuating an intricate, casteized, abyssal epistemicidal divide. While these aspects could be identified under ancient and colonial times, it is undeniable that caste has shown remarkable adaptability under coloniality. Caste "rearranges the field of visibility; that is, caste is not just an act of casteized laborer, but rather a structural imperative, such that spaces are casteized, perspective is casteized, gestures and languages" (Gajarawala, 2012, p. 81), as are the non-existences.

However, the invisible visibility of caste—odd as it might be—is also produced in specific, counter-hegemonic Eurocentric approaches. I have defined this issue as reversive epistemicide (Paraskeva, 2016, 2018a, 2018b, 2021, 2022a, 2022b, 2022c). Such reversive epistemicide epitomizes an overt 'hysterical blindness' (Jal, Chapter 8). In the struggle against the functionalist and non-dialectical view of the caste system, many counter-hegemonic movements and groups ended up falling into a functionalist trap. This happens with analyses that erroneously place caste, race, and class as identical categories. This identical yoke speaks volumes about the epistemological despotism that frames counter-hegemonic, Eurocentric perspectives, which dare to determine which system defines structures of domination, power, and oppression of 'the other' based on Eurocentric models and categories wholly disconnected from the historical context. Uma Chakravarti and Maithreyi Krishnaraj (2020) argue that caste fosters social formations framed by modes and conditions of production. It is not an assimilative system but an aggregative matrix (Chakravarti and Krishnaraj, 2020). To put it simply, caste is caste.

Caste is Caste. Not Class!

> *We do not want money, nor do we want prestige.*
> *We do not want education, nor do we want knowledge*
> *We only wish for the recognition of our caste*
> *We only want our cast to be alive.*
> —*(Bandyopadhyay Sekar, 1987)*

To claim that the history of all hitherto Hindutva society is the history of caste struggle, Karl Marx would have disagreed, though, is not an overstatement. Caste is caste, and it "transcends class, race, and labor" (Sampath, Chapter 7). Following Hinduism, in the beginning—whatever the beginning was—it was the Purusha Hymn of the Rig-Veda, 'thy' hymn, that describes the creation of castes. Caste precedes the known modern Empire. There is no possible radical change in India, Teltumbde (2018, p. 19) claims, "without confronting caste." He (2018, p. 19) adds, "without the annihilation of caste, there can be no revolution in India, and at the same time, without a revolution, there can be no annihilation of caste." Caste needs to be confronted in caste terms, not in class and racial terms—although these categories are not absent from the caste system. Class and caste "are intertwined," though (Teltumbde, 2018, p. 19; Béteille, 1965). However, it is one thing to acknowledge the intertwined character of such intricate dynamics; it is another to proclaim that they are identical. A casted society is not a copy-paste of a classed or racialized society.

It has become a dangerous truism—within the fields of liberal arts, humanities, and education, fundamentally designed within a Eurocentric matrix within and beyond the Global North—to grasp the dynamics of caste in the light of the dynamics of race and class. In other words, caste has been constructed, interpreted, unpacked and re-packed based on the dynamics that underlie those of race and class that structure the terrains of Eurocentric modernity and in Eurocentric terms. This, I reiterate, is an error from a historical and theoretical point of view. The historical roots of caste are quite distinct from those of class and race, and although there are some theoretical similarities, the differences are undeniably abysmal and irresoluble. In what follows, and briefly, I challenge such a truism—what I would call 'samenessization'—the forced agglutination of different social dynamics, which exemplifies a superior form of the epistemicidal nature of both dominant and counter-dominant Eurocentric epistemological traditions—a symptom of the eugenic praxis of what Santos (2018) calls the monumentalism of Eurocentric reason.

In Erik Olin Wright's (1994) terms, one cannot understand poverty, inequality, oppression, and exploitation out of the class matrix that structures the capitalist system. That is, poverty, inequality, oppression, and exploitation are not "unfortunate consequences of the pursuit of material interests; they constitute an essential condition for the realization of the material interests of the privilege and powerful actors" (Wright, 1994, p. 38). This relatively complex wrangle between poverty, inequality, oppression, and exploitation and the control of the modes of production, the access to the fruits of labor as well as the material assets usurped by a tiny minority constitutes the ideological matrix of the class system, finds a parallel within the caste system. Undeniably, class and caste—and I would add gender and race—undergird a particular mode of material production, pumping social systems deeply framed on exploitation, poverty, inequality, and slavery. Teltumbde (2010, pp. 67–68) articulates such a parallel by stating that caste is deeply a social capital that—like class—"unites in economics, but it divides in politics." Caste "is unified from the outside, yet divided within" (Dumont, 1970, p. 34). Caste, like class, paves the way to glue the endless diverse angles of the "political economy of atrocities" (Teltumbde, 2010, p. 54). Like any classed or racialized society, caste societies are also flooded with patriarchal codes linked to exploitive production modes (Chakravarti and Krishnaraj, 2020). Like class, caste is intimately related to the consequences of graded cultural politics and political economy that pumped a graded system of dominance. Naturally, like class, caste, for instance, is at the core of the "direct causes of much of the unemployment" (Ambedkar, 2016, p. 236, 2018, p. 17) and other social sagas.

Wright (1994, p. 51) also unpacks the Marxist tension between 'class-in-itself,' a purely economic category, and 'class-for-itself,' a broader political dynamic. Following Wright (1994), like class, caste also needs to be de-constructed from a reductive economic category into the political and ideological dynamic. Such political existence has responded to the persistence of caste since ancient times (Teltumbde, 2010). Here, one finds another apparent similarity between caste and class—in terms of the eugenic role played in a mercilessly segregated society, a role deeply related to caste structure, formation, and struggles. However, such parallels—which don't make both categories identical—do not overshadow their conceptual differences. The characteristics that bring class and caste together also distance them, primarily when one examines both class and caste in the light of the historical text and context, their structure, formation, and bloody struggles. Like understanding class, understanding caste is also about unpacking its structure, shape, and struggles.

While class structure, Wright (200b, p. 19; see also 2000a; 2015) argues, "refers to the structure of social relations into which individuals enter which determine their class interests," class "formation relates to the formation of organized collectivities within the class structure based on the interests shaped by that class structure" (Wright 2000b, p. 19; see also 2000a; 2015). More to the point, "if social relations between classes define the class structure, class formation is defined by social relations within classes, social relations which forge collectivities engaged in struggle" (Wright 2000b, p. 19; see also 2000a; 2015). Like class, debating caste also dissects its structure, formation, and sanguinary existence. However, I would argue that caste structure and formation trigger different metamorphoses. Caste closeness, endogamic, hereditary, and spiritual *quasi-irreversible* dynamics introduce different radical elements to the graded equation—a misrepresented aspect in too many approaches—among others, by Gunnar Myrdal (1944, 1967), Allison Davis et al. (1941),[10] Robert Havingusrt, (1945),[11] W. Lloyd Warner (1936), W. Lloyd Warner and Allison Davis (1939), Davis (1945) Nicholas Dirks (2002), Immerwahr (2007), Isabel Wilkerson (2000), Loïc Wacquant (2002, 2022). I would highlight, though, that such radical differences at each category's core do not prevent "a unifying emancipatory struggle" (Teltumbde, 2018, p. 91)—as class and caste struggles constitute a non-negotiable commitment to equality, justice, freedom, and emancipation. Such commitment is grounded historically within irresolvable lack of commonalities that cannot be diluted within the commonalities.

Caste, unlike class, carries a lethal religious and spiritual structure and formation—triggering different dynamics that provide caste with the pillars of alleged irreversibility. Moreover, for this reason, caste—unlike class—is also constructed as an act of faith with millenary roots and, therefore, without any place in the rational human matrix—whatever it may be—an endemic metaphysical drift. Although there is a divine desire underlying slavery—to spread the Christian faith to the barbarous, discovered peoples—the dynamics of class and race—triggered as soon as the first Prosperous met the first Caliban (Henry, 2000)—were quickly aligned as a pillar of a necessary, brutal economic and cultural politics.

However, while we can affirm a spiritual aspect to the gestation of these two categories, the fact is that, in the case of caste, the religion/spiritual matrix occupies a verticality that we do not find in the class. While Hindutva remains the major logic underpinning caste, one cannot argue that Christianity remains the central logic undergirding the class system. Moreover, conversely to class, a counter-hegemonic spiritual avenue such as Buddhism is advocated as a way to smash caste dynamics (Ambedkar, 2016, 2018; Teltumbde, 2010, 2018).

This is not a minor issue and helps one understand other distinct metamorphoses inherent to both eugenic categories. The Marxist concept of 'lumpenproletariat,' so well unpacked by Eric Wright (1994) and Clyde Barrow (2020), is crucial here. The idea of the lumpenproletariat, which refers to underclasses devoid and devoiced of any political consciousness, is undeniably quite structural in both eugenic categories. However, while the class system relies on underclasses, "a category of social agents who are economically oppressed but not consistently exploited within a given system" (Wright, 1994, p. 48), the caste system is not only about upper caste and undercaste, but also, abominably, it is about the outcaste (Ambedkar, 2016, 2018; Teltumbde, 2010, 2018; Teltumbde and Yengde, 2018). Caste is a brutal wrangle between upper, lower, and outcastes, a ruthless clash between 'touchability and untouchability' and between 'existence and non-existence'—as Santos (2014) would have put it. Such conflict also integrates class matters, making caste a more intricate dynamic. While 'Marxism, provided a critical language for challenging caste's dehumanizing effects' (Rao, Chapter 5) clearly, in the minds of the doyens of the anti-Caste movement, caste was never a class matter. However, the class was a dynamic, meandering, and undergirding caste as the "veneer of

India's historical bloody trajectory," which precedes the Empire and pervades coloniality (Teltumbde, 2018, p. 19). Caste is the matrix of Hinduism "that was always unable to absorb the untouchables or remove the bar of untouchability" (Ambedkar, 2009). No society was so "casteized as India" (Teltumbde, 2018, p. 93), a distinctive feature crossing the conditions and modes of production. In this context, Ambedkar (2016, pp. 233–234, 2018, pp. 15–16) defines the caste system as a system pumped by the division of laborers, not through a division of labor like the class system.

> The Caste System is not merely a division of labor. It is also a division of laborers. Civilized society undoubtedly needs a division of labor. But in no civilized society is the division of labor accompanied by this unnatural division of laborers into watertight compartments. The Caste System is not merely a division of laborers, which is quite different from the division of labor—it is a hierarchy in which the divisions of laborers are graded one above the other. In no other country is the division of work accompanied by this gradation of laborers.

Such a division of laborers, he (2016, p. 233, 2018, p. 16; see also Rao, Chapter 5) argues, "is not spontaneous; it is not based on natural aptitudes." That is, the principle of social and individual efficiency "is violated in the Caste System, in so far as it involves an attempt to appoint tasks to individuals in advance—selected not based on original trained capacities, but on that of the social status of the parents" (Ambedkar, 2016, p. 233, 2018, p. 14). The division of laborer is about casteized labor, one that produces the "casteized subject" (Gajarawala, 2012, p. 71). In fact, the "real difference between classes lay in the manner in which one class labors and produces wealth, while another, which exercise private rights of ownership over the means of production, lived more or less of the toil of the laborers" (Teltumbde, 2018, p. 96). Sampath (Chapter 7) argues that the phenomena of caste "lies beyond the Western historical modalities of alienation, oppression, and expropriation of the human essence in the commodification of labor."

Marx and Ambedkar unpack class differently. While, for the former, "class was an essential and universal element spiraling down history through revolution" (Teltumbde, 2018, p. 101), for the latter, "it was a culture-specific interest group that could accomplish its goal by forcing through a series of changes in its situation" (Teltumbde, 2018, p. 101). Despite being sentient of such disparagements, Ambedkar "recognizes class as the basic constituent of society" (Teltumbde, 2018, p. 99), although he argues that there is no class until caste contradictions are resolved (Ambedkar, 2016, 2018; Teltumbde, 2018). Ambedkar tirelessly challenges hardcore leftists "that maintain class primacy as a social category" (Teltumbde,

2018, p. 113). As Teltumbde (2010, p. 65) argues, "even trade unions and staff associations where class interests should be the ground for solidarity, we see Dalits being forced to form caste-based associations."

The materiality of caste "needs some emphasizing due to the tendency to treat it as either a mask for class or economic exploitation or as an idealized social structure without any material basis—i.e., as kinship or religious system" (Natrajan, 2005, p. 228). Rao (Chapter 5) shrewdly unpacks the dangers and challenges of equating class and caste—'*claste*' as I would put it—within the Anti-caste struggle as historical and theoretical imprecisions. Caste saturates Indian society in which class plays a key role. Caste doesn't flood class-saturated societies, though (Subedi, 2013). 'Samenesszation' implies synonymizing class and caste, an overt mistake establishing sharp differences between Dalit and left movements—within and beyond the so-called Global South (Santos, 2018). Caste "is a concrete reality, the lifeworld of the people of the subcontinent. Caste often encompasses classes within it. Class, on the other hand, is a conceptual category; an abstraction based on one's relations to the means of production" (Teltumbde, 2018, p. 20). Thus, any "class analysis of Indian society cannot be done without taking cognizance of the overriding reality of caste" (Teltumbde, 2018, p. 20). Ambedkar (1979, p. 4) defines caste as an "enclosed endogamous class," which "cannot absorb caste identities" (Basu, 2003, p. 112), though.

Caste "did not constitute the core concern of Marx's struggle" (Teltumbde, 2018, p. 106). While admitting caste as the logic of a patriarchal system traditionally functioned as hereditary guilds, Marx falls into his base-superstructure trap, laboring in a dichotomic, yarn-class caste (Teltumbde, 2018; see also Syamprasad, Chapter 11). He soon hastened to kick caste to the nimbus of the superstructure. Inequality, poverty, and segregation are key categories targeted by Dalit intellectuals. The anti-caste struggle never gave up on unpacking the inner logic fostering social segregation. The debate between caste and/or class as the enzymes of inequality, poverty, and dehumanization was always an essential debate between "the Marxists and the Ambedkarists" in India since its independence (Syamprasad, Chapter 11). However, caste was never a subalternized category.

Like any other oppressive category, caste has relative autonomy—something Eurocentric counter-hegemonic impulses erroneously minimized. The fact "that someone else previous life is the harbinger of a future person's pain, torment, and anguish when born into the lowest cast" (Sampath, Chapter 7) is one of the distinctive features of the caste system. While the increase of urban migration and the development of urban infrastructure somehow mitigate caste distinctions—after all, it was impossible to maintain caste taboos or regulate contact in public conveyances—the fact is that these new spaces were also in constant danger of being overwhelmed by social pressure to reproduce caste distinctions through 'new technologies of spatial segregation' (Rao, Chapter 5).

Although trapped in a dichotomous discipline, the Marxist counter-hegemonic dialectic did not prevent it from proclaiming Indian history as the history of caste struggle (Teltumbde, 2018; Marx & Engels, 1853), a position penciled by Bukharin as well. In his terms, while "class is a category of persons united by a common role in the production process, caste is a group of persons united by their common position in the juristic or legal order of society. While the landlord is a class, the nobility are a caste" (Teltumbde, 2018, p. 97). Moreover, while class "potentially brings people together, the very nature of caste is to divide them by seeking hierarchy" (Teltumbde, 2018, p. 98). To be more precise, while the "the proletariat would include most of the Shudras and Dalits, they would not automatically form a class until the caste contradictions between them is eradicated" (Teltumbde, 2018, p. 98). To argue that class analysis, in a caste-based society, "would necessarily subsume caste" is an egregious error (Teltumbde, 2018, p. 98).

Whereas one can identify an organic nexus between caste, class, and race—overtly visible within the polemic constitutionalized reservations and socially and educationally backward classes, which constitute a point of "intersection between caste and class" (Teltumbde, 2018, p. 82)—it is undeniable that caste is an ascribed status (Pathania and Tierney, 2018, p. 3); it is "a collection of endogamous groups whose membership is hereditary and who bear a common name, follow a common occupation and claim a common origin" (Pathania and Tierney, 2018, p. 3; Pankaj, 2021). Reservations are a "face of social justice; they ended up proliferating caste identity" (Teltumbde, 2018, p. 53). Teltumbde (2018, p. 53) adds that untouchability "will not go away unless castes were destroyed." Although reservations were designed as a tool to eradicate poverty and improve the economic status of lower castes, the truth is that, under reservations, Dalits experienced "various hardships, discrimination, and exclusion" (Pankaj, 2021, p. 931).

The "distributions of power create a hierarchy different from the hierarchies of caste and class" (Béteille, 1965, p. 187; Tamás, 2006, p. 243: Subedi, 2013). Caste differs from class, as it is a system that is not defined essentially in terms of social honor; upward and downward movements are, in theory, inadmissible, and mobility is thus much slower in a graded system that "enjoys both legal and religious sanctions" (Béteille, 1965, p. 191). Contrary to caste and class, (Béteille, 1965, p. 190; Srinivas, 1962; Pathania and Tierney, 2018, p. 10; Chaudhry, 2013) adds that it is an open system. Classes are "*de facto* categories; they do not enjoy the legal and religious sanctions associated with Castes" (Béteille, 1965, p. 191). With the risk of oversimplifying, Béteille (1965, p. 191) posits, "the class system is largely subsumed under the caste structure."

Thus, the claims of the death of the caste system—as advocated by Ramkrishna Mukherjee (2000) and others—are quite a precipitation. Moreover, it does not do justice "to the large body of critical work on the social production of identities, forms of social distinction, and formation of group interests other than class that exists in ideological space and competition with class, all of which show that phenomena such as caste are not simply imagined and propped up by scholars and politicians" (Natrajan, 2005, p. 229).

I do agree with Wilkerson (2000, p. 23) "that caste is not a term often applied to the United States." That caste—as she (2000, p. 11) so well defined—is "one of the silent earthquakes" within the US as a nation and its public institutions; however, I have strong reservations with how she was voicing such eugenic silence. While I commend Wilkerson (2000) for bringing caste to the table, I contest the articulation and re-articulation she jazzed between caste and race and class, which misrepresents the historical idiosyncrasies of such dynamics. I will return to this issue later. Caste is caste. It is not class. It is not race, either.

Caste is Caste. Not Race!

> *Caste is not the same as race.*
> *—(Meena Dhanda, 2015)*

If equating caste with class as identical categories is a theoretical and historical misrepresentation, to do so with race—and above all, using as a matrix the deplorable racialized US society still struggling to be freed from the consequences of slavery—is a theoretical aberration and historical rape (see Phule, 1911). To say that US and Indian societies are historically segregated is one thing. To say that they were and are segregated in the same way—and to transplant unpardonable eugenic models from the Asian continent to the US and vice versa—is quite another and manifestly wrong. Indian and US societies were and are brutally segregated—a blatant historical carnage unbelievably 'scientifically' justified for centuries—but they were and continue to be in radically different ways. Race and caste saturate US and Indian societies differently. The stubbornness—which is not innocent—in interpreting historical and theoretical frameworks in the Global South based on the epistemological matrix of the global north is incomprehensible.

Slavery, poverty, rape, genocide, inequality, exploitation, and oppression are pivotal characteristics in the US and Indian societies as graded societies. However, they are historically and theoretically woven differently, yet with the same eugenic brutality. To construct the blunt, racialized, foundational aspects of US society as a caste system not only misrepresents the racialized historical reason underpinning US society but also incurs a dangerous theoretical, historical error because it deracializes the nation's original sin—racialized and genderized slavery. To place slavery out of race is unacceptable. Disposing of slavery as a dynamic of race to put it in a supposedly broader category—i.e., caste—is precipitation. Race is a general category that, together with class and gender, makes up the US matrix as an enslaved society. There is a tendency within particular, critical, progressive sectors and approaches woven within the Eurocentric epistemological matrix to assert that there is only one form of domination and, concomitantly, proclaim that there is only one form of resistance. This proved a lethal mistake (Santos, 1999; Paraskeva, 2021, 2022a, 2022b).

Such inaccuracy did not go unnoticed by Dalit intellectuals who fought tenaciously against it. Ambedkar (2016, p. 238, 2018, p. 20) argues that the caste system "does not demarcate racial division. The caste system is a social division of people of the same race." The caste system, as we know it today, "is admittedly not based in Aryo-Dravidian racial antagonism. It is a social system of an entirely different nature" (Cox, 1959, p. 84). Caste is not class. Caste is not race either; it is worse. Caste is caste. Ambedkar (2016, p. 236, 2018, p. 17) stresses that, to hold that distinction of castes "are distinctions of race, and to treat different castes as though there were so many different castes, is a gross perversion of facts."

What is the racial affinity between the Brahmin of the Punjab and the Brahmin of the Madras? What is the racial affinity between the untouchable of Bengal and the untouchable of Madras? What racial difference is there between the Punjab Brahmin and the Punjab Chamar? What racial difference exists between the Brahmin of Madras and the Pariah of Madras? The Brahmin of Punjab is racial of the same stock as the Chamar of Punjab, and the Brahmin of Madras is of the same race as Punjab is racially of the same stock as the Chamar of Punjab. The Brahmin of Madras is of the same race as the Pariah of Madras.
(Ambedkar, 2016, p. 236; 2018, p. 17)

The caste system, he adds, "cannot be said to have grown as means of preventing the admixture of races, or as a means of maintaining purity of blood." However, Western intellectuals "opted for race at the root cause of the problem of caste because they were themselves impregnated by color prejudice" (Ambedkar, 1979, p. 22).

There is no parallel, in the bloody struggle for black emancipation in the US, to the gotra system, a hallmark of the Brahmin graded social structure—"a system that reflects an exogenous division whose members are believed, particularly among Brahmins, to be agnatically decent from a saint or seer" (Béteille, 1965, p. 48). The sanguinary wrangle of "light-skin beneficiaries *vs*. dark-skin victims" (Hall and Mishra, 2018, p. 15) frames caste and race differently. Gary Tartakov (2018, pp. 33–36) argues that, while in practice, Dalit and African Americans are victims of a segregated yarn, "by contrast, the internal explanations of the U.S. race system and India's caste system are quite different." The Indian caste system, as we argued before, "is based on religious myth, while the U.S. ideology of race is pseud-scientific" (Tartakov, 2018, p. 36).

Approaches such as those of Warner, Myrdal, and others reduce caste in the US as a separation of whites and blacks, and "while the purpose was to oppose the color line to class distinctions, they accept the idea that caste is a particular and extreme form of class" (Dumont, 1970, p. 243). They could not be more wrong; for "caste is a social phenomenon and not a racial one" (Jaffrelot, 2003, 2005, p. 32). Teltumbde (2010, p. 11) insightfully highlights the specificity of the caste system, which notoriously distances caste from race and class.

While systems of social division have existed throughout history across the world, the form prevalent in India was not to be found anywhere else. Caste, as such, is a form of social stratification involving a mode of hierarchically arranged, closed endogamous strata, membership to which is ascribed by descent and between which contact is restricted and mobility impossible. The Indian word for caste is *jati*. When we refer to 'caste,' we speak of jati, although many tend to confuse it with *varna*, which refers to the basic 'classes,' four in number, established in Hindu scripture.

One should remember Meena Dhanda (2015) alerts that using the word 'caste' to describe the many groups, or 'jatis,' in India does not connote a racial differentiation between them, as the original meaning of the word 'caste' might imply. Without any euphemisms, Dhanda (2015, p. 40) argues that

The visibility of caste is not the visibility of skin color but of the clothed body, the body in the space of action, meaning, and vulnerability—where 'being clothed' includes wearing expressions as well as being dressed, projecting a voice, carrying the smell of clothes, body odors, being armed with the tools of the trade, marked or unmarked by scars, wrinkles and other signs of toil, age, exposure to the elements, displaying or hiding one's possessions. In our clothed encounters, other bodies are first marked not by skin color but by these identity markers that run ahead as we approach each other. Our bodies reside within social spaces—it is the acting body we see or hear first, not a colored, white, brown, or black face.

Caste is not the same as race (Dhanda, 2015). Moreover, The African American claim that blends caste and race is an inaccuracy produced by an African American belief system that "is centered on their historical struggle against racial oppression" (Brown, 2018, p. 45).

Thus, castes in a singular number are unreal, a non-reality, as "castes exist only in the plural number. There is no such thing as caste. There always castes" (Ambedkar, 1979, p. 20). Moreover, the caste system is "a negative thing. It merely prohibits persons belonging to different castes from intermarrying. It is not a positive method of selecting which two among a given caste should marry" (Ambedkar, 2016, p. 238, 2018, p. 19). Endogamy, Christopher Jaffrelot, 2005, p. 32) argues, was and is "the main springboard of caste, and the caste crystallized after the Brahmins turned inwards, henceforth refusing all matrimonial unions save those among their community." As Senart (1930, pp. 12–13) argues, "castes have often been compared—particularly by Hindus of English upbringing, who are very anxious at heart to lessen the distance between our races and theirs and to lower the barriers which separate India from Europe—whit the social distinctions that exist among us"—which is a blunt mistake. Caste, however, he (1930, p. x) adds, "corresponds only very remotely to our social classes, or race. Its constitution is far stronger, and its implications far more precise. It is an institution and an essential one." The question of caste "is not one of race at all" (Risley, 1892, p. xxi).

As I have been flagging, too many scholars, working from and within a Eurocentric epistemological matrix, erroneously mobilize "European ideas of race to unpack taxonomies related to *the Global* South" (Jayawardene, 2016, p. 332).[12] In doing so, they forcibly see a caste-graded system in class and racial terms as a racial and class wrangle, showing blunt incapability to engage in what Santos (2018) calls a process of 'translation'—one that respects the endless, different onto-epistemological diversity of the world (Paraskeva, 2016, 2018a, 2018b, 2021, 2022a, 2022b; Santos, 2014). One thing is to claim that "oppressed groups communities have historically shared critical, post-colonial and anti-colonial critiques, conceptualizations of social justice, and methods for mass resistance across national borders" (Goodnight, 2017); quite another is to argue, for instance, the accuracy of approaches such as critical race theory to unpack caste segregation in India. While 'critical race theory' provides 'approximations' with 'Dalit theories' the truth is that not caste, but "race is CRT's main conceptual framework for analyzing discrimination" (Goodnight, 2017, p. 666). As we examined before, "the caste system is a social division of people of the same race" (Ambedkar, 2016, p. 237, 2018, p. 18). Thus, if caste means race, then differences of sub-castes cannot mean differences of race because sub-castes become ex-hypothesia sub-divisions of one and the same race (Ambedkar, 2016, p. 237, 2018, p. 18).

While critical theory approaches might help unpack a caste system, "exploring the viability of CRT for analyzing inequities in India requires analysis of how race and caste and gender have been linked in discrimination in India." (Goodnight, 2017, p. 673). Such implies a move to deterritorialize, to de-link, and to commit to a non-derivative theory of translation, a decolonial zone of intersectionality—an itinerant educational and curriculum theory. Any attempt to examine the dynamics of caste segregation exclusively in terms of critical theories of race or gender—or even class, as we discussed earlier—not only omits glaring inconsistencies and "does not address potential incongruences between race and caste or key differences in the sociopolitical environments of India and the USA" (Goodnight, 2017, p. 674) but also, concomitantly, it is overtly epistemicidal.

To recapture and complexify Jayawardene's (2016, p. 331) proclamation, I would argue that caste dynamics cannot be "castigated reducing it to a raced and classed phenomenon"—although race and class are not absent categories within the caste dynamics. Unpacking caste within a Eurocentric classed and raced taxonomy wrongly parallels caste, class, and race as identical and speaks volumes to the epistemic despotism of Eurocentric perspectives (Santos, 2018; Paraskeva, 2021). This malaise crosses dominant and counter-dominant views. It is dangerous that this process that equates caste, class, and race as the same thing is built, "promoting the absoluteness" of class and/or race—as Jacques Rancière (2010) would put it. And, erroneously, one understands caste by understanding race or simplistically reducing the grapheme 'caste' to 'class' and/or 'race.' Counter-dominant Eurocentric approaches absolutize class and race—an egregious error.

As I have mentioned, specific literature—academic or not—claims this dangerous tendency. Attempts to 'synonymize' caste, class, and race are pretty palatable in the works of DuBois and Sumner—as we have examined previously—but also in approaches crafted by Warner (1936)—which was quite influential in Myrdal's masterpiece "An American Dilemma"—who argues that caste should be viewed as a form of absolutely rigid class; "it was more appropriate to describe blacks and whites in the U.S. as castes than as races or classes" (Béteille, 1990, p. 489, 1971). In Myrdal's terms, caste replaces race in the US "as pure practical manner" (Dumont, 1970, p. 243). For Warner (1936), though, the caste system entails a variety of classes.

US sociologists relied on "the same conceptual scheme as Warner and justified the characterization of blacks and whites as castes rather than races on the ground that they were socially, and not biologically, defined categories" (Béteille, 1990, p. 489). The work of Allison Davis and colleagues (1941, pp. 16–17; also, Davis, 1945) also echoes Warner's matrix as it dichotomizes the racialized, bloody war in the US as a caste issue between whites and blacks, "an inherently racial division of superior and inferior individuals as a will of God that edified society based on socialized and unsocialized individuals."

The most recent example of such a tendency—arguably the most popularized—frames Wilkerson's (2000) bestseller, "On Caste." Wilkerson's (2000) approach, like many others in the past—and she echoes some of them—completely nullifies the US original sin: racism. This tendency can be seen immediately in the opening chapters of her oeuvre and becomes more acute throughout her diegesis. Either through the language in which she practically replaces the term 'race' with 'caste' ("the African American as a man of a lower caste" [p. 6]) or through a completely misplaced global, historical analysis, in abusively drawing human history in three great castes ("the caste system of Nazi-Germany, India and the U.S." [p. 17]) or even through the eight pillars through which she proclaims the US as a caste society, Wilkerson (2020) does nothing more than lose herself in the contradiction she crafted. She (2020) ignored how the caste system globally was viewed from an Untouchable perspective.

Wilkerson's (2020) historical simplism opens the door to other crucial questions. For example, Ambedkar (2016, pp. 221–222, 2018, pp. 9–10) places the "social problem between Ulster and Southern Ireland, as a problem between Catholics and Protestants, which is essentially a problem of Caste which prevented the solution of the political problem." The fact that caste is also—but not only—simplistic analysis obliterates a graded dynamic among people of the same race. Mia Couto, the great Mozambican novelist—and who already deserves a Nobel—unleashes a scathing critique of the idyllic and parsimonious vision of the peoples of Africa, permanently portrayed as pure, tainted purity and taint only violated in the first 'encounter' with the white individual. Many African leaders were deeply involved in the slave trade—a reality that can no longer be covered up—and that has changed the debate on reparation policies. There is this tendency to read the non-Eurocentric, African, Asian, and Latin American past as 'clean,' 'ethereal,' a movement that reveals an ideological cult of condescension and, therefore, epistemicidal that allows affirming that beyond the equator, there are no sins (Santos, 2014). What Wilkerson (2020) does is to eviscerate from the centrality of the history of human civilization the tremendous historical processes that map African, Asian, and Latin American cultures—forged through struggles as noble and bloodthirsty as those of the West.

Wilkerson (2020) persistently and wrongly places "caste as the grammar that structures the language of race" (Gilda and Horn, 2021, p. 21). In her (Gilda and Horn, 2021, p. 21) understanding, "race is the visible decoy, the primary tool, the front man for the caste system, doing its heavy lifting, or a visual cue, a historical flashboard, indicting to what cast an

American should be assigned." Her (2021) approach and many others fall into an egregious swamp, ignoring that "to call American blacks a caste need not imply that whites composed one too." It is one thing to invoke Martin Luther King Jr. when he, in a sharp stereophony, parallels caste and untouchability within the African American struggle in the US ("I am untouchable and every negro in America in an untouchable"); it is quite another to assume that, for Dr. King Jr., Indian caste untouchability and US racial untouchability are identical. Also, it is one thing to say that "the untouchables cannot forget the fate of the Negroes" (Ambedkar, 2009. p. 171); it is quite another to claim that Dalits and Untouchables replaced their outcaste identity by the African American raced subject position.

It is one thing "to sail on a journey to reach out across the oceans" (Gilda and Horn, 2021, 20); it is quite another not realizing that it is only by force that the dynamics of segregation in the United States and India can be equated as identical. Wilkerson (2021) regards the immense African American community as Dalits—a grandiose mistake. While admitting that the US and India are profoundly different from each other, she (2021) argues that "they operate under the same instruction manual" (Gilda and Horn, 2021, p. 20). Did she not think it is defensible to say that the Dalits in the United States are the blacks and that the blacks in India are the Dalits? Can't she see that her own life story destroys her argument? How many bi-millionaire Dalits does Wilkerson know? Also, if the US "caste hierarchy is so powerful, how did the country elect a two-term black president?" (Gilda and Horn, 2021, p. 23)—a sharp contrast with India in which "someone like Ambedkar could never win an election in post-independence India" (Teltumbde, 2018, p. 82). Wilkerson's (2021) *On Caste* "is not a formally or analytically structured work but a collage of short sermons, poetic flights, social philosophizing, potted history, journalistic sketches, personal anecdotes, and meditations, across thirty-plus uneven chapters. The result is as conceptually thin as it is stylistically over-egged" (Gilda and Horn, 2021, p. 23). Wilkerson (2020) surrenders caste to the absolutism of race or class. Also, she (2020) ignores that 'African Americans' is a social construction whose roots go back to when the first white conqueror faced the Native Americans and slavery. African Americans were brought to the US, while Dalits were in India already. Unquestionably—I repeat—there are very strong points of contact—and approximations—between the anti-racial and anti-caste struggles. There are irrefutable similarities and mutual influences both in black and Dalit reasons and in the emergence of powerful movements such as the Black/ Dalit Panthers. However, going beyond the similarities and approximations and claiming that, if we are facing identical metamorphoses, is a step forward toward the precipice. Caste unveils very particular archeology; one that doesn't fit orthodox social models; one that "becomes intelligible in the social context, where every other person appears as a stranger to every other person in opaque social relations. The urban context makes it difficult for the pure untouchable to remain in touch with the despicable untouchable" (Guru, Chapter 4).

Could it be that we were all wrong? Does racism—the original sin of the US that structures our schools and curricula—continue to persist because we treat it as a matter of race or class rather than caste? And if so, how was it possible for us to plow on this error for decades? Could the triumphalism and popularity of racialized analyses such as Charles Herrnstein and Richard Murray's "The Bell Curve" (1995) capture long percentages of common sense because they are not challenged in terms of caste?

A close reading of crucial works such as Chancellor Williams's (1987) "The Destruction of Black Civilization" or Martin Bernal's (1987) "The Black Athena" documents the inaccuracy of approaches that subsume racial struggles under inexistent caste categories and vice versa. There is a lack of historical, critical, and ideological precision in these analyses, in which our educational institutions are not innocent, and as Asa Hillard (2001, p. 12) argues, "it is crucial to gain clarity, first, about the meaning of the topic of race and education, and then about the nature of the problem in education that is related to."

While Wilkerson's (2020) volume on *Caste* is quite timely—under the ferocious awakening of eugenic impulses in the US and elsewhere—and helps to place 'caste' at the debate table, it is undeniable that it shows sharp conceptual and historical inaccuracies. There is the historical existence of an Afro-Solidarity between African Americans and Dalits in the racialized and casteized struggles against segregation (Purakayastha, 2019); it is undeniable—the existence of common paths, movements, strategies, as well as accomplishments and challenges. However, commonalities are just commonalities, and they cannot cancel out the historical and theoretical differences between two battlefields that, on a global scale, fight against social segregation. Referring to Latinos and Asians as 'middle caste,' thus 'a-racializing' such graded communities or the similarities created between the Black Panther and anti-caste struggles, is a theoretical oversight and an apparent misreading of history. Can one argue that a black African who stayed in Africa—not being chained and thrown aboard a ship like his compatriots—and was brutally exploited, raped, and oppressed—sees slavery, exploitation, and oppression in the same way as relatives and friends who were chained and brought to the American continent? With *Žižekean* glasses, Wilkerson (2020) laudably tells us, 'Yes, please.'

The more we dig into Wilkerson's (2020) diegesis, the more we get the idea that what was/is caste in India is race, and race in the US is caste. The absolutism of the caste in the United States curiously intersects with the absolutism of the race in India in a heartbreaking paradox and one of the symptoms of what I have already examined in other spaces (Paraskeva, 2016, 2018a, 2018b, 2021, 2022a, 2022b)—and pointed out earlier—as the monumentality of white reason. This monumentality dares to determine who and how the other is within the Global North and the Global South, thus rewriting its history.

Despite some commonalities, caste, class, and race differences are glaring. Caste, Dhanda et al. (2014, p. iv, 2015) proclaimed, "is distinct from class, race, and various forms of ethnicity. Caste and race have long been interlinked, but caste hierarchy cannot have originated in social gradations based on skin color." While at the center "of race and caste superstructures sits dehumanization, inequality and condemnation" (Yengde, 2022, p. 348), caste "is more insidious" (Yengde, 2022, p. 349). Equating caste with race/or class is what Mosse (2020, p. 15) defines as "externalization as it misrepresents—maliciously transmutes—caste as a racist idea." Such misrepresentation makes caste "appears benign. To Dalits though caste is not benign, but brutal" (Natrajan, 2022, pp. 309–310). While "race divides, caste subdivides" (Harney, 2015, p. 45); North American and Latin American graded systems "do not exactly conform to those of the Indian caste system" (Harney, 2015, p. 117); whereas "Brahminhood is a no-entry zone, untouchability in a no-exit zone" (Manoharan, 2017, p. 87).

Kheya Bag and Susan Watkins (2021) summarized such differences rather accurately. First, they (2021) argue, is history. The history of "African-Americans has been packed with jarring shifts every two generations between different political-economic regimes: from slave labor to sharecropping to urban-proletarian life, and thence to the present class bifurcation between educated professionals and low-paid work or joblessness." Quite different is the case of India's caste system. It is an ancient system that "change has been molecular at best." Also, secondly, one is before "the richest, most technologically developed, compared to one of the poorest" (Bag and Watkins, 2021, p. 56). Thirdly, "while the U.S. racial order is also *sui generis* there is no prevailing religiously sanctioned pyramid." The US and India show radical forms of social mobility, as India "forms the world's most elaborate, hierarchical and fetishized system of social stratification, with many thousands of regional *jati* (birth communities) ranked in order of holiness and purity, from the highest brahmins to the lowest untouchables" (Bag and Watkins, 2021, p. 56). Fourthly, the racial dynamic is different. While, in the US, "the marker is ethnic: presumed ancestral descent from the African slave population, in India, it may be surname, neighborhood, job or even bearing and demeanor—anything that signals birth into an endogamous regional *jati*, once linked to hereditary occupation, or origin" (Bag and Watkins, 2021, p. 57). Finally, caste, race, and class framed different cultures and societies. The socio-economic conditions triggered by 'manual scavengers,' their hereditary task to clean up human excrement, simply do not exist in the US (Bag and Watkins, 2021, p. 57).

As Appadurai (2021a) argues, one thing is the understandable "mutual admiration in human history among both oppressors and oppressed"; quite another is establishing a deep 'structural comparison' between caste and race or class. To begin with "caste crystallized over several millennia of Indian history, primarily as a cosmology which allowed pastoral and agricultural colonizers from the Northwest of the subcontinent to gradually colonize thousands of groups and communities who were previously not organized into castes" (Appadurai, 2021a, p. 2). That is, Appadurai (2021a) adds, caste dynamics "allowed many locally dominant groups to organize their local subordinates into a system which conflated rank, occupation, and purity into a single status system." Moreover, "purity and pollution, constitute a driving source of caste ideology in India, (O'Hanlon, 1985), whereas, in the US, the polluting status of black Americans is an effect of racialized ranking and not a cause" (Appadurai, 2021a, p. 2). The Indian caste system, he (2021) adds, "is geared to an infinity of caste ranks"—a sharp difference from the US racialized system. Finally, while the top of the Indian caste system, usually composed of Brahmins, "is permanent, closed, and unquestionable, the bottom, which is certainly defined by Dalits (Untouchables), is strangely porous since every Indian caste, including the lowest, has someone or some group, usually in a neighboring village, who performs polluting services (like cremation, scavenging and hair-cutting) for them, and is, therefore, lower than they are" (Appadurai, 2021a, p. 2). This is very different from "the exclusionary logic of race, which is binary (black versus white) and lacks any cosmological basis for one black person to feel racially superior to another black" (Appadurai, 2021a, p. 2). Caste dynamics, Appadurai (2021a, p. 20, 2021b) argues, are "very different from the creation of whiteness as a category of domination in the context of the colonial and later independent U.S." Teltumbde (Chapter 3) makes no euphemisms: 'caste is caste, not race,' as race and caste relations are different.

> While in some sense, the racial oppression appears severer than caste oppression, simply because a black person cannot escape his or her physical identity, whereas a lower caste person can easily do that, there is more to the caste oppression than meets the eye. Like the visibility of race, the racial oppression is also visible; the caste oppression is deep drawn, subtle and, therefore, far more vicious.
>
> (Teltumbde, Chapter 3)

So far, we have examined how imprudent it is to define caste, class, and race as identical categories. We reiterate that rashness incurs a serious historical, theoretical, and political error. The argument is weird, however. Ultimately, there is no caste! There is 'only' class and race; caste is constructed as synonymous with race and class, thus nullifying the idiosyncrasy of each social category. From the perspective of the millions oppressed by caste dynamics, this amalgamation is, at the very least, abusive and obscene. Welcome to the violence of the identical, as Byung Chul Han (2018) would have put it. Such violence twists the ethnographic, ideological, and political understandings of caste (Basu, 2003) and misrepresents historical and theoretical matters; it is, according to Ranajit Guha (1997, p. 85), "an act of violence." Our educational institutions and curriculum field are not innocent of such violence.

This tendency to grant oneself the right to perceive the 'other' better than the 'other' can perceive itself is a vital characteristic of the egotism of Western thought; an arrogance that dares to describe the real 'of the other'—that 'other' situated, as I examined earlier, on the other side of the line—either as non-existent or through social constructions only possible in perspective on this side of the line and in a language—in most cases—only perceptible within the text and context on this side of the line. And with this, concomitantly, a blatant historical foresight is produced. The pilfering of history, so well denounced by intellectuals like Jack Goody (2006) and Andre Gunder Frank (1998)—although crafted from a different perspective—fits perfectly in this context. This arrogance overtly mirrors the true epistemological colors of white reason—a reason that saturates both dominant and counter-dominant Eurocentric views.

The Monumentality of White Reason

> *The West is not the West. It is a project, not a place.*
> *—(Edouard Glissant, 1992)*

The monumentality of white, Eurocentric reason is structured in its divisive matrix, which—as we had the opportunity to examine—among other issues, promotes abyssal thinking. This divisive thinking promotes the epistemological despotism that much more than creating the 'other,' 'their social categories,' and 'the other side of the line,' eugenically grants itself the right to determine how and where the other could and should be defined—as if the 'other' were devoid of any cognitive capacity and their own epistemological matrix. Unfortunately, specific sectors of the counter-hegemonic hemisphere cannot get out of this straitjacket that is the monumentalism of Eurocentric thought, which prevents thinking the 'other' of and about the 'other' in terms of the 'other'; that is, to commit to what Santos (2014) calls epistemologies from the South—going to the South, living in the South and learning from and with the South.

Slavoj Žižek provides us with a graphic example of such an inability, not just to stop talking on behalf of the other but also to show 'just' knowledge about otherness. One day, Žižek states that, in Montana, one Indian refers to himself as Indian. Immediately a white, well-meaning liberal interrupted him and said, "No, you are Native American; don't you know you are humiliating yourself!" The Indian, Žižek adds, gave a perfect answer. "No, I am sorry, Native American is, for me, much more racist. Native American means part of nature and part of your own culture. I prefer to be called Indian; in this way, my name is a sign of white man's stupidity as they thought they were in India when they arrived in my land."

This blunder is so evident in the way the caste system is interpreted. That is like the "the Indian is not Indian but a Native American"; millions of Dalits are confronted with the error of focusing on caste. Like the Indians, Dalits also do not realize how that is 'humiliating,' and they were told—through the monumentalism of Eurocentric science—that they were/are wrong and do not understand what is happening historically and theoretically. The Dalit saga is not the caste system, nor even how the racialization of the caste system takes place. The way out of Dalits' malaise relies on class and/or race; that is, the answer depends on Caliban's reason (Henry, 2000) which has the master key to unlock the problem.

While Wilkerson's (2002) volume raised many reservations, other approaches deeply surprised me. I got used to seeing intellectuals like Perry Anderson and Loïc Wacquant as 'comrades in arms,' allies in the struggle against the brutality triggered historically and daily by the capitalist system. Their analysis is crucial to better understanding the failure of our educational and curriculum approaches. Their expeditions into caste dynamics somehow triggered the same feeling I learned from Aijaz Ahmad (2008) in his reaction to Frederic Jameson. I got used to seeing Anderson and Wacquant as Ahmad got used to seeing Jameson—"as birds of the same feeder" (Ahmad, 2008, p. 96)—or probably birds of close feeders, yet different nests. Seeing that Anderson and Wacquant—although through different and deeper avenues—fall into the tendency to 'read' the 'other side of the line' (Santos, 2014) with glasses and dyopteries of 'this side of the line' (Santos, 2014), wasn't "a good feeling" (Ahmad 2008, p. 96) as well.

In Wacquant's (2002, p. 45) words, "the systematic enslavement and dehumanization of Africans and their descendants on North American soil was the creation of a racial caste line separating what would later become labeled 'blacks' and 'whites.'" He (2002, pp. 54–55) further adds that the "Jim Crow regime reworked the racialized boundary between slave and free into a rigid caste separation between 'whites' and 'Negros'—comprising all persons of known African ancestry, no matter how minimal—that infected every crevice of the postbellum social system in the South." Wacquant (2002) places slavery not just within the matrix of the caste system, but he puts caste as the logic undergirding slavery. To be confronted with such a claim was, I admit, a very puzzling feeling. It was my 'Ahmad momentum.'

Aijaz Ahmad (2008, pp. 95–96) reacted to Frederic Jameson's "rhetoric of otherness." In Jameson's proclamation, "the teaching of the World literature in the U.S. academic should be informed by a sense not only of Western literature but of world literature" (Ahmad, 2008, p. 95). While Jameson's take needed to be seen in the context of his diegesis (Jameson, 2005, 2016)—one committed to social justice—the fact is that it came across as egregiously celebratory, to say the least. Jameson's plea for syllabus reform pushed Ahmad to "an awkward position" (Ahmad, 2008, p. 95). He deserves to be quoted in length.

> If I were to name the one literary critic/theorist writing in the U.S. today whose work I generally hold in the highest regard, it would surely be Jameson. I am a Marxist. I always thought of us, Jameson and myself, as birds of the same feather, even though we never quite flocked together. But then, when I was on the fifth page of his text (specifically, on the sentence starting with 'All third-world texts are necessarily . . .'), I realized that what was being theorized was myself, among many other things. I was born in India and wrote in Urdu, a language not commonly understood among US intellectuals. So, I said to myself: 'All . . . necessarily?' It felt odd. The further I read, the more I realized with no bit of chagrin that the man whom I had for so long, so affectionally, albeit from a physical distance, taken as a comrade, was, in my own opinion, my civilizational Other. It was not a good feeling.
> (Ahmad, 2008, pp. 95–96)

I call such the 'Ahmad momentum,' the same momentum I experienced when I read Wacquant's argument. Far from me was I able to imagine that one of the most influential public intellectuals for me, with an unavoidable work for the understanding of the monstrosity of a racialized society, in the challenge to racial segregation and inequality, would fall into the tendency to refuse to read 'the other' beyond the Eurocentric epistemological hemisphere. Why, Hamid Dabashi (2015, p. 5) argues, "Europeans should not be able to read even when we write in the language they understand?" Because

> as 'Europeans' caught in the snare of an exhausted but self-nostalgic metaphor, they are assimilating what they read back into the trap and to what they already know—and are thus incapable of projecting it forward into something they may know and yet might be able to learn.
> (Dabashi, 2015, pp. 5–6)

Like Jameson, Wacquant (2002) not only theorizes racism in the United States as a caste issue but also theorizes the racialized subject, a-racializing it and formatting racial maladies as a caste issue. The sensation was one of strangeness. As I delved into the text, I tried to understand what positive things could be achieved by framing eugenics in US society as a matter of caste rather than race. I tried to understand how the scourge of slavery would be viewed in the light of caste and not race—either in the US or on the African continent itself. I also tried to understand the question of caste in the light of punishment as an institution, one of the most brilliant avenues of his great precursor, Pierre Bourdieu. For example, in my understanding, framing Jim Crow as "caste terrorism" (Wacquant, 2022, p. 81) subalternates racial dynamics right at the core of Crow's matrix. I understand the nexus between race and ethnicity, unpacked by Wacquant (2002, 2022). However, I have difficulty understanding the racialization of the US as a caste phenomenon. Sampath (Chapter 7) uses no euphemisms in his deconstruction of caste, arguing that "caste like a tribe-edification elevate to a persona based on the accident of birth and symbol of false pride." The ethnic, tribal nature of caste is not de-linked to particular caste idiosyncrasies; some of them are irreversibly different from those of class, race, tribe, and ethnicity. To argue race as the logic undergirding caste, thus deploying caste instead of race or vice versa, is a simplistic excavation of the wrangle signifier signified. Caste, race, class, or gender are not mechanical signs.

Recapturing an argument raised before, and as highlighted in Raj Sampath (Chapter 7), caste makes it "impossible to move from one level to another across generations; there is no predecessor or successor system in human societies, including intergenerational slavery through the ages, Western feudalism, or Jim Crow white-Black segregation in America, that compares with the caste system." I do reiterate my disquiet, especially when he denounces the monumentality of Eurocentric thought that frames the civic debate. According to him (2022, p. 71) "academic and civic debates on race globally are dominated by American categories, assumptions, and claims—as illustrated recently by the international diffusion of intersectionality in the academy and Black Lives Matter on the streets. But the American definition of race as a civic felony and blackness as public dishonor transmitted through strict hypodescent is historical outliers." Like Wilkerson (2021), Wacquant (2002, 2022) also frames the caste system as a 'black-and-white division', and he undermines the US racialized society's imparity with the 'outcaste.' While a parity could be crafted between 'undercaste' and 'underace,' there is no 'outraced' in the U.S.—at least, in the same terms as it exists in India and diaspora.

I was expecting a different take, however. To my disquiet, just like Ahmad (2008, p. 96), "it was not a good feeling." As Linda Smith (1999) argues, the oppressed is the most researched subject on the planet; however,

Wacquant (2002) and others ignore that the eyes of the other "are bound to be different eyes because they are trained in another culture" (Santos, 2018, p. 175).

The epistemicide is not only related to the killing of knowledge but also the concomitant construction of a non-real reality, a reality that promotes certain events, legitimizes specific historical structures, band builds and encourages certain myths, heroes, and martyrs who fit into the definitions and parameters defined by Eurocentric rationality, relegating others to unforgivable ostracism, throwing them into the nimbus of nothingness, of non-existence. The epistemicide is at the root of why "we know little about social and educational change" (Popkewitz, 1992, p. 309). On this level, the visibility and existence conferred on Mahatma Gandhi must be framed, visibility and existence that produces Ambdekar's invisibility and nonexistence—one of the most acute symptoms of the epistemic nature that saturates Eurocentric common sense. Raj Sampath (Chapter 7) nails it when he coins caste as a crucial hallmark of prosperous reason and its social apparatuses. He states:

> Caste, in many respects, defies any current Western intuitions of reason and madness (as an object of scientific reason) and therefore traditional anthropologies or sociologies of caste. Caste hides the name of something that is neither reason nor madness. Caste is the other side of social stratification as a purely material structure of culture that relies on religious myths to propel itself; rather, caste has to do with a speculative, metaphysical realm of temporality and the transmigration of souls that punish bodies in their lived states. Caste has nothing to do with culture, despite all anthropological bias. A phantom-like quality pulses within the material core of caste as a continuous dividing of divisions in social space
>
> (Sampath, Chapter 7)

Another example of the accurate epistemological colors of the monumentality of modern Western reason is visible in Perry Anderson's (2013) approach—and for me, another unpleasant 'Ahmad momentum.' Anderson's (2013) approaches not only—inadvertently—subalternate Indian intellectuals and offer a condescending and unnecessary, parsimonious, immaculate, naïve view of Indian onto-epistemological veins, but in doing so, for example, they prevent the needed recognition and critical examination, from the perspectives of the epistemologies from the South (Santos, 2014)—of 'Gandhi and Gandhism.' He (2013) underscores crucial aspects of Gandhi's and Ambedkar's positions on varna *vs.* caste.

Conversely to Gandhi, Ambedkar (2016, p. 288, 2018, p. 46) claims that "caste had a divine basis" that needed to be destroyed. A "social endosmosis" (Ambedkar, 2016, p. 260, 2018, p. 29) could not be achieved in a society "in which caste has made public opinion impossible" (Ambedkar,

2016, p. 260, 2018, p. 29). Menon (2014, p. 36) frames Anderson's (2013) approach as "a crassly Orientalist analysis" (p. 36), using unreliable sources, a "pitiless exposure of Indian ideology, showing a method of engaging with non-Western modes of thought jeering like a schoolboy at funny foreign notions to make sarcastic jibes" (pp. 44–45).

The altercations between Gandhi and Ambedkar were profound and revealed two different visions of society. They exposed Gandhi's conservative, reactionary, sexist impulses—paradoxically erased in the mystified image produced by the West. Gandhi is crafted based on the epistemological parameters of the West. And in this process, his polemical and disgusting positions regarding the caste system, gender and sexuality, and religious matters are completely obliterated (Roy, 2016). In fact, the anti-caste struggle did not ignore gender segregation. Jyotirao Phule becomes a leading voice in the struggle against the "exploitation of women and underprivileged classes and protection of human rights" (Malik-Goure, 2015). Phule (1911, p. 18) frames "the history of Brahmin domination in India" as a matrix of gendered caste dynamics as well. In doing so, Ambedkar's thoughts and work are not only erased from the map, but the historical legacy of great anti-caste intellectuals in the struggle against the caste system is also produced as non-existent. Unlike Gandhi, "who finds the solution of untouchability in the moral surgery of the heart, Ambedkar suggests the annihilation of caste of which untouchability is just the existence" (Guru, Chapter 4)

The sublime exponent of the wrangle between Gandhi and Ambedkar erupts during the famous Poona Act[13] with irreversible splinters in the Jat-Pat Todak Mandal of Lahore, a scandal—a forum for breaking up the caste system (Roy, 2016). Gandhi's position on the 'Dalit' question is, at minimum, very faltering. Gandhi, Arundathi Roy (2016, p. 26) argues, was "an admirer of the caste system," and he was not necessarily in favor of smashing such a system, but "he believed that should be no hierarchy between castes and all castes should be considered equal and brought into the varna system." He also never concedes to Ambedkar as the representative of the "whole of the Untouchables of India" (Omvedt, 1994, p. 171). While arguing that "he would rather that Hinduism died than that untouchability lived" (Omvedt, 1994, p. 171), Gandhi, however, argues about the fallacy of Ambedkar as leading the Dalit cause, which "creates a division in Hinduism which he cannot possibly look forward" (Omvedt, 1994, p. 171). Gandhi's tottery is not unnoticed by Ambedkar, who questions his commitment and solidarity to the Dalit's struggle for emancipation. If Gandhi is the real friend of the Untouchables, he (Ambedkar, 2009, pp. 243–245) argues, why did he

> Go on fast many a time to achieve a variety of objects which are dear to him, but he never fast even once for the sake of the Untouchables? Why did he go to the length of making a pact with the Muslims to isolate

and defeat the untouchables? Why did he declare a fast unto death, the object of which was to deprive the untouchables of the benefit of the Communal Award by this extreme form of coercion? After accepting the Poona Act, why did Gandhi not keep up the gentlemen's agreement and instruct the Congress High Command to include representatives of the Untouchables in the Congress Cabinets? How can the Untouchables regard Gandhi as being earnest who, when in 1924 he got an opportunity to impose upon the Hindus the obligation to remove Untouchability, did not do so even though he had the power and the occasion to reinforce it?

Gandhi and *Gandhism* offer no hope to the Untouchables (Ambedkar, 2009). Gandhi and his follower, Ambedkar (2009, p. 285), frame caste "as an anachronism. They did not say caste is evil, they did not say that it is an anathema." While "he might say/imply that it is not supportive of the caste system, he does not say that he is against the Varna system" (Ambedkar, 2009, p. 285).

Another irreversible fracture erupted when, on December 12, 1935, Ambedkar accepted an invitation from Sam Ram, the secretary of Jat-Pat Todak Mandal, to produce a lecture for the forum; upon receiving a written draft of the lecture, the committee decided to cancel Ambedkar's speech due to his refusal in addressing an issue, which was viewed as being "undoubtedly outside of the scope of the Mandal" (Ambedkar, 2016, p. 196, 2018, p. xix). That issue was Ambedkar's blunt criticism of Hindutva logic and his call to walk away from Hinduism, blaming the endemic malaise of the caste system.

In this undelivered address—published subsequently as the "Annihilation of Caste"— Ambedkar uses no euphemisms and blasts Hinduism as a non-religion and at the root of the caste system. He (2016, p. 254) argues that the so-called Hindu religion "ceased to be a missionary religion when the caste system grew among the Hindus." That is, he (2016) adds, "the Hindu society, as a collection of castes, and each caste being a closed corporation, there is no place for a convert. Thus, the caste has prevented the Hindus from expanding and absorbing other religious communities. So long as Caste remains, Hindu religion cannot be made a missionary religion." Moreover, Hinduism and the Hindu society are 'myths' and he proclaimed that

> The effect of caste on the ethics of the Hindus is simply deplorable. Caste has killed the public spirit. Caste has destroyed the sense of public charity. Caste has made public opinion impossible. A Hindu's public is his caste. His responsibility is only to his caste. His loyalty is restricted only to his caste. Virtue has become caste-ridden, and morality has

become caste-bound. There is no sympathy for the deserving. There is no appreciation of the meritorious. There is no charity for the needy. Suffering as such calls for no response. There is charity, but it begins with the caste and ends with the caste. There is sympathy, but not for men of other castes.

(Ambedkar, 2016, p. 259, 2018, p. 26)

The "Annihilation of Caste" didn't go unnoticed by Gandhi (2016), who reacted vehemently against it. While arguing that "no reformer could ignore the delivered address" (Gandhi, 2016, p. 322), he (2016, p. 322) opens the hostilities by arguing that "Ambedkar was a challenge to Hinduism." He (2016, p. 333) questions Ambedkar's (2016) claims that "the vast majority of Hindus had not only conducted themselves inhumanly against those of their fellow religionists whom they classed as Untouchables, but they based such conduct on the authority of the scriptures." While flagging that Ambedkar was "not alone in his disgust" (Gandhi, 2016, p. 323), he also vehemently challenges Ambedkar's erroneous historical interpretation of Hinduism, undermines the tolerant characteristic of Hinduism, and argues that "caste has nothing to do with religion, but it is a custom whose origins I do not know, and do not need to know for the satisfaction of my spiritual hunger" (Gandhi, 2016, p. 326). Gandhi (2016) ends his critique on Ambedkar stating that "the profound mistake he did was to pick out texts of doubtful authenticity and value."

Ambedkar's rebuttal was no less sophisticated and ballistic. He (2016, p. 333, 2018, p. 71) argues that, with his address, he wanted "to provoke the Hindus to think" that Gandhi had missed his argument entirely and that the issues he had raised "are not the issues that arise out of what he is pleased to call his indictment to Hindus." After advocating the authenticity of the texts—"they are all taken from the writings of late Mr. Tilak who was a recognized Sanskrit authority" (Ambedkar, 2016, p. 335, 2018, p. 73)—Ambedkar (2016, 2018) argues that "not only none of the Saints ever attacked the caste system, on the contrary, they were staunch believers in the system of castes, but also the masses have been taught that a Saint might break caste, but the common man must not" (Ambedkar, 2016, pp. 334–335, 2018, p. 73). Moreover, Ambedkar (2016, p. 340, 2018, p. 75) was against the idea that "Hindus could be persuaded to follow a high standard of morality" and thus be engaged and committed to more tolerant approaches and attitudes.

In his (2016, p. 340, 2018, p. 75) terms, "anyone who relies on an attempt to turn the members of the caste Hindus into a better man by improving his character is wasting energy and hugging and illusion." Ambedkar proceeds with the devasting attack on Gandhi, questioning his coherence. "Does the Mahatma practice what he preaches?" He unpacks Gandhi's overt contradictions, not just on heredity but also on the caste system itself, arguing that Gandhi, in a piece entitled "Caste versus Class," had defended "that the caste system was better than the class system on the ground that caste was the best possible adjustment for social stability" (Ambedkar, 2016, p. 347, 2018, pp. 78–79). Ambebdkar (2016, 2018) ends his diegeses by arguing that Gandhi "appears not to believe in thinking as he prefers to follow the Saints" and labors in irreversible confusion. Such confusion, on the one hand, is because "he was in almost everything the simplicity of a child, with the child's capacity for self-deception, and like a child, he can believe in anything he wants to believe"; on the other hand, such confusions is triggered by "the double role he wants to play—of Mahatma and a politician" (Ambedkar, 2009, p. 351). Caste, Ambedkar (2009) argues "is a notion; a state of mind," and under Gandhi and *Gandhism*,

> The common man must keep toiling ceaselessly for a pittance and remain a brute. Gandhism, with its call back to nature, means back to nakedness, squalor, poverty, and ignorance for the vast majority of the people. Class structure in *Gandhism* is not an accident. It is its official doctrine. (p. 269)

The praise for Gandhi and inclusively for Gandhian pedagogies—shows the conundrum of a one-dimensional matrix, a vivid example of the eugenic abyssal reason. This 'side of the line' notarized what is valid and legit on 'the other side of the line.' The praise for Gandhi comes with a tag price: The 'Ambekaricide.'

I am not tossing Gandhi's legacy into the dustbin of history. Neither am I drafting here an Ambedkarite *vs.* Gandhian map (see Biswas, 2021). I question how the monumentality of Western reason produces Gandhi as an icon, giving him certain visibility at the expense of the invisibility of other figures or of some of the issues related to caste and gender he championed in very unacceptable and deplorable ways. While Gandhi could be considered—in certain hemispheres—a critical 'card' within the 'dialectic intercultural translation' (Santos, 2018, p. 33) that cannot be accurately grasped—from an epistemology from the South perspective—dashing Ambedkar and the caste struggle toward emancipation to the nimbus of nowhere, to "the abyssal line, the zone of non-being" (Santos, 2018, p. 20). The clash between Gandhi and Ambedkar—and their respective followers—is a wrangle that persisted throughout history. While the former advocated "eradicate the discrimination based on caste, the latter championed eradicating the caste system itself" (Sampath, Chapter 7; Yengde and Teltumbde, 2018).

The examples provided by Wilkerson, Zižek, Wacquant, Anderson, and others speak volumes about the temerity to impose a one-dimensional epistemological matrix—capable of packing and unpacking every social construction in human history—thus killing any other epistemological existence beyond the Eurocentric hemisphere. It provides a real example of the authentic colors of the epistemicidal nature of such a reason.

An Absence Presence in Our Field

> *[The silence on caste in the field] is cacophonous.*
> —*(Murzban Jal, Chapter 8)*

One of the most prominent symptoms of the monumentality of Western thought relates to the absence of caste in education, curriculum, and teacher education debates. Such monumentality depends on the perpetuation of 'this' type of absence. It reflects the arrogance of hegemonic and counter-hegemonic movements. While the former is not even predisposed to interpret the curriculum phenomena as a political arena and within the context of class, race, or gender dynamics—much less caste—the latter incomprehensibly either silences caste or, when they address it, makes it subsumed in a perspective of class or race. In each case, caste is treated as non-existent, a non-issue. This monumentality enacts the eugenics conception of single dominant and counter-dominant visions, both monolithically designed based on the Western matrix and which delimits what is, should, and has been the theory and history of education, curriculum, and teacher education. Such epistemological arrogance "translates itself into normative dualisms such as 'truth/false,' 'knowledge/opinion'" (Santos, 2018, p. 38). Imposing a distorted view of reality can only reflect a malformed theory and history. Welcome to the hemisphere of Occidentosis (Al-l-Ahmad, 1984).

The monumentality of modern reason is granted in its eugenic scientific matrix, it is a form of violence, a symptom of its violence. This monumentality is an epistemic scandal (Chow, 2006). The violence of modernity is the violence of modernity's reason, it is the violence of modernity's science. The violence of modernity is the naturalization of the violence of its reason and its science as non-violent reason and, at the limit, a violent reason, but necessary. The science of modernity subscribes to the eugenic codes of "vivisection, indifference, triage, disassembling of the body" (Visvanathan 1997)—banal socialized codes, scientifically. This is not a minor issue since the much-vaunted scientific management has its roots 'in the vivisection of the animal body—a management that determined what would come to be defined by Taylor and Ford as an assembly line' (Visvanathan, 1997)—and which would become dominant in our field. The reason and science of modernity "are not sacred cows but fat cows" (Visvanathan, 1997, p. 40) in the curriculum temple. Such reason and science impose like a cult, an act of faith, a particular graded view of society and humanity; like a temple of a sacrosanct verb that conveys the only scientific truth, it scandalously builds a non-existence multitude "hereness of the Other as subjects of history" (Lionnet and Shi, 2011, p. 9); odd as it might be, such monumentality reason and science vandalizes its own epistemological temple—as Venturini (2023) would put it. The absence of caste in the curriculum debate desecrates the conventional Eurocentric curriculum 'liturgies'—dominant and counter-dominant. Reason and the experimental eugenic science of modernity were also constructed through the curriculum as an epistemic laboratory, promoting the production, development, and consolidation of a modern (I would add curriculum) theory not only as a system of political control but, above all as a vehicle for incorporating a very concrete form of violence – vivisection – fabricated as inevitable in the face of development challenges (Visvanathan, 1997). The absence of caste in debates in our field—or the recurrent inaccuracy of theorizing it in the Eurocentric matrices of 'class' or 'race' in too many spheres of the social sciences (as is the case of Wilkerson, and as this volume challenges) demonstrates the eugenic violence of the monumentality how the theory of modernity has been unable to be more than a modernity theory (Eagleton, 1999).

Even though the caste system affects millions of the oppressed scattered throughout the world, and although it is also found in many of the nation's classrooms—given its diasporic nature—the truth is that its absence in the field of curriculum studies is a symptom of a catalectic theoretical framework and of the eugenic way in which the historical course of the field has been fabricated. Caste sits in the classrooms of our country and too many other nations throughout the world. But not in terms of a corset between whites and blacks, as one would surreptitiously make out. Caste is sitting in our country's classrooms. It is one of the carbs of one of the most deplorable segregating logics of humanity because it structures a casteized disposition that flourishes in the nation. After all, it helps us better understand the limits of other segregating dynamics such as class, race, and gender; to speak of race is not to talk about caste. Caste—like class, race, and gender—is a world of oppressed subjects who could not see themselves in textbooks. Untouchability crosses our classrooms because it crosses our education, curriculum, and teacher education institutions. The Untouchable sympathizes with the battles around the Critical Theory of Race and the LGBTQ+ quest for equality but knows that 'the untouchables' face a surplus burn as their experience—despite some proximities—is quite different. The LGBTQ+ untouchable community faces sharper graded differences and challenges than the LGBTQ+ racialized community. Untouchability exhibits a radically different archeology (Guru, Chapter 4).

In other contexts, I have had the opportunity to examine (Paraskeva, 2021) this glaring absence as a symptom of an apparent theoretical insufficiency that is not entirely innocent. There is an evident theoretical incapacity of counter-hegemonic movements in our field—who champion so many laudable battles for a just education and curriculum—to detach themselves from a chilling epistemological submission to Western models, as if in these models were the language, the concept, the matrix to respond to the many different challenges facing humanity. As I have examined (Paraskeva, 2021), there is an apparent inability on our counter-hegemonic platforms to think of the word and the world beyond the Western epistemological matrix. Counter-hegemonic movements act like they own their only epistemological yarn. Thus 'the other' and its challenges are either scrutinized from Western, Eurocentric lenses or produced as 'non-existent' (Santos, 2014). Surprisingly or not, not even spaces like the John Dewey Society paid careful attention to Ambedkar's thoughts and work, given the enormous influence Dewey had on his intellectual formation (Mahadevan, Chapter 9).

This silence becomes more cacophonous (Jal, Chapter 8) and an embarrassment, especially in the heyday of one of the greatest contemporary fallacies in the field—its internationalization under the elasticity promoted by complicated celebratory conversations—in itself epistemicidal (see Huebner, 2021) and unable to provoke communicative pedagogies (Mahadevan, Chapter 9). How is it possible that, even within the scope of the much-vaunted internationalization of the field, the caste system has not jumped to the table of the field's debate? Whose/what theory—if any—gave rise to this internationalization? Who benefited and has benefited from this internationalization? What circuits of cultural production emerged from this internationalization? In other spaces—along with others—I was very critical of how the internationalization of the field was processed. I have alerted the reader in my work (Paraskeva, 2015, 2016, 2018a, 2021) how the spirit of the complicated conversation had been twisted and how the internationalization of the field looks more like a Frankenstein momentum.

Under the internationalization of the epistemicidal consulate—a kind of 'sss' momentum where the same talk about the same to the same—the absence of the other side of the line and caste persists. Such 'sss' momentum needs to be challenged, as it perpetuates "myths that crystalize certain hopes, values, and beliefs into universal truths, yet upon closer examination of scientific communities, these interpretations are found to be incomplete and erroneous, distorting the very nature of disciplined inquiry" (Popkewitz, 1976, p. 317). The internationalization wave is just another evidence of an apparent theoretical deficiency of our field to recognize that 'the other side of the line' cannot be grasped with epistemological tools from 'this side of the line.' Along with Santos (2018, p. 175), I argue that the monumentality of Eurocentric reason ignores that "casted eyes are bounded to be different eyes because they are trained in another graded cultural matrix." Caliban's reason cannot be insultingly explained from and with Prosperous logic (Henry, 2000). The caste system crosses both sides of the line and persists as an absent, non-existent dynamic. Under the heyday of globalization and internationalization, caste is a master key to unpacking sociological shadows. Such monumentality ignores the very matrix of Dalit thinking and the existence of a Dalit critique that 'understands several layers of discrimination,' including caste, class, race, and gender (Mahadevan, Chapter 9).

The noisy silence on caste is a vivid example of a field lost in time, historically and theoretically mutilated, a producer of erratic, reckless, and dangerous avenues, a field hostage to abyssal intellectuals and theorists who can only produce an abyssal theory and fabricate a divisive history. It is thus crucial to open the epistemicidal canon of the field's internationalization, dismantling the abyssal divide by placing caste at the center of the curriculum debates. Such a move begs for a commitment to the epistemologies from the South a radical co-presence of different and diverse epistemological avenues, leading to a total blast, a critical Dalit curriculum theory, a sublime example of the ecology of—curriculum—knowledges. A post-abyssal—or non-abyssal—momentum also helps to bring the approach back to the curriculum debates. I will return to this issue later. Our critique will always be catalectic, inconsequential, and out of touch in a field that persistently remains out of joint by ignoring crucial categories—such as caste—affecting how they are faced with a blatant production of caste as a non-existent category, where education and curriculum are not innocent.

The way the caste system has been either rarely debated or absent from the curriculum debates speaks volumes to a manifest theoretical insufficiency from counterhegemonic, Eurocentric platforms, which is not innocent and is responsible for what I call reversive epistemicide; that is, in the struggle against epistemicide, another epistemicide is committed (Paraskeva, 2016, 2018a, 2018b, 2021, 2022a, 2022b, 2022c). It is thus crucial to open the canon of silence in our field and pave the way for Critical Dalit Curriculum Theory, the river of the Untouchables, to break the eugenic silence on the caste system. An excellent way to address such unpardonable absence is to engage in what I have championed as itinerant curriculum theory (ICT). This non-derivative approach will place 'caste' face to face with other eugenic dynamics such as race, class, and gender.

Itinerant Curriculum Theory: Toward Critical Caste Curriculum Theory

> *Critical Caste Curriculum Theory champions the struggle against the epistemicidal nature of our field. It situates Dalit reason at the core of the anti-caste struggle through education, curriculum theory, and development.*
> —*(João M. Paraskeva, Chapter 1)*

Caste, Arundathi Roy (2016, p. 17) argues, has been an uncracked, millenary, deplorable, graded system, which is "implied in people's names, in the way people referred to each other, in the work they did, in the clothes they wore, in the marriages they were arranged, in the language they spoke and yet one never encounters the notion of caste in a single school textbook." The absence of caste debate within the so-called 'complicated conversation' is undeniably one of the sublime examples of the epistemicidal nature of the field, which historically has been "one of the labs of casteocracy" (Yengde, Chapter 6).

The coloniality of caste is also irrefutable evidence that "there are no unique historical agents or a unique form of domination, and since the faces of domination are manifold, the resistances and the agents that lead it are manifold" (Santos, 1999, p. 202). Hence "it is not possible to bring together all resistances and agencies under a common grand theory" (Santos, 1999, p. 203). To be more precise, and as this volume shows, while caste, class, and race exhibit common points of contact (Cox, 1959), which provide common metamorphoses in the struggle towards emancipation, one would be far from the truth ignoring their sharp historical and theoretical differences and claiming that one is before identical collective forms and agendas of dominance and counter-dominance. Thus, along with Santos (1999, p. 203), I argue that "more than a common theory, what we need is a theory of translation that makes the different struggles mutually intelligible and allows collective actors to talk about the oppressions they resist and the aspirations they animate." Such is not possible without the debate on caste—'as caste'—at the table.

The itinerant curriculum theory (ICT)—"which thinks against itself", as Eagleton (1990, p. 47)—paves the way for such intercultural inter/intra-political theory of translation (Santos, 2018; Paraskeva, 2022c), fostering a non-derivative Critical Caste Curriculum Theory (CCCT), one that first and foremost champions the struggle against the epistemicidal nature of our field. It is a call against the curriculum epistemicide and reversive epistemicide (Paraskeva, 2011, 2016, 2018a, 2018b, 2021, 2022a, 2022b, 2022c), unpacking the functionalist nature of both hegemonic and counter-hegemonic, Eurocentric curriculum traditions. CCCT is "Dalit *Chetna*,[14] obsessed with touching" (Gajarawala, 2012, pp. 68–69), bringing messier material to the table (Elam, 2021b, p. 611) and putting Dalit reason at the core of the anti-caste struggle through education and curriculum. CCCT epitomizes a diverse praxis of 'worlding' (Rao, Chapter 5); it echoes the crucial features of the "three waves to the Dalit reason" (Pathania and Kalyani, Chapter 10), addressing some of its strengths and inconsistencies; it challenges the "pathologization of Dalit subjects as inadequate or abnormal" (Vijay and Nair, 2019, p. 329). CCCT is about "Dalit life which is was street life, defined by the lack of privacy, and proximity to shit and garbage" (Rao, Chapter 5); it brings and reinforces the legitimacy of Dalit *Sahitya*,[15] which, although a labor of love, it is, however, "not about pure aesthetics, but pain and anguish" (Pathania and Kalyani, Chapter 10). Drawing on ICT, CCCT challenges the 'indeginestoude malaise' on both

Global North and South epistemological hemispheres (see Teltumbde, Chapter 3). CCCT is the theory of Dalit liberation (Omvedt, 1994), echoing Phule's recognition that 'the material context of caste's transformation also carried the potential for immanent critique.' (Rao, Chapter 5). CCCT helps one to deconstruct non-derivatively why counter-hegemonic Eurocentric hemisphere is not empowering (Ellsworth, 1989).

CCCT voices and places caste as caste, not race and class, and respects the relative autonomy of each socially graded category. It stands and walks shoulder to shoulder with other graded dynamics in the struggle for a just and equal education and curriculum. CCCT is a non-abyssal commitment to bringing a global outcaste theory and praxis to our curriculum debate's 'momentist tone.' CCCT is thus an itinerant curriculum isonomia (Karatani, 2017; Paraskeva, 2021). It is much more than a challenge or a denunciation of the silence and absence of caste in our pedagogical apparatuses; it is the proclamation of a non-aligned epistemological river that breaks with what Jal (Chapter 8) frames as 'Freudian hysterical blindness' and 'constructed ignorance' and occupies its legitimate space in the debates on education and the curriculum. It short-circuits and challenges the celebratory swamp into which the discussion on the internationalization of the field has sunk. Any dispute—especially—in the current world context about the internationalization of the field that does not have at its epicenter the epistemic nature of the curriculum is a deception and an intellectual hoax. CCCT is Dalit pedagogies from the Global South and its diaspora (Mahadevan, Chapter 9)

CCCT responds to Ambedkar's (1989, p. 9) call to pave the way "to change the Touchable Hindus" and a commitment to "theorize Hindutva nationalism" (Sampath, Chapter 7); to deconstruct it as a form of "epistemic violence" (Natrajan, 2022, p. 303); to unpack how it "proliferates in the symbolic with the popularization and normalization of a language that represents others" (Natrajan, 2022, p. 303). CCCT is an anthem to smash Hindutva as a myth, a sublime form of barbaric ignorance, through our curriculum, pedagogies, teacher education, and evaluation. Santos (2018, p. 40) argues that all ignorance "is ignorance of a given kind of knowledge, and all knowledge is overcoming a certain kind of ignorance." CCCT dismantles the convenient comfortability of such constructed ignorance and attacks caste right at the core of its sociological lab, Hinduism and Hindutva. It brings Hinduism/Hindutva to justice. It challenges Sanskritization and emulation of the upper-class culture; it defies Hindutva as 'the praxis' of existence and thinking (Reddy, 2011).

In doing so, it also reacts against the violence and cruelty of the identical (Han, 2018) that pervades Global North forms of reason, thus masking caste, race, class, and gender. It counters the 'resignification' (Gajarawala, 2012, p. 93) errors that place class, race, and caste as identical. CCCT does not minimize class, race, or gender, however. Quite the opposite. It champions caste as irreversibly intertwined with such graded categories and respects its relative autonomy and idiosyncrasies. It established a dialogue with such segregated dynamics, which are predominant elsewhere, and runs away from any absolutist, segregated matrix. Hence, it challenges the absolutism of class, race, and gender, over caste—and vice versa—and pronounces the relative political sovereignty of each graded category, thus establishing not necessarily a radical co-presence, but a radical 'co-habitance' of different parallel and non-parallel forms of domination and struggle. The notion of 'radical co-habitance' complicates Santos' notion of radical co-presence, as it provides a latitude and longitude to disarticulate from Eurocentric reason's fundamentalism and re-articulate with non-Eurocentric epistemological perspectives, while doing so paves the way for a 'theory of translation' that walks away from conventional notions of 'translation' as a "translingual and/or transcultural practice crossing and equivalizing two languages, epistemes, cultures, or practices entangled within the issue of power and resistance" (Zhao et al., 2022, p. 9). Instead, the 'radical co-habitance' implies a 'radical itinerant co-habitus' from itinerant co-habitants advocating a 'radical co-translation' as "mediating between cross-cultural differences on the principle of transparency, precisely produces 'the partly opaque relationship called difference'" (Zhao et al., 2022, p. 9). That is, "cultural episteme are entangled practices, with one not reducible to the other. Thus 'entangled-ness' allows for seeing different epistemes as existing side by side in the sense that each has its own integrity and historical sensibility in forming a relational rather than the hierarchical notion of difference" (Zhao et al., 2022, p. 9). Critical Caste Curriculum Theory helps counter dominant Eurocentric approaches to decolonize, to de-link from the Eurocentric matrix.

CCCT counters the epistemologies from the Global North edified in a eugenic monumentality that "have crucially contributed to converting the scientific knowledge developed in the Global North into the hegemonic way of representing the world and one's own and transforming it according to one's own needs and aspirations" (Santos, 2018, p. 6). CCCT advocates the Global South onto-epistemological matrix as an asset within various emancipatory solutions. In doing so, and from a crucial angle, CCCT opens the canon of Eurocentric reason that frames our field, its history, and the theory that occupies our schools and classrooms. It challenges the abyssal nature not just of dominant curriculum theory and history crafted and taught in Eurocentric terms but also of counter-hegemonic curriculum approaches that, despite noteworthy accomplishments, remain overtly divisive, derivative, and so despotic as the despotism they criticized. CCCT deconstructs hegemonic and counter-hegemonic knowledge regulation forms, paving the way for epistemological emancipation out of

'Occidentosis' (Al-l-Ahmad, 1984). CCCT is an itinerant "emotional and rational emancipation of the critical," as Susan Sontag (2010, p. 29) would put it.

Influenced by ICT, CCCT is a theory that itinerantly 'destabilizes' (Eagleton, 1990, p. 27; see also 2003) and 'clarifies' (Pinar, 2015, p. 1) social life. It is a theory of a sub-field but not a sub-theory. It addresses Ayyathurai's (2022) calls for a new field of theoretical inquiry that frames caste as a dynamic with relative autonomy. CCCT advocates 'critical caste studies,' however, non-derivatively. It is a field 'committed to examining diverse cultural, religious, political, and economic mechanisms by which caste power is produced and dispersed through a putatively inviolable caste structure' (Ayyathurai, 2022). A radical itinerant co-habitus field devoted to zealously 'unraveling the discursive and non-discursive counter-caste practices of women, men, and children as well as their organic intellectuals and movements' (Ayyathurai, 2022; see also Paik, 2014). An itinerant approach that advocates a just theory of translation, one that not only understands that caste dynamics cannot supersede any other graded dynamics—such as class, race, ethnicity, and gender; but also is quite sentient for the need of non-abyssal intersectionality between the epistemologies of the Global North and the Global South. CCCT is a 'radical co-habitance' of endless diverse caste epistemological traditions; a 'radical co-habitus' that "harmonizes what could be a cacophonous confrontation across incalculable cultural complexity" as William Pinar (2015, p. 3) would have put it. It's a full-blast itinerant curriculum theory, which is "in the first place, a political rather than an intellectual one," as Eagleton (1990, p. 32) would put it.

CCCT moves away from celebratory 'superficial analogical juxtapositions' within and beyond the caste system, breaks void parallels forcibly established between caste and other categories such as class, race, and gender; it is a 'degree zero commitment'—as Sampath (Chapter 7) rightly proclaims—one that dissects the undergirding pillars that 'propel only one group in the name of metaphysical reason endowed at birth, namely the 'trick' known as the Brahmin,' to be the sole pursuer of transcendence through the subjection, humiliation, and destruction of others who are lowest in the system and even outside it, namely the Dalit/'untouchable' (Teltumbde, 2010; see also Sampath, Chapter 7). The search for this 'degree zero' (Sampath, Chapter 7) allows us to frame caste not only "in the ambit of stratification and hierarchy combined with a form of racism, but also as a form of racist schizophrenia where not only cannot hear but were the terror of 'silent blindness' is hurling India into intellectual backwardness from where there can be no return" (Jal, Chapter 8). CCCT unveils how caste is not just about eugenics as it historically reconfigures the eugenicist matrix—the 'eugenic eugenicism.' In doing so, CCCT provokes a significant casualty within the caste system, as it unmasks Hinduism as a lethal myth.

> The first and foremost thing that must be recognized is that Hindu society is a myth. The name Hindu is itself foreign. Hindu society, as such, does not exist. It is only a collection of castes . . . A caste does not feel affiliated with other castes except when there is a Hindu-Muslim riot. There is no Hindu consciousness of kind. In every Hindu, the consciousness that exists is the consciousness of his caste. That is the reason why the Hindus cannot be considered to form a society or nation.
>
> (Ambedkar, 2016, p. 241)

As a degree zero—which is a decoloniality itinerant zone—CCCT is a first 'act' towards a post-abyssal momentum; it is an itinerant, non-abyssal, radical co-presence of endless epistemological rivers on caste, an itinerant theory of translation that, through a "comparative dialogue of the West and East and everything in between utilizing the resources of poststructuralist phenomenology and deconstruction" (Sampath, Chapter 7) weaves a diverse epistemological ecology as the riverbed of an ecology of knowledges (Santos, 2014). It doesn't knock at the door of this side of the line. It breaks the door and occupies such turf. It challenges the visibilities, the non-existences.

CCCT is thus an itinerant "exercise of intercultural translation and dystopic hermeneutics through which the reciprocal limitations of alternative conceptions of human dignity can be identified, thus opening the possibility of new relations and dialogues among them" (Santos, 1999, 2009, p. 18, 2014). CCCT implies knowledge emancipation that does not aim "a great theory, it aims a theory of translation that works as epistemological support for the emancipatory practices, all of them finite and incomplete, and because of that, only sustainable once interconnected as a web" (Santos pp. 206–207).

CCCT is made itinerantly by itinerant CCC*theorists* who understand that "there is an epistemological foundation to the capitalist and imperial order that the global North has been imposing on the global South" (Santos, 2004, p. ix). It implies a CCC*theorist* that de-links from derivative pedagogical approaches and peregrinates itinerantly toward non-abyssal, communicative, pedagogical approaches (Mahadevam Chapter 8). What we need, the CCCT advocates, is to engage in a battle against "the monoculture of scientific knowledge [and fight for an] ecology of knowledges" (Santos, 2004, p. xx) that colonizes specific avenues within both the Global North and Global South. An ecology of knowledge is

> an invitation to promote non-relativistic dialogues among knowledge, granting equality of opportunities to the different kinds of knowledge

engaged in ever broader epistemological disputes aimed at maximizing their respective contributions to building a more democratic and just society and decolonizing knowledge and power.

(Santos, 2004, p. xx)

Such ecology of knowledges is just the outcome of CCCT as a praxis of anti-caste critique (Rao, Chapter 5), short-circuiting epistemological untouchability (Jal, Chapter 8) CCC*theorists* are post-divisive and post-derivative intellectuals, "not obsessed with originality or authorship, not aspiring to be a super author" (Santos, 2018, p. 148). Such an itinerant theorist is a craftsperson seeking "the adoption of alternative avenues" (Santos, 2018, p. 149). Working within itinerant theoretical malleability, CCC*theorists* deconstruct; they don't look at the stage lights but at the shadows these lights cast. They seek to understand the meanders and labyrinths of the cultural industrial produced and dominated by modern Western epistemological tentacles—the pure touchables 'on this side of the line'—and deeply dissected, albeit in a derivative way, by intellectuals such as Antonio Gramsci and the heavy artillery of the Frankfurt school. That is why CCC*theorists* commitment to a non-derivative itinerant posture provokes a 'co-habitus' of 'both sides of the line'(Santos, 2014), challenging romanticizing views and illuminating the missing pieces in some counter-hegemonic approaches, the eloquent ideological silences in the word and the world, and how such silences are eugenic. CCC*theorists* know full well the importance of making a distinction between craft and methodology. While the latter "was rigor mortis, dead rigor, rigor fossilized into arcanely of statistical practice so fetishized as to have eclipsed the real stakes of research, the former, partook rigor but rigor could not guarantee craft." CCCT is not about how complicated a conversation is but about how relevant, how non-regulatory, how 'non-abyssal,' and how 'such' conversation transposes diverse and different scales of analysis (Santos, 2018). CCCT is a non-abyssal struggle done by non-abyssal thinkers. A CCC*theorist* knows that the damage paved by Hindutva-praxis is so deep that, even if Hinduism were extinct today, the battle for the emancipation of caste would continue. CCCT is the unavoidable and irreversible epistemological color framing the emancipation of the Untouchables. CCCT is a tout court *Ambekarite* theory; an ethics of resilient persuasion, the ability to "imagine oneself as different from the untouchable self" (Guru, 2017). CCCtheorists know that the future needs to go beyond *Ambekdaritism* without avoiding it.

CCCT is a vivid example of epistemology from the South (Santos, 2014) that is "a non-derivative thinking that involves a radical break with modern Western ways of thinking and acting" (Santos, 2007b, p. 65). To think in non-derivative terms "means to think from the perspective of the other side of the line, precisely because the other side of the line has been the realm of the unthinkable in Western modernity" (Santos, 2007b, p. 65). CCCT is a caste struggle from the endless, diverse epistemological rivers of the 'other side of the line' placed at the table of the educational and curriculum debates—its history and theory. It confronts the dominant and counter-dominant Eurocentric reason for 'this side of the line' with the epistemological legitimacy of the 'other side of the line.' Caste cannot be explained and smashed with Eurocentric lenses and diopters. CCCT helps one to understand that "caste by nature is an intersectionally and epistemologically complex object, in contradistinction to the intersectional analyses of class, race, ethnicity, gender, and sexuality and disability in purely Western contexts" (Sampath, Chapter 7).

CCCT itinerant path helps excavate the caste system as a "phenomenologically complex object of 'non-existence' in the intermixture of a non-Abrahamic, polytheistic, ritually based religious culture in the South Asian-Indian context: one that blurs thresholds of what is visible and invisible to an outsider's view." In CCCT terms, Eurocentric, counter-hegemonic notions of state, power, labor, exploitation, oppression, while important, are not "sufficient to tackle the complexity because caste is at once material and immaterial, yet caste is also neither since it requires the embodiment of a non-linear temporality whereby past, present, and future do not follow a simple sequence. Caste lies beyond any material-immanent or immaterial-transcendental distinctions" (Sampath, Chapter 7)

CCCT is concomitantly an "artisanship of a pluriversal polyphony of praxis" (Santos, 2018, p. 12) against the coloniality power matrix (Quijano, 1992, Mignolo, 2008), a struggle against the coloniality of power, knowledge, being, and labor. In fighting this battle, CCCT de-links from "Eurocentric views that create and describe diversity and difference within the framework of the nation-states of the Northern hemisphere, the prime expression of the cultural logic of multinational or global capitalism, capitalism without homeland at last, and a new form of eugenics, tending to be quite descriptive and apolitical thus suppressing the problem of power relations, exploitation, inequality, and exclusion" (Santos, 2004, pp. xx—xxi). CCCT echoes and engages in an itinerant radical cohabitance of different forms of resistance and struggle. CCCT is a political act, an anti-casteist "ideological critique of various mystifications that mask the inequalities of caste-governed lives." As an anti-casteism commitment, CCCT challenges foundational myths used to support the necessity or inescapability of 'making caste differentiations' (Dhanda, 2019, p. 72); it is an engagement against the coloniality of the diaspora (Martinez-San Miguel, 2014).

As an archeology of anti-castecized ways of knowing from the South, CCCT, by definition, is against the romanticization of South ways of perceiving the world; it challenges any form of indigenoustude (Paraskeva, 2011, 2021, 2022a, 2022b); it counters anti-casteism casteism (Manoharan, 2017); that is, CCCT is not bacteriologically pure and understands that any theory carries with it all the purity and impurity of the reality that builds it and for which it is intended. Along with Phule and other anti-caste intellectuals, the CCC*theorist* fully recognizes "that the material context of caste's transformation also carried the potential for immanent critique" (Rao, Chapter 5). CCCT is not 'the' theory, as it is sentient about the impossibility of a general epistemology for a general epistemology (Santos, 2014). In this context, CCCT is a struggle for recognition and legitimacy (Fraser, 1997), and it is sentient to the dangerous absolutism of other alternative approaches and challenges such absolutism. CCCT unpacks traditional ways to produce and frame theory. CCCT is an itinerant, emancipatory praxis against curriculum occidentosis (Paraskeva, 2021, 2022a, 2022b). It de-links from absolutist epistemological perspectives 'on this side of the world towards a polycentric world' (Amin, 1990). CCCT echoes a multiplicity of anti-colonial and decolonial approaches, such as Amilcar Cabral's 'return to the source' (Cabral, 1973) and Kwame Nkrumah's Global South 'philosophical consciencism' (Nkrumah, 1964), to help emancipate the mind the colonized (Césaire, 2000), Dussel's 'ethics of liberation' to torpedo the monumentality of Eurocentric reason crafted within the hemisphere of both dominant and counter dominant traditions. CCCT jazzes Nkrumah's 'consciencism,' Mariátegui's 'consciousness,' and Ambedkar's social *Chetna*[16]—a praxis completely devoid of dogmatism (Angotti, 1986, p. 38)—as the *sine qua non* 'pre-requests' for just emancipation. In doing so, CCCT challenges dominant Hindutva reasoning that "isolates consciousness and therefore prevents common collective activity and by preventing common activity, it has prevented the Hindus from becoming a society with a unified life and a consciousness of its being" (Ambedkar, 2018, p. 19; also, Elam, 2021a, 2021b).

CCCT dismantles caste as an idea (Ambedkar, 2016); it de-monumentalizes the one-dimensional, Eurocentric epistemological yarn; it is about unassembling the monumentality of Prosperous reason; it deconstructs the cult that it is in the Global North that the solution is found not only for the problems created by the Global North but also for the problems that the Global North did not necessarily create. CCCT understands that the other cannot just be researched by those who—directly, indirectly, consciously, and unconsciously—made the other or are not helping deconstruct the theoretical and historical conditions that perpetuate the other (Teltumbde, 2018). CCCT exposed the insufficiencies of Eurocentric theory. Audre Lorde (2007) taught us that the master's tools could not dismantle the master's house. CCCT doesn't see caste from the African American belief system (Brown, 2018, p. 45). CCCT deconstructs the icons that arise through the theft of history and theory (Goody, 2006; Frank, 1998, Amin, 2011; Paraskeva, 2016, 2018), kidnapping reality into space and time that, in fact, never existed. CCCT is thus committed to de-Gandhian Gandhi—framing Gandhi from an epistemology from the South—de-iconizing him. Jazzing Gramsci and Ambedkdar's epistemological ethos, CCC*theorists* counter perspectives "who relied in "wild mumblings and stylistic affection to survive; they decry the idolizing of human personalities" (Teltumbde and Yengde, 2018, p. xxiv).

CCCT, as I have highlighted, speaks the Dalit reason, verbalizes the pain, the rights, and the heterotopia (Santos, 2018) of "the minor and the minority uniquely so unapologetically, so forcefully and so persuasively that it mimics and confounds the confidence of the majoritarian state and its acolytes" (Appadurai, 2021b, p. 15). CCC*theorists* speak and act "in the voice of conscience and of truth, and refuse to grant to the Hinduized state the monopoly of the conscience" (Appadurai, 2021b, p. 15).

CCCT is a wakeup call for all of those who refuse to get out of the strait-jacket of Eurocentric reason; it masters, as Bernadette Baker (2007) would put it, a new wave of research, thus making visible the eloquent silences that were petrified (and sometimes ossified) by secular occlusion. CCCT is a challenge for all of those who hide in their language deficiencies to justify the impossibility of engaging with the other side of the line. CCCT is about a decent education and a decent curriculum for a decent life, for a world we all wish to see (Amin, 2008). In doing so, CCCT places an itinerant theory at the center of the curriculum debates, helping build alternative ways to think and do education curriculum theory alternatively (Santos, 2014). CCCT is a praxis of an itinerant curriculum theory. It brings theory back to the table, challenging the 'field's regression,' or what I have called *theorycide*, or curriculum involution (Paraskeva, 2018a, 2021, 2022a, 2022b). The battle for social and cognitive justice (Visvanathan, 1997; also, Santos, 2014) cannot be triumphalistically accomplished out of the caste debate.

As I have flagged earlier, this is the first volume that places caste 'as caste' at the epicenter of the struggle for a more just curriculum. In doing so, it examines and proclaims caste as an autonomous socio-political device that cannot be reduced to class or race dissected out of the epistemologies from the South. In Chapter 2, "Caste: A Division of Labour and Labourers," Bhimrao Ramji Ambedkar unpacks how Hindutva is a graded system based on the division of laborers, arguing caste as a unique, graded category with sharp historical and theoretical differences from class and race. He challenges counter-hegemonic forces and groups to commit to radical social reform—that will address caste dynamics—stressing the impossibility of economic and political reform without social reform.

In Chapter 3, "The Caste Context," Anand Teltumbde excavates caste dynamics historically. While there are caste dynamics everywhere,

Teltumbde frames caste as a defining feature of Indian society. He digs deep within the Hindutva-graded cult, grasping the origins of caste. Teltumbde highlights the role of intellectuals, such as Bhimrao Ramji Ambedkar and Pokala Lakshmi Narasu, in the anti-caste struggle and some responsible for Dalit caste consciousness. The chapter places caste as a socially graded dynamic that "come into being because the material conditions demand them."

In Chapter 4— "Archeology of Untouchability"—Gopal Guru unveils how the available descriptions of untouchability are often inaccurate in grasping the totality of the meaning of such oppressive praxis. The chapter explores two crucial frameworks—the philosophical and the archaeological—that could open to us much richer and more nuanced meanings of the phenomenon of untouchability.

Anupama Rao, in her chapter, "The Word and the World: Dalit Aesthetics as a Critique of Everyday Life," provides a prehistory of the 1950s and 1960s Dalit *sahitya* and argues that Dalit writing is a form of immanent critique that addresses the changing relationship of caste, capital and Bombay's distinctive urbanity. Rather than focus on the 'literariness' of Dalit *sahitya*, the chapter argues that one should bracket the question of the literariness of Dalit literature, and focus instead on those forms of linguistic concreteness, or practices of naming and description that politicized key aspects of subaltern life.

In Chapter 6, "Casteocracy: A Millennium Standard of Merit and Tests," Suraj Yengde dissects merit and meritocracy as a social construction. In so doing, Yengde unpacks how "its original idea of individual achievement in a collective environment is being discounted to advance certain misapprehended notions of merit disguised as talent." The chapter examines how meritocratic fever feeds into the structure of casteocracy. Rajesh Sampath's Chapter 7, "Reading Foucault's *History of Madness* to Obliterate Caste in Hindu-Majority Indian Society," engages in a critical de-construction of Hindutva. Sampath develops a series of phenomenological theories on the 'phantasm of Hindu myth as caste mutating a materialist spiritual power in the form of an undifferentiated social body of divisions.' The chapter frames caste as a tribe-like deification elevated to a persona based on the accident of birth and a symbol of false pride. Sampath weaves powerful analogies to Foucault's (2009) *History of Madness*.

In Chapter 8, "Epistemological Untouchability: The Deafening Silence of Indian Academics" Murzban Jal examines Indian academics as a 'transformed feudal ideology,' a transformation in the form of deceptive metamorphosis. Jal claims that there is not merely the silence of caste but blindness that is a '*Freudian* hysterical blindness.' The chapter unveils how caste has to be seen not only in the ambit of stratification and hierarchy, combined with a form of racism, but also as a form of racist schizophrenia, where not only can one not hear but where the terror of 'silent blindness' is hurling India into intellectual backwardness from where there can be no return. Kanchana Mahadevan, in "Critical and Caring Pedagogies: Habermas and Ambedkar at the Intersections of Caste and Gender," explores crucial pedagogical spaces to scrutinize knowledge systems developed through privileges of caste, class, gender, tribe (and others). Mahadevan brings to the table Jyotirao Phule's articulations of the 'third eye' as the first step in his version of the pedagogy of the oppressed, as well as Sharmila Rege and Shailaja Paik's empirical footprint related to the basis of contemporary Dalit-feminist pedagogical practice. The chapter examines prospects for pedagogies of critical care and caring critiques through Ambedkar's notion of critique as embedded in care. It argues that he offers a richer notion of critique about Habermas, given his appropriation of the Buddhist idea of *karuna* (compassion). The latter can respond to critiques of care by engaging with care at the intersection of caste and gender.

Chapter 10, "Contextualizing the Emergence of Dalit Studies in Indian Academia," from Gaurav J. Pathania and Kalyani, examines how the phenomenology of anti-caste resistance has been one of the powerful ways through which Dalit question has been re-centered within the academic engagement. The chapter explores various forms of ideological opposition in the emergence of Dalit literature and its protracted struggle to gain acceptance in academic departments. Based on interviews with Dalit scholars and activists, it unfolds the epistemologies of anti-caste writings in curricula. It traces the emergence of young Dalit writers, artists, and musicians within pedagogic practices. It presents narratives from Dalit women's literature and their struggle to include this literature in institutional practices, its resistance to subaltern studies, and mainstream feminism. The chapter concludes that the introduction of Dalit Studies in academia challenges the dominant ideologies impeding social justice and integration of an anti-caste consciousness in academia and beyond. To conceptually understand this integration, the paper uses Jeffrey Alexander's concept of 'civil repair' and argues that the arrival of Dalit Studies in Indian academia not only challenges the idea of 'civil' but also upends the scope of the term.

In the final chapter, "Economic Reservation as Caste and Cultural Power: Posing Challenges to Representation, Equality and Diversity in Kerala, India," K. V. Syamprasad exposes the habitual dispositions of 'economic reservation' policies that pose challenges to the core principles of affirmative action, such as representation, equality, and diversity in education, in employment, and in electoral politics in Kerala by offering a critique of the classical Marxist economic theory of power. Bourdieu's concepts of *habitus*, reproduction, cultural capital, and power form the theoretical framework of analysis. First, the chapter revisits Marx's theory of economic extremism to present the debates revolving around the position of caste in the base or the superstructure as determinant forces of the Indian social system. Second, the chapter continues to expose the habitual dispositions of economic determinism and how they marginalize critical discussions about caste inequality and reservation. Third, the chapter explores the extent to which educational, employment, and electoral bodies together become the guardian of *habitus* reproducing the upper caste culture with 'economic reservation' policies in favor of the 'economically backward' but 'socially forward overrepresented' communities, putting affirmative action at risk at the theoretical and at the policy levels.

I end this introduction with a story that is important to share. This book was conceptualized and produced at a time when Anand Teltumbde and other anti-caste intellectuals were fervently fighting for their freedom. All over the world, voices were raised denouncing the injustice of the sentence and trying at all costs to reverse it. I express my gratitude to the European Member of Parliament Ana Gomes, whom I alerted to the fact that the arrest of Anand Teltumbde constituted one of the many serious violations of human rights in India. She did not hesitate to activate the diplomatic mechanisms of the European Union, 'requesting the intervention' of the High Representative of the European Union for Foreign Affairs and Security Policy and Vice-President of the European Commission, Federica Mogherini, in a letter dated February 20, 2019. It goes without saying that Anand Teltumbde and his comrades ended up arrested. The condemnation of Teltumbde through 'fabricated evidence' demonstrates only that 'there is more to the caste oppression than meets the eye' (Teltumbde, Chapter 3). This volume is dedicated to him and to all of those who have perished under the brutality of the caste system, as well as to all of those who have resiliently challenged such a 'chamber of horrors.'

Acknowledgments

Every manuscript has its 'history' and is always a challenge that becomes more acute when the text takes over the hermeneutical process. Reading, thinking, and writing today in the academy—or in what some call the academy—is an act of courage and intellectual honesty. In his lecture on "The Death of Criticism" at the University of Edinburgh, Terry Eagleton describes with sublime irony—yet rigor—the institutional bewilderment facing academia today. He states that critics today in academia 'live in a permanent state of dread, a fear that one day some clerk somewhere in a government office turning over a leaf will stumble into a shameful truth: that we have been actually paid to read poems, novels, and plays. The clerk will throw himself on the phone to his superior and blow the whistle on many of us, and soon experts like Jean Austin will be fixing computers. Our work is far too pleasurable an activity to be bonafide. The scandalous cuts deeper than that, though. It is not that we have been paid for reading books. We have been paid outrageously for reading books about people who never existed and events that never took place. In ordinary life, talking about people who never existed is known as psychosis; in university it is literary criticism.' The life of a pedagogue as a public intellectual in academia fits Eagleton's bill. In too many nations, faculty "are inundated by a myriad of often-minuscule obligations that take away time for even their most basic professional duties: reading scholarship of colleagues" (Pinar, 2015, p. 3). Anti-intellectual intellectualism saturates academia (Paraskeva, 2013, 2012, 2009). This volume, like countless others, imposes itself against such a prevailing current, and it is only possible due to countless colleagues' support. I have repeatedly argued that our work in academia is collective. This book is no exception.

Although I run the risk of forgetting some colleagues who have helped me so much along my path, I dare to leave here a heartfelt and profound thank you to Anthony Brown, Antonia Darder, Angela Valenzuela, Boaventura de Sousa Santos, Bernadette Baker, Cameron McCarthy, Cathryn Severino, Clyde Barrow, David Hursh, Dwayne Huebner, Fatma Mizikaci, James Jupp, José Felix Rasco, Jurjo Torres Santomé, Maria Alfredo Moreira, Maria Luiza Süssekind, Maria Nikolakaiki, Inês Oliveira, Mike Peters, Nelson Maldonado Torres, Paget Henry, Peter McLaren, Ramon Grosfoguel, Richard Quantz, Todd Price, Thomas Pedroni, Thomas Popkewitz, Weilli Zhao, and William Schubert, as they helped me to refine my arguments. I owe Dwayne more than I can ever say. Special thanks to the contributors of the book—Anand Teltumbde, Anupama Rao, Gopal Guru, Gaurav J. Pathania, and K. Kalyani, Kanchana Mahadevan, K. V. Syamprasad, Muzban Jal, Raj Sampath, and Suraj Yengde—for their strong commitment and solidarity. As I write this volume, Anand Teltumbde and other intellectuals were released on bail after being in jail for 31 months. This volume is dedicated to him and to all of those who have been resiliently challenged and who have perished under the brutality of the caste system. A word of thanks to David Hursh for writing the foreword. Also, I am grateful to my doctoral students in Educational Leadership and Policy Studies. Our seminars are always moments of contentious discussion about education and curriculum as a political phenomenon permeated by dynamics of class, race, gender, and caste intertwined with economic and cultural categories. I also thank my sharp Routledge editors, AnnaMary Goodall, Alice Salt, and Katherine Tsamparlis, for their patience and crucial insights related to manuscript production. A word of gratitude also to Spandana P. B., from Apex Covantage (P) Ltd. for the tremendous editing support provided in the last stages of this volume's production. My endless indebtedness to my dear wife Isabel and my daughter Camila for the common commitment, knowing so well, as Matsuo Bashō argues, that "every day is a journey, and the journey itself is home." Also, a word of gratitude to my siblings, Pandelis and Jorge, whose lives are vivid examples of the outcome of what was once a promised revolution. Last but not least, to my beloved parents and best friends, who, sadly, did not live long enough to see so many of our conversations reflected in this book. While I confess such a myriad of crucial mentors, for the record, I must state that they are unrelated to the potential crimes produced in the manuscript.

Notes

1. University of Strathclyde, U.K.
2. I am indebted to Bill Wraga for bringing to my attention the work of Davis, Allison, Gardner, Burleigh, and Gardner, Mary (1941) *Deep South. A Sociological Anthropological Study of Caste and Class.* Charlotte, SC: The University of South Carolina Press.
3. I am indebted to Dwayne Huebner for exposing me to the work of Robert Havingusrt and the discussions we had on his work and Allison Davis.
4. I draw on two editions of Ambedkar's germinal piece "Annihilation of Caste." One dated 2018 and published in Triplicane, Chennai: MJP Publishers/Moven Books; the other from 2016 published in London through Verso, with a precious annotated critical introduction by Arundhati Roy.
5. Francis Galton first used the term eugenics in his *Inquiries into Human Faculty* (1883, p. 25). However, while he "was the founder of the eugenics movement, the analysis of his work alone does not establish the nature of eugenics as a whole." In this regard, see Mackenzie (1976, p. 509)
6. The Rig Veda is an ancient Indian collection of Vedic Sanskrit hymns. It is one of the four sacred canonical Hindu texts known as the Vedas. The Rigveda is the oldest known Vedic Sanskrit text. Its early layers are one of the oldest texts in any Indo-European language.
7. See Walter Mignolo, Retrieved, www.youtube.com/watch?v=0R_qA6R4lns
8. Italic mine.
9. Caste division.
10. I am indebted to Bill Wraga for bringing to my attention the work of Davis, Allison, Gardner, Burleigh, and Gardner, Mary (1941) *Deep South. A Sociological Anthropological Study of Caste and Class.* Charlotte, SC: The University of South Carolina Press.
11. I am indebted to Dwayne Huebner for flagging for me the work of Robert Havingusrt, as well as for the discussions we had on his work and Allison Davis.
12. Italic mine.
13. A crucial and historic agreement was signed in 1932 between Mahatma Gandhi and Babasahed Ambedkar on behalf of depressed classes and upper caste Hindu leaders on the reservation of electoral seats for the depressed classes.
14. Consciousness.
15. Literature.
16. Consciousness.

References

Abu-Lughod, Janet (1989) *Before European Hegemony. The World System A.D. 1250–1350*. New York: Oxford University Press.

Abu-Lughod, Janet (2001) Territorially-Based Nationalism and the Politics of Negation. In E. Said and C. Hitchens (eds) *Blaming the Victims: Spurious Scholarship and the Palestinian Question*. New York: W. W. Norton, pp. 193–206.

Ahmad, Aijaz (2008) *In Theory. Classes, Nations, Literature*. London: Verso.

Al-l-Ahmad, Jalal (1984) *Occidentosis: A Plague from the West*. Iran: Mizan Press.

Ambedkar, Bhimrao (1979) Castes in India. Their Mechanism, Genesis and Development. In *Dr. Babasaheb Ambedkar Writings and Speeches*, Vol. 5. Bombay: Government of Maharashtra, pp. 3–22.

Ambedkar, Bhimrao (1989) Untouchables or the Children of India's Ghetto and Other Essays. In *Dr. Babasaheb Ambedkar. Writings and Speeches*, Vol. 5. Mumbai: Education Department, Government of Maharashtra.

Ambedkar, Bhimrao (1991) *Dr. Babasaheb Ambedkar. Writings and Speeches*, Vol. 9 (V. Moon, ed.). Bombay: Education Department, Government of Maharashtra.

Ambedkar, Bhimrao (2009) *What Congress and Gandhi Have Done to the Untouchables*. Delhi: Gautam Boom Centre.

Ambedkar, Bhimrao (2016) Annihilation of Caste. In Arundhati Roy (ed) *Annihilation of Caste. B. R. Ambedkar*. London: Verso.

Ambedkar, Bhimrao (2018) *The Annihilation of Caste*. Triplicane, Chennai: MJ Publishers/Moven Books.

Amin, Samir (1990) *Delinking. Towards a Polycentric World*. London: Zed Books.

Amin, Samir (2008) *The World We Wish to See*. New York: Monthly Review Press.

Amin, Samir (2011) *Global History: A View from the South*. Cape Town: Pambazuka Press.

Anderson, Perry (2013) *The Indian Ideology*. London: Verso.

Angotti, Thomas (1986) The Contributions of José Carlos Mariátegui to Revolutionary Theory. *Latin American Perspectives*, 13 (2), pp. 33–57.

Appadurai, Arjun (2021a) Comparing Race to Caste Is an Interesting Idea, But There Are Crucial Differences between Both. *The Wire*. www.thewire.in/books/book-review-isabel-wilkerson-caste-racism-america

Appadurai, Arjun (2021b) Fear of Small Disciplines: India's Battle against Creative Thought. *Postcolonial Studies*, 24 (91), pp. 11–15.

Apple, Michael (1999) Review Symposium. *Race Ethnicity and Education*, 2 (2), pp. 303–307.

Apple, Michael, and Weis, Lois (eds) (1983) *Ideology and the Practice of Schooling*. Philadelphia, PA: Temple University Press.

Ayyathurai, Gajendran (2022) It is Time for a New Sub-field; Critical Caste Studies. *London School of Economics*. https://blogs.lse.ac.uk/southasia/2021/07/05/it-is-time-for-a-new-subfield-critical-caste-studies/

Bag, Kheya, and Watkins, Susan (2021) Structures of Oppression. *New Left Review*, 132, pp. 55–79.

Baker, Bernadette (2007) Animal Magnetism and Curriculum History. *Curriculum Inquiry*, 37 (2), pp. 123–158.

Banerjee-Dube, Ishita (2014) Caste, Race and Difference. The Limits of Knowledge and Resistance. *Current Sociology Monograph*, 62 (4), pp. 512–530.

Barrow, Clyde (2020) *The Dangerous Class. The Concept of Lumpenproletariat.* Ann Arbor, MI: University of Michigan Press.

Basu, Swaraj (2003) *The Dynamics of the Caste System. The Rajbansis of North Bengal, 1910–1947.* New Delhi: Manohar.

Bernal, Martin (1987) *Black Athena: The Afroasiatic Roots of Classical Civilization.* New Brunswick, NJ: Rutgers University Press.

Béteille, Andre (1965) *Caste, Class and Power.* Berkeley: University of California Press.

Béteille, André (1971) Race, Caste and Ethnic Identity. *International Social Science Journal,* 23 (4), pp. 519–535.

Béteille, André (1990) *Society and Politics in India: Essays in a Comparative Perspective.* London: The Athlone Press Ltd.

Biswas, Suyai (2021) Gandhi and Ambedkar against *Untouchability. South Asia Research,* 41 (2), pp. 259–278.

Black, Edwin (2003) *War against the Weak: Eugenics and America's Campaign to Create a Master Race.* New York: Four Walls, Eight Windows.

Blunt, E. A. H. (1969) *The Caste System of Northern India.* Delhi: S. Chand & Co.

Bob, Clifford (2007) Dalit Rights Are Human Rights. Caste Discrimination, International Activism, and the Construction of a New Human Rights Issue. *Human Rights Quarterly,* 29, pp. 167–193.

Bonilla-Silva, Eduardo (2003) *Racism without Racists.* Washington: Rowman and Littlefield.

Bouglé, Célestin (1908) *Essais sur Le Régime du Caste.* Paris: Félix Alcan Éditeur.

Bourdieu, Pierre (1980) *The Logic of Practice.* Stanford, CA: Stanford University Press.

Bourdieu, Pierre (1984) *Distinction: A Social Critique of the Judgement of Taste.* London: Routledge.

Bressey, Caroline (2013) *Empire, Race and the Politics of "Anti-Caste."* London: Bloomsbury.

Brown, Kavin (2018) African American Perspective on Common Struggles. In S. Yengde and A. Teltumbde (eds) *The Radical Ambedkar. Critical Reflections.* New York: Penguin, pp. 43–60.

Burkholder, Zoë (2021) *An African American Dilemma. A History of School Integration and Civil Rights in the North.* New York: Oxford University Press.

Cabral, Amilcar (1973) *Return to the Source. Selected Speeches of Amilcar Cabral.* New York: Monthly Review Press.

Camus, Albert (2005) *The Myth of Sisyphus.* New York: Penguin Books.

Carnegie Institution of Washington (1939) *Yearbook No. 38.* Washington, DC: Carnegie Institution of Washington.

Césaire, Aimé (2000) *Discourse on Colonialism.* New York: Monthly Review Press.

Chakravarti, Uma, and Krishnaraj, Maithreyi (2020) *Gendering Caste: Through a Feminist Lens.* Los Angeles: SAGE.

Chatterjee, Partha (2018) Ambedkar's Theory of Minority Rights. In S. Yengde and A. Teltumbde (eds) *The Radical Ambedkar. Critical Reflections.* New York: Penguin Books, pp. 107–133.

Chaudhry, Prashant (2013) Caste as an Institutionalised System of Social Exclusion and Discrimination: Some Evidence. *International Journal of Gender and Women's Studies*, 1 (1), pp. 56–63.

Chitty, Clyde (2013) The Educational Legacy of Francis Galton. *History of Education*, 42 (3), pp. 350–364.

Chow, Rey (2006) *The Age of the World Target. Self-Referentiality in War, Theory and Comparative Work*. Durham: Duke University Press.

Cox, Oliver Cromwell (1959) *Caste, Class and Race: A Study in Social Dynamics*. New York: Monthly Review Press.

Crooke, William (1896) *The Tribes and Castes of the North-Western Provinces and Oudh*. Calcutta: Office of the Superintendent of Government Printing.

Čvorović, Jelena. (2007). Caste behaviors among Gypsies in Serbia. *Культура у трансформацији (Culture in Transformation)*, pp. 151–168.

Dabashi, Hamid (2015) *Can Non-Europeans Think?* London: Zed Books.

Davenport, Charles (1923) *Eugenics, Genetics, and the Family*. Baltimore, MD: Williams and Wilkins.

Davenport, Charles, and Laughlin, Harry (1915) *How to make a Eugenical Family Study* (Project Report. Carnegie Institution of Washington). New York: Cold Spring Harbor.

Davis, Allison (1945) Caste, Economy and Violence. *American Journal of Sociology*, 51 (1), pp. 8–9.

Davis, Allison, Burleigh, Gardner, and Mary, Gardner (1941) *Deep South. A Sociological Anthropological Study of Caste and Class*. Charlotte, SC: The University of South Carolina Press.

de Certeau, Michel (1988) *The Practice of Everyday Life*. Berkeley, CA: University of California Press.

Derrida, Jacques (1973) *Speech and Phenomena and Other Essays on Husserl's Theory of Signs*. Evanston: Northwestern University Press.

Derrida, Jacques (1976) *Of Grammatology*. Baltimore: The Johns Hopkins University Press.

Dhanda, Meena (2015) Anti-Casteism and Misplaced Nativism: Mapping Caste as an Aspect of Race. *Radical Philosophy*, 192, pp. 33–43.

Dhanda, Meena (2019) The Philosophical Foundations of Anti-Casteism. *Proceedings of the Aristotelian Society*, cxx, Part 1, pp. 71–96.

Dhanda, Meena, Waughray, Annapurna, Keane, David, Mosse, David Green, Roger, and Whittle, Stephen (2014) Caste in Britain. In *Sociological Review. Equality and Human Rights Commission, Research Report 91*. Manchester: Equality and Human Rights Commission.

Diop, Cheikh Anta (1970) The Birth of the "Negro Myth." In I. L. Markovitz (ed) *African Politics and Society*. New York: Free Press.

Dirks, Nicholas (2002) *Castes of Mind. Colonialism and the Making of Modern India*. Princeton, NJ: Princeton University Press.

Douglass, Frederick (1845) The State Convention in Ohio. *Douglass' Monthly*, L (VIII), pp. 4–5, p. 4.

Douglass, Frederick (1859) Equal Suffrage or Equal School Rights? *Douglass' Monthly*, p. 37.

DuBois, William E. B. (1911) The Economic of Negro Emancipation in the United States. *Sociologial Society*, 18, pp. 303–313.
Dumont, Louis (1970). *Homo Heirarchicus: An Essay on the Caste System*. Chicago, IL: University of Chicago Press.
Dussel, Enrique (2000) Europe, Modernity and Eurocentrism. *Nepantla: Views from South*, 1 (3), pp. 465–478.
Dussel, Enrique (2013) *Ethics of Liberation. In the Age of Globalization and Exclusion*. Durham, NC: Duke University Press.
Eagleton, Terry (1990) *The Significance of Theory*. Oxford: Blackwell.
Eagleton, Terry (2003) *After Theory*. London: Verso.
Elam, J. Daniel (2021a) *Impossible and Necessary Anticolonialism, Reading, and Critique*. Himayatnagar: Orient Blackswan.
Elam, J. Daniel (2021b) Conscience and Conscious in the Global South: B.R. Ambedkar, Kwame Nkrumah, and Anticolonial Sociology. *Comparative Literature Studies*, 58 (3), pp. 604–622.
Ellsworth, Elizabeth (1989) Why Doesn't This Feel Empowering? Working Through the Repressive Myths of Critical Pedagogy. *Harvard Educational Review*, 59 (3), pp. 297–324.
Fanon, Frantz (1963) *The Wretched of the Earth*. New York: Grove.
Fanon, Frantz (1967) *Black Skin White Masks*. New York: Grove.
Flannery, Kent, and Marcus, Joyce (2012) *The Creation of Inequality. How Our Pre-Historic Ancestors Set the Stage for Monarchy, Slavery, and Empire*. Cambridge, MA: Harvard University Press.
Forrest, Derek (1974) *Francis Galton: The Life and Work of a Victorian Genius*. New York: Taplinger Publishing Company.
Frank, Andre Gunder (1998) *Reorient. Global Economy in the Asian Age*. Berkeley, CA: University of California Press.
Fraser, Nancy (1997) *Justice Interrupts. Critical Reflections on the "Postsocialist" Condition*. New York: Routledge.
Gajarawala, Toral Jatin (2012) *Untouchable Fictions: Literary Realism and the Crisis of Caste*. New York: Fordham University Press.
Galton, Francis (1883) *Inquiries into Human Faculty*. London: Macmillan.
Galton, Francis (1892) *Hereditary Genius. An Inquiry into the Laws and Its Consequences*. London: Macmillan.
Galeano, Eduardo (1997) *Open Veins of Latin America: Five Centuries of Pillage of a Continent*. New York: Monthly Review Press.
Gandhi, Mahatma (2016) A Vindication of Caste. Dr. Ambedkar's Indictment. In Bhimrao Ambedkar (ed) *Annihilation of Case*. London: Verso, pp. 321–326.
Gil, José (2018) *Caos e Ritmo*. Lisboa: Relógio D'Água.
Gilda, Sujatha, and Horn, Alan (2021) Caste, Race . . . and Class. *New Left Review*, 131, pp. 15–34.
Glissant, Edouard (1992) *Caribbean Discourse: Selected Essays*. Charlottesville, VA: University of Virginia Press.
Goodnight, Melissa Rae (2017) Critical Race Theory in India: *Theory Translation* and the Analysis of Social Identities and Discrimination in Indian Schooling. *Compare: A Journal of Comparative and International Education*, 47 (5), pp. 665–683.
Goody, Jack (2006) *The Theft of History*. Cambridge: Cambridge University Press.

Gordon, June (2017) Caste in Japan: The Burakumin. *Caste and Life Narratives*, 40 (1), pp. 265–287.

Grosfoguel, Ramon (2003) *Colonial Subjects. Puerto Ricans in a Global Perspective*. Berkeley: University of California Press.

Grosfoguel, Ramon (2011) Decolonizing Post-Colonial Studies and Paradigms of Political Economy: Transmodernity, Decolonial Thinking, and Global Coloniality. Transmodernity. *Journal of Peripheral Cultural Production of the Luso-Hispanic World*, 1 (1), pp. 1–38.

Guha, Ranajit (1997) *Dominance without Hegemony. History and Power in Colonial India*. Cambridge, MA: Harvard University Press.

Guru, Gopal (2017) Ethics in Ambedkar's critique of Gandhi. *Economic & Political Weekly*, 52 (15), pp. 95–100.

Hall, Ronald, and Mishra, Neha (2018) Ambedkar and King. The Subjugation of Caste or Race vis-à-vis Colourism. In S. Yengde and A. Teltumbde (eds) *The Radical Ambedkar. Critical Reflections*. New York: Penguin, pp. 4–16.

Han, Byung-Chul (2018) *The Expulsion of the Other*. Medford: Polity.

Harney, Michael (2015) *Race, Caste and Indigeneity in Medieval Spanish Travel Literature*. New York: Palgrave Macmillan.

Harvey, David (2005) *A Brief History of Neoliberalism*. Cambridge: Oxford University Press.

Havingusrt, Robert (1945) Caste, Class in a Democracy. *Childhood Studies*, 22 (3), pp. 116–123.

Henry, Paget (2000) *Caliban Reason*. New York: Routledge.

Herrnstein, Charles, and Richard, Murray (1995) *The Bell Curve. Intelligence and Class Structure in America*. New York: Free Press.

Hillard, Asa (2001) Race, Identity, Hegemony, and Education. What Do We Need to Know Now? In W. Watkins, J. H. Lewis, and V. Chou (eds) *Race and Education. The Roles of History and Society in Educating African American Students*. Boston, MA: Allyn and Bacon.

Holmes, Samuel J. (1939) The Opposition to Eugenics. *The Scientific Monthly*, 89, pp. 351–357.

Huebner, Dwayne (2021) A Foreword—Second Edition: Theory Not as a Schema for "Acting," But for "Looking." In João M. Paraskeva (ed) *Conflicts in Curriculum Theory* (2nd edition). New York: Palgrave, pp. v–x, p. vii.

Huebner, Dwayne (2022) A Curriculum Afterword: The Dialogue Dwayne Huebner and João M. Paraskeva. In João M. Paraskeva (ed) *The Curriculum. A Comprehensive Reader*. New York: Peter Lang, pp. 529, 559.

Hursh, David (2015). *The End of Public Schools: The Corporate Reform Agenda to Privatize Education*. New York: Routledge.

Immerwahr, Daniel (2007) Caste or Colony?: Indianizing Race in the United States. *Modern Intellectual History*, 4 (2).

Jackson, Edmund (2019) *Report of the Minority of the Committee of the Primary School Board on the Caste Schools in the City of Boston*. Miami: Hardpress.

Jackson, Edmund, and Bowditch, Henry Ingersoll (2019) *Minority Report*. Miami: Hardpress, pp. 3–20.

Jaffrelot, Christophe (2003) *Indians Silent Revolution. The Rise of Lower Castes in North India*. London: C. Hurst & Co.

Jaffrelot, Christophe (2005) *Dr. Ambedkar and Untouchability*. London: C. Hurst & Co.

Jameson, Fredric (2005) *Archaeologies of the Future: The Desire Called Utopia and Other Science Fiction*. New York: Verso.

Jameson, Fredric (2016) *American Utopia: Dual Power and the Universal Army* (S. Žižek, ed.). New York: Verso.

Jayawardene, Sureshi M. (2016) Racialized Casteism: Exposing the Relationship between Race, Caste, and Colorism Through the Experiences of Africana People in India and Sri Lanka. *Journal of African American Studies*, 20 (3/4), pp. 323–345.

Kapoor, Shivani (2021) The Smell of Caste: Leatherwork and Scientific Knowledge in Colonial India. *South Asia: Journal of South Asian Studies*, 44 (5), pp. 983–999.

Karatani, Kojin (2017) *Isonomia and the Origins of Philosophy*. Durham, NC: Duke University Press.

Kumar, Kapil (ed.) (1998) *Congress and Class. Nationalism, Workers, and Peasants*. New Delhi: Manohar.

Leach, Edmund R. (1960) Introduction: What Should We Mean by Caste? In E.R. Leach (ed) *Aspects of Castes in South India, Ceylon and North-west Pakistan*. Cambridge: Cambridge University Press, pp. 2–10.

Lionnet, Francoise & Shiv, Shu-mei (2011) Introduction. In Francoise Lionnet, & Shu-mei Shiv (Eds) *The Creolization of Theory*. Durham: Duke University Press, pp. 1–33.

Lombardo, Paul A. (2014) When Harvard Said No to Eugenics: The J. Ewing Mears Bequest, 1927. *Perspectives in Biology & Medicine*, 57 (3), pp. 374–392.

Lorde, Audre (2007) *Sister Outsider*. Berkeley, CA: Crossing Press.

Lowe, Roy (1980) Eugenics and Education: A Note of the Origins of the Intelligent Testing Movement in England. *Educational Studies*, 6 (1), pp. 1–8.

Lowe, Roy (1998) The Educational Impact of the Eugenics Movement. *International Journal of Educational Research*, 27 (8), pp. 647–660.

MacKenzie, Donald (1976) Eugenics in Britain. *Social Studies of Science*, 6, pp. 499–532.

Maldonado-Torres, Nelson (2008) *Against War: Views from the Underside of Modernity*. Durham, NC: Duke University Press.

Maldonado-Torres, Nelson (2012) Decoloniality at Large: Towards a Trans-Americas and Global Transmodern Paradigm (Introduction to Second Special Issue of "Thinking through the Decolonial Turn"). *Transmodernity. Journal of Peripheral Cultural Production of the Luso-Hispanic World*, 1 (3), pp. 1–10.

Malik-Goure, Archana (2015) Jyotiba Phule. Modern Philosopher and Maker of Modern India. *Journal of East-West Thought*, pp. 73–81.

Manoharan, Kartchik Ram (2017) Anti-Casteist Casteism. *Interventions. International Journal of Postcolonial Studies*, 19 (1), pp. 73–90.

Mariátegui, José Carlos C (2011) Peru's Principal Problem. In H. E. Vanden and M. Becker (eds) *José Carlos Mariátegui: An Anthology*. New York: Monthly Review Press.

Martinez-San Miguel, Yolanda (2014) *Coloniality of Diasporas*. New York: Palgrave Macmillan.

Marx, Karl and Engels, Friedrich (1853) *On Colonialism*. Moscow: Foreign Language Publishing House.

Mbembe, Achile (2014). *Critica da Razão Negra*. Lisboa: Antigona, p. 147.
Mbembe, Achile (2017) *The Critique of the Black Reason*. Durham, NC: Duke University Press, p. 83.
McCarthy, Cameron (1998) *The Uses of Culture. Education and the Limits of Ethnic Affiliation*. New York: Routledge.
McCarthy, Cameron, and Apple, Michael (1988) Race, Class and Gender in American Education. Toward a Nonsynchronous Parallelist Position. In L. Weis (ed.) *Class, Race and Gender in American Education*. Albany, NY: State University of New York Press, pp. 3–39.
Mclaren, Peter (2022) *Critical Theory, Rituals, Pedagogy and Resistance*. Boston: Brill.
Memmi, Albert (1999) *Racism*. Minneapolis: University of Minnesota Press.
Memmi, Albert (2000) *The Colonizer and the Colonized*. Boston, MA: Beacon Press.
Menon, Nivedita (2014) Perry Anderson and the British Ideology. In Partha Chatterjee, Sudipta Kaviraj, and Nivedita Menon (eds) *The Indian Ideology. Three Responses to Perry Anderson*. Himalayana: Orient Blackswan, pp. 13–60.
Mignolo, Walter (2008) The Geopolitics of Knowledge and Colonial Difference. In M. Morana, E. Dussel, and C. Jauregui (eds) *Coloniality at Large. Latin America and the Postcolonial Debate*. San Antonio, TX: Duke University Press, pp. 225–258.
Mignolo, Walter (2018) The Invention of the Human and the Three Pillars of the Coloniality Matrix of Power. In C. Walsh and W. Mignolo (eds) *On Decoloniality: Concepts, Analytics, Praxis*. Durham, NC: Duke University Press, pp. 153–176.
Mignolo, Walter (2022) Por Qué es Necesaria la Analítica de la Colonialidad y Desprenderse. *Occidente. Retratos, Visoes y Utopia*. www.bioeconomy.tv
Morgan, Thomas Hunt (1925) *Evolution and Genetics*: Princeton, NJ: Princeton University Press.
Mosse, David (2020) Outside Caste? The Enclosure of Caste and Claims to Castelessness in India and the United Kingdom. *Comparative Studies in Societies and History*, 62 (1), pp. 4–34.
Mukherjee, Ramkrishna (2000) Caste in Itself, Caste and Class, or Caste in Class. *Journal of World-Systems Research*, 6 (2), pp. 332–333.
Muthu, Sankar (2003) *Enlightenment against Empire*. Princeton, NJ: Princeton University Press.
Myrdal, Gunnar (1944) *An American Dilemma: The Negro Problem and Modern Democracy*. New York: Routledge.
Myrdal, Gunnar (1967) Analogues and Homologues of Caste Systems: Discussion. In A. De Reuck and J. Knight (eds) *Caste and Race: Comparative Approaches*. Boston: J & A Churchill, pp. 74–91.
Natrajan, Balmurli (2005) Caste, Class, and Community in India: An Ethnographic Approach. *Ethnology*, pp. 227–241.
Natrajan, Balmurli (2022) Racialization and Ethnicization. Hindutva Hegemony and Caste. *Ethnic and Racial Studies*, 45 (2), pp. 298–318.
Naumenko, Olga, and Naumenko, Evgeny (2018) Transformation of Caste Consciousness of Siberian Gypsies in XVIII—at the Beginning of XX Centuries as a Factor of Their Cultural Socialization. *International Network Center for Fundamental and Applied Research*, 10, pp. 1397–1405.
Nkrumah, Kwame (1964) *Consciencism*. New York: Monthly Review Press.

O'Hanlon, Rosalind (1985) *Caste, Conflict, and Ideology*. Cambridge: Cambridge University Press.
Omvedt, Gail (1994) *The Dalits and the Democratic Revolution. Dr. Ambedkar and the Dalit Movement in Colonial India*. New Deli: SAGE.
Osborne, Henry (1921) The Second International Congress of Eugenics. Address of Welcome. *Science*, LIV/1397, pp. 311–313.
Paik, Shailaja (2014) *Dalit's Women's Education in Modern India*. New York: Routledge.
Pankaj, Ajeet Kumar (2021) Caste Amid Aspiration and Opportunity: Everyday Struggles of Dalits to Gain Access to Education. *American Journal of Economics and Sociology*, 80 (3), pp. 931–947.
Paraskeva, João M. (2009) *Unaccomplished Utopia. Neoconservative Dismantling of Public Higher Education in the European*. Rotterdam: Sense.
Paraskeva, João M. (2011) *Conflicts in Curriculum Theory* (1st edn). New York: Palgrave.
Paraskeva, João M. (2012) Challenging the Neoliberal Global Minotaur. *Policy Futures in Education*, 10 (6), pp. 700–716.
Paraskeva, João M. (2013) The Need for a Higher Education Carnival. *Policy Futures in Education*, 11 (4), pp. 478–483.
Paraskeva, João M. (2014) *Conflicts in Curriculum Theory* (Paper Back 1st Edition). New York: Palgrave.
Paraskeva, João M. (2015) The Curriculum: Whose Internationalization? In João M. Paraskeva (ed.) *The Curriculum: Whose Internationalization?* New York: Peter Lang, pp. 1–12.
Paraskeva, João M. (2016) *Curriculum Epistemicides* [Preface by A. Darder]. New York: Routledge.
Paraskeva, João M. (2018a) *Towards a Just Curriculum Theory. The Epistemicide* [Foreword by N. Chomsky]. New York: Routledge.
Paraskeva, João M. (2018b) Against the Scandal: Itinerant Curriculum Theory as Subaltern Momentum. *Qualitative Research Journal*, 18 (2), pp. 128–143.
Paraskeva, João M. (2021) *Curriculum and the Generation of Utopia* [Preface by A. Darder]. New York: Routledge.
Paraskeva, João M. (2022a) *Conflicts in Curriculum Theory* (2nd edn). New York: Palgrave.
Paraskeva, João M. (2022b) The Original Sin. A Critique of the Curriculum Reason: Towards a 'Non-Derivative' Critical Curriculum Reason. In João M. Paraskeva (ed) *The Curriculum: A Ne Comprehensive Reader*. New York: Peter Lang, pp. 1–62.
Paraskeva, João M. (2022c) The Generation of the Utopia: Itinerant Curriculum Theory Towards a 'Futurable Future'. *Discourse: Studies in the Cultural Politics of Education*, 43 (3), pp. 347–366.
Pathania, Gaurav J., and Tierney, William G. (2018) An Ethnography of Caste and Class at an Indian University: Creating Capital. *Tertiary Education and Management*, pp. 1–12.
Phule, Jyotirao (1911) *Slavery. In the Civilised British Government under the Cloak of Brahmanism*. Bombay: The Education Department.
Pinar, William (2015) Introduction. In William Pinar (ed) *Curriculum Studies in India. Intellectual Histories, Present Circumstances*. New York: Palgrave, pp. 1–34.

Plato (1968) *The Republic.* New York: Basic Books.

Popkewitz, Thomas (1976) Myths of Social Science in Curriculum. *The Educational Forum,* 40 (3), pp. 317–328.

Popkewitz, Thomas (1992) *A Political Sociological Critique of Teacher Education Reforms: Evaluation of the Relation of Power and Knowledge. Focus on Evaluation and Measurement. Volumes 1 & 2.* Proceedings of the National Research Symposium on Limited English Proficient Student Issues, Washington, DC, September 4–6.

Purakayastha, Anindya Sekhar (2019) W.E.B Du Bois, B.R. Ambedkar and the History of Afro-Dalit Solidarity. *Journal of Literary and Cultural Inquiry,* 6 (1), pp. 20–36.

Quijano, Anibal (1992) Colonialidad y Modernidad/Racionalidad. *Perú Indígena,* 29 (1), pp. 11–21.

Quijano, Anibal (2008) Coloniality of Power, Eurocentrism, and Latin America. In M. Morana, E. Dussel, and C. Jauregui (eds) *Colonialiy at Large. Latin America and the Postcolonial Debate.* San Antonio, TX: Duke University Press, pp. 181–224.

Ramesh, Hari (2022) B. R. Ambedkar on Caste, Democracy and State Action. *Political Theory,* 50 (5), pp. 723–753.

Rancière, Jacques (2010) *Chronicles of Consensual Times.* New York: Continuum.

Rao, C. Hayavadana (1931) *Indian Caste System. A Study.* New Delhi: Asian Educational Services.

Reddy, Deepa (2011) Hindutva as Praxis. *Religion Compass,* 5/8, pp. 412–426.

Risley, Herbert (1892) *Tribes and Castes of Bengal. Ethnographic Glossary, Volume 1.* Calcutta: Bengal Secretariat Press.

Roy, Arundhati (2016) The Doctor and the Saint. In B. R. Ambedkar. In *Annihilation of Caste.* London: Verso, pp. 17–179.

Santos, Boaventura de Sousa (1999) Porque é tão difícil construir uma teoria crítica? *Revista Crítica de Ciencias Sociais,* 54 (Junho), pp. 197–215.

Santos, Boaventura de Sousa (2001) Nuestra America: Reinventing a Subaltern Paradigm of Recognition and Redistribution. *Theory, Culture, and Society,* 18 (2–3), pp. 185–217.

Santos, Boaventura de Sousa (2004) *A Gramatica do Tempo.* Porto: Afrontamento.

Santos, Boaventura de Sousa (2007b) Beyond Abyssal Thinking. From Global Lines to Ecologies of Knowledges. *Review,* XXX (1), pp. 45–89.

Santos, Boaventura de Sousa (2014) *Epistemologies from the South.* Boulder, CO: Paradigm.

Santos, Boaventura de Sousa (2018) *The End of the Cognitive Empire.* Durham, NC: Duke University Press.

Sekar, Bandyopadhyay (1987) Protest and Accommodation: Two Caste Movements in Eastern and Northern Bengal. *The Indian Historical Review,* XIV (1–2), p. 227.

Selden, Steven (1999) *Inheriting Shame. The Story if Eugenics and Racism in America.* New York: Teachers College Press.

Selden, Steven (2000) Eugenics and the Social Construction of Merit, Race and Disability. *Journal of Curriculum Studies,* 32 (2), pp. 235–252.

Senart, Émile (1930) *Caste in India. The Facts and the System.* London: Methuen & Co.

Senghor, Leopold (1970). *Negritude: A Humanism of the Twentieth Century. The African Reader.* New York: Vintage.

Senthilkumar Solidarity Committee (2008) Caste, Higher Education and Senthil's 'Suicide'. *Economic and Political Weekly*, 43 (33), pp. 10–12.

Sinha, Surajit (1967) Caste in India: Its essential pattern of socio-cultural integration. In Reuck, Anthony and Julie Knight (eds) *Caste and Race*. London: J & A Churchill Ltd, pp. 92–105.

Sirohi, Rahul, and Gupta, Sonya Surabhi (2020) The Political Economy of Race and Caste: Revisiting the Writings of Mariátegui and Ambedkar. *Labor and Society*, 23, pp. 399–413.

Sirswal, Desh Raj (2013) Mahatma Jyotirao Phule. *A Modern Indian Philosopher*, pp. 1–13. www.researchgate.net/publication/272303358

Smith, James (1845) Civilization. *Douglass Monthly*, L (X), pp. 26–29, p. 28.

Sofair, A. N., and Kaldjian, L. C. (2000) Eugenic Sterilization and a Qualified Nazi Analogy: The United States and Germany, 1930–1945. *Annals of Internal Medicine*, 132, pp. 312–319.

Sontag, Susan (2010) *Renascer. Diários e Apontamentos 1947–1963*. Lisboa: Quetzal.

Srinivas, M. N. (1962) *Caste in Modern India and Other Essays*. New York: Asia Publishing House.

Stroud, Scott (2023) *The Evolution and Pragmatism in India. Ambedkar, Dewey and the Rhetoric of Deconstruction*. Chicago: University of Chicago Press.

Subedi, Madhusudan (2013) Some Theoretical Considerations on Caste. *Dhaulagiri Journal of Sociology and Anthropology*, 7, pp. 51–86.

Sumner, Charles (1845) *His Complete Works, Volume 1*. Boston, MA: Lee and Shepard.

Sumner, Charles (1900a) *His Complete Works, Volume 20*. Boston, MA: Lee and Shepard.

Sumner, Charles (1900b) *His Complete Works, Volume 14*. Boston, MA: Lee and Shepard.

Swapnil, Singh (2015) Caste and Diaspora. *International Journal of Social Sciences and Humanity*, 5 (1), pp. 80–82.

Tamás, Gáspár Miklós (2006) Telling the Truth about Class. *Socialist Register*, pp. 228–268.

Tamim, Tayyaba (2018) Caste, Costs and Educational Access in Rural Punjab. *Journal of Education and Economic Development*, 1, pp. 25–41.

Tartakov, Gary (2018) Criminalized Castes. Dalits, African Americans, and the Jews of Christian Europe. In S. Yengde and A. Teltumbde (eds) *The Radical Ambedkar. Critical Reflections*. New York: Penguin, pp. 32–42.

Teltumbde, Anand (2010) *The Persistence of Caste. The Khairlanji Murders and India's Hidden Apartheid*. New York: Zed Books.

Teltumbde, Anand (2016) *The Republic of Caste. Thinking Equality in the Time of Neoliberal Hindutva*. Delhi: Navayana.

Teltumbde, Anand (2017) *Dalits. Past, Present, and Future*. New York: Routledge.

Teltumbde, Anand (2018) Umar Khalid and the Hate Republic. *Economic and Political Weekly*, September 8, pp. 1–3.

Teltumbde, Anand and Yengde, Suraj (2018) Introduction: Reclaiming the Radical in Ambedkar's Practices. In Sure Yengde and Anand Teltumbde (eds) *The Radical Ambedkar. Critical Reflections*. New York: Penguin, pp. xi–xxvi.

Thorat, Amit, and Joshi, Omkar (2015) The Continuing Practice of Untouchability in India: Patterns and Mitigating Influences. *India Human Development Survey Working Paper No. 2015–2*. National Council of Applied Economic Research.

Thorat, Sukhadeo (2020) Editorial. Why a Journal of Caste? Part 2 An Introduction to Caste. *Caste—A Global Journal on Social Exclusion*, 1 (1), pp. i–vii.

Todd, D. M. (1977) Caste in Africa? *Journal of the International African Institute*, 47 (4), pp. 398–412.

Venturini, Roger (2023) *Curriculum, Spirituality, and Human Rights. Towards a Just Public Education*. Boston: BRILL.

Vijay, Devi, and Nair, Vivek G. (2019) In the Name of Merit: Ethical Violence and Inequality at a Business School. *Journal of Business Ethics*, 11, pp. 315–337.

Visvanathan, Shiv (1997) *A Carnival for Science. Essays on Science, Technology and Development*. Delhi: Oxford University Press.

Wacquant, Loïc (2002) From Slavery to Mass Incarceration. *New Left Review*, 13, pp. 41–60.

Wacquant, Loïc (2022) Resolving the Trouble with Race. *New Left Review*, 133–134, pp. 67–88.

Walsh, Catherine (2018) Insurgency and Decolonila Prospect, Praxis and Project. In Catherine Walsh and Walter Mignolo (eds) *On Decoloniality: Concepts, Analytics, Praxis*. Durham: Duke University Press, pp. 33–56.

Walsh, Catherine, and Mignolo, Walter (2018) *On Decoloniality: Concepts, Analytics, Praxis*. Durham: Duke University Press.

Warner, W. Lloyd (1936) American Caste and Class. *American Journal of Sociology*, 42 (2), pp. 234–247.

Warner, W. Lloyd, and Davis, Allison (1939) A Comparative Study of American Caste. In E. Thompson (ed.) *Race Relations and the Race Problem*. Durham, NC: Duke University Press.

Wa' Thiong'o, Ngugi (2005) *Decolonizing the Mind*. New York: Boydell and Brewer.

Watkins, W. (1993) Black Curriculum Orientations. *Harvard Educational Review*, 63 (3), pp. 321–338.

Watkins, W. (2001) *The White Architects of Black Education*. New York: Teachers College Press.

Wilkerson, Isabel (2020) *Castes and the Origins of our Discontent*. New York: Random House.

Williams, Chancellor (1987) *The Destruction of Black Civilization*. Chicago, IL: Third World Press.

Wright, Erik Olin (1994) *Interrogating Inequality: Essays on Class Analysis, Socialism, and Marxism*. London: Verso.

Wright, Erik Olin (2000a) *Interrogating Inequality*. New York: Verso.

Wright, Erik Olin (2000b) *Class Counts*. Cambridge: Cambridge University Press.

Wright, Erik Olin (2015) *Understanding Class*. London: Verso.

Yengde, Suraj (2022) Global Castes. *Ethnic and Racial Studies*, 45 (2), pp. 340–360.

Zhao, Weili, Popkewitz, Thomas and Autio, Tero (2022) Historicizing Curricuoum Knowledge Transition and Onto-Epistemic Coloniality. In Weili Zhao, Thomas Popkewitz, and Tero Autio (eds) *Epistemic Colonialism and Transfer of Curriculum Knowledge Across Borders*. New York: Routledge, pp. 3–18.

2 Caste

A Division of Labour
and Labourers

Bhimrao Ramji Ambedkar[1]

Why Social Reform is Necessary for Political Reform

The path of social reform, like the path to heaven (at any rate, in India), is strewn with many difficulties. Social reform in India has few friends and many critics. The critics fall into two distinct classes. One class consists of political reformers, and the other of the Socialists.

It was at one time recognized that, without social efficiency, no permanent progress in the other fields of activity was possible; that, owing to mischief wrought by evil customs, Hindu society was not in a state of efficiency; and that ceaseless efforts must be made to eradicate these evils. It was due to the recognition of this fact that the birth of the National Congress was accompanied by the foundation of the Social Conference. While the Congress was concerned with defining the weak points in the political organisation of the country, the Social Conference was engaged in removing the weak points in the social organisation of the Hindu Society. For some time, the Congress and the Conference worked as two wings of one common activity, and they held their annual sessions in the same pandal.

But soon, the two wings developed into two parties: a 'political reform party' and a 'social reform party', between whom there raged a fierce controversy. The 'political reform party' supported the National Congress, and the 'social reform party' supported the Social Conference. The two bodies thus became two hostile camps. The point at issue was whether social reform should precede political reform. For a decade, the forces were evenly balanced, and the battle was fought without victory on either side.

It was, however, evident that the fortunes of the Social Conference were ebbing fast. The gentlemen who presided over the sessions of the Social Conference lamented that the majority of the educated Hindus were for political advancement and indifferent to social reform; and that, while the number of those who attended the Congress was very large and the

DOI: 10.4324/9781003155065-2

number who did not attend but who sympathized with it was even larger, the number of those who attended the Social Conference was very much smaller.

This indifference, this thinning of its ranks, was soon followed by active hostility from the politicians. Under the leadership of the late Mr. Tilak, the courtesy with which the Congress allowed the Social Conference the use of its pandal was withdrawn, and the spirit of enmity went to such a pitch that, when the Social Conference desired to erect its own pandal, a threat to burn the pandal was held out by its opponents. Thus, in the course of time, the party in favour of political reform won, and the Social Conference vanished and was forgotten.

The speech delivered by Mr. W. C. Bonnerji in 1892 at Allahabad, as President of the eighth session of the Congress, sounds like a funeral oration on the death of the Social Conference and is so typical of the Congress attitude that I venture to quote from it the following extract. Mr. Bonnerji said:

> I for one have no patience with those who say we shall not be fit for political reform until we reform our social system. I fail to see any connection between the two . . . Are we not fit (for political reform) because our widows remain unmarried and our girls are given in marriage earlier than in other countries? because our wives and daughters do not drive about with us visiting our friends? because we do not send our daughters to Oxford and Cambridge?
>
> (Cheers [from the audience])

I have stated the case for political reform as put by Mr. Bonnerji. There were many who were happy that the victory went to the Congress. But those who believe in the importance of social reform may ask, is an argument such as that of Mr. Bonnerji final? Does it prove that the victory went to those who were in the right? Does it prove conclusively that social reform has no bearing on political reform? It will help us to understand the matter if I state the other side of the case. I will draw upon the treatment of the untouchables for my facts.

Under the rule of the Peshwas in the Maratha country, the untouchable was not allowed to use the public streets if a Hindu was coming along, lest he should pollute the Hindu by his shadow. The untouchable was required to have a black thread either on his wrist or around his neck, as a sign or a mark to prevent the Hindus from getting themselves polluted by his touch by mistake. In Poona, the capital of the Peshwa, the untouchable was required to carry, strung from his waist, a broom to sweep away from behind himself the dust he trod on, lest a Hindu walking on the same dust should be polluted. In Poona, the untouchable was required to carry an earthen pot hung around his neck wherever he went—for holding his spit, lest his spit falling on the earth should pollute a Hindu who might unknowingly happen to tread on it.

Let me take more recent facts. The tyranny practised by the Hindus upon the Balais, an untouchable community in Central India, will serve my purpose. You will find a report of this in the Times of India of 4th January 1928. The correspondent of the Times of India reported that high-caste Hindus—viz., Kalotas, Rajputs and Brahmins, including the Patels and Patwaris of the villages of Kanaria, Bicholi-Hafsi, Bicholi-Mardana, and about 15 other villages in the Indore district (of the Indore State)—informed the Balais of their respective villages that if they wished to live among them, they must conform to the following rules:

1. Balais must not wear gold-lace-bordered pugrees.
2. They must not wear dhotis with coloured or fancy borders.
3. They must convey intimation [=information] of the death of any Hindu to relatives of the deceased—no matter how far away these relatives may be living.
4. In all Hindu marriages, Balais must play music before the processions and during the marriage.
5. Balai women must not wear gold or silver ornaments; they must not wear fancy gowns or jackets.
6. Balai women must attend all cases of confinement [= childbirth] of Hindu women.
7. Balais must render services without demanding remuneration and must accept whatever a Hindu is pleased to give.
8. If the Balais do not agree to abide by these terms, they must clear out of the villages.

The Balais refused to comply; and the Hindu element proceeded against them. Balais were not allowed to get water from the village wells; they were not allowed to let go their cattle to graze. Balais were prohibited from passing through land owned by a Hindu, so that, if the field of a Balai was surrounded by fields owned by Hindus, the Balai could have no access to his own field. The Hindus also let their cattle graze down the fields of Balais. The Balais submitted petitions to the Darbar [= Court of Indore] against these persecutions; but, as they could get no timely relief and the oppression continued, hundreds of Balais with their wives and children were obliged to abandon their homes—in which their ancestors had lived for generations—and to migrate to adjoining states; that is, to villages in Dhar, Dewas, Bagli, Bhopal, Gwalior and other states. What happened to them in their new homes may, for the present, be left out of our consideration.

The incident at Kavitha in Gujarat happened only last year. The Hindus of Kavitha ordered the untouchables not to insist upon sending their children to the common village school maintained by Government. What sufferings the untouchables of Kavitha had to undergo for daring to exercise a civic right against the wishes of the Hindus is too well known to need detailed description. Another instance occurred in the village of Zanu, in the Ahmedabad district of Gujarat. In November 1935 some untouchable women of well-to-do families started fetching water in metal pots. The Hindus looked upon the use of metal pots by untouchables as an affront to their dignity and assaulted the untouchable women for their impudence.

A most recent event is reported from the village of Chakwara in Jaipur State. It seems from the reports that have appeared in the newspapers that an untouchable of Chakwara who had returned from a pilgrimage had arranged to give a dinner to his fellow untouchables of the village as an act of religious piety. The host desired to treat the guests to a sumptuous meal, and the items served included ghee (butter) also. But, while the assembly of untouchables was engaged in partaking of the food, the Hindus in their hundreds, armed with lathis, rushed to the scene, despoiled the food, and belaboured the untouchables—who left the food they had been served with and ran away for their lives. And why was this murderous assault committed on defenceless untouchables? The reason given is that the untouchable host was impudent enough to serve ghee, and his untouchable guests were foolish enough to taste it. Ghee is undoubtedly a luxury for the rich. But no one would think that consumption of ghee was a mark of high social status. The Hindus of Chakwara thought otherwise, and in righteous indignation, avenged themselves for the wrong done to them by the untouchables, who insulted them by treating ghee as an item of their food—which they ought to have known could not be theirs, consistently with the dignity of the Hindus. This means that an untouchable must not use ghee, even if he can afford to buy it, since it is an act of arrogance towards the Hindus. This happened on or about the 1st of April 1936!

Having stated the facts, let me now state the case for social reform. In doing this, I will follow Mr. Bonnerji as nearly as I can, and ask the political-minded Hindus, "Are you fit for political power even though you do not allow a large class of your own countrymen like the untouchables to use public schools? Are you fit for political power even though class of your own countrymen like the untouchables to use public schools? Are you fit for political power even though you do not allow them the use of public wells? Are you fit for political power even though you do not allow them the use of public streets? Are you fit for political power even though you do not allow them to wear what apparel or ornaments they like? Are you fit for political power even though you do not allow them to eat any food they like?" I can ask a string of such questions. But these will suffice. I wonder what would have been the reply of Mr. Bonnerji. I am sure no sensible man will have the courage to give an affirmative answer. Every Congressman who repeats the dogma of Mill that one country is not fit to rule another country must admit that one class is not fit to rule another class. How is it, then, that the 'social reform party' lost the battle? To understand this correctly, it is necessary to take note of the kind of social reform which the reformers were agitating for. In this connection, it is necessary to make a distinction between social reform in the sense of the reform of the Hindu family and social reform in the sense of the reorganisation and reconstruction of the Hindu Society. The former has a relation to widow remarriage, child marriage, etc., while the latter relates to the abolition of the Caste System.

The Social Conference was a body which mainly concerned itself with the reform of the high-caste Hindu family. It consisted mostly of enlightened, high-caste Hindus who did not feel the necessity for agitating for the abolition of caste, or had not the courage to agitate for it. They felt quite naturally a greater urge to remove such evils as enforced widowhood, child marriages, etc.—evils which prevailed among them and which were personally felt by them. They did not stand up for the reform of the Hindu Society. The battle that was fought centred round the question of the reform of the family. It did not relate to social reform in the sense of the break-up of the Caste System. It [=the break-up of the Caste System] was never put at issue by the reformers. That is the reason why the Social Reform Party lost.

I am aware that this argument cannot alter the fact that political reform did, in fact, gain precedence over social reform. But the argument has this much value (if not more): it explains why social reformers lost the battle. It also helps us to understand how limited was the victory which the 'political reform party' obtained over the 'social reform party'; and to understand that the view that social reform need not precede political reform is a view which may stand only when by social reform is meant the reform of the family. That political reform cannot, with impunity, take precedence over social reform in the sense of the reconstruction of society is a thesis which I am sure cannot be controverted.

That the makers of political constitutions must take account of social forces is a fact which is recognised by no less a person than Ferdinand Lassalle, the friend and co-worker of Karl Marx. In addressing a Prussian audience in 1862, Lassalle said:

The constitutional questions are in the first instance not questions of right but questions of might. The actual constitution of a country has its existence only in the actual condition of force which exists in the country: hence political constitutions have value and permanence only when they accurately express those conditions of forces which exist in practice within a society.

But it is not necessary to go to Prussia. There is evidence at home. What is the significance of the Communal Award, with its allocation of political power in defined proportions to diverse classes and communities? In my view, its significance lies in this: that political constitution must take note of social organisation. It shows that the politicians who denied that the social problem in India had any bearing on the political problem were forced to reckon with the social problem in devising the Constitution. The Communal Award is, so to say, the nemesis following upon the indifference to and neglect of social reform. It is a victory for the Social Reform Party, which shows that, though defeated, they were in the right in insisting upon the importance of social reform. Many, I know, will not accept this finding. The view is current—and it is pleasant to believe in it—that the Communal Award is unnatural and that it is the result of an unholy alliance between the minorities and the bureaucracy. I do not wish to rely on the Communal Award as a piece of evidence to support my contention, if it is said that it is not good evidence.

Let us turn to Ireland. What does the history of Irish Home Rule show? It is well-known that, in the course of the negotiations between the representatives of Ulster and Southern Ireland, Mr. Redmond, the representative of Southern Ireland, in order to bring Ulster into a Home Rule Constitution common to the whole of Ireland, said to the representatives of Ulster: "Ask any political safeguards you like and you shall have them." What was the reply that Ulstermen gave? Their reply was, "Damn your safeguards, we don't want to be ruled by you on any terms." People who blame the minorities in India ought to consider what would have happened to the political aspirations of the majority if the minorities had taken the attitude which Ulster took. Judged by the attitude of Ulster to Irish Home Rule, is it nothing that the minorities agreed to be ruled by the majority (which has not shown much sense of statesmanship), provided some safeguards were devised for them? But this is only incidental.

The main question is, why did Ulster take this attitude? The only answer I can give is that there was a social problem between Ulster and Southern Ireland: the problem between Catholics and Protestants, which is essentially a problem of caste. That Home Rule in Ireland would be Rome Rule was the way in which the Ulstermen had framed their answer. But that is only another way of stating that it was the social problem of caste between the Catholics and Protestants which prevented the solution of the political problem. This evidence, again, is sure to be challenged. It will be urged that here too the hand of the Imperialist was at work.

But my resources are not exhausted. I will give evidence from the History of Rome. Here, no one can say that any evil genius was at work. Anyone who has studied the History of Rome will know that the Republican Constitution of Rome bore marks having strong resemblance to the Communal Award. When the kingship in Rome was abolished, the kingly power (or the Imperium) was divided between the Consuls and the Pontifex Maximus. In the Consuls was vested the secular authority of the King, while the latter took over the religious authority of the King. This Republican Constitution had provided that of the two Consuls, one was to be Patrician and the other Plebian. The same Constitution had also provided that, of the Priests under the Pontifex Maximus, half were to be Plebians and the other half Patricians. Why is it that the Republican Constitution of Rome had these provisions—which, as I said, resemble so strongly the provisions of the Communal Award? The only answer one can get is that the Constitution of Republican Rome had to take account of the social division between the Patricians and the Plebians, who formed two distinct castes. To sum up, let political reformers turn in any direction they like; they will find that, in the making of a constitution, they cannot ignore the problem arising out of the prevailing social order.

The illustrations which I have taken in support of the proposition that social and religious problems have a bearing on political constitutions seem to be too particular. Perhaps they are. But it should not be supposed that the bearing of the one on the other is limited. On the other hand, one can say that, generally speaking, history bears out the proposition that political revolutions have always been preceded by social and religious revolutions. The religious Reformation started by Luther was the precursor of the political emancipation of the European people. In England, Puritanism led to the establishment of political liberty. Puritanism founded the new world. It was Puritanism that won the war of American Independence, and Puritanism was a religious movement.

The same is true of the Muslim Empire. Before the Arabs became a political power, they had undergone a thorough religious revolution started by the Prophet Mohammad. Even Indian history supports the same conclusion. The political revolution led by Chandragupta was preceded by the religious and social revolution of Buddha. The political revolution led by Shivaji was preceded by the religious and social reform brought about by the saints of Maharashtra. The political revolution of the Sikhs was preceded by the religious and social revolution led by Guru Nanak. It is unnecessary to add more illustrations. These will suffice to show that the emancipation of the mind and the soul is a necessary preliminary for the political expansion of the people.

Why Social Reform is Necessary for Economic Reform

Let me now turn to the Socialists. Can the Socialists ignore the problem arising out of the social order? The Socialists of India, following their fellows in Europe, are seeking to apply the economic interpretation of history to the facts of India. They propound that man is an economic creature; that his activities and aspirations are bound by economic facts; that property is the only source of power. They therefore preach that political and social reforms are but gigantic illusions; and that economic reform by equalisation of property must have precedence over every other kind of reform. One may take issue with every one of these premises—on which rests the Socialists' case for economic reform as having priority over issue with every one of these premises—on which rests the Socialists' case for economic reform as having priority over every other kind of reform. One may contend that the economic motive is not the only motive by which man is actuated [=motivated]. That economic power is the only kind of power no student of human society can accept.

That the social status of an individual by itself often becomes a source of power and authority is made clear by the sway which the Mahatmas have held over the common man. Why do millionaires in India obey penniless Sadhus and Fakirs? Why do millions of paupers in India sell their trifling trinkets which constitute their only wealth and go to Benares and Mecca? That religion is the source of power is illustrated by the history of India, where the priest holds a sway over the common man often greater than that of the magistrate, and where everything, even such things as strikes and elections, so easily takes a religious turn and can so easily be given a religious twist.

Take the case of the Plebians of Rome as a further illustration of the power of religion over man. It throws great light on this point. The Plebians had fought for a share in the supreme executive under the Roman Republic and had secured the appointment of a Plebian Consul elected by a separate electorate constituted by the Commitia Centuriata, which was an assembly of Plebians. They wanted a Consul of their own because they felt that the Patrician Consuls used to discriminate against the Plebians in carrying on the administration. They had apparently obtained a great gain because, under the Republican Constitution of Rome, one Consul had the power of vetoing an act of the other Consul.

But did they, in fact, gain anything? The answer to this question must be in the negative. The Plebians never could get a Plebian Consul who could be said to be a strong man and who could act independently of the Patrician Consul. In the ordinary course of things, the Plebians should have got a strong Plebian Consul, in view of the fact that his election was to be by a separate electorate of Plebians. The question is, why did they fail in getting a strong Plebian to officiate as their Consul?

The answer to this question reveals the dominion which religion exercises over the minds of men. It was an accepted creed of the whole Roman *populus* [=people] that no official could enter upon the duties of his office unless the Oracle of Delphi declared that he was acceptable to the Goddess. The priests who were in charge of the temple of the Goddess of Delphi were all Patricians. Whenever, therefore, the Plebians elected a Consul who was known to be a strong party man and opposed to the Patricians—or 'communal', to use the term that is current in India—the Oracle invariably declared that he was not acceptable to the Goddess. This is how the Plebians were cheated out of their rights.

But what is worthy of note is that the Plebians permitted themselves to be thus cheated because they, too, like the Patricians, held firmly the belief that the approval of the Goddess was a condition precedent to the taking charge by an official of his duties and that election by the people was not enough. If the Plebians had contended that election was enough and that the approval by the Goddess was not necessary, they would have derived the fullest benefit from the political right which they had obtained. But they did not. They agreed to elect another, less suitable to themselves but more suitable to the Goddess—which, in fact, meant more amenable to the Patricians. Rather than give up religion, the Plebians gave up the material gain for which they had fought so hard. Does this not show that religion can be a source of power as great as money, if not greater?

The fallacy of the Socialists lies in supposing that, because, in the present stage of European Society, property as a source of power is predominant, the same is true of India or that the same was true of Europe in the past. Religion, social status, and property are all sources of power and authority, which one man has, to control the liberty of another. One is predominant at one stage; the other is predominant at another stage. That is the only difference. If liberty is the ideal, if liberty means the destruction of the dominion which one man holds over another, then obviously, it cannot be insisted upon that economic reform must be the one kind of reform worthy of pursuit. If the source of power and dominion is, at any given time or in any given society, social and religious, then social reform and religious reform must be accepted as the necessary sort of reform.

One can thus attack the doctrine of the Economic Interpretation of History adopted by the Socialists of India. But I recognise that the economic interpretation of history is not necessary for the validity of the Socialist contention that equalisation of property is the only real reform and that it must precede everything else. However, what I would like to ask the Socialists is this: Can you have economic reform without first bringing about a reform of the social order? The Socialists of India do not seem to have considered this question. I do not wish to do them an injustice.

I give below a quotation from a letter which a prominent Socialist wrote a few days ago to a friend of mine, in which he said, "I do not believe that we can build up a free society in India so long as there is a trace of this ill-treatment and suppression of one class by another. Believing as I do in a socialist ideal, inevitably I believe in perfect equality in the treatment of various classes and groups. I think that Socialism offers the only true remedy for this as well as other problems."

Now, the question that I would like to ask is: Is it enough for a Socialist to say, "I believe in perfect equality in the treatment of the various classes?" To say that such a belief is enough is to disclose a complete lack of understanding of what is involved in Socialism. If Socialism is a practical programme and is not merely an ideal, distant and far off, the question for a Socialist is not whether he believes in equality. The question for him is whether he minds one class ill-treating and suppressing another class as a matter of system, as a matter of principle—and thus allowing tyranny and oppression to continue to divide one class from another.

Let me analyse the factors that are involved in the realisation of Socialism, in order to explain fully my point. Now, it is obvious that the economic reform contemplated by the Socialists cannot come about unless there is a revolution resulting in the seizure of power. That seizure of power must be by a proletariat. The first question I ask is: Will the proletariat of India combine to bring about this revolution? What will move men to such an action? It seems to me that, other things being equal, the only thing that will move one man to take such an action is the feeling that other men with whom he is acting are actuated by a feeling of equality and fraternity and—above all—of justice. Men will not join in a revolution for the equalisation of property unless they know that after the revolution is achieved, they will be treated equally, and that there will be no discrimination of caste and creed.

The assurance of a Socialist leading the revolution that he does not believe in caste, I am sure, will not suffice. The assurance must be the assurance proceeding from a much deeper foundation; namely, the mental attitude of the compatriots towards one another in their spirit of personal equality and fraternity. Can it be said that the proletariat of India, poor as it is, recognises no distinctions except that of the rich and the poor? Can it be said that the poor in India recognise no such distinctions of caste or creed, high or low? If the fact is that they do, what unity of front can be expected from such a proletariat in its action against the rich? How can there be a revolution if the proletariat cannot present a united front?

Suppose, for the sake of argument, that, by some freak of fortune, a revolution does take place and the Socialists come into power; will they not have to deal with the problems created by the particular social order prevalent in India? I can't see how a Socialist State in India can function for a second without having to grapple with the problems created by the prejudices which make Indian people observe the distinctions of high and low, clean and unclean. If Socialists are not to be content with the mouthing of fine phrases, if the Socialists wish to make Socialism a definite reality, then they must recognise that the problem of social reform is fundamental and that, for them, there is no escape from it.

That the social order prevalent in India is a matter which a Socialist must deal with; that, unless he does so, he cannot achieve his revolution; and that, if he does achieve it as a result of good fortune, he will have to grapple with the social order if he wishes to realise his ideal; this is a proposition which, in my opinion, is incontrovertible. He will be compelled to take account of caste after the revolution if he does not take account of it before the revolution. This is only another way of saying that, turn in any direction you like, caste is the monster that crosses your path. You cannot have political reform, you cannot have economic reform, unless you kill this monster.

Caste is Not Just a Division of Labour; it is a Division of Labourers

It is a pity that caste, even today, has its defenders. The defences are many. It is defended on the ground that the Caste System is but another name for division of labour; and if division of labour is a necessary feature of every civilised society, then it is argued that there is nothing wrong in the Caste System. Now, the first thing that is to be urged against this view is that the Caste System is not merely a division of labour. *It is also a division of labourers.* Civilised society undoubtedly needs division of labour. But in no civilised society is division of labour accompanied by this unnatural division of labourers into watertight compartments. The Caste System is not merely a division of labourers, which is quite different from division of labour—it is a hierarchy in which the divisions of labourers are graded, one above the other. In no other country is the division of labour accompanied by this gradation of labourers.

There is also a third point of criticism against this view of the Caste System. This division of labour is not spontaneous, it is not based on natural aptitudes. Social and individual efficiency requires us to develop the capacity of an individual to the point of competency to choose and to make his own career. This principle is violated in the Caste System, in so far as it involves an attempt to appoint tasks to individuals in advance—selected not on the basis of trained original capacities but on that of the social status of the parents.

Looked at from another point of view, this stratification of occupations which is the result of the Caste System is positively pernicious. Industry is never static. It undergoes rapid and abrupt changes. With such changes, an individual must be free to change his occupation. Without such freedom to adjust himself to changing circumstances, it would be impossible for him to gain his livelihood. Now, the Caste System will not allow Hindus to take to occupations where they are wanted if they do not belong to them by heredity. If a Hindu is seen to starve rather than take to new occupations not assigned to his caste, the reason is to be found in the Caste System. By not permitting readjustment of occupations, caste becomes a direct cause of much of the unemployment we see in the country.

As a form of division of labour, the Caste System suffers from another serious defect. The division of labour brought about by the Caste System is not a division based on choice. Individual sentiment, individual preference, has no place in it. It is based on the dogma of predestination. Considerations of social efficiency would compel us to recognise that the greatest evil in the industrial system is not so much poverty and the suffering that it involves as the fact that so many persons have callings [=occupations] which make no appeal to those who are engaged in them. Such callings constantly provoke one to aversion, ill will, and the desire to evade.

There are many occupations in India which, on account of the fact that they are regarded as degraded by the Hindus, provoke those who are engaged in them to aversion. There is a constant desire to evade and escape from such occupations, which arises solely because of the blighting effect which they produce upon those who follow them, owing to the slight and stigma cast upon them by the Hindu religion. What efficiency can there be in a system under which neither men's hearts nor their minds are in their work? As an economic organisation, caste is therefore a harmful institution, inasmuch as it involves the subordination of man's natural powers and inclinations to the exigencies of social rules.

Caste Cannot Preserve a Nonexistent 'Racial Purity'

Some have dug a biological trench in defence of the Caste System. It is said that the object of caste was to preserve purity of race and purity of blood. Now, ethnologists are of the opinion that men of pure race exist nowhere and that there has been a mixture of all races in all parts of the world. Especially is this the case with the people of India. Mr. D. R. Bhandarkar, in his paper on "Foreign Elements in the Hindu Population", has stated that "There is hardly a class or Caste in India which has not a foreign strain in it. There is an admixture of alien blood not only among the warrior classes—the Rajputs and the Marathas—but also among the Brahmins who are under the happy delusion that they are free from all foreign elements." The Caste System cannot be said to have grown as a means of preventing the admixture of races or as a means of maintaining purity of blood.

As a matter of fact, the Caste System came into being long after the different races of India had commingled in blood and culture. To hold that distinctions of castes are really distinctions of race and to treat different castes as though they were so many different races is a gross perversion of facts. What racial affinity is there between the Brahmin of the Punjab and the Brahmin of Madras? What racial affinity is there between the untouchable of Bengal and the untouchable of Madras? What racial difference is there between the Brahmin of the Punjab and the Chamar of the Punjab? What racial difference is there between the Brahmin of Madras and the Pariah of Madras? The Brahmin of the Punjab is racially of the same stock as the Chamar of the Punjab, and the Brahmin of Madras is of the same race as the Punjab, who is racially of the same stock as the Chamar of the Punjab, and the Brahmin of Madras is of the same race as the Pariah of Madras.

The Caste System does not demarcate racial division. The Caste System is a social division of people of the same race. Assuming it, however, to be a case of racial divisions, one may ask: What harm could there be if a mixture of races and of blood was permitted to take place in India by intermarriages between different castes? Men are no doubt divided from animals by so deep a distinction that science recognises men and animals as two distinct species. But even scientists who believe in purity of races do not assert that the different races constitute different species of men. They are only varieties of one and the same species. As such, they can interbreed and produce an offspring that are capable of breeding and that are not sterile.

An immense lot of nonsense is talked about heredity and eugenics in defence of the Caste System. Few would object to the Caste System if it was in accord with the basic principle of eugenics because few can object to the improvement of the race by judicious mating. But one fails to understand how the Caste System secures judicious mating. The Caste System is a negative thing. It merely prohibits persons belonging to different castes from intermarrying. It is not a positive method of selecting which two among a given caste should marry.

If caste is eugenic in origin, then the origin of sub-castes must also be eugenic. But can anyone seriously maintain that the origin of sub-castes is eugenic? I think it would be absurd to contend for such a proposition, and for a very obvious reason. If caste means race, then differences of sub-castes cannot mean differences of race because sub-castes become *ex hypothesia* [= by hypothesis] sub-divisions of one and the same race. Consequently, the bar against intermarrying and interdining between sub-castes cannot be for the purpose of maintaining purity of race or of blood. If sub-castes cannot be eugenic in origin, there cannot be any substance in the contention that caste is eugenic in origin.

Again, if caste is eugenic in origin, one can understand the bar against intermarriage. But what is the purpose of the interdict placed on interdining between castes and sub-castes alike? Interdining cannot infect blood, and therefore, cannot be the cause either of the improvement or of the deterioration of the race.

This shows that caste has no scientific origin and that those who are attempting to give it a eugenic basis are trying to support by science what is grossly unscientific. Even today, eugenics cannot become a practical possibility unless we have definite knowledge regarding the laws of heredity. Prof. Bateson, in his "Mendel's Principles of Heredity", says, "There is nothing in the descent of the higher mental qualities to suggest that they follow any single system of transmission. It is likely that both they and the more marked developments of physical powers result rather from the coincidence of numerous factors than from the possession of any one genetic element." To argue that the Caste System was eugenic in its conception is to attribute to the forefathers of present-day Hindus a knowledge of heredity which even the modern scientists do not possess.

A tree should be judged by the fruits it yields. If caste is eugenic, what sort of a race of men should it have produced? Physically speaking, the Hindus are a C_3 people. They are a race of pygmies and dwarfs, stunted in stature and wanting in stamina. It is a nation nine tenths of which is declared to be unfit for military service. This shows that the Caste System does not embody the eugenics of modern scientists. It is a social system which embodies the arrogance and selfishness of a perverse section of the Hindus who were superior enough in social status to set it in fashion and who had the authority to force it on their inferiors.

Caste Prevents Hindus from Forming a Real Society or Nation

Caste does not result in economic efficiency. Caste cannot improve and has not improved the race. Caste has, however, done one thing. It has completely disorganised and demoralised the Hindus.

The first and foremost thing that must be recognised is that Hindu society is a myth. The name 'Hindu' is itself a foreign name. It was given by the Mohammedans to the natives for the purpose of distinguishing themselves from them. It does not occur in any Sanskrit work prior to the Mohammedan invasion. They did not feel the necessity of a common name because they had no conception of their having constituted a community. Hindu society as such does not exist. It is only a collection of castes. Each caste is conscious of its existence. Its survival is the be-all and end-all of its existence. Castes do not even form a federation. A caste has no feeling that it is affiliated to other castes, except when there is a Hindu-Muslim riot. On all other occasions, each caste endeavours to segregate itself and to distinguish itself from other castes.

Each caste not only dines among itself and marries among itself, but each caste prescribes its own distinctive dress. What other explanation can there be of the innumerable styles of dress worn by the men and women of India, which so amuse the tourists? Indeed, the ideal Hindu must be like a rat living in his own hole, refusing to have any contact with others. There is an utter lack among the Hindus of what the sociologists call 'consciousness of kind'. There is no Hindu consciousness of kind. In every Hindu, the consciousness that exists is the consciousness of his caste. That is the reason why the Hindus cannot be said to form a society or a nation.

There are, however, many Indians whose patriotism does not permit them to admit that Indians are not a nation; that they are only an amorphous mass of people. They have insisted that, underlying the apparent diversity, there is a fundamental unity which marks the life of the Hindus, inasmuch as there is a similarity of those habits and customs, beliefs and thoughts, which obtain all over the continent of India. Similarity in habits and customs, beliefs and thoughts, there is. But one cannot accept the conclusion that, therefore, the Hindus constitute a society. To do so is to misunderstand the essentials which go to make up a society. Men do not become a society by living in physical proximity, any more than a man ceases to be a member of his society by living so many miles away from other men.

Secondly, similarity in habits and customs, beliefs and thoughts, is not enough to constitute men into society. Things may be passed physically from one to another like bricks. In the same way habits and customs, beliefs and thoughts of one group may be taken over by another group, and there may, thus, appear a similarity between the two. Culture spreads by diffusion, and that is why one finds similarity between various primitive tribes in the matter of their habits and customs, beliefs and thoughts, although they do not live in proximity. But no one could say that, because there was this similarity, the primitive tribes constituted one society. This is because similarity in certain things is not enough to constitute a society.

Men constitute a society because they have things which they possess in common. To have similar things is totally different from possessing things in common. And the only way by which men can come to possess things in common with one another is by being in communication with one another. This is merely another way of saying that society continues to exist by communication—indeed, in communication. To make it concrete, it is not enough if men act in a way which agrees with the acts of others. Parallel activity, even if similar, is not sufficient to bind men into a society.

This is proved by the fact that the festivals observed by the different castes amongst the Hindus are the same. Yet these parallel performances of similar festivals by the different castes have not bound them into one integral whole. For that purpose, what is necessary is for a man to share and participate in a common activity, so that the same emotions are aroused in him that animate the others. Making the individual a sharer or partner in the associated activity, so that he feels its success as his success, its failure as his failure, is the real thing that binds men and makes a society of them. The Caste System prevents common activity; and by preventing common activity, it has prevented the Hindus from becoming a society with a unified life and a consciousness of its own being.

Note

1. Bhimrao Ramji Ambedkar (April 14, 1891, Mhow, India—December 6, 1956, New Delhi) is the most prominent Dalit intellectual and leader of the Dalit struggle. A champion of social justice and civil rights, Ambedkar did his studies at Columbia—under the mentorship of John Dewey and others—and received his Ph.D. in economics in 1927. In 1952, Ambedkar received an honorary degree from Columbia University. He also studied at the London School of Economics, where he got his master's degree in 1922 and D.Sc. in economics in 1923.

3   The Caste Context

Anand Teltumbde[1]

Dalits are a product of India s caste system. For castes to last, the Dal-its are necessary. Their emancipation, as diagnosed by Ambedkar, is thus homologous with castes. The castes thus constitute an intimate context for the Dalits. This chapter, therefore, focuses on understanding the essential features of the caste system: its origin, its evolution into a unique system of stratification, its comparison with other such systems and also the com-parison between its victims, the Dalits, with those of others. While it will necessarily deal with some prominent theories and opinions, it will also explain how understanding castes in their evolutionary perspective is still a work in progress.

Caste, *Jati* and *Varna*

Simply put, caste is a defining feature of the Indian society. Etymologically, the English word 'caste' derives from the Spanish and Portuguese *casta*, with its roots in Latin *castus*. It meant 'race, lineage, or breed.'[2] The Indian name for castes is *jati*.

There is much confusion even in scholarly literature between *jati* and *varna*,[3] which together constitute the basis for the caste system. *Varnas* were brought into India by the conquering tribes of Aryas during the dark period of history. Initially, there were three *varnas* (classes)[4] sans hierar-chy, which evolved into four (Brahman, Kshatriya, Vaisya and Shudra) *varna* system (*Chaturvarna*) by the end of Rigvedic period with a notion of hierarchy and then went on to designate the excluded ones as the *avarnas* (non-*varna*) or *pancham* (fifth) *varna*.[5] Thus, *varnas* were finite and with a definitive hierarchy. Castes (*jatis*), in contrast, are countless and (because of it) with fluid notions of hierarchy.[6] *Varna* is the *vedic* classification of the four ranked occupational order, whereas caste refers to ranked heredi-tary, endogamous and occupational groups separated from each other by the ideas of purity and pollution.[7] Classically, *varnas* defined the borders of Hinduism, whereas *jatis* were local and are rarely found beyond the

DOI: 10.4324/9781003155065-3

borders of ethnolinguistic regions. The *varnas* may be taken as theoretical, whereas castes (*jatis*) are real and concrete. Besides, Brahman and the *avarna* Dalits, which bracket an overall Hindu social order, all other *varnas* are rarely found everywhere. Castes though are found all over. As a result, the mapping of castes with intermediate *varnas* remains hazy and is not accepted by many castes. Many castes reject the legitimacy of the *varna* hierarchy and/or the places assigned to them by others. In the Brahmanical strongholds of South India itself the intermediate *varnas* hardly exist. Where they exist, they do so with local variations. Even historically, the village roost was not necessarily ruled by any Brahman caste; when it was, one could find wealth and power rather than its ritual status being instrumental in its placement. Many Brahmans did not enjoy any such reputation.[8] Second, even their explanation for the advent of *varnashram dharma* also is unconvincing as it does not explain why it only survived in India and not elsewhere.

Origin of Castes

Scholars have proffered theories of the origin of castes, which are at best hypotheses without any agreement. They may be broadly classified into as many as nine classes based on their thrust: (i) traditional or Indological theory, (ii) racial theory, (iii) political theory, (iv) religious theory, (v) occupational theory, (vi) racial/functional theory, (vii) guild theory, (viii) mana theory and (ix) evolution or multi-factor theory.

According to the traditional or Indological theory, the caste system is of divine origin. It is based on the allegorical explanation in *Purushsukta* in *Rig Veda* for the origin of four *varnas* as parts of the cosmic being *purusha* or the supreme creator (God).[9] Castes were born later as a result of different types of marriages between *varnas* in ancient India. Although of little intellectual value, it underlies the popular belief in castes. The racial theory propounded by Sir Herbert Risely[10] held that caste system was due to racial differences between migrant Aryas and Anaryas (native people). G. S. Ghurye[11] and Westermarck[12] appear to support this theory. The political theory held that caste system was the result of political conspiracy of the Brahmans to secure control over the functions of the society. This theory was originally propounded by a French scholar Abbe Dubais[13] and found tacit support in many scholars like Denzil Ibbetson and also S. G. Ghurye. The religious theory was advocated by Hocart[14] and Senart.[15] Hocart postulated that castes were a hierarchy of ritual offices centred on a king (or a local lord) having as their purpose the performance of the royal ritual for the benefit of the entire community. The king, as the representative of the God and religion, allotted positions to different functional groups. Senart tried to explain the caste system on the basis of prohibitions regarding sacramental food. Occupational theory, originally propounded by Nesfield,[16] held that occupations were the main base of the caste system. The notion of hierarchy of castes stemmed basically from the superiority or inferiority of occupations. The racial/functional theory put forth by Slater[17] combines both the racial and functional origins, postulating that the caste system was created to safeguard the professional and occupational secrets of different races. The Aryan invasions intensified and developed the existing structure making occupations hereditary and marriages only within the same occupation groups, sanctified later by ritual practices and religious ceremonies. The guild theory put forth by Denzil Ibbeston[18] holds that castes are the modified forms of guilds and the caste system was the product of three forces, (i) tribes, (ii) guilds and (iii) religion. The guilds evolved into castes imitating the endogamy of the prestigious class of priests. The *mana* theory based on the views of J. H. Hutton[19] accords the caste system pre-Aryan origin and suggests that the primitive belief in *mana* among tribes accounted for the origin of the caste system. *Mana* was associated with magical and harmful powers, and hence the ancient tribes evolved elaborate taboos or restrictions to protect themselves from other tribes' *mana*. Lastly, the evolutionary or multi-factor theory propounded by sociologists held that a complex phenomenon of the caste system could not be explained by a single factor and rather was a result of many factors such as beliefs in racial superiority, geographical isolation, metaphysical concepts, belief in *mana*, desire to maintain racial purity of blood and manipulation by Brahmans.

As could be seen, none of these theories, save for the last one, which does not claim a specific factor and hence is flexible enough to accommodate any of the above or entirely new one within its fold, are able to explain the origin of the caste system. They rather explain the *varna* system and take for granted that caste system is born out of the *varna* system.

Ambedkar on Caste

In relation to the Dalits, Dr Ambedkar assumes extraordinary importance because of his lifelong devotion to the cause of their emancipation. While engaged with practical struggles he simultaneously worked on theorising many aspects of the caste system. His seminal paper, *Castes in India: Their Mechanism, Genesis and Development*, which Ambedkar presented as a student, at an Anthropology Seminar taught by Dr A. A. Goldenweizer in Columbia University on 9 May 1916, dealt with some of these views and also of Dr Ketkar and dismissed them as *Petitio Principii* of formal logic.[20] It was here that he observed, 'A caste is an Enclosed Class'.

He disagreed with Senart that the 'idea of pollution' was a peculiarity of caste as it was 'a particular case of the general belief in purity'.[21] For Ambedkar, the idea of pollution could be ignored without affecting the working of castes. It was attached to the institution of caste only because the priestly caste enjoyed the highest rank. To Nesfield's theory highlighting absence of messing with outside the caste, Ambedkar would say that it was mistaking the effect for the cause. Being a self-enclosed unit, caste naturally limits social intercourse, including messing. He did not find Risley's views deserving of a comment. He rather included Ketkar who had defined caste in its relation to a system of castes, and had focused his attention only on those characteristics which were absolutely necessary for the existence of a caste within a system. Ambedkar, however, critiqued Ketkar for taking 'prohibition of intermarriage and membership by autogeny' as the two characteristics of caste and argued that they were but two aspects of one and the same thing. If intermarriage is prohibited, the membership of those born within the group also shall be automatically limited.[22]

Ambedkar argues that Hindu society like other societies was essentially a class system, in which individuals, when qualified, could change their class. However, at some time in history, the priestly class socially detached itself from the rest of the people and through a closed-door policy became a caste by itself. The other *varnas*, which were subject to the law of social division of labour, developed subdivision with social mobility of the class system. However, as he argued, they too lost the open-door character of the class system and have become self-enclosed units called castes. He explained their becoming castes, saying 'Some closed the door: Others found it closed against them.'[23] He proffered a psychological explanation for the former saying that since the Brahmans or priestly class occupied the highest position in the social hierarchy of the Hindu society, the other classes simply *imitated* them by adopting endogamy.[24] Over the years, endogamy became a fashion since it originated from the priestly class, who were venerated and idolised in the scriptures. Endogamy was thus practised by all the classes, which ultimately resulted in the rigid formation of castes.[25] The custom of endogamy superimposed on exogamy, which prevailed in all ancient tribes, became the creation of castes.[26] He points out that without the practice of endogamy, the caste system cannot survive. Along with endogamy, Brahmans followed the custom of *sati* and enforced widowhood which later spread to other castes. The mainstream sociology never acknowledged this analysis of Ambedkar, although it predated the thesis by G. S. Ghurye, celebrated as the first sociological treatise on caste by a decade and anticipated many of the ideas of the later scholars.

Ambedkar developed his theory of untouchability on the basis of 'broken men' (broken from their tribes during the tribal wars), who, since they were Buddhists, and did not respect Brahmans, were made untouchables. He wrote,

the Broken Men were Buddhists. As such they did not revere the Brahmins, did not employ them as their priests and regarded them as impure. The Brahmin on the other hand disliked the Broken Men because they were Buddhists and preached against them contempt and hatred with the result that the Broken Men came to be regarded as Untouchables.[27]

They were made untouchables because they continued eating beef when the Gupta kings made cow killing a criminal offence and beef eating a sin in fourth century AD.[28] This theorisation that attributed untouchability to the struggle for supremacy between Buddhism and Brahmanism helped him to endow the Dalits with Buddhist past.

Ambedkar's theorisation of untouchability is as problematic as his analysis of castes was profound. It is pivoted on 'broken men' being Buddhist, which, as candidly admitted by Ambedkar, does not have any evidential support. He just concludes it saying, 'No evidence is . . . necessary when the majority of Hindus were Buddhists. We may take it that they were.'[29] Besides, it raises many natural questions such as: why was cow killing and beef eating banned, and why did the broken men still persist with eating beef risking being rendered untouchables?

Narasu's Study on Caste

The other notable activist scholar on caste to have been similarly ignored is Pokala Lakshmi Narasu (1851–1954), whose *A Study of Caste* distinguishes itself from others by its rigorous analysis.[30] Narasu's views are important because unlike others his prime concerns were to restructure the society on scientific and rationalist foundation.[31] Narasu adopts a methodology of elimination of the existing theories and arrives at his own proposition. He rejects the theory that ascribes the origin of castes to the cunning of ambitious priests, who modelled Hindu society wholly to their advantage. He considers preposterous ascribing the design of the caste system to Brahmanism for the purpose of developing *satvic* qualities whose acquisition is posited as the source of all progress. He positively considers the theories likening castes to the guilds of medieval Europe but observes the failure of these 'petrified' guilds confirming to the three features peculiar to caste, viz., forbidding intermarriage, interdining and acceptance of others into the caste. He therefore looks for reasons in the idea of taboo and in the theocracy at the bases of systems of caste.[32] After introducing classes into the Dravidian society on a basis similar to the *pistras* of their original home Iran, he argued, the Brahmans established their supremacy as the mediator between gods and humans.

Narasu considers and eliminates the possibility of professional guilds as in medieval times to be the basis of castes as they did not have any of the three features (endogamy, acceptance of outsiders and interdining) peculiar to caste.[33] He thus veered around to seeing the idea of taboo 'so common among primitive people and in the theocracy at the basis of the system of caste'. He also rejected the idea that Aryan tribes created castes.[34] He saw the ritualistic worship of fire combined with the magic and the introduction of the *soma* drink to be common to the Iranian and the Vedic Aryans. It is with this ritual of *soma-homa*[35] the class of Brahman clergy was born in India and gradually led up to the division of society into classes along the lines of the four *pistras* of the *Avesta*.[36] But he rightly observed that these divisions represented only classes (*varna*) and not castes. The Aryan immigrants came among the Dravidians as astrologers and sorcerers carrying with them their *Indra-Agni* cult, but they seem to have brought with them few women or none at all. They influenced the elite among the darker Dravidians, established themselves as priests and took women according to their needs.[37] When they bred families enough to serve their purposes and to establish a distinct *jus connubii* (right to marry), they closed their ranks to further intermixture of blood, what Ambedkar called enclosing itself. Unlike all ancient societies where priests hailed the highest rank and enjoyed special privileges but the material control was still retained by the royal sovereign, in India the priestly class of Brahmans had its influence so deeply permeate the community that it has been able to prescribe under the sanction of religion a code of elaborate prescriptions on domestic and personal conduct which is accepted by all as the ideal, the relative conformity to which settles the status of every group of the Hindu society from top to bottom.[38]

Thus, although Narasu started off looking for material basis for castes, he ended up in locating them in accidental supremacy of the Brahmans very similar to Ambedkar.

A Materialist Hypothesis

While the ideological contrivance surely plays a role in sustaining a social order, ideology cannot create social order. The fact that *varna*-like systems of stratification found elsewhere in ancient times were not ordained by any religious ideology, a purely ideological explanation for the origin of the caste system, is problematic. Social systems come into being because the material conditions demand them. The ideological superstructure develops later to preserve them. A section of society that benefits from the system develops vested interests and wants to preserve it through an ideological apparatus. The pervasiveness of the caste system over the vast subcontinental space and its becoming a 'lifeworld' of people must lead us to search for some more enduring material factors than purely ideological ones.

These factors can perhaps be located in the uniquely rich natural endowment of the Indian subcontinent for the biotic mode of production extant in ancient times. In terms of plentiful flat, fertile land; rivers and water bodies; abundant sunshine and congenial climate, the Indian subcontinent may scarcely have a parallel on the planet in its richness for agriculture. These factors might be seen to be the key to fathoming the mystery of the unique system of stratification in the form of the caste system. When nomadic tribes began settling for agriculture, they necessarily underwent change in their social structure everywhere confirming to their material conditions. For instance, the places where the land was hostile and not so fertile; where water sources were scanty and seasons were erratic; and sunshine had a narrow window of a few months, as for instance in England, it gave rise to a system of serfdom. To cultivate vast tracts of lands within a small time-window you needed a huge army of serfs to work and a lord to control them. In contrast, Indian tribes did not have to undergo such a structural transformation and had settled down with their tribal identities intact. These tribal identities were rather castes, albeit sans hierarchy or any stigma.

The notion of hierarchy and stigma (purity and pollution) was rather superimposed by the post-Rigvedic *varna* system. Thus, contrary to the proposition of the traditional ideological theory, it is not the *varnas* that came first and they evolved into castes, but quite the opposite. The castes in the form of tribal identities with some amount of magico-religious development, natural to agricultural communities, already existed in India, which were later overlain by the *varna* system brought in by the vanquishing Aryan tribes. With the growth of surplus production, it needed an intricate ideological contrivance, appealable to agricultural society as it purported to solve their myriad knowledge problems about natural events on which agriculture depended. The priestly class of Brahmans assumed the role of a mediator between people and gods, and slowly became 'gods on earth' themselves to establish their hegemony. They propounded a theory of *karma* to justify the present order and fortify their own supremacist position. While it made people to accept their caste statuses as their destinies according to their past *karma*, it also motivated them to adhere to the caste *dharma* in order to be born into a better caste in the next birth. Besides this self-propellant, there was a cobweb of rules as in *Manusmriti* that prescribed their behaviour and punishments for any deviation from the prescribed code. This entire superstructure would stabilise making castes as the lifeworld of people.

The Dalits beyond this four-*varna* system comprised the vanquished tribes. Iyothee Thassa Pandithar (1845–1914)[39] and Ambedkar claimed that they were the Buddhists. Their denigration as untouchables was a reflection of the degree of animosity and hatred Brahmans had for Buddhism. A system of total exclusion was instituted to keep them at bay. When castes became the lifeworld of people with internalised notion of hierarchy, they unleashed perennial contention within the vicinity of each caste for superiority, effectively securing the broad *varna* structure from any challenge. The structure worked well for the largely autonomous and insular villages, assuring ordered subsistence for all in exchange of their acceptance of the order, which lent it a self-organising, self-regulating property of the modern cybernetic system. The caste system as such survived all kinds of changes—political, technological, economical and cultural—only adjusting itself here and there, at times giving rise to new castes and at others accommodating outsiders within, that would earn itself the dubious epithet of being the longest-living man-made system in the world.

Other Dalit-Like People

Some systems with caste-like features, even associated with untouchability, are extant in a few pockets of the world, which make their victims appear like India's Dalits. For instance, the Osu people in Nigeria and southern Cameroon are treated by the *Igbo* indigenous religious system to be a 'living sacrifice', an outcaste, untouchable and subhuman people.[40] There are other caste-like stratifications in other African countries with their own lower strata which can be likened to the Dalits in some respect. For instance, in Mande societies in Senegal, Gambia, Guinea, Sierra Leone, Liberia, Ivory Coast, and Ghana, previously Ancient Manden, the Jonows (meaning slave), whose ancestors were enslaved by other Africans during tribal wars, make up the lowest strata. There is a *varna*-like system among the Borana in north-east Kenya and southern Ethiopia wherein Borana *Gutu* (pure) are treated as the highest, followed by Gabbra, Sakuye and Watta, a traditional hunter-gatherer caste, being the lowest. The Wattas are considered unwanted, worthless and condemned to lifelong servitude for members of the higher castes.[41] The intercaste clashes between castes, particularly between Borana and Gabbra, the two upper-caste groups, continue even today.[42] In Yemen there exists a caste-like system that keeps the Al-Akhdam (*Akhdam* means servants) social group as the perennial manual workers (scavengers) for the society through practices that mirror untouchability. Though practising Islam over 1,000 years, they are treated quite like the Dalits, and prefer to be called Al Muhamasheen, or the 'marginalized ones'. Likewise, there are people in Japan known as Burakumin (*Buraku*, meaning community or hamlet, and *min*, meaning people), or

Hisabetsu (*Buraku* meaning 'discriminated communities/hamlets'). Studies comparing the caste systems in India and Japan have noted similar discriminations.[43] Like the Burakumins, the Baekjeong were an 'untouchable' outcaste group of Korea. The condition of the Baekjeong in pre-colonial Korean society was quite similar to the Dalits. They too began their resistance movement beginning in the late 19th and early 20th centuries, first aiming at reform and later at more radical change. The system, however, disappeared in the turbulence the Korean society underwent.[44]

Based on these similarities some people tend to belittle the problems of the Dalits. They forget the fact that not just these but all societies sometime in the past had some kind of stratification and discriminatory practices which might even include untouchability. However, as they developed, only the residue of the old structure and practices survived in a few. In a superficial way, these structures may outwardly appear like India's caste system but they are essentially different. First, they feature in a small section of the society and apply to a miniscule minority as in the case of the Barakumin and do not reflect a subcontinental feature of the Indian caste system. Second, none of these systems are sourced from religious sanction. Third, unlike them, the Indian caste system is not just based on stratification but reflects a continuum of infinite castes strung loosely within the *varna* framework with a notion of hierarchy that unleashes million contentions within but leaves the macro-structure unchallenged. Fourth, none of these systems have influenced the behaviours of the larger society and remained an island within the latter. Indian caste system, though stemming from Hinduism, has infected other religious societies too that came up in India. Therefore, the Indian caste system becomes a gigantic, complex and intricately evolved continuum of simultaneously loose and rigid hierarchy—rigid in the macro framework of *varna* and loose within it—pervasively practised over a vast geographical area as the lifeworld of the people. It is quite unlike others both in qualitative and in quantitative terms.

Dalits and Slaves

Among the victims of *four* major forms of stratification in complex societies, namely the *caste* systems with rigid borders, highly differentiated statuses and limited possibility of mobility; the system of *estates* characteristic of European feudal societies, which distinguished between the clergy, the nobility and the broad category of peasants, merchants and artisans; the slavery referring to the condition in which a person is owned as property by another to be sold and bought like any commodity, and the *class systems*, more common in modern societies, the slaves in slavery which evokes intense disgust in modern times could be compared with the Dalits.

Slavery was an accepted institution in the old world, widely practised in ancient Mesopotamia, Egypt, Greece, Israel, Persia, Rome and Byzantium, as well as among the Chinese, Mayans, Aztecs, Indians and the people of a number of African, Polynesian and Melanesian countries.[45] The invention of agriculture 10,000 years ago led to surplus production and engendered conflicts among people to control it. Those who succeeded in overpowering others in this conflict had surplus with which they could make other people work for them. This was the rudimentary form of slavery, which compared well with the origination of the Dalits. Since land was the main biotic source of surplus in those times and hence a source of power, people set out to conquer lands from other people. The vanquished people in such wars became big source of slaves for the victors to till these lands and, thus, came into being the institution of slavery. The other sources were the fugitives, the delinquents and the outlaws from within the society. The offspring of these enslaved people became slaves themselves and provided a vast workforce.[46]

While this was the approximate origin of slavery anywhere, in each country it appears to have developed specific features. For instance, in Mesopotamia, although slaves under the code had the status of property or merchandise (meaning they could be traded), they had rights. Slaves were permitted to own property, conduct business and even marry free women.[47] Manumission was allowed through both self-purchase or adoption by the owner. There was no racial component to Egyptian and Roman slavery. Many of the slaves in Egypt were Israelite Jews and neighbouring African blacks, while those in Rome were drawn from blonde, blue-eyed Anglo-Saxons from Britannia or blacks from Sahara as well as every other racial type including those of Italian stock.[48] Although, there was a notion of slaves being inferior in most civilisations, generally speaking, the ancient world does not seem to have had racial association with inferiority.[49] There are even references from the past which suggest that slaves were indistinguishable from other people. For instance, although the Romans felt the need to distinguish them with a distinctive appearance for control purposes, they could not do so for fear that this identity might induce unity among slaves and inspire them to revolt.[50] Roman history is still littered with slave rebellions, particularly in the first and second centuries BC, in some of which slaves managed collectively to free themselves from their masters.[51]

There are references to slavery in India in literary sources during the sixth century BC to the beginning of the Christian era. Thereafter the references disappear indicating that it might have been replaced by a more intricate and efficient caste system. Again, the reference to slavery surfaces during the Islamic period.[52] Generally, when the Muslims arrived as per their customs, they would have imported African slaves to India. There is no further information on Indian slavery beyond the bonded labour system, which still prevails in India. It can be clearly seen as an outgrowth of the caste system, as most bonded labourers belong to the Dalit communities.[53] A report by the Anti-Slavery International in 2008 revealed that Dalit bonded labourers are employed to carry out the most physically straining and menial types of work in industries such as silk farms, rice mills, salt pans, fisheries, quarries and mines, tea and spice farming, brick-kilns, textile industry and domestic work.[54] In any case, the reference to slavery in its comparison with the caste system is of a general nature, as discussed earlier.

In the Indian caste system, however, since the direct producers were split up into different castes and *jatis*, the division remained deeply hierarchical. Most importantly, slavery did not rob slaves of consciousness of their human selves, which occasionally erupted into revolts. While such revolts are found aplenty in the history of slavery, there is not a single comparable instance in the long history of the caste system in India. Although castes also did not have a racial association, in the microcosm of villages that they operated, everybody's caste was known. Even in the modern urban setting, which provides a huge space for anonymity, Dalits can barely hide their castes. As in the case of slavery, the caste system also granted caste-specific rights to people: the uppermost caste having all of them and the lowest ones without any. Unlike a slave, who could set himself free, a caste man could never escape his destiny. Moreover, caste consciousness, unlike consciousness of a slave that impels him or her to revolt against slavery, further enslaves a person into his or her caste. In slavery, there is an intrinsic hope of transcending the system, whereas in the caste system one does not have any such hope. Dr Ambedkar himself elaborately compared the situation of slaves in classical Rome and in Europe and the Americas with that of the untouchables in India and established that untouchability was much worse than slavery.[55]

The worst feature of the caste system vis-à-vis slavery is the opposite consciousness they produce and also their processes of production. While caste consciousness strengthens the caste system, slave consciousness resists the system of slavery. Dr Ambedkar once said, 'Tell a slave, he is a slave and he will rise in revolt'. This was not possible with the untouchables, who willingly endured their untouchability for centuries. Untouchability induced a sense of self-deprecation in untouchables, and killed their spirit of revolt. The process of producing this consciousness basically differed because of the differential structures of the two systems. In slavery, the system had two dominant parts in contradiction: slaves and masters. The structure of the caste system depicts a continuum that obviates the neat division between the oppressor and the oppressed. The contradiction is pushed down to the local levels, not for elimination of the oppression but for becoming an oppressor. The castes contend within their locale with the castes which suffer similar oppression as them, for superiority. This eliminates the possibility of any rebellion against the system as a whole.

Dalits and Racial Victims

Beyond slavery, the caste system gets compared with the racism practised in the Western world, particularly in the United States in respect to the African Americans. The African Americans also faced discrimination and humiliation from the white majority and had to wage a very long battle for securing their civil rights. While in some sense, the racial oppression appears severer than caste oppression, simply because a black person cannot escape his or her physical identity, whereas a lower caste person can easily do that, there is more to the caste oppression than meets the eye. Like the visibility of race, the racial oppression is also visible; the caste oppression is deep drawn, subtle and, therefore, far more vicious. On the experiential plane caste discrimination is quite like racial discrimination and, hence, there is a vocal tendency among Dalit activists to treat caste as race.[56]

Race relations are physical, whereas caste relations are cultural. As Cox (1945) observed, 'As distinguished from a bipartite interracial adjustment, the caste system is ancient, provincial, culturally oriented, hierarchical in structure, status conscious, non-conflictive, non-pathological, occupationally limited, lacking in aspiration and progressiveness, hypergamous, endogamous and static.'[57] There are fundamental differences in the ways in which race and caste relations are patterned, which produces a differential impact on society.[58] Race sentiment and interest tend to be universal, while caste sentiment and interest tend to be circumscribed and localised. Unlike the Dalits in India, the African Americans have been seeking to increase their participation and integration in the dominant culture. The absence of such striving is an inseparable feature of the caste system.[59]

There is a sense of inferiority associated with the black race, but the important thing is that it does not have any religious sanction as castes claim. The blacks in America in a short time could dispel the notion of inferiority in them, first, with glorious resistance to Jim Crow legislations and later movements like the Garvey movement, by far the largest mass movement of the African Americans of the 1920s, that challenged entrenched ideas of white supremacy. It promoted the ideas of black culture and black history that Africa was noble and black people had created great civilisations that rivalled Western civilisation on every front, which led to the Harlem Renaissance giving birth to their confident expression in the form of black literature, music, drama and so on, and the movements like 'Black is Beautiful' in the 1960s that demolished the remnant traces of inferiority of 'black being ugly and low' and made the blacks take pride in being black. Unlike the Dalits in India, the blacks no more carry any baggage of social disapproval. Therefore, they tend to strive for more and more participation in mainstream culture. It is relatively difficult for the Dalits to shake off their baggage of inferiority in the social environment of pervasive caste prejudices.[60]

Note

1. Goa Institute of Management, India.
2. The *Oxford English Dictionary* quotes John Minsheu's Spanish dictionary (1599). When the Portuguese arrived in India in 1498 and encountered thousands of in-marrying hereditary Indian social groups, they called them 'castas', which became 'castes' in English in 1613. (Editors of the American Heritage (ed.), (2005) *Word Histories and Mysteries.* Boston: Houghton Miffin Company, p. 210.
3. They are used interchangeably by most scholars. For instance, Corbridge, Stuart; Harriss, John and Jeffrey, Craig (2013) *India Today: Economy, Politics and Society.* Cambridge: Polity Press; Also see Jhunjhunwala, Bharat (1999) *Varna Vyavastha: Governance through Caste System.* New Delhi: Rawat Publications, p. 183; Agrawal, Binod C. (1982). Anthropological Approaches to the Study of Complex Societies. *Ethnographic & Folk Culture Society*, Lucknow, p. 44; Dutt, N. K. (1931) *Origin and Growth of Castes in India*, Vol. 1. Calcutta: The Book Co. Ltd., p. 4.
4. If the lineage of Aryans is traced to the Iranian society, *Avesta* mentions only three classes of people based on economic functions in society. See Ahmed, Mukhtar (2014) *Ancient Pakistan: An Archaeological History*, Vol. V. Reidsville: Foursome Group, p. 149.
5. Pappala, Appalanaidu (2015) *Tribes vs Castes*, Lulu.com.
6. The rough estimate of castes runs into thousands, but no one for sure can vouch for those numbers. Louis Dumont deals with this question but leaves it unanswered because of its infeasibility. See Dumont, Louis (1970) *Homo Hierrachicus.* Chicago: University of Chicago Press, p. 33.
7. Geetha, K. A. (2014) *Contesting Categories, Remapping Boundaries.* Cambridge: Cambridge Scholar Publishing, p. 15.
8. Stern, Robert W. (1993) *Changing India: Bourgeois Revolution on the Subcontinent.* Cambridge: Cambridge University Press, p. 64.
9. Dundes, Alan (1997) *Tales of Crow and Sparrow: A Freudian Folkloristic Essay on Caste and Untouchability.* Lanham: Rowman & Littlefield Publishing, p. 56.
10. Risley, Herbert Hope (1915) *The People of India.* London: Thacker, Spink & Co.
11. Ghurye, S. G. (1932) *Caste and Race in India.* New York: Alfred Knopf.
12. Westermarck, E. (1901) *History of Human Marriage.* London: Macmillan.
13. Dubois, Abbe J. A. (1992) *Hindu Manners Customs and Ceremonies.* New Delhi: Rupa.
14. Hocart, Arthur Maurice (2010) *Caste: A Comparative Study.* Minneapolis: University of Minnesota Press, pp. 17–19.
15. Senart, Emile (1930) *Caste in India: The Facts and the System.* Sherborne: Verandah Books; Senart, Emile and Hegglin, A. (1912) *The Castes in India.* London: British India Press.

16. Nesfield, J. C. (1885) *Brief View of the Caste System of the North-Western Provinces and Oudh*. Allahabad: Government Press.
17. Slater, Gibert (1987) *The Dravidian Elements in Indian Culture*. New Delhi: Asian Educational Services.
18. Ibbeston, Denzil (2010) *Panjab Castes*; Being a Reprint of the Chapter on 'The Races, Castes and Tribes of the People' in the Report on the *Census of the Panjab* published in 1883, Nabu Press, 2010. Reprinted by Nabu Press, Charleston.
19. Mana is a form of supernatural energy in Polynesian religion that inheres in things or people. See http://pollex.org.nz/entry/mana1/. Last accessed: 9 May 2016; Hutton, John Henry (1963) *Castes in India*. New Delhi: Oxford University Press.
20. See Moon, Vasant (2014) (ed.), *Babasaheb Ambedkar Writing and Speeches*, Vol. 1. Mumbai: Government of Maharashtra, p. 17.
21. Ibid., p. 7.
22. Ibid., p. 8.
23. Ibid., p. 18.
24. '. . . Classes have become Castes through imitation and excommunication.' Ibid., p. 22.
25. Ibid., p. 13.
26. '*Thus the superposition of endogamy on exogamy means the creation of caste*'. Emphasis in original. Ibid., p. 9.
27. Ambedkar, Bhimrao Ramji (2013) 'The Untouchables Who Were They and Why They Became Untouchables?', in Vasant Moon (ed.), *Babasaheb Ambedkar: Writings and Speeches*, Vol. 7. Mumbai: Government of Maharashtra, p. 315.
28. Ibid., p. 379.
29. Ibid., p. 315.
30. Narasu, P. Lakshmi (2003) *A Study of Caste*. New Delhi: Asian Educational Service.
31. He was a part of triumvirate of Tamil country of his day along with Shingarvelu and Iyothee Thassar Pandithar, which pursued what came to be known as *engaged Buddhism* half a century later. See Aloysius, G. (2002) *The Religion of Modern Buddhist*. New Delhi: Pharos.
32. Ibid., p. 11.
33. Ibid.
34. Ibid., p. 12.
35. *Soma* (Sanskrit), or *Homa* (or *Haoma*) (Avestan), refers to a ritual drink of importance in ancient Vedic and Persian culture. It was most likely hallucinogenic, which caused an overwhelming and empowering feeling of intoxication, perceived to be a quality of the gods. See New World Encyclopedia at www.newworldencyclopedia.org/entry/Soma. Last accessed on 9 May 2016.
36. Ibid., p. 14.
37. Ibid.
38. Ibid., p. 15.
39. Ahir, D. C. (1992) *Buddhism in South India*. New Delhi: South Asia Books, p. 149; Bergunder, Michael (2004) 'Contested Past: Anti-Brahmanical and Hindu Nationalist Reconstructions of Indian Prehistory', Historiographia Linguistica, Vol. 31, No. 1, pp. 59–104.
40. Teltumbde, Mahad (2016) *The Making of the First Dalit Revolt*. New Delhi: Aakar, p. 7.
41. Ibid.

42. Ibid.
43. Ibid.
44. Ibid.
45. Acher, Leonie (1988) *Slavery and Other Forms of Unfree Labour.* London: Routledge; Hartmann, Thom (1999) *The Last Hours of Ancient Sunlight.* London: Hodder & Stoughton.
46. Bradley, Keith and Cartledge, Paul (2011) (eds.), *The Cambridge World History of Slavery*, Vol. 1: *The Ancient Mediterranean World.* Cambridge: Cambridge University Press.
47. Rodriguez, Janius P. (1979) *The Historical Encyclopedia of World Slavery*, Vols 1 and 7. Santa Barbara: ABC-CLIO, p. 67; Mehta-Jones, Shilpa (2004) *Life in Ancient Mesopotamia.* Saint Catharines: Crabtree Publishing, p. 12.
48. Stratification: http://social.jrank.org/pages/2978/stratification. html. Last accessed: 16 August 2010.
49. As one Trinidadian historian of slavery Eric Williams puts it: 'Slavery was not born of racism: rather, racism was the consequence of slavery', in Williams, Eric (1980) *Capitalism and Slavery.* New York: Perigee Books, p. 7. Also, one should note that while slavery existed as an economic system for thousands of years before the conquest of America, racism as we understand it today did not exist.
50. There was no visible marker to identify a slave. For instance, C. L. R. James writes, 'Historically it is pretty well proved now that the ancient Greeks and Romans knew nothing about race. They had another standard—civilized and barbarian—and you could have white skin and be a barbarian and you could be black and civilized'. C. L. R. James quoted in Alexander, Pete (1987) *Racism, Resistance and Revolution.* London: Bookmarks, p. 5.
51. William Blair writes, 'A passage in Seneca, which alludes to a proposal once made, to distinguish slaves by a peculiar dress but abandoned, from the danger if showing the numbers of the free, conveys, necessarily an impression, that numerical excess was much on the side of slaves.' Blair, William (2007) *An Inquiry into the State of Slavery Amongst the Romans: From the Earliest Period Till the Establishment of the Lombards in Italy.* New York: Native American Books Distributor, p. 274.
52. There are many studies such as Lal, K. S. (1994) *Muslim Slave System in Medieval India.* New Delhi: Aditya Prakashan; Kidwai, Salim (1985) 'Sultans, Eunuchs and Domestics: New Forms of Bondage in Medieval India', in Utsa Patnaik and Manjari Dingwaney (eds.), *Chains of Servitude: Bondage and Slavery in India.* Madras: Sangham Books; Chattopadhyay, Anal Kumar (1959) *Slavery in India.* Calcutta: Nagarjuna Press; Chatterjee, Indrani (1999) *Gender, Slavery and Law in Colonial India.* New Delhi: Oxford University Press; on slavery in India under the Islamic period.
53. The Denmark-based International Dalit Solidarity Network cites cases of caste-based slavery in all the countries of the Indian subcontinent. See for example the section of Caste-Based Slavery on their web site: http://idsn. org/caste-discrimination/keyis sues/bonded-labour/india/. Last accessed: 21 January 2014.
54. Upadhyaya, Krishna Prasad (2008) *Poverty, Discrimination and Slavery: The Reality of Bonded Labour in India, Nepal and Pakistan.* London: Anti-Slavery International.
55. Ambedkar, Bhimrao Ramji (1989) 'Untouchables or the Children of India's Ghetto', in Vasant Moon (ed.), *Dr. Babasaheb Ambedkar: Writings and Speeches*, Vol. 5. Mumbai: Government of Maharashtra, p. 15.

56. The first loud representation of it was heard in the 2001 World Conference against Racism (WCAR) in Durban. See Anand Teltumbde. (2020) *Dalits. Past, Present and Future*. New York: Routledge, chapter 8.
57. Cox, Oliver C. (1945) 'Race and Caste: A Distinction', *The American Journal of Sociology*, Vol. 50, No. 5, March, pp. 360–368.
58. Ibid., p. 46.
59. Ibid., p. 363.
60. Ibid., p. 366.

4 Archaeology of Untouchability[1]

Gopal Guru[2]

Untouchability as a dynamic reality is bound to produce experience which is always in excess of its description. Hence, the available description is often inadequate to capture the totality of the meaning of the experience. To capture the full experience of untouchability, one is required to invoke other perspectives and methods. This chapter argues that at the moment there could be two such frameworks—the philosophical and the archaeological—that could open to us much richer and nuanced meanings of the phenomenon of untouchability.

Debating Sarukkai[3] acquires significance, especially in an intellectual context, where the discourse on untouchability in contemporary times has received only lopsided attention in different quarters. For instance, it has elicited some degree of academic interest among historians (Jha 1974) and substantially more attention from sociologists and social anthropologists. Arguably, sociology and social anthropology look impressive inasmuch as these disciplines offer quite a detailed description of untouchability (Dumont 1988; Desai 1976; Shah *et al* 2006). On the other hand, it is interesting to note that untouchability as a social concern finds its most profound expression in a different discipline—the non-Dalit[4] and Dalit literature.[5] On the flip side, in some of the influential disciplines like political science (Rudolph & Rudolph 1967; Rajshekhariah 1976), it figures only marginally, while in others like economics and philosophy,[6] it is completely blacked out. Even sociological or anthropological descriptions of untouchability, which may look fascinating to some, do not exhaust all the reference points. To put it differently, untouchability as a dynamic reality tends to produce experience, which is always in excess of these textualised sociological and anthropological descriptions. Hence, available descriptions are often inadequate to capture the totality of the meaning that emanates from this dynamism. This dynamism warrants a fresh perspective that could enable us to tap excess meaning embedded in untouchability as a dynamic practice.

At the moment, I can think of two such frameworks—the philosophical and archaeological, that could reveal a much richer and nuanced meaning

DOI: 10.4324/9781003155065-4

of the phenomenon of untouchability. Sarukkai's article in my opinion succeeds in assigning both height and depth to the understanding of untouchability thus elevating it from its mere descriptive/empirical, and therefore, more routinised and familiar understanding to its much richer and wider philosophical context.

Sarukkai, in his article "Phenomenology of Untouchability," offers a wider philosophical grasp of the notion of untouchability. This he does by drawing on both Indian and western philosophical traditions. In Sarukkai's understanding of untouchability, the idea of touch (and skin) becomes important. For touch and skin, as he says, form a primal sense of the body. Sarukkai (2009) gives a fascinating insight into the phenomenological understanding of untouchability and argues, "the notion of untouchability is an essential requirement of brahminhood." (p. 39) For Sarukkai (2009), brahminhood, as a part of this requirement, seeks not just the need to outsource untouchability to others, but most importantly, it also involves a philosophical move to supplement untouchability into others.

I would argue that Sarukkai's article, particularly this new understanding of untouchability as outsourcing and supplementation, questions the final vocabulary that has almost acquired a settled status, particularly in the authoritative sociological work of Louis Dumont. Sarukkai's take on untouchability thus provides a counter argument to Dumont's (Dumont 1988, p. 54), who says, "It is clear that impurity of the untouchable is conceptually inseparable from the purity of Brahmin". Sarukkai's perspective on untouchability, thus, provides a counter argument to this Dumontian understanding of untouchability. In addition to this, it also opens up the possibility of solving some of the "sociological puzzles".[7] Further more, his notion of outsourcing offers us an opportunity to theoretically understand the political dynamics of anti-untouchability movements led by Ambedkar, and subsequently, by the Dalit movement in India. Finally, it will not only help us in detecting the spaces that inhabit the upper castes' anxious self, but it also offers an opportunity to foreground the moral significance of this notion of supplementation and its contestation.

Dealing with Select Issues

Sarukkai's (2009) approach thus offers several insights embedded in his rather capacious reading of untouchability. However, the height and depth that he has assigned to the understanding of untouchability makes it all the more difficult to take on board all the important issues that Sarukkai (2009) has raised in his article. Hence, in the first part of this chapter, I will engage with select issues like metaphysics of the body, the distinctive relationship between contact and touch, the concept of supplementation, and finally, the structural logic that unites both the brahmins as "deferential" or ideal untouchables and the Dalit as "despicable" or real untouchables. Let me offer another clarificatory point that the choice to engage with some issues is informed more by my own convenience and less by the need to seek refutation of Sarukkai's argument. At best, I can claim that my own take on the issue under consideration is modestly aimed at seeking an extension of Sarukkai's position. Thus, the first part will involve a dialogue that pertains to the issues as mentioned above.

The second part of this chapter deals with the possibility of this expansion. I would like to argue that there are different types of archaeological methods deployed by different scholars, perhaps, for different purposes. However, I plan to choose one that would be more appropriate in making sense of the complex relationship between untouchability and caste. Taking the cue from Vitthal Ramji Shinde (Shinde 1976, p. 129), one of the leading non-brahmin social thinkers from modern Maharashtra, who says, *Asprushtechi malmal, manachy talashi dadun basil ahe* ("Untouchability is a kind of repulsive feeling, a sort of nausea, that sits deep at the bottom of brahminical mind"). I would like to argue that modernity forces untouchability to descend deep down at the bottom of "brahminical mind". As I would argue in the second part, archaeological method seems to be the most appropriate one to detect the nausea-like attitude.

It is also interesting to note that Sarukkai's understanding of untouchability goes close to the understanding of Shinde. As we have seen in the above section, Sarukkai also locates the source of untouchability in the brahminical self. I would further argue in the second part that due to the compulsion of the modern conditions, untouchability both as practice and as consciousness, finds it difficult to remain on the surface of social interaction as was the case in the feudal past.[8] Modernity forces it to slide further down to the bottom of the hierarchical mind. Differently put, untouchability as a discursive practice, plays itself out in a much subtler form than ever before. Untouchability in modern times is forced to hide itself behind certain modern meanings and identities. Hence, a mere sociological or anthropological description does not seem to be effective enough to access untouchability thus located. Archaeology as a method seems to be more effective in accessing this complex mind because it deals not so much with a need to invent, but to discover an essence or truth of caste that gets covered with a subtle form of untouchability.

Let me initiate a dialogue with Sarukkai (2009) by engaging first with what he describes as metaphysics of body and later explore what implications this idea has for untouchability when understood in the Indian context. Sarukkai (2009) offers us different notions of body, that as he says, appear in different Indian philosophical traditions. In the Nyaya tradition, as he continues to argue in his essay, the body is the locus of senses and the body feels through the senses. Sarukkai (2009) suggests the need for further exploration in this regard, but from the phenomenological point of view. Sarukkai (2009) quoting from Lang, further observes that for the Buddha, the body was indeed the world in that it is within the body that there is the arising and ceasing of the world. Sarukkai (2009) further quoting from Buddhism, particularly its Madhyamika tradition from the Buddhist compendium, observes that the notion of impurity of body is all pervading. From Buddhism, he elaborates five impurities of body: womb, seed, body's nature, bodies' characteristics and corpse.

Extended Sense of the Impurities of the Body

Taking the cue from Sarukkai (2009), it is possible to make an extended sense of impurities of the body and argue that, in addition to these five impurities, organic body also contains another set of impurities, which seek to undercut the moral significance of both the sacred (in ritual sense) and perfect (physical sense) bodies. All the organic bodies contain within them negative properties like sweat, excreta, urine, mucus and gases. In the material sense, they are the source of foul smell and unpleasant feeling. Thus, at the metaphysical level, the organic body as the source of impurities suggests a kind of ontological equality—that everybody is dirty, both in moral sense as well as material sense. Ontological equality suggesting equal distribution of these impurities or organic refuse sitting underneath the skin of everybody is supposed to bring out in every person a moral insight that in turn will compel him/her to acknowledge this ontological equality. To put it differently, this insight is supposed to create a sense of self-realisation among people who then can find no reason to produce pernicious classification of bodies into repulsive and attractive (of course, this is bad news for the cosmetic industry). This insight, which can generate a sense of moral relativism, in effect creates the possibility to restrain, and perhaps, totally eliminate the morally offensive capacity that a person may use for producing the classification as mentioned above. To put it differently, moral relativism can make it difficult to produce a negative judgment that often is deployed to seek condemnation of other's body as filthy.

Metaphysics of the body, leading to moral relativism, has significance inasmuch as it seeks to relativise the notion of the perfect body or "even out" excess moral Value that makes some bodies superior to others. Assigning an egalitarian value to everybody becomes a possibility, what is called ontological mirroring of other bodies. It is in this sense that my understanding of the metaphysics of body makes a complementary reading with Sarukkai's (2009) reading of metaphysics of body. I suppose both of us suggest a redescription of untouchability that can have implications for the discourse on disability.

Five Principles

Conversely, it is also possible to argue that everybody is respect worthy, simply because it is constitutive of five principles that are present in every organic body with equal quantity. These are earth, water, fire, air and *akāsa* (space). In Indian philosophy (Sānkhya school), these are called *Panchamahabhute*.[9] At the metaphysical level, these *Panchamahabhute* assign affirmative meaning to "filthy" body as mentioned above. These five principles, which are naturally endowed with internal purity, form the necessary physical conditions for the very organic existence of any body. It is in this sense *Panchamahabhute* establish an ontological unity among bodies across time and space. Ontological equality as an underlying principle, therefore, should make all the organic bodies worthy of respect without discrimination. Thus, any cultural construction dividing egalitarian bodies into pernicious gradation could be decisively refuted by invoking the metaphysics of body. Metaphysics of body, in turn, can create moral capacity among those who lack this capacity that is so necessary for assigning moral worth to everybody. Mutual affirmation of bodies becomes a possibility through acknowledgement of *Panchamahabhute* as an essential need of every organic body. Those who have the ability to use *Panchamahabhute* to mirror through others' body, ultimately acquire a moral capacity to shade off some surplus moral value that they attach to their own personality. Self-preservation as morally integrated self finds its basis not in surplus moral value but equal worth—one person one value. The lower caste struggle was aimed at achieving this principle of "one person one value". Thus, *Panchamahabhute* can contribute to the creation of egalitarian order in bodies. *Panchamahabhute*, to paraphrase Aristotle, seeks to provide an ontological mirror, through which people can look at themselves not with the dominant sense of having an excess moral value, but the same value as the other (in Aristotelian sense a friend) would have. This moral capacity which flows from these five principles in effect radically undercuts the very basis of Hobbesian self-preservation, which is ontologically related to the superior self.

Politics of self-preservation in the Hobbesian sense, therefore, suggests an unwillingness to step out from brahminhood. Interestingly, brahminhood seeks to preserve itself through the process of Sanskritisation. Sanskritisation as a cultural process involves the efforts on the part of the people at the lower layer to emulate brahminhood. The lower orders instead of rejecting brahminhood seek to perfect it. Practitioners of brahminhood seem to have adopted a much rigorous and all pervading process that has helped the former to preserve brahminhood in entrenched form. To put it differently, brahminhood requires not just Sanskritisation, which as a preservative option could be a little unreliable, but structurally a much more stable device to redeem this self-preservation.

Conversion of the Ecological into Sociological

This structural device involves the conversion of the ecological ("five principles") into the sociological (hierarchical). The sociologist assigns different, and perhaps, negative meaning to *Panchamahabhute* through deploying the ideology of purity-pollution, which is so central to the former. This conversion is sustained by the asymmetries of power that robs the *Panchamahabhute* of their positive meaning. People do not follow the moral basis of metaphysics of body when they act. They are not sufficiently motivated by the exalted, and therefore, the egalitarian meaning that is implied in the metaphysics of *Panchamahabhute*. In fact, their material interest and the cultural need to draw relative superiority over others seriously undermine the validity of metaphysics as the universal framework that provides moral orientation to social interaction among people. The failure of religio-theological discourse represented by different saint traditions proves this and has to be understood in terms of the corresponding failure of the common people to respond to the appeal of different saints, particularly Kabir. Put yet differently, the need to remain socially superior has led the upper castes to convert the ecological into sociological or natural into cultural. Let me explain this in terms of the politics of converting the *Panchamahabhute* into an instrument that is deployed to reduce some social section to "walking carrion" (Naipaul 1988, p. 37), a degraded entity filled with a deep sense of repulsion. This transmutation, which is produced by the politics of preservation of the hierarchically superior self, has serious implication for these five principles. They stand discredited; they are robbed of their egalitarian meaning. Let us see how.

According to *Manusmriti*, the physical association of the upper castes, which is still under the social influence of ritual orders, with the earth is considered to be ritually polluting. According to *Manusmriti*, members of the top layer in social hierarchy are not supposed to soil their hands with either the earth or mud. Using ritual pollution to assign negative quality to the earth goes completely against the Gandhian naturopathy, which treats the earth with much respect on account of its having a healing value. Gandhi considers it as healing inasmuch as it helps in pumping out the excess heat from the body. But the Manu strictures deny this medicinal value to the earth. The earth, thus, suggests a broad division based on purity-pollution thus dividing the top of the twice-born on the pure side and the *shudras* and ati-*shudra* on the impure side. Generally speaking, conversion of water as a natural, therefore, pure substance into a polluted substance should be considered as objectionable. Similarly, the use of water for maintaining physical hygiene should not be considered as objectionable. But how can one understand the efforts made by some socially privileged sections to use water for constructing morally painful asymmetry in social and cultural life?

Using Water

The upper castes, taking their cue from the Manu code, use water for constructing a perennial division thus rendering some bodies ritually pure and others as eternally impure. Such people treat sea water as ritually polluting[10] and also as a source of ritual purification. According to this understanding, water, unlike the earth, becomes a standard by which it then becomes possible to measure how deeply the essence of caste has penetrated and perverted the social relations across castes. Water, unlike the earth, is available to every caste, which uses it to reproduce untouchability practices so as to retain relative social superiority on the scale of ritual hierarchy. Thus, water determines the scale of untouchability. Water, in fact, forms the lifeline or provides the most important precondition for the survival of untouchability. Just imagine if there was no water, the untouchability would not have originated at the first instance or it would have gone long ago if the water resources had dried up. Thanks to the water sources or long living Himalayas, water is still available for practicing untouchability!

According to the laws of Manu (Dumont 1988, p. 50), fire is considered as another source of purification. In *Manusmriti*, fire is intrinsically pure, and this is proved by the social strictures that prevent Hindu women to mount her deceased husband's funeral pyre if she is menstruating (ibid). Fire, according to the Manu Dharma, also acts as the purification agent. The ritual practice in Hindus known as *Agni Pariksha* underscores the point. Within the Hindu social/cultural practices, the untouchables and women are forced to take this *Agni Pariksha* for different reasons. The upper castes use fire not only to punish untouchables, but also to purify the vicinity through seeking displacement of the untouchables as "walking carrion".

The social history of caste riots in the recent past clearly shows how the upper castes have used fire for devastating the little shanty huts of Dalits all over the country. Thus, water purifies the upper caste bodies, while fire indirectly maintains the purity of space or the *akasa*. Fire, as a weapon of the strong upper caste, is deployed by them to destroy not only the untouchables themselves, but their dwellings as well.[11] In this regard, it is interesting to further note that fire as a purifying resource is also available to Ambedkar, but for emancipatory purposes. As is well known, during the Chavdar water tank struggle in March 1927 at Mahad in Ratnagiri district of Maharashtra, he set Manusmriti on fire in 1927. However, it has to be noted that there is a difference between the two social usages of fire. The socially dominant deploys fire only to perpetuate the division between the ideal untouchable (twice-born) and the despicable untouchable, while Ambedkar uses it to symbolically destroy this division.

'Air' as an Objectionable Substance

Under what conditions should "air" become an objectionable substance? It can be objectionable when it is converted from its natural status as a pure substance into a source of contamination. However, air in itself does not constitute a source of contamination. On the contrary, it can become a source of contamination, particularly when it is filled with foul smell, deadly gas or dangerous bacteria which are quite harmful to the general health of the people. Thus, locating hazardous factories away from human habitation is quite understandable from a certain perspective. But how does one understand the location of Dalit *bastis* on the eastern side of a village? This location of Dalits to the east of the main village has been empirically confirmed by several anthropological studies on India.[12] Is it natural or the part of a social design? I would like to argue that this morphology is part of the social design which has been done by the upper castes. Why? There is an ideology of purity-pollution behind this morphology. The *bastis* of the untouchables on the eastern side of the village form a part of this deliberate design that is deployed by the upper castes to avoid pollution crossing over from the west to the east should the Dalit *bastis* happen to be situated on the west side of the village. Since the upper castes cannot control the direction of air which flows from the west to the east, they are forced to change the social morphology of the village in such a way so as to situate themselves on the west, while pushing the untouchables to the east.

Radial Impact of Sound

According to the Nyaya philosophical tradition in India, sound accesses the space. Even in modern times one can actually measure the radial impact of sound. Excess production of sound leads to noise, which ultimately leads to noise pollution. Thus, space comes to be filled with noise pollution. In this context, it might look completely bizarre to believe that at least a few decades before, sound created by untouchables was considered a source of ritual pollution. During the feudal social set-up, the untouchables in most parts of India were forced to announce their arrival before they could enter the main village.[13] The reason behind such precautionary measure was that the upper castes sought to avoid listening to the sound of an untouchable that the former considered polluting. The notion of the sacred sought to turn sound into the source of ritual pollution. Taking evening meals was considered as the most sacred occasion, particularly by the priestly class from the village (Dumont 1988, p. 54). The upper castes, particularly the brahmin priests from the village, found the sound of an untouchable as a source of interruption in the most sacred occasion. During the night patrolling in the village, the untouchable was permitted to shout only at a low-pitched voice. This was done to avoid the undesirable interruptions. The link between untouchability and morphology of expression (different levels of expression) was firmly established and strictly followed by the upper caste in the village (Kamble 2008). In one of the leading autobiographies of Babytai Kamble, the *veskar* (the village servant), the Mahars (ex-untouchable caste in Maharashtra) were not allowed to use high-pitched sounds during the evenings as it was considered a major source of interruption of sacred functions.

Sarukkai (2009) has argued that there is a contact between body and words. Thus, chanting words while bathing, according to Sarukkai (2009) establishes this contact. But in case of the untouchables as 'walking carrion' with a concentrated expression of repulsion (even today some Indian people feel nauseated after seeing the untouchables and they cover their noses whenever they walk past the untouchables), there is a complete denial of this contact. This is because the words do not belong ontologically to the brahmin body. They flow from the mouth of the walking carrion; a potent source of pollution. Thus, at one level, the untouchables were prohibited from producing high-pitched sounds as it was considered polluting as far as the pure untouchables are concerned. At another level, even the low-pitched sound is considered polluting by the upper castes. Since the sound accesses the space, it can become the source of pollution as well. In order to avoid the menace of words coming from the untouchables, the upper castes, particularly the brahmins forced the untouchables to eliminate the word and replace it with sound. This was done by forcing the untouchables to announce their arrival in the public sphere, not by shouting their words but by beating the drum.[14] The top of the twice-born castes seem to have used these *Panchamahabhute* to produce "walking carrion", a concentrated expression of untouchability. Since the untouchable was a walking danger, there was a need to quarantine this danger in an isolated place called the Chamrauti in Uttar Pradesh, Halgeri in Karnataka, Cherry in Tamil Nadu and Mahar/Mangwad in Maharashtra.

In the above sections, we have seen that the *Panchamahabhute* do have a capacity to assign universal meaning (ontological equality) to a body which might look particular in terms of its outer constitution. But at another level, it can also deny a particular body, for example, an untouchable or walking carrion a moral significance. A walking carrion can acquire moral significance in two major ways. First, it can turn a passive, helpless, quarantined body into a potent weapon not so much to produce destruction, on the contrary, for liberating the upper caste bodies that otherwise would remain folded into an estranged being—privileged untouchables. The touch of the despicable untouchable seeks to convert the folded bodies into freely flowing bodies.[15] It can liberate the 'privileged untouchables,' as Sarukkai (2009) would like to call them, from the constraining sense of anxiety. The physical or corporeal or material touch of the hygienic bodies could also be liberating for these bodies to fold into themselves. The touch, ranging from a simple handshake to innocent hugging or intensive hugging (inter-caste marriage consummated as a result of sheer love or that which is led by conviction and reason to produce a decent society) can democratize the very idea of touch. The touch, therefore, can help overcome the mutual reification of culturally folded bodies. Secondly, the untouchable as the actual entity ironically seeks to establish a reverse control on the sacred bodies that are treated as ideal. To put it differently, it is the ideal untouchable who feels vulnerable to the threat of the "sociological danger". We shall discuss this point in greater detail in the second part of this chapter.

Mutually Exclusive

Touch and contact can acquire mutually exclusive meanings depending on the particular social context. Thus, touch, which is active purely in private and personal contexts, does not possess any special significance except that it has a functional value. Thus one hand touching other part of the body has only such a functional value. This touching the touched as Sarukkai (2009) puts it, has a functional value. However, there is another context, in which folding both the hands together acquires a definite social meaning. Thus, the act of touching/folding both the hands can communicate different, perhaps, contradictory messages. For example, in the Indian context, greeting people with both hands from a distance is considered safe as it serves the purpose of avoiding the touch of others, perhaps, the repulsive other, namely, the untouchables. This point becomes relevant in the context of Sarukkai's observation that it is only the contact with the other through touch that can define the touched and the untouched. Similarly, Sarukkai's (2009) attempt to elevate untouchability much beyond the binary of pure and impure, by invoking the metaphysics of body, as mentioned earlier, plays an important role in collapsing the cultural hierarchy that divided these bodies. Also his invocation of Merleau-Ponty becomes quite instructive to appreciate the role that an untouchable as an invisible plays in illuminating the touchable.

One can further build on to this insight, and argue that the untouchable is forced to become the repository of the impurities of the touchable. While this elevation of untouchability beyond the contours of purity-pollution is desirable, at the same time, it also tends to undermine the moral significance of untouchability based on the ideology of purity-pollution. I would like to argue that the untouchable as supplementation of the touchable has contradictory value. This is so because it is available for conservative as well as subversive purposes. On a conservative reading, it could be argued, that untouchability has a moral significance. Just imagine what would happen to the touchable, if the untouchable were to refuse to become the dumping ground for somebody's moral dirt or refuse to illuminate the touchable. It perhaps would lead to the moral decomposition or atrophy of the touchables' body or they would get crushed under the accumulated weight of these impurities. (Thank god, there has been an untouchable around to carry this burden!) The untouchables as repository of impurities also have a moral significance for another reason. The upper caste politicians, including some of the left politicians, should thank the untouchables for providing a vocabulary to express either their agony or anger against their political opponents or beat the opponents with untouchability as a poison weapon. Look at the expression that political leaders use almost every day. "We are not untouchable", "Do not treat us as untouchable". It seeks to undercut the social significance of the twice-born by making the latter realize that they are either parasites or free riders resting their burden on the body of the untouchables. The moral depletion of these free riders becomes total when the latter refuses to take any responsibility for the untouchable after he deposits moral dirt in the former.

Idea of Moral Significance

However, the idea of moral significance could be deeply problematic as far as the emancipatory project of the untouchable is concerned. A person who prefers to stay in untouchability for moral significance summarily loses the capacity to question the asymmetrical social relationship between the touchables and the untouchables. In fact, moral significance becomes a possibility only in the context of this asymmetry. Hence, it lacks transformative potential. The sacrifice made for maintaining the superiority, for example, of the top layer of the twice-born, may have only an instrumental value to the extent that it provides vocabulary to the self-serving politicians, but it hardly has any transformative value for the slave and untouchable. Thus, staying in an asymmetrical relationship necessarily subverts the self-understanding that is fundamentally so important for the freedom and ultimate emancipation of the person in question. Those, in question, however, do not stay tied with the master just because they get some spiritual advantage or moral significance. In fact, the force of new aspirations motivates them to walk out from this constraining relationship. They refuse to become the dumping ground for somebody's garbage. This new emancipatory rationality could be very well-captured in the modern mood characterizing the subversive politics of Ambedkar and his followers. His mood could be paraphrased in the following sentence, "It may be in your interest to deposit your impurities in us, but how can it be in our interest to remain repository of your dirt (moral)". In the post-Ambedkar Dalit movement, the critique of untouchability as supplementation (Sarukkai's expression) is best captured in the term "Ghamdya"[16] that subverts this Dalit rationality which is the hallmark of Ambedkar's emancipatory politics.

Ambedkar's politics seeks to annihilate caste. But before he attacks its roots, he very systematically seeks to prune its branches—various untouchability practices. For carrying out this attack against casteism through untouchability, Ambedkar does follow an archaeological method. That is to say, through the social struggle he first seeks to question untouchability practices which are the manifestation of the essence of caste. Also, for Ambedkar, the solution lies not in morality; on the contrary, it is fundamentally political. It is because of this primacy of the political that he does not lose sight of caste, while he attacks its existence, i e, untouchability. But for Gandhi, the solution lies not in the political but the moral. Gandhi chooses the moral route which does not centrally take on the essence of untouchability, i e, caste. In the Gandhian moral framework of action against untouchability, the contestation, if any, does not encircle the essence of caste but its existence—untouchability. This shift in focus from essence to existence invokes naturally a moral response rather than a political one.

Seva (service) as the moral category in Gandhian discourse on untouchability makes sense in the context of this shift. *Seva* as a moral category, does not seek to attack the roots of the problem, instead it chooses to prune its rough edges. In Gandhi, it is pruning rather than uprooting, while in Ambedkar, the reverse is the case. Although Gandhi looks less interested in establishing the link between untouchability and its essence (caste), it has to be acknowledged that his moral category seva looks certainly radical when compared to Vedantic thinking, which rules out resolution of untouchability through material and corporeal touch.

Gandhian Approach

Look at Gandhi's body language which is so relaxed and flows freely across time and spaces. Reverse is the case for the Shankaracharya, whose body is folded into itself, it is completely frozen. It is in this sense the significance of corporeality of touch that makes Gandhian approach to untouchability analogous to Ambedkar. Because both of them insist that an untouchable must enter the temple with his/her physical body and not through a spiritual mind, which is what the Vedantic view suggests. However, Gandhi and Ambedkar differ from each other quite substantially on other counts. Unlike Gandhi, who finds the solution of untouchability in the moral surgery of the heart, Ambedkar suggests the annihilation of caste of which untouchability is just the existence. According to Ambedkar, the "brahminical mind" produces opaque forms of untouchability, which can be detected either through sociology or anthropology. Untouchability exists beyond mere description, and hence, requires archaeology that could access untouchability, which as Shinde has very perceptively pointed out, sits at the bottom of this mind. Ambedkar's thinking and politics follows the archaeological method of discovering the essence of untouchability. Let us explore the question what is archaeology? And why is it relevant for understanding untouchability in "elegant India"?

Archaeology of Untouchability

Archaeology, in recent times, has become a generic term that appears in different fields of inquiry ranging from the social sciences to humanities to physical sciences like geomorphology. For example, medical practitioners have been using archaeology to understand the diminishing height (physical) of persons across generations. Parentage with nutritional deficiency, leads to diminishing height in the successive generation. Similarly, in geomorphology, archaeology is an important method to access the natural substance that due to changes in nature gets hidden underneath water bodies, earth and snow.[17] In fact, changes occurring in the natural substance can best be captured with archaeology as a method of analysis. For example, in the region experiencing snowfall, one finds peaks getting covered with snow and becoming denuded during the hot weather. The importance of archaeology in history deals not so much with invention, but discovering historical evidence in different forms (artefacts, even quantitative data) so as to provide the background for making conjectures and their refutation. The debate among the Indian historians over certain disputed historical structures proves this point quite adequately. Archaeology in history thus involves extracting the truth from the past by "carefully" discovering and analysing the historical data (Nicole 2005). Some of the sociologists also find archaeology as a useful method to study social relations in India.[18]

Interestingly, archaeology also finds its relevance in the debates between two leading Marxist thinkers: Hobsbawm and Althusser. Hobsbawm finds in Althusser an archaeological operation and identifies in the latter different layers of theoretical thinking, which gradually accumulated on top of Marx's original thought (Hobsbawm 1994, p. 1). Finally, and most importantly, in the Foucauldian sense, archaeology tries to define

> not the thoughts, representation, images, themes, preoccupations that are concealed or revealed in discourse, but those discourses themselves, those discourses as practices obeying certain rules. It does not treat discourses as document, as a sign of something else, as an element that ought to be transparent, but where unfortunate opacity must often be pierced if one is to reach at least the depth of the essential in the place in which it is held in reverse, it is connected with discourses in its own

volume as a monument. It is not interpretative discipline, it does not seek another, better hidden discourse, it refuses to be allegorical (Foucault 1994, p. 136).

A Foucauldian take on archaeology would also help us to distinguish archaeology from architecture. In the Indian context, Dalits used the metaphor of the pyramid to describe the caste system, and more particularly, the *varna* system, while the Marxists put caste and untouchability as located at the superstructure. In the archaeological sense, caste and untouchability are not a kind of order or an open design. In fact, as we shall see in the following pages it plays out quite secretly and subtly. For example, in public discussion, themes on Dalits come to be listed at the far end of a seminar/conference or at the end of a research journal.[19] This preferential order looks natural, because those who have the power to put Dalits in an irreversible order, do not find it necessary to provide any reason for such preferential arrangement.

Thus, archaeology seeks to access this inalterability of the "Indian mind". It seeks to reveal or fathom the untouchability-ridden "Indian mind" that hides within itself a persisting element of caste. The Indian mind essentially operates through the subtle act of transferring value from one sphere to another. Thus, archaeology is a generic concept that appears relevant to different scholars in different contexts. However, covering and discovering or melting and freeing are essential and defining features of archaeology common to all the perspectives on archaeology. Secondly, archaeology for its definition requires a hidden context with opacity or anonymity. That is to say it does not become relevant in a transparent context. Let us explore what is this context for untouchability.

The Context of Archaeology of Untouchability

Let me in the beginning argue that archaeology as a method of discovering the essence or the truth of caste becomes intelligible only in certain contexts. For example, archaeology may become redundant in the rural context, where caste hierarchies play out openly by resorting to blatant untouchability practices, and hence, caste does not require untouchability to adopt subtle forms for its own expression. Let me make this point further clear by citing some evidence from some villages in Tamil Nadu and Maharashtra.[20] In these villages, where the upper castes have raised a physical wall of separation between the touchables and the untouchables, archaeology does not need to discover anything more. To put it differently, archaeology requires a spatially ambiguous context for its success. Similarly, archaeology would become ineffective in the rural context, where the untouchables still have to appear in the public with body markers (with a broom and basket of filth on the head, certain dress codes, black ribbon on the wrists) constituting them into walking carrion with a concentrated expression of repulsion. To put it differently, archaeology does not make sense, particularly in the face to face or intimate social context. Rather, archaeology becomes intelligible in the social context, where every other person appears as a stranger to every other person in opaque social relations. The urban context makes it difficult for the pure untouchable to remain in touch with the despicable untouchable. I am already suggesting, as does Sarukkai (2009), that the despicable untouchable provides a subjective condition for self-preservation of the "pure untouchables".

The growing dilution of the interactive sphere leading to growing anonymity makes the domestic space within the urban context as the only sphere for the protection of the "pure untouchable". The domestic sphere provides an opportunity for the resolution of anxiety that continues to grip the urban upper castes. Let me further argue how the domestic space offers a stable context for the pure untouchable to overcome his/her anxiety.

Domestic Sphere

First, the domestic sphere offers the space for conducting purificatory functions. The touchables or the twice-born persons use the domestic sphere for both physical and ritual purification. It is quite revealing to note that some of the parents hose down their children after they return home from school, not because their bodies are mired in mud or dust, but because they might have messed up with the untouchable children, while in the school.[21] Second, the domestic sphere also provides an opportunity for the upper castes to feel sovereign over controlling the domestic space. Practicing untouchability at home becomes the major source of the sovereignty. The need to realize this sovereignty cannot be fulfilled in the public sphere, which can offer only an abstract sense of sovereignty as citizen of the Indian Republic. This becomes clear from following moves that the pure self makes in protecting the domestic sphere as a sphere of sovereignty. First, he invites only those about whose background he is absolutely sure. He enjoys discretionary, power. Second, the twice-born host uses money power to retain his ritual power in case the twice-born host commits the mistake by inviting a person with ambiguous social identity, gets food from the hotel, and finally, he knows the invitee is from the lower caste, but since he cannot avoid inviting the latter he offers him a tender coconut. The shell of the used tender coconut is a safe device for avoiding ritual pollution because the shell can be disposed of.

Interestingly, the axis between the domestic and the public spheres provides space for archaeological articulation. As mentioned above, the domestic sphere is the sphere of sovereignty for the upper caste. He/she, due to the pressure of social vigilance, can enjoy sovereignty only the fragmented time and space and not in continuous time. In fact, the pressure of social vigilance, forces him/her to don universal masks, while he is in the public domain. Thus, he becomes co-worker, teacher, citizen, consumer, and so on, depending on the spheres. In the journey back home, these sacred souls begin to drop each of these universal identities. He becomes completely denuded in the domestic. This is analogous to the archaeology of the glacier as mentioned above. It is in this sense that the domestic becomes the sphere of deflation of pretension. For the untouchables, therefore, it is the domestic sphere which is the testing ground for the morally integrated or genuine personality. This has been further confirmed by some of the anthropologists (Khare 1984, p. 14). How does one get an insight into this deflation of the "pure self" who hides behind the universal identities? While there are several Dalit autobiographies that offer an insight into this archaeological insight, let me cite an interesting conversation between the upper caste landlord and the prospectus untouchable tenants:

Landlord: May I know your name?

Tenant: My name is Bhagvan. (This Hindu sounding name anticipates a subsequent question from the landlord.)

Landlord: Which region are you from?

Tenant: I am a Maharashtrian. (This does not give any idea of his social background.)

Landlord: Which language do you speak?

Tenant: Hindustani or English.

Landlord: Are you a vegetarian or a non-vegetarian? (This is true in some regions only.)

Tenant: Vegetarian. (This does not help the landlord to overcome landlord's reservations, and hence, he uses the last question.)

Landlord: Where do you work? (This is the last but sure source of knowing the caste of a tenant because as Harkishan Santoshi has observed in his testimonies, the caste of a person reaches to working place earlier than his/her transfer papers

(Guru 1986)

Contradictory Move

The conversation between the landlord and the prospective tenant underlies an archaeological move, which is deeply contradictory in nature. The landlord's archaeology involves a set of questions, which are authoritative, irrational, and hence, offensive. This archaeology, which is aimed at restoring inalienability between the sacred self and the modern enterprise acquires an offensive character, particularly on the normative ground. The prospective tenant, instead of rejecting the irrational question on rational grounds, chooses to cope with it by adopting a defensive archaeology, which involves universal answers for the particular questions. This withdrawal into guided universalism thus suggests a loss of self-esteem as far as the tenant is concerned.

The tenant fails to put a counter question to the landlord, thus exposing the latter's failure to follow market rationality. It is by this primacy of the irrational over the rational or ritual value over the monetary value, that the offensive archaeology adopted by the upper caste landlord cannot be reduced to mere psychology, because the landlord does not ask these questions for satisfying his psychological curiosity. In fact, in this case, the offensive archaeology establishes an ontological link with the ritually superior self. The offensive archaeology, which operates through coercive questioning, in the process tends to render the landlord completely denuded, of course, on moral ground. The prospective tenant also suffers from a painful skinning off layers of different universal identity, which he puts on himself as defence mechanism. Thus, archaeology suggests a double bind.

This offensive archaeology has implications at three levels. First, at the phenomenological level, the social attitude of the ideal untouchable (the upper caste) does point out the social relations rather than the knowledge conditions. Second, this archaeology suggests the irresoluble tension between a good citizen and a good person. To put it differently, an upper caste person may be a citizen good enough to grant at least a temporary recognition to an untouchable, but he/she may not be a good person. Third, the domestic as the private sphere cordoned off by the ideology of purity-pollution effectively denies the private the benign quality of being the space for healing and recuperating necessitated by the ravages of the public world.[22] Fourth, this Janus-faced ideal untouchable thus violates the Aristotelian principle that suggests an interconnection between the private and the public which is bound by the totality of moral qualities of the good "man". Finally, the ideal untouchable and his/her attitudes towards the real untouchable confirms Sarukkai's (2009) main argument, according to which the self-definition of the upper caste or the ideal untouchable becomes possible only in relation to the as criptive identity of the untouchable. This sacred self cannot exist without the presence of other—the despicable untouchable. This tense coexistence becomes a possibility only through outsourcing untouchability to the other. However, those who supplement untouchability into others continue to suffer from endless anxiety. That is to say they can neither completely detoxify themselves of an element of untouchability, nor can they brandish it openly. Ironically, the predicament makes the archaeological method inevitable for the detection of untouchability, which sits deep in the anxious self.

Notes

1. This work has evolved through long and insightful discussions with Sundar and Dhanu. I thank them for showing unfailing interest in my work.
2. Centre for Political Studies, Jawaharlal Nehru University, Delhi, India.
3. Sarukkai, Sundar (2009) 'The Phenomenology of Untouchability', *Economic and Political Weekly*, Vol. 44, No. 37, pp. 39–48.
4. Anand Mulk Raj's *The Untouchables*, Shivaram Karanth's *Choma's Duddi*, Thakazhi Shivashankara Pillai's *Scavenger's Boy*, U R Ananthamurthy's *Samskara* are some of the prominent literary texts that centrally touch upon the question of untouchability.
5. Baburao Bagul, *Jevanha Me Jat Chorali Hoti* (short story collection) (Nagpur: Siddarth Publication) 1978, Om Prakash Walmiki, *Jhootan* (tran) Prabha Mukherjee (Calcutta: Samya Publication), 2002.
6. It is only in Bhimrao Ramji Ambedkar's collective writings and speeches that one come across a thick discussion on the impact of untouchability on economics.
7. The sociological puzzle could be understood in terms of intense practices of untouchability that is found in the regions with negligible Brahmin population. Or, less intense untouchability practices with larger Brahmin population, particularly in Uttar Pradesh. I have dealt with this issue in my power of touch, published in *Frontline*, December 2007.
8. In the 19th century, Pune in Maharashtra, the untouchables were forced to appear in public with an earthen pot hanging around their neck and broom sticking around their waist. The untouchables were forced to use the pot as spittoon, as their spit was also considered as polluting. The broom was supposed to erase their footprints which were considered as polluting.
9. See *The Samkhya Karika*, translated by Nandalal Sinha (1915) Oriental Books, Delhi.
10. In the orthodox Hinduism, although there are umpteen number of references that suggest crossing the sea is a taboo, one can also argue that some of the orthodox Hindus do treat sea water as polluting, which is why they do not immerse the ashes of the dead into sea water, even if they are close to sea water (particularly, from the coastal region).
11. Forty-three untouchable agricultural labourers were burnt alive by the upper caste landlords in Kilvenmani in Thanjavur district of Tamil Nadu in 1962. Several houses of Valmikis from Gohana in Harayana were set on fire by the upper castes in January 2007.
12. Karve, Irawati, makes this observation in her seminal work on Maharashtra. Even research study on the *Dignity Index in Maharashtra*, Vlkas Adhyayan Kendra, Mumbai, 2009, proves this point.
13. This has been the common practice among the upper caste Indians from different parts of India. Interestingly, e.g., Thomas Isaac's *India's Ex Untouchables*, Michael Walzer also reconfirms this in his work on *Spheres of Justice: A Defence of Pluralism and Equality*.
14. Baby Kamble (2008), this has also been confirmed by Mehbubhai from Behat block in Saharanpur district, UP.
15. U R Ananthamurthy, *Samskara*, The Janpith Award Winning work.
16. For more discussion, Guru (1996). This term could also be understood through the literary imagination of Dalit literary writers like Prahlad Chendwankar, who has written the poem "The Cup".

17. I benefited from the discussion I held with Harjit Singh, an expert in glaciology.
18. Kramer C, I E Douglas quoted in Nicole 2005, P 242.
19. *Bibilio*, VII, Nos 9 and 10, October 2002.
20. *Frontline*, December 2008.
21. My own fieldwork from the villages from Sawantwadi block from the Tal (deep) Konkan region of Maharashtra.
22. Michael de Certan, quoted in Gupta (2003: p. 56).

References

Desai, I P (1976): *Untouchability in Rural Gujarat* (Mumbai: Popular Prakashan).

Dumont, Louis (1988): *Homo Hierarchicus* (New Delhi: Oxford University Press)

Foucault, Michel (1994): *Archaeology of Knowledge* (London: Routledge).

Guru, Gopal (1986): "Social Discrimination and Sanskritisation: Some Theoretical Issues", *Sociological Bulletin*.

— (1996): *Dalit Cultural Movement in Mahrashtra* (Mumbai: Vikas Adhyayan Kendra)

Gupta, Dipankar (2003): "Domesticated Public: Tradition, Modernity and the Public/Private Divide" in Gurpreet Mahajan, *The Public and the Private: Issues of Democratic Citizenship* (Delhi: Sage).

Hobsbawm, E J (1994): "The Structural of Capital" in Gregory Elliot (ed.), *Althusser: A Critical Reader* (Oxford: Blackwell).

Jha, Vivekananda (1974): "From Tribe to Untouchability: The Case of Nisad" (New Delhi: People's Publishing House).

Kamble, Baby (2008): *The Prison We Broke*, Marathi translation by Maya Pandit (Delhi: Orient Longman).

Khare, R S (1984): *The Untouchables as Himself, Ideology, Identity and Pragmatism among the Lucknow Chamers* (Cambridge: Cambridge University Press).

Naipaul, V S (1988): *India: A Wounded Civilisation* (Delhi: Picador).

Nicole, Boivin (2005): "Orientalism, Ideology and Identity: Examining Caste in South Asian Archaeology", *Journal of Social Archaeology*.

Rudolph, S H and L I Rudolph (1967): *The Modernity of Tradition: Political Development in India* (Chicago: University of Chicago Press).

Rajshekhariah, A M (1976): *Politics of Untouchability* (New Delhi: Ashis Publishers).

Sarukkai, Sundar (2009): "Phenomenology of Untouchability", *Economic and Political Weekly*, 12 (18), pp. 39–48.

Shah, Ghanshyam, H Mander, S Thorat, S Deshpande and A Baviskar (2006): *Untouchability in Rural in India* (Delhi: Sage).

Shinde, Vitthal Ramji (1976): *Bhartatil Ashprushctecha Prashna* (Mumbai: Social Welfare and Cultural Department, Government of Maharashtra).

5 The Word and the World

Dalit Aesthetics as a Critique of Everyday Life[1]

Anupama Rao[2]

The most iconic text that announced Dalit writing as an event in Marathi literary history is surely Dhasal's (1972) *Golpitha*. As is well known, the critic and playwright Vijay Tendulkar noted his inability to understand Dhasal's Marathi because he lacked access to the life of everyday violence and sudden intimacies that Dhasal described:

> This is a world where the night is reversed into the day, where stomachs are empty or half-empty, of desperation against death, of the next day s anxieties, of bodies left over after being consumed by shame and sensibility, of insufferably flowing sewages, of diseased young bodies lying by the gutters braving the cold by folding up their knees to their bellies, of the jobless, of beggars, of pickpockets, of holy mendicants, of neighbourhood tough guys and pimps.
>
> (Quoted in Dhasal and Chitre 2007, p. 10)

Dalit life was street life, defined by the lack of privacy, and proximity to shit and garbage. In Dhasal's writings, Dalit existence was indistinguishable from life in the city: Bombay was the protagonist of Dalit *sahitya* (literature), but it was a Bombay marked by informal livelihoods and lumpen lives.[3]

Dhasal was working as a taxi driver when he wrote *Golpitha*. His family had migrated from Khed taluka in Pune, to the Dhor Chawl in Arab Galli near Golpitha, the black hole of Bombay's traditional red-light district. He would describe this world as one populated by small-time smugglers, drug-traffickers, *supari* (contract) killers, thieves, loan-sharks' henchmen and goons living on protection money. By the time he started the little magazine *Vidroha* in 1968, Dhasal, a key founder-leader of the Dalit Panthers, was recognizable by his "Castro"-type *topi* (cap) and a shoulder bag, which were imitated by many Dalit men. His open admission of desire for liquor, *charas* (hashish), and women from Kamathipura, the famous red-light district of central Bombay, earned him a fair degree of notoriety.[4]

DOI: 10.4324/9781003155065-5

Dhasal embraced an aesthetic politics: his investment in violent visibility was predicated on the symbolic efficacy of violent language, not to
mention the Panthers' commitment to the instrumental efficiency of street
fighting. Dalit precarity and informality—rather than being viewed as an
aberration from the narrative of class formation—increasingly enabled
Dalits to assert their right to the city because they existed as a form of
political life or stigmatized humanity whose claim to recognition was the
mere fact of their survival. That they existed on a continuum with the city's
detritus (excreta, garbage, scraps)—scarred by human violence (theft,
rape, child abuse), and excised from sanctioned circuits of production and
reproduction—enabled a set of associations between Dalit life and urban
materiality. More important, it showcased the unique mutuality between
Dalit *sahitya* and Bombay modern as a project of political aesthetics, distinguished by its powerful assault on the hegemony of caste as a proscription on the seeable and the sayable.

Dalit Writing: Between the Urban and the Insurgent

Dalit *sahitya* is typically viewed as a paradigmatic example of Marathi
modernism, and a literary practice that exemplifies the social experience of
urban subalterns. This chapter explores how we might connect the space
called Bombay with those forms of literary representation that go under
the rubric of Dalit writing. Therefore this chapter excavates something like
the prehistory of a recognizable Dalit literature, itself a product of both the
self-conscious identification of writers with a style and content associated
with the representational strategies of Dalit *sahitya*, and the artifact of a
vigorous market in publishing that has seen enormous growth in the last
40 years.

Dalit literature's ready identification with literatures of protest makes
it difficult to contend with the distinctiveness of its social critique and its
insurgent aesthetics. Standard narratives of an identifiable Dalit literary
movement might date the event to the publication of the magazine *Asmita*
(1963) soon renamed *Asmitadarsh* (1967–68) under the editorship of Gangadhar Pantawane after conflict within the editorial board—followed by
the writings of the Dalit Panthers. Yet a different history might be told,
one that begins in a rather different place, and with a different set of char-
acters. This alternative genealogy approaches the fraught issue of Dalit
sahitya—that is, its status as the literary, or cultural practice of a group of
persons identified as Dalit, with secret, insider knowledge about the life of
their community—from a fresh perspective. In this regard, Jaaware (2012)
has argued rather strongly against the identitarianism lurking behind this
literary form: he argues that the assumption that Dalit literature is written
by Dalits about the Dalit condition engages with its radical implications *as*

literature precisely because of the conventions of social realism that guide our engagement with it. Instead Jaaware's own efforts to read Dalit literature as "destitute literature"—"It is" extremely important to remember that the "de" [in destitution, deprivation] is a *privative*, it takes away, it's *not* merely a negative" (p. 33), he reminds us—views Dalit *sahitya* as forcing the reader to confront the question of ethics in a situation where the social structuring of caste enacts a persistent and brutal dehumanization of all its subjects. Thus staging the impossibility of ethics would constitute Dalit *sahitya*'s real achievement, rather than its role in giving voice to a reified "Dalit experience" as such.

I echo Jaaware's argument regarding Dalit *sahitya*'s capacity to stage the ethical relation in a radical manner. However this chapter approaches the problem of Dalit writing differently, via a longer-term accounting of the practices of radical empiricism that politicized everyday life, and by asking how the social relations of caste were altered (and re-inscribed) in the context of urban migration, and modern work: that is, the chapter argues that the social transformations of caste also altered the experiences of caste and its (literary) expression. My chapter situates the entry of Dalit *sahitya* as critical practice and publishing phenomenon in the institutional apparatus of friendship circles, literary organizations and the *sahitya sammelan* (literary gatherings) that grew around Dalit cultural producers starting in the 1950s and 1960s. However, I also extend my gaze back to the turn of the 20th century and the interwar period to explore Dalit and lower caste migration to Bombay in the context of rural immiseration as an important turning point that can be calibrated with their exposure to new modes of critical thought. The divergence between the constraints of social life, and the reception of ideas of emancipation produced a distinctive form of critique, that was predicated on efforts to specify the inequities of caste. The early phase of Dalit *sahitya* drew quite centrally on descriptive and critical practices associated with both anti-caste thought and Marxism to produce a particular kind of urban literature which had as its central figure the Dalit subaltern as an agent of social transformation. A reconsideration of Dalit *sahitya* thus requires that we bracket the question of the literariness of Dalit literature, and focus instead on those forms of linguistic concreteness, or the practices of naming and description that politicized key aspects of subaltern life. Herein lies the prehistory of a recognizable Dalit poetics, one that relates writing with urbanity and Dalit Bombay with Bombay modern.

Bombay Modern

It is well known that Bombay's meteoric rise as British India's most important port city coincided with the boom and bust of the cotton economy.

This was directly connected to the American Civil War and the problems faced by British industry in procuring southern cotton, on the one hand, and the opening of the Suez Canal to steam shipping on the other. Their combined impact on the subcontinent was twofold. First, the rich black soil of the Khandesh and Berar regions of western India was taken over by cotton. New technologies for rationalizing production and accelerating the circulation of Bombay cotton soon followed, creating new linkages between the rural hinterland and the city, and between Bombay and the British Empire (see Hazareesingh 2007; Beckert 2014). Thus Bombay's late 19th-century cotton economy coincided with the broader commercialization of Indian agriculture and peasant production for global markets. As a consequence, Bombay's social world would come to be categorized by an ongoing set of cyclical migrations, new forms of labor mobilization, and distinctive forms of critique amongst which Marxist internationalism played a critical role.

Two points require emphasis in this regard, and will function as governing assumptions for this chapter:

(1) First, the politics of caste became legible as a *politics* in the context of colonial capitalism, and the specific forms of abstraction to which capitalist society gives rise. When I speak of social abstraction, I have in mind Marx's explanation of how the commodity form comes to stand in for social relations of exchange and exploitation, so that a critique of the social must necessarily proceed through a critique of political economy, and the idea of value. This is why the commodity form is so significant to Marx. In the form lies the "secret" to the organization of capitalist social relations and its potential critique. We could say that this structure of argumentation—the way that an analytics also functions as a politics—becomes available with the birth of political economic thinking, and the social abstraction on which it is based: the supplementarity of property and personhood. (Recall that Locke predicates personhood, having possession of oneself, on the model of property, or the right to alienate that portion of nature that has been improved by one's labor.) In this regard, Dalit literature succeeded in positing the link between personhood and property— a relationship that was crucial to the birth of modern subjectivity— *negatively* by forefronting degradation, humiliation, impoverishment and destitution as governing conditions of social life. For this reason Dalit literature is both a quintessentially modern form and amongst the most severe critics of modernity in its content.

(2) Second, the introduction of Marxism made it possible to rethink the materiality of caste in a new way, and this was essential to the aesthetic experimentation undertaken by Dalit cultural producers. Indeed, one

of the aims of this chapter is to explore how as Dalits began to theorize their own labor—R.B. Moré (1903–72), Annabhau Sathe (1920–69), Baburao Bagul (1930–2008) and Namdeo Dhasal (1949–2014) among others—the category of labor disappeared into the forms of its concrete manifestation and unfolding, in order to re-emerge as a form of "inhabitation". Dalits' struggles to revalorize stigmatized life also functioned as a practical critique of subaltern urbanity. It is this distinctive relationship between political concept and aesthetic practice that makes Dalit literature a practice of insurgent thought, and gives it an incendiary concreteness.

New Words for Old Worlds: Phule's *Satyashodh* and Practice of Anti-Caste Critique

In his important study of the impact of the commodification of agriculture on the 19th-century Deccan, Jairus Banaji (2011) argued that the subjugation of Indian small peasantry to the usury capital of Marwari and Gujarati merchants, as well as to a nascent capitalist class emerging from the big peasantry in the Deccan, was accomplished by repurposing prior modes of production such that they could perform in a different historical environment but nevertheless serve the requirements of surplus extraction. Essentially, peasant indebtedness to local moneylenders had alienated them from the means of production, and it could be argued that like the industrial proletariat, the peasant, too, was now working for a wage. Agrarian indebtedness, rather than a sign of backwardness, was the historically specific mode by which the peasant received a wage for his own reproduction, whether in the form of an advance on the crop to be delivered, or as a share of the crop. In essence, under conditions of colonial capitalism, peasant production for a global market coupled with his reliance on usurious loans for basic survival meant that the peasant has become dependent on the capitalist, that he had become a worker (Banaji 2011, pp. 308–309; see also Harootunian 2015).

The anti-caste activist Jotirao Phule (1827–90) describes this same world in vivid detail. His attention to agrarian distress as the combined outcome of native rent seeking and colonial surplus extraction is remarkable; so too his sensitivity to peasants enforced mobility, and the urban-rural linkages that structured the colonial economy of the time. He writes:

> In the past, those farmers who had very little land and could not survive on its produce, would go into the nearby forest and would gather wood, fruits and leaves . . . But now the cunning European employees of our honourable government have spent all their foreign and multifaceted intelligence to establish a massive Forest Department; including

all mountains and hills and valleys. . . . Now if they want to fill their bellies they [the poor farmers] have to work in the factories as weavers, iron-smiths or carpenters or as casual laborers. . . . [Because English artisans are selling machine produced goods here]. The goods produced here have lost their market, and many weavers and julahas and momins are so poor they are forced to near starvation.

(Phule 2002a, p. 132)

In *Gulamgiri*, Phule notes that the Indian peasant

has been in fact a proverbial Milch Cow . . . Those who successively held sway over him cared only to fatten themselves on the sweat of his brow, without caring for his welfare or condition. It was sufficient for their purposes that they held him safe in their clutches for squeezing out of him as much as they possibly could.

(Phule 2002b, p. 31)

Phule goes on to link agrarian distress with various states of transient and impoverished existence. He notes, "Many farmers who cannot subsist on their fields alone will leave home and become vagrant (*paraganda*), working for wages in a big city instead of starving" (Phule [1969] 1991, p. 242). The alienation of rural labor from its own labor-power is depicted in Phule's world by figures such as the moneylender, who index the commodification of social relations in a colonial economy.

Phule recognized that the material context of caste's transformation also carried the potential for immanent critique. Phule's painstaking descriptions delineate key aspects of the agrarian sensorium: in his writings he describes a world of routinized deprivation with specific attention to figures that embody vulnerability and impoverishment. His vignette about a day in the life of a farmer describes a scene of destitution that merges an account of deformed bodies with descriptions of a depleted, unhygienic environment: "The women's clothes are in tatters and they are forced to wear ancient bedsheets bought for marriage" (Phule 2002a, p. 159). Outside the house is a cattle shed, and near it a crude bathing shed: "Beyond, under the chafa tree, there are a few children dancing, half-naked, with all manner of stains on their bodies, noses running, sweating and stinking, playing with lumps of mud" (p. 159).

Not much later, a *pada* (poem) written by the president of the Bombay Shri Somavanshi Mitra Samaj (Association for Friends of the Somavanshi), Pandit Kondiram, a key exponent of *Satyashodak* ideology, drew on this same imagery to communicate the horrors of untouchability. In addition to wearing the black thread, Dalit Mahars could own no new clothes or jewelry. They dressed in clothes from corpses, wore iron jewelry, ate from broken clay pots and owned only "dogs and asses; rats and mice". They were dispossessed, shadowy figures reduced to begging and eating food unfit even for animals:

The [Mahars] condition is so deplorable, that they come begging
For the rotten food scraps that have been thrown to the cows[5]
Which even the cattle will not touch.
(Kondiram verse 4, quoted in Valangkar 1984)

Kondiram ends with the powerful image of Mahar children sitting on a dung heap, their bodies covered with ash, sores on their eyes, rags covering their buttocks, their stomachs "sunken and empty". Like Phule s excruciatingly detailed picture of the cultivator s life, Kondiram's attention to the wretched condition of the Mahars utilizes social description as a practice of (social) critique.

Anti-caste activists contended that *jatibhed* (caste division) was not merely a social arrangement, but a mode of thought, indeed a *social abstraction* along the lines of the property-personhood relation instituted by classical liberalism. Radical empiricism was the response: naming, description and the experimental practices of *satyashodh* (truth-seeking) were key to intellectual emancipation because they helped focalize the experience of injustice and indifference. In Phule's and Kondiram's resonant imagery, the exploitation of labor and the humiliated body of caste are collapsed into each other to produce figures of destitution. These figures would accrete new meaning over time, as the contexts of exploitation were transformed: what requires emphasis is the power of such word-images to convey the exploitative character of caste, and to signal the emergence of a (modern) critique of caste inequality.

Caste and Class: Marx in Maharashtra

In 1907, the newspaper *Dinbandhu* (Friend of the Impoverished), an organ of the working-class and lower-caste movement in western India, carried an important essay on the city as a space of transformed (caste) sociality.[6] The essay's anonymous author noted: "[In Bombay] we all drink water from the same tap, in hotels and Irani stores we sit at the same table and drink tea and eat bread and biscuits. On trains and steamboats we sit with our thighs and shoulders touching". Urban migration and urban infrastructure—especially everyday technologies of travel and communication that appeared to shrink, even obviate, social distance—provoked key transformations of lower caste and Dalit selfhood. Modern travel, "sitting with thighs and shoulders touching", obliterated caste distinctions because it was impossible to maintain caste taboos or regulate contact in public conveyances. However, these new spaces were also in constant danger of being overwhelmed by social pressure to reproduce caste distinctions through new technologies of spatial segregation.

The relationship between space and social difference was also politically consequential: it would expose Dalits to Marxism, which provided a critical language for challenging caste's dehumanizing effects. The chawls (tenements) of the Bombay City Improvement Trust (BCIT) and, later, of the Bombay Development Directorate (BDD; 1919–26) were important sites of Dalit activism at the time. These included marches and political processions of the Samata Sainik Dal (formed in 1924 by Dalit military pensioners to protect Ambedkar) and the first celebration of Ambedkar Jayanti (Ambedkar's Birthday) on the open grounds of the BDD chawls in 1933. Additionally, study circles were organized by Dalit Communists associated with the Delisle Road Friends' Circle; there were performances of Ambedkari *jalsa*, a form of pedagogic folk theatre, by the Scheduled Caste Federation (formed in 1942), and the offices of the Independent Labour Party and the Municipal Kamgar Sangh (Municipal Workers' Union) were established in the area. B.R. Ambedkar lived in a BCIT chawl until he moved to Dadar's middle-class Hindu Colony: almost all his organizational and publishing efforts were located in this area.

The area was also associated with an earlier phase of Dalit activism: struggles for public access; institutional initiatives by the Depressed Classes Mission, which started separate schools in response to Dalit students' continued inability to enter mixed government or government-aided schools; and activism of the Bombay Millhands Union, formed in 1894 by the non-Brahmin leader, N.M. Lokhande. Additionally, the area was home to nonconformist missionaries, and the non-denominational Hindu reformist organizations such as the Prarthana Samaj. The area had an historic association with anti-caste and anti-poverty activism, which rendered it amenable to working-class politics. The Dalit communist R.B. Moré began to conduct classes on Marxism and Leninism in this area during the 1930s in the *Lal Chawl* (Red Tenement) or Building Number 14 with communist leader S.V. Deshpande and three other comrades (Moré and Moré 2003, p. 15). The Delisle Road Friends Union was thus formed in an area historically associated with anti-caste and anti-poverty activism, but now focused on drawing Dalit young people into the working-class movement.

Caste and the Colonial City

R.B. Moré was born near Dapoli, in the Ratangiri District, famous for its long history of anti-caste thought and activism. Military pensioners from the Mahar and Chambhar castes had purchased land in Dapoli to create a unique community of financially empowered, educated Dalits in the region. Gopalbaba Valangkar, a radical Dalit thinker of the late 19th century and a direct associate of Jotirao Phule, resided there and played an important role in focalizing caste injustice. Moré s exposure to this anticaste protest tradition combined with his experience of caste exclusion had a powerful effect on him. A brilliant student, Moré had received a coveted scholarship to attend high school, yet was unable to take full advantage of the opportunity: he was educated while sitting on the school verandah to respect upper-caste sentiment regarding caste pollution, and writes of having exam papers flung at him while taking the entrance exam so caste Hindus could avoid physical contact.[7] He played a key role in organizing a local movement for public access to water tanks and government property, which was the inspiration behind the famous Mahad water *satyagrahas* of 1927 led by B.R Ambedkar. By 1930, he was a trade unionist, labor organizer and card-carrying member of the Communist Party. Though a lifelong member of the Communist Party, he was a consistent critic of its avoidance of the caste question: of caste's role in structuring hierarchical relations within the party and between the workers who were the target of its outreach.

The accounts of Moré's life—narrated in his words, and those of his son, Satyendra—illuminate a deeper conflict between the promise of Marxist emancipation, on the one hand, and communists reluctance to apprehend the complex roots of caste inequality on the other.[8] His anomalous role as a Dalit communist who was committed to a radical critique of caste hierarchy and class emancipation became evident in the late interwar period when Left and Ambedkarite politics parted ways, and episodic efforts at joint political action gave way to often violent conflict between supporters of Ambedkar and of Marx. However, Moré's account also counters the foreclosures of cultural nationalism, Stalinism and caste identitarianism; it takes us back to a time when Marxism was reinvigorated by caste radicalism, and vice versa.

Moré's account is as much about the city that enabled such political crossings and cross-fertilization as it is about the lives of Bombay s destitute and dispossessed. It is significant that R.B. Moré's narrative does not carry the impress of properly "political" categories of identity and identification: his account describes the peregrinations of an urban dandy, albeit an impoverished one, through the city of money and machines. As is well known, Bombay, more than any other subcontinental city, attracted large groups of people from across India. The spatial organization of Bombay's neighborhoods reflected both the cultural mixing that was responsible for Bombay's famed cosmopolitanism and the practices of spatial separation that had developed to demarcate communities by caste, region and religion: spatial proximity and regulated social contact were thus two sides of the same coin in this demographically dense city. Bombay's 19th-century expansion coincided with Dalit migration. Members of the Mahar caste formed the bulk of Dalits who came to Bombay seeking to escape exploitative caste relations, and to embrace new economic possibilities. By the turn of the 19th century—indeed between 1872 and 1881 alone—the number of Dalits in Bombay rose by about 66 percent. Dalits worked on the railways, in textile mills and colonial public works. The 1921 census noted that outcaste labor constituted 12 percent of the total workforce. Urban life and modern contexts of labor transformed outcaste identity by disembedding caste from rural contexts of caste servility, and re-inscribing it onto practices of social and spatial segregation. Caste's transformation was the result of broader social processes, including the commercialization of agriculture and the commodification of labor, which had enormous impact on western India at the turn of the century. Struggles over self-making, with roots in longer-term traditions of anti-caste protest, also took on a distinctively urban complexion with the sizeable migration of Dalits to Bombay. Thus urban experience did not neatly map onto material processes. Rather, Moré's account confirms urban outcastes' paradoxical experience of social emancipation and practices of segregation: we see the key role they played in the public and political culture of Bombay's working-class neighborhoods, and in imagining worker dignity and social equality, but we also witness their exclusion from those narratives and their distinctive struggles for dignity and self-respect.

R.B. Moré's narrative thus gains traction against the backdrop of a late colonial Bombay which saw the rise of popular nationalism, trade unionism and worker protest, and which became a key site for incubating B.R. Ambedkar's political projects. In particular, Moré's account suggests an important role for Dalits in the development of a popular or "vernacular Marxism" and the cultural forms through which it circulated. By linking R.B. Moré's life with the successes and failures of the Ambedkar movement and the Communist Party as these transitioned from late colonial into postcolonial politics, we also get a bird's-eye view of the social structure and political ideologies that governed the everyday life of Bombay's working poor.

Precarity and the Everyday

Moré's description of work and conscientization does not resemble "class formation" in the classical sense. Rather, the details of his life resemble Jacques Rancière's (1989) description of "the aleatory population of precarious workers" (p. 147). Moré's entry into wage labor is episodic—he works at the Seaman's Lodge collecting monies as a porter on the docks, and finally gets steady work at a munitions factory in Pune. These periods of waged work are interspersed by periods of activism back in Dapoli as well as in Bombay. This leads to extended periods of homelessness, when he is sleeping on park benches or taking shelter with friends and relatives. His married life, too, is marked by periods of economic uncertainty and precarious existence: unable to pay their rent, the family is put onto the streets while he remains "underground" due to the ban on the Communist Party during most of the late-colonial period. Satyendra Moré and R.B. Moré (2003) record an especially poignant account of the family sitting under Elphinstone Bridge in central Bombay on a handcart containing all their belongings, after they were evicted from their home. The upper-caste leadership of the Communist Party chances on the family in this desperate situation and expresses surprise at their visible poverty.

Moré's descriptions of labor are contiguous with his descriptions of life in the neighborhood, from visiting *tamasha* performances and frequenting the chawls where these socially disreputable performers lived, to smoking *bhang* (cannabis) and stealing to survive. An interesting account features "visiting" different restaurants where Moré and his friends order food and rush out before they are made to pay. In Moré's narrative precarity distinguishes Dalit life, and it is defined by the anxiety surrounding informal and episodic labor. Many anecdotes speak of waiting, waiting for work, waiting to become permanent or just waiting for something eventful to happen: this is a discourse of exhaustion and tiredness. Even the eventful politics of the 1920s and the 1930s make their appearance in Moré's book through an account of conscientization in Dalit and working-class neighborhoods; that is, through practices of everyday life.

Dalits, Labor and Dalit Labor

In his famous address at the Dalit Sahitya Sammelan of 1958, the performer Annabhau Sathe associated the invisibility of outcaste labor with the devaluation of labor more generally, and argued that Dalits' capacity for struggle and hardship, *kashta*, produced wealth: Dalits' labor, because it created the world, also made Dalits the *malaks*, or proprietors, of that world. In his famous words, "*Hi prithvi dalitanchya talahatavar tarleli ahe* (This world turns/dances to the Dalits tune)" (quoted in Gaikwad 2013, p. 1).

Sathe was from the Matang caste, historically associated with subaltern performative traditions, and known for his hard living and brilliant extempore performances. One of the three founders of the Lal Bavta Kalapathak (Red Flag Performing Troupe) Sathe had survived in the city by performing odd jobs before he was "discovered" by R.B. Moré via the Construction Workers' Union. Like Moré, Sathe was haunted by the Left's exclusion of Dalit worlds, so much so that he argued in 1958 for the necessity of a separate convention for Dalit literature. We know

Moré's lifelong commitment to Ambedkar was effectively prior to his entry into Left politics. Sathe dedicated his novel, *Fakira*, to Ambedkar, noting, *"Jag badal ghaluni ghav/Maz Sangun gela Bhimarao* (Bhimarao told me/Change the world by force)" (Sathe 1959). This is Ambedkar the audacious thinker who struggled with caste and class, stigma and labor as supplemental, yet incommensurable categories. For Ambedkar, as for Moré and Sathe, untouchability was ultimately a peculiar kind of body history: the recourse to terms such as class and labor ultimately forefronted the "difference" of caste, and the specificity of its social experience. The emancipatory potential of labor universalism created the possibility of Dalit utopia but simultaneously foreclosed it.

Like Phule and the *satyashodaks*, Moré, Sathe and the cultural producers who came after them combined street politics with a turn towards the word and its capacity for world making. If Phule had been inspired by accounts of radical republican thought, and American anti-slavery, it was Marx in the interwar period. Ambedkar's newspaper, *Janata* (1930–56), reprinted translations of "Wage, Labour, and Capital", as "Mol Mazuri Bhandval", from communist pamphlets well before this, and published Soviet social realism, especially Gorky's *Mother*, which attained iconic status. Meanwhile, the Independent Labour Party formed by Ambedkar in 1936 had explicitly argued for a caste-class critique, and mobilized workers in colonial public works (railways, trams, sanitation) who came from the Dalit castes. In this regard, the re-signification of caste through approximation with class (and colonial capitalism) is the story of a brief opening when interwar internationalism and colonial urbanism collided to engender powerful experiments in "vernacularizing" Marxist thought. The history of Dalit communism is a reminder of those possibilities and their powerful closures. These hidden histories would be resuscitated by the cultural production and activism of the 1970s and the formation of the Dalit Panthers.

Incendiary Speech and the Political Project of the Dalit Panthers

In June 1972, the newspapers *Navakal* and *Prajasattak* noted the formation of the Dalit Panthers under the leadership of Arjun Dangle (b. 1945), Namdeo Dhasal and J.V. Pawar. Another leader, Raja Dhale, had been politicized by the socialists' youth wing, the Yuvak Kranti Dal (Revolutionary Youth Movement) started in 1969. The Panthers, who expressed antagonism to the Republican Party of India (RPI), were vitriolic in their criticism of corrupt Dalit politicians and consistently challenged state violence. Their claims to self-representation and their anti-establishmentarianism also brought the Dalit Panthers into direct conflict with the Shiv Sena (Mane 1976).

A complex and highly politicized world of subaltern neighborhoods, Congress co-optation, and internal debate shaped Dalit politics in the 1970s. Urban expansion had produced an extended cityscape subject to informalization as efforts to shift the urban poor out to newly emerging suburbs along the Central Railway line intensified. Spaces of central Bombay marked by the history of Dalit activism and agitation now expanded to include areas such as Matunga Labour Camp, and the suburbs of Chembur, Ghatkopar, Vikhroli and Ulhasnagar: now this constituted the real and imagined boundaries of the "Dalit city".

Within a year, the Panthers had established 32 Bombay *chhavanis* of 25 members each, and by 1974 they had branches all over Maharashtra. *Chhavanis* were local groups that were largely autonomous, and the Panthers often announced impromptu meetings and *morchas* (processions) in progressive newspapers such as *Navashakti* and *Navakal* (Murugkar 1995, p. 79). Public meetings served as ecstatic commemorations and public affirmations of a despised and denigrated identity now redefined as political potentiality.

Ambedkar's complex legacy—his fraught engagement with Marx, and the proto-historicist engagement with Buddhism as ethics, and political philosophy—divided the Panthers between Buddhist and Marxist interpretations of Dalit history, the Dalit self, and conflict over the best strategy for Dalit emancipation. Supporters of Namdeo Dhasal were drawn to Marxism, while Buddhism—and an emphasis on the separate cultural and religious identity of Dalit Mahars predominated among the supporters of Raja Dhale. Dhale argued in *Dr Ambedkar and Revolution* that Ambedkar was a revolutionary leader whose greatness was evident in his political leadership and Buddhist conversion (Dhale 1976). Dhasal argued instead that Ambedkar's ideas had to be rendered adequate to changing historical circumstances and re-interpreted for the times. Firmly convinced of the material basis of caste exploitation, he wanted to recess Buddhist identity and form coalitions with the Left.[9] His support for the CPI (Communist Party of India) in the 1974 elections became the most visible bone of contention. Dhale warned against trusting the communists who were out to expand their political base by diverting Dalits from the fight against untouchability. As one Panther wrote: "There cannot be a merging of Ambedkarvad and Marxvad" (Dhamankar 1974, n.p.). Dhasal was thrown out of the unified Dalit Panther Party in October 1974.[10]

This extended discussion of the Dalit Panthers points to the inherent tension between a sociological analysis of Dalit *sahitya*'s origins on the one hand, and the measure of its literary challenge on the other. In the case of the latter, it is true that the specific potency of Dalit speech was related to the materiality of Dalit life and its identification with the life of the slum, *zhopadi*. However, this was no easy association between social location and social realism. Rather, slum life denoted a struggle for social recognition, an *aesthetic politics* that functioned as a challenge to the *labor theory of value* (and the aspiration for upward mobility exhibited by the majority of educated Dalits). In turn, it was the experimental nature of modern Dalit *sahitya*, its efforts to *disrupt* the association between (literary) form and (social) identity that was significant at the moment of its inception instead of the prevalent understanding of Dalit literature as giving "voice" to Dalit experience.

Forms of Life

Baburao Bagul's depictions of slum life in *Maran Svast Hot Ahe* (Death is Becoming Cheaper; Bagul 1980) present a space teeming with visual difference: the mob, or the lumpen proletariat here appear as so many life forms deformed, drunk, violent and violated, but also capable of giving "care" to others who are equally dispossessed and downtrodden. Here the "slum" achieves a sort of thick description and begins to exist as form of life. Unlike the sentimental critique of earlier Dalit poetics, Bagul's writing established him as a singular experimental voice whose literary writing underscored the unbearability of (caste) ethics (Jaaware 2012).

When the Marx and Engels's *Communist Manifesto* was translated by G. Adhikari, who had returned from Germany, as the *Communist Jahirnama* (Marx and Engels [1848] 1931), class was associated with the social experience of hardship through the use of terms such as *kashta* (hard work), *daridryata* (impoverishment, destitution), *bekar* (unemployed, worthless) and *bhukekangal* (pauperized). Class identity was also related to social forms such as the degraded Dalit classes, *dalit varga*, Pathans (popularly associated with the "flesh trade", moneylending, extortion and other parasitical activities that further impoverished working people) and the wild, rowdy *mavali*, identified with the communities of the hilly Sahyadri mountain range (and their traditions of banditry and guerrilla warfare). Each of these was imprecisely identified with class and constituted something like an excessively dispossessed multitude rather than a proletariat class per se.

Bagul certainly drew on these kinds of description and elaborated on them in his own writings. While the (Marathi) translation of class had recourse to an ethical discourse of exploitation (and its visual staging) in the *Jahirnama*, Bagul appears to have extended those descriptions in the interest of creating a social world teeming with figures for whom class exploitation, caste humiliation and gendered violence exist as social facts of daily life: the association between *Dalit* as a caste identity and *dalit*-ness as a general condition of abjection and destitution of slum living appears fungible, as if the Dalit perspective was a form of empathetic identification with all those wretched and destitute lives that testified to the city's cruel 20th-century history of industrialization and urbanization.

By then, familiarity with African-American literature was as important as Bagul's exposure to Dalit Marxism. One of the founding members of the journal *Asmita*, M.N. Wankhede, professor of English at Milind College (Aurangabad), was among 14 students selected by Ambedkar in 1953 to receive a scholarship and go abroad for further study. Wankhede was unable to go abroad at the time, but he did go as a Fulbright Fellow later, completed a Masters degree at Indiana University (1962) and received a PhD in English from the University of Florida-Gainesville (1965). Wankhede was exposed to the African-American literary canon, beginning with Stowe s *Uncle Tom's Cabin*, and the works of Richard Wright, James Baldwin and LeRoi Jones, and argued that they ought to be a significant source of inspiration for Dalit writers.[11]

African-American literature inspired the emergence of a self-conscious Dalit literature in the period, but other trends were also visible. The Dalit Sahitya Sangh, which focused on recovering early Dalit cultural history as the predecessor to contemporary Dalit literature, incubated young writers like Raja Dhale (see Bansode *et al.* 1963; Waghmare 1959). The Siddharth Sahitya Sangh, formed in 1950, comprised students who lived in the hostel of Siddharth College. Other writers traced their genealogy back to the Pragati Sahitya Sabha, which had a presence in the Matunga Labour Camp area. Baburao Bagul, and the key publisher of Dalit and radical literature V.V. Bhatt of Abhinav Prakashan, were both associated with this group. It is from these early literary associations that writers began moving into the experimental orbit of little magazines, contributed to *Asmita* (later *Asmitadarsh*) and then went on to publish independent collections of prose and poetry once Dalit *sahitya* became marketable. Indeed, upper-caste progressive writers associated with the Little Magazine movement (and with trends in Marathi modernism)—writers like Dilip Chitre, Satish Kalshekar and Narayan Athavale—publicized Dalit writing and created a reading public for whom proximity to subaltern urbanism was increasingly mediated through (male) Dalit writers.

In Conclusion

Dalit *sahitya* was born out of diverse practices of "worlding": what remained constant across its long and creative journey was the manner by which caste and capital came together at distinct moments to enable modes of representation that privileged the materiality of urban existence. The literary qualities of Dalit writing surely require engagement on their own terms albeit through a genealogy of aesthetic experiment in Marathi literature. However, the focus of this chapter has been different: to place the urban condition and colonial capital as mutually entailed, significant aspects of the concrete writing, and depiction of a violent everyday that distinguishes the force and power of Dalit writing. Forms of description and figures of deprivation with a long genealogy in the anti-caste repertoire were repurposed, one might say, in the interest of a political ethics that spoke on behalf of the urban disenfranchised who demanded to be seen and recognized on their own terms as so many forms of life whose strange, deformed multiplicity indicted hegemonic social structures. By politicizing everyday life, Dalit writing also managed to claim Bombay as Dalit Bombay.

Notes

1. No potential conflict of interest was reported by the author.
2. Columbia University, U.S.A.
3. Namdeo Dhasal's political autobiography, *Ambedkari Chalval Ani Socialist, Communist* (Ambedkar Movement and Socialists, Communists; Dhasal 1981) presents an account of his engagement with the two parties and their ideologies. He is quoted as saying: "These are my people—these lumpen; I am one of them. My poetry is about life here" (Dhasal and Chitre 2007, 162).
4. Details of Dhasal s life are taken from his account, "Dalit Pantherchi Ganagaulan" (Dhasal 1974), and Dilip Chitre,"Namdeo's Mumbai, in *Namdeo Dhasal: Poet of the Underworld* (Dhasal and Chitre 2007, 149–180).
5. Literally, "thrown into the cow shed".
6. *Dinbandhu*, which began publication in 1877, was associated with Phule's *Satyashodak Samaj*. *Dinbandhu*'s focus shifted to the social experience of urbanity and the problems of industrial labor when Narayan Meghaji Lokhande, founder of the Bombay Millhands Association, took over the newspaper's publication in 1880.
7. I have argued elsewhere (Rao 2009, chapter 1) that the *verandah* was a colonial technology of segregation that responded to new juridical demands for equal access, even as these were redefined to accommodate caste prejudice.
8. The production of this autobiography is both complex and interesting. R.B. Moré stands at the head of a "red family" that stretches across three generations; each generation has had a hand in shaping his life narrative. Moré's son, Satyendra, completed the narrative of the father's life. The recognizable genre of communist hagiography intervenes, albeit with a twist. Satyendra underscores Moré's personal sacrifices and selfless dedication, and works within a recognizable narrative tradition that conflates activists lives and party history. Yet Satyendra Moré cannot help but emphasize R.B. Moré's decision to maintain extensive contact with the Ambedkarite movement, even after he joined the Communist Party and Moré's criticism of the communists evasion of the caste question. Satyendra Moré's act of memorialization is thus a severe indictment of the political exclusions that structure the divide between heterodox histories of political emancipation, on the one hand, and its subsequent "flattening" and homogenization, on the other. Meanwhile, Moré's grandson, Subodh, a tireless researcher in his own right, combined the Marathi autobiography, S. Moré's biography and primary material (comprising photographs and journal covers) in order to locate R.B. Moré in his many worlds: as a link

figure between broader worlds of Dalit protest and activism that predated him, and as a key actor in shaping Dalit Bombay.
9. Dhale and Dhasal were initially associated with communists and socialists respectively; their first formulations of the Dalit was in materialist terms. Many scholars and activists associated with the Left believed that the Panthers had radicalized Dalit politics with their "total critique" and that "[i]f there had been an autonomous, grass-roots Dalit leadership, then the seeds of revolution would have sprouted amongst the Panthers" (Omvedt 1979, 58).
10. *Blitz* carried news of the Panther split on July 20, 1974, then *Maratha* on July 23, 1974.
11. *Prabuddha Bharat*, "*Dalitano Vidrohi Vangmaya Liha* (Dalits Should Write Revolutionary Literature)". Wankhede's exhortations to Dalit writers to emulate this radical literary tradition also provoked a split between Wankhede and Gangadhar Pantawane on the editorial board of *Asmita*.

References

Bagul, Baburao (1980) *Maran Swasta Hot Ahe.* 2nd ed. Pune: Continental Prakashan.
Banaji, Jairus (2011) *Theory as History: Essays on Modes of Production and Exploitation.* Chicago: Haymarket Books.
Bansode, Hira, Janardhan Waghmare, Bhausaheb Adsul, and Appa Ranpise, eds. (1963) *Nave Kshitij* [New Horizons]. Bombay: Pragnya Prakshan, Maharashtra Bauddha Sahitya Parishad.
Beckert, Sven (2014) *Empire of Cotton.* New York: Knopf.
Dhale, Raja (1976) *Dr. Ambedkar and Revolution.* Bombay: Mohan Mudranalaya.
Dhamankar, Vasant. 1974. *Gair Republican Pudhari, Bichari Paddalit Janata, ani Dalit Panther* [False Republican Leaders, The Unfortunate Dalit Masses, and the Dalit Panthers]. n.p.
Dhasal, Namdeo (1972) *Golpitha.* Bombay: Lokvangmaya Griha Pvt.
Dhasal, Namdeo (1974) *Dalit Pantherchi Ganagaulan* [The Dalit Panther's Call. ganagaulan is lit. invocation]. Abakadai: Divali Ank.
Dhasal, Namdeo (1981) *Ambedkari Chalval Ani Socialist/Communist* [The Ambedkar Movement, Communists, and Socialists]. Bombay: Ambedkar Prabodhini.
Dhasal, Namdeo, and Dilip Chitre (2007) *Namdeo Dhasal, Poet of the Underworld: Poems, 1972 2006.* Pondicherry: Navayana.
Gaikwad, B. N. (2013) "Manifestation of Caste and Class in Anna Bhau Sathe's *Fakira* and Baburao Bagul's *Jenvha Mi Jaat Chorli Hoti*". *The Criterion: An International Journal in English* 12: 1–7. www.the-criterion.com/V4/n1/Baliram.pdf
Harootunian, Harry (2015) *Marx After Marx.* New York: Columbia University Press.
Hazareesingh, Sandip (2007) Chasing Commodities over the Surface of the Globe. "*Ferguson Centre for African and Asian Studies*, The Open University. Commodities of Empire Working Paper No. 1. www.open.ac.uk/Arts/ferguson-centre/commodities-of-empire/working-papers/WP01.pdf
Jaaware, Aniket (2012) *Destitute Literature: The First Annual Jotirao Phule Oration.* Mumbai: University of Mumbai.
Mane, Lakshman (1976) "Dalitanchya Bhashanache Bhandval [The Value of Dalit Discourse]." *Maharashtra Times*, June 14.

Marx, Karl, and Friedrich Engels. [1848] (1931) *Communist Jahirnama (The Communist Manifesto)*. Translated by G. Adhikari. Bombay: Kamgaar Vangmaya Prasarak Mandal.

Moré, R. B., and Moré, Satyendra (2003) *R.B. Moré: Dalit va Communist Calvalicha Sashaktha Duva* [Comrade R. B. Moré: A Powerful Link Between the Dalit and Communist Movements]. Mumbai: Paryay Prakashan.

Murugkar, Lata (1995) *Dalit Panther Chalval* [The Dalit Panther Movement]. Pune: Sugawa Prakashan.

Omvedt, Gail (1979) "Varga Ladha Ki Jati Yuddha [Class Struggle or Caste War]." *Kranti Jyoti* 2 (10–12): 58.

Phule, Jotirao [1969] (1991) "Shetkaryacha Asud [Cultivator s Whipcord]." In *Samagra Vangmay: Mahatma Phule Samagra Vangmay* [Collected Works of Mahatma Jotirao Phule], edited by Dhananjay Keer S. G. Malshe, and Y. D. Phadke, 2nd ed. Mumbai: Mumbai Rajya Sahitya ani Samskriti Mandal.

Phule, Jotirao (2002a) "Cultivator s Whipcord." Translated by Aniket Jaaware. In *Selected Writings of Jotirao Phule*, edited by G. P. Deshpande. New Delhi: Leftword Books.

Phule, Jotirao (2002b) *Slavery. Selected Writings of Jotirao Phule*. Translated by Maya Pandit and edited by G. P. Deshpande. New Delhi: Leftword Books.

Rancière, Jacques (1989) *The Nights of Labor: The Workers Dream in Nineteenth-century France*. Philadelphia, PA: Temple University Press.

Rao, Anupama (2009) *The Caste Question: Dalits and the Politics of Modern India*. Berkeley, CA: University of California Press.

Sathe, Annabhau (1959) *Fakira*. Pune: Surya Agency.

Valangkar, G. B. (1984) "*Anarya Dosh Pariharak Mandali: Petition to His Excellency the Commander-in-Chief of Bombay Presidency in Poona, July 1984*" *(Marathi)* [Petition to his Excellency, the Commander-in-Chief of Bombay, July 1894, on behalf of the Society to Redress the Condition of the Non-Aryans]. Khairmode Collection, Bombay University.

Waghmare, Janardhan (1959) *Loksahityacha Nava Drishtikon* [New Perspectives in Folklore]. Worli: Maharashtra Dalit Sahitya Sangh.

6 Casteocracy

A Millennium Standard of Merit and Tests

Suraj Yengde[1]

Snacking on the freshly baked bread that was still hot with creamy butter, I found myself surrounded by fellow Indians—mostly students—at a dinner sponsored by the South Asian Studies Department at Harvard at Cambridge's exotic restaurant, Harvest. I arrive a tad late, so I greet everyone at the dinner table and introduce myself. There is a warmth of spring air at the gathering. Tarun Khanna, the director, invites me to a chair next to him. As we engage in conversations with our neighbors Tarun intervenes, "Why don't we each introduce", pointing to the person next to me indicating that she should begin. After the introductions, we establish reasons for people to be there at that particular dinner. It is random! Orders are served. Winery and booze entertain the conversation.

Two hours in, biting the juicy, tender lamb steak, I pose a question to the students—freshman, sophomore and some graduates—as to why do they think they are selected for Harvard, or rather, why did you select Harvard? For the earlier question, everyone is baffled but certainly not unprepared. Many are cautious but equipped to answer. And for the second question, the answer was simple. They had applied to multiple institutions, including Harvard, and they had Harvard as their first option. As we dug deep, it came to the realization that, notwithstanding their individualized, test-inspired, "marked" merit, they also brought to Harvard what Harvard desperately needed—diversity. Diversity of color, nationality, gender, sexuality, class, talent, lived-experiences, people with disabilities, among others.

In this chapter, I will concentrate on various aspects of merit-making by arguing that its original idea of individual achievement in a collective environment is being discounted to advance certain misapprehended notions of merit disguised as talent. This concept was once looked down upon as making a bourgeois, aristocratic elite who then claimed ownership of the bureaucratic and monarchial entitlements. In the rapacious strides against any form of inheritance acting as virtue, middle-class society is fed into acknowledging the virtues of "merits" as it portends a view of "earning"

DOI: 10.4324/9781003155065-6

something, as opposed to the inheritance of "caste" feeding into the structure of casteocracy.

Talent and Merit

Michael Young, a British sociologist and Labor Party activist, coined the term "meritocracy" in his book *The Rise of the Meritocracy 1870–2033 An Essay on Education and Equality*[2] to vilify the growing assertion of the aristocratic class into the British social order. By critiquing the evolving methods of testing and grading, which defined merit, Young observed that the calculation of one's success through the narrow yardstick of civil service-oriented results was insufficient. This, he argued, was breaking the traditional codes of nepotism and plutocracy of wealth by the emergence of meritocracy of talent. Is this the case? Young's work spoke to the growing resistance in the society that separated the students of the elites with the rest in regard to access to education.

Author of the bestselling *The Meritocracy Trap*,[3] Daniel Markovits argues that meritocracy breeds new aristocracy. Instead of being a fascination of the non-elite to pull their bootstraps, meritocracy is a kernel of "concentrated advantage and toxic inequalities", argues Markovits. The notion that opportunities develop from one's toil doesn't fully expand to include the pain of the laborer who is undergoing the process of producing value. It becomes an unnecessary competition weighing on the welfare and personal development of the trapped, meritocratic subject.

The rise of an elite class that was deemed to be talented—under the arbitrary qualifiers of "talent"—received the cold shoulder. T S Eliot commented that, if talent is prioritized, then it would "disorganize society and debase education". Some looked at it as a religious conspiracy, a model "invented by Jews for the advancement of Jews", observed Cambridge scholar Edward Welbourne. Some argued that the emphasis on talent was just another method to nest the children of privileged parents.[4]

Casteocracy

Following meritocracy came a phase of "testocracy", a term coined by an African American Harvard Law professor, Lani Guinier, in her provocative *The Tyranny of Meritocracy Democratizing Higher Education in America*, which states that testocracy is an aristocracy in action. A "twenty-first century cult of standardized, quantifiable merit, (that) values perfect scores but ignores character".[5] Extreme competitiveness has put the notion of "entitlement" into the very foundations of a meritocratic society that privileges individualized merit over the manifold hands that remain invisible in the individual-centric celebration of achievements.

This chapter will give an overview of the concepts of meritocracy and testocracy by looking at the case of casteocracy that is global yet a millennium phenomenon. Casteocracy carries in itself important histories of greater depth and lived experiences of the present that is burdened with felt-past. So far, the idea of merit and test was promoted and critiqued as a shallow predicament of societal developments. By overlooking caste classifications in societies, the analysis thus far has fallen short of calling it out loud and invariably has maintained a silence on casteocracy.

Casteocracy, like meritocracy, is a mixture of two languages, to give the condition a proper sense. Meritocracy was a mashup of Latin and Greek words.[6] Similarly, casteocracy advances on the terminology given by the Portuguese and Greek words. Casteocracy is the advancement of inherited caste privilege without competing in the equally distributive merit market. It is a strategic move of the oppressive elite whose accumulation of wealth is conditioned upon the oppressed labor and hard-earned capital of the oppressed castes gathered over 3,800 years. Due to the imposed caste injunctions, the exploited wealth remained unaccounted for in the feudal and religiously ordained caste structures.

The Ruling of the Meritocracy

Young, in his chapter "Rich and Money, Merit Money", declared that the "Castes and classes are universal".[7] In the introduction, he observed that castes could not cohere with development. Britain had to do away with the caste society because, "if it had to survive as a great nation, in comparison with others, in the international competition" it had to go otherwise.[8] Thus, the inherited prevalence of certain jobs was now decided by merit.

The question of merit provided stabilities in various degrees. Citing the example of the British model, Young observed that there was a phenomenon of earned and unearned income—unearned income being inheritance. Taxing such incomes by the state settled the most important aspect and, through this, the "root of this criticism was cut away".[9] This led to the belief that few members of the lower classes had any objection because the formula was simple: if you win, you land a good job after fighting your way up in the tremendously unwelcoming and unfavorable educational system, and in return you receive a huge salary. If this formula is followed, then probably you deserved it. This right to self-achievement and ownership of the discourse as *deserving* in a free market still persists in the minds of the people.

The concept that Young designed is now in circulation to his "disappointment". In a *Guardian* newspaper article aptly titled "Down with meritocracy", Young expressed his apathy over the deployment of meritocracy by the ruling elite that was now subverted from the original meaning to suit the convenience of the elite.[10] The concept of "merit rating", Young observed, was a measurement of comparisons of one job with the another.

One fact that remains still in meritocratic society is the post-1870s phenomenon wherein compulsory education meant competitive civil service entry. This facilitated the idea of education's relation to competitiveness over few coveted jobs and the status it brought. However, the distribution of jobs is now hardened by the factors of education. Education paves a way for maintaining the status quo. The purpose of education seems to be subversive too. Young observes that, by involving the general public in the models of education, it has become a public norm to assign an "approval on the minority" to rule and govern.[11]

Appointments on the basis of "merit" merits the ideated norm of belonging and non-belonging. The ones who pass the tests harden into a social class that acts against the one who is not appointed or selected. The "unselected ones"—i.e. the majority—vanish out of the picture and memory. This same selection should have been a catalyst to harness potential leaders of each class, meaning equal representation. Instead, it facilitates the reality of excluding the many. The social revolution of this order brought education's position into the "narrow band of values". This meant the governance of the "selected" class is undisputed and largely under its command and control. It further emboldens it by reproducing. Thus, the phenomenon of meritocracy along with aristocracy paves a way for undisputed governance of the elite. Civil services equated with merit continue to fall short time and again with an overwhelming emphasis on the quest for talent. This is evident with the growing bureaucrat-controlled organizations. The European Union, for example, is the epitome of such a situation that warrants unelected children of the elite to decide for the rest of the "unselected" ones.

To emulate the elitism of the ruling classes in India, many candidates of the 1.1 million appear to the civil service tests, only to prove that they are not less than anyone.[12] As if this is the only test that defines one's character. There is little scope to expose the major part of corruption that is rooted in the process of finding merit and talent. The Kafkaseque model of democracy relies on bureaucracy to treat individuals as commodity manufacturing units where cumbersome procedures and unending processes dominate the life of a human being.

A visit to any government-controlled department will reveal the depressing space of shared animosity and discordance in the red tape model of governance.[13] Civility is inverted to diminish the fluidity of movement in the government edifice. By converting the people into citizens, the government then makes itself an absolute arbiter of its citizens. This helps the government to keep its people in check; and secondly, it controls its actions and manipulates the functions.

We have now come to a stage of casteocracy which upholds histori-cal/traditional elitism with an admixture of testocracy and meritocracy. Casteocracy dovetails with the impacts of the measures of the merit-oriented bureaucratic set-up along with test-centered quality-testing meth-ods. Reviewing the impacts of such a disturbed order that is maintained, encouraged and promoted to stabilize the destabilized caste habitus, I prof-fer critical analysis of the Indian model that has been and is increasingly asserted into the casteocratic tendencies without acknowledging its over-whelming presence.

The Selection of Testocracy

The present age is a prodigy of meritocracy that is testocracy. Lani Guinier, in her landmark work *The Tyranny of Meritocracy*, put forth this vision. Guinier observed the undercurrents that took us from the suffocating ideal of Young's meritocracy to the current age of testocracy, a grim picture of ungrateful narcissists who are rewarded for their arrogance.

Testocracy, as Guinier puts it, teaches cocky boys—and, we may add, girls—to "internalize success and to take personal credit for the trap-pings of privilege, including the educational resources and networks of his college-educated parents".[14] In short individualized and individual-oriented achievement is considered as the measurement of success. The phenomenon of reaching the finish line first by scoring the best grades and demonstrating one's capacity to acquire better grades gives more bragging rights.

The architecture of grading—meaning separating individuals on the basis of their "talent"—becomes a norm of measuring one's self. Society feels the need to establish itself with someone else. It does not have the confidence to measure through individual character. It always relies on the other's inability or lack of capacity to organize the relationship. The demo-cratic charter doesn't feature in establishing a neutral association.

In a globalized, competitive world, we are constantly trying to firm up our scores and grades and parade them as demonstrative of our personal-ity. This is departing from the ethical standard of education, which is to develop character and instill wisdom and humility. In the market-driven economy, the race to acquire the best is a norm. Getting into better-paying jobs by having a certain diploma or degree acts as a decider of one's fate for the rest of one's life. This all begins with the testing machinery that grades the individual talent in scores, which are then utilized to grant access to specific institutions and organizations, which eventually translates into entitlements. This is acknowledged and granted by the general public and everyone around. The purpose of education has evolved into fixed com-petitions to show how one is more incapable than the other. The scheme of competitive testing is to drive one set of pre-destined, privileged kids to reaffirm their position. As a consequence, "merit" is guarded as a defense. The quality of tests and their grading system is not challenged. Instead, the working class and underprivileged caste parents are forced to fit their children into the caricature of mythical merit. Of the many millions, a handful make it through. These handfuls are considered as the best of the rest. In this competition, the ones who could not make it are termed outrightly as "the failures". This imprints a lifelong stigma in the mind of the child. Society commits such gross violence without adequately taking notice of it. The few who make it through the caricature are not necessarily smarter than the rest. One can notice this in the testimonies of success stories. Many reiterate that they are the same as other people and not extraordinary. By "selecting" them into coveted positions, the system manages to showcase the myth of the egalitarian mission of education. This handful of representatives serve as the poster boys and girls for the education mafias or the elites of the society to impinge upon the undemocratic merit set-up. In such a merit-based system, students are forced to excel into something that is not taught to them and neither is it tutored adequately. More importantly, these testing methods are dissociated from student's social and personal life. Students are made to face an oppressive and fear-mongering regime of such testocratic merit in India that they have to perform and behave in certain avatars that is not the representation of their true character.

In order to survive the cobweb of a complex education system, parents force their children through the hurricane of prep schools, tuitions and coaching centers ahead of time. Their fate is decided in a three-hour, life-deciding test. One has to gamble the future in those doomsayer three hours. Rather than focusing on the educational experiences in the college, test-based methods pass on as secret codes of the ruling elite—and these eventually become the "accurate reflectors of wealth".[15] The success of a student is defined by the amount of wealth acquired or the position one is escalated to.

The case study of education in India that is driven by admissions is based on undemocratic merit—i.e. casteocratic merit. There is little hope to develop moral models in society. If the test-centered caste-class-focused exams were anything but an indicator to demonstrate failure, then we have ample evidence to see the demurral of society. The selected few elites carry no archetype of being the leaders of ethical character. The rampant corruption, failed policies, nepotism, and reproduction of elitism is what underscores the phenomenon of casteocracy. "Periyar" EV Ramaswamy, the *shudra* anti-caste reformer from Tamil Nadu, commented on the idea of separate tests (which are apart from the regular exams) being used to prove the ability and merit of the pupil as a coarse strategy to exclude the backward and scheduled caste students. These strategies, Periyar commented, were "cumbersome, unjust an unwanted practice created by Brahmins".[16]

In another article titled *Why Brahmins Hate Reservation?* Periyar lays out the categorical arguments of Brahmins' quest against equality given to backward classes. He subverts the regulating narratives of Brahmins who look down upon the backward classes as "job hunters". Periyar sees no wrong in hunting for a job. It is the Brahmins who hunt for the jobs, but when it comes to the realization of the distribution of jobs to the backward and scheduled castes, Periyar notices a Brahmin conspiracy in demeaning the work aspirations among the educated subaltern youth. Hence, aspirations are subverted as "hunters"—scavengers of sorts—undermine the equal representation call of the backward classes.[17]

Periyar declared that merit and efficiency could be found among all the people. He promoted reservation policies in proportion to the total population. So much was his reliance on proportional representation that he often lamented the overrepresentation of 3% Brahmins in all the faculties of Indian life—in particular, his concern was public services where reservation policy was being hotly debated. He had quit the Congress party over its indifference toward communal representation for Dravidians in public services.

Tests in Caste Guise

Testocracy builds upon the notion that the idea of merit is now a settled fact. It is considered as the most essential part of a developing society. Thus, the normalizing of such merit has turned us to looking for test-based qualities. This essentially is a monopolistic reservoir of the privileged and elites of our society. Therefore, certain amounts of tests as qualifiers to decide a student's fate has upended the purpose of education, which was to nurture the community and not produce an idiosyncratic *personal*. Guinier comments that such testocratic merit prizes "production and reproduction of privilege but without shame or obligation".[18]

There is an evasion from the political and moral accountability if viewed through the lens of merit. Merit begets entitlements. Entitlement becomes vital to ascertain one's responsibility to society. For as long as entitlements soothe the power hunger of the "cocky boys" and girls, there remains a fundamental gap in accountability that risks the rise of rampant corruption.[19] The elites who have no accountability to the society they live in have very little investment in paying back society. This radically alters the original meaning and purpose of merit.

However, with the marginalized groups, we find differing experiences. In the case study of African American students who got admitted to schools, it was observed that these students often took responsibilities of their community. Many students in this category turned out to become leaders in their communities and representatives of their cause in business and social sectors. We do not yet have a detailed study of the contribution of the Dalit students to society.

The tests, too, do not measure the smartness of students, and they disregard the immense cultural, economic and, most importantly, family factors. Guinier quotes a study by economist Rothstein Jesse, which states that the SAT is a common qualifier as a reasoning test that only indicates how students cope in the first year of their college program. These tests do not have the capacity to predict the future performances of the students. This essentially brings a rude and disgraced behavior among the breed of graduates who harbor the feeling of deservingness, which is to negatively ascribe their primary and sole ownership, all the while remaining unaccountable to the unpredictable future.

The SAT-oriented model is also an assumption-based strategy which is based on hunches. The entrance exams and multiple-choice questions are given to select the right answer from a misleading set of options and opinions. You cannot guarantee the selection of talent and merit by selecting the right answer. After all, what is right is not right unless it is proven right. President of the Bard College Botstein, in his widely popular article in the *Times* magazine, pointed out the limitations of the SAT as "a bizarre relic of long outdated twentieth century" assumptions. He continued, "As every adult recognizes, knowing something or how to do something in real life is never defined by being able to choose a 'right' answer from a set of possible answers (some of them intentionally misleading) *put forward by faceless test designers who are rarely eminent experts.* No scientist, engineer, writer, psychologist, artist, or physician—and certainly no scholar, and therefore no serious university faculty member—pursues his or her vocation by getting right answers from a set of prescribed alternatives that trivialize complexity and ambiguity" (emphasis mine).[20]

The SAT-like entrance exams in India are the "near monopoly on tests".[21] Botstein charges these tests as violating the basic justification of tests. Many a time, it is not the educational curriculum that is tested in these tests. It is not judging the student's capacity to develop and contribute to their field. If it was, it still remains an unfair test. Because schooling is a method of developing the necessary skills so the person can eventually contribute to the field. If one is already armed with skills and is aware of its utility, then that person does not deserve to be in school, because one is already aware of the knowledge. However, in the current system, entrance exams are just mandates that do not necessarily invest in developing the amateur student's curiosity; rather, they are quick to assimilate the test-proven, merit-driven wealthy, dominant-caste students.

It is also a moneyed business. The coaching institutes and pre-coaching classes prey on their vulnerable subjects. The entrance exam fiasco in India is becoming a solution for the ruling elite because it became a norm to compete under certain circumstances—which is to go to expensive private classes, hire a tutor, go to summer schools, attend overseas seminars and conferences and connect with the professors at private events through unbreakable caste networks. This separates the dominant-caste students from their peers of non-privileged backgrounds. The entrance exam then becomes the right of the elites to claim their undefeated and unchallenged position through self-defined "merit". These entrance exams go further by disparaging the quality of a student that is determined by the status of merit, which gestalts from aspects of smartness and talent. Therefore, admitting students into certain colleges and into certain institutions does not suggest that they deserve but just that they can manufacture the norm of merit. If *Indian Institute of Managements* (IIMs) and Indian Institute of Technology (IITs)—the elite colleges of India, for example—are any indication, then the formation of test-oriented merit is nothing but a caste merit. The entrance exams are caste exams. The school tests are caste tests privileging the dominant and suppressing the oppressed. This can be better explained from the lack of caste diversity in the faculty positions at the 13 IIMs. Of the 642, four belonged to the Scheduled Castes while one belonged to the Scheduled Tribe.[22] Similarly, at the 23 IITs, of the total 8,856 faculty members, only 149 belonged to the Scheduled Castes and merely 21 to Scheduled Tribes.[23]

The pre-admission exams permitted the ruling elite to seek their self-centered goals without worrying about being charged for the corrupt practices of exclusion. This spate of workable conditions provided them an upper hand to pass as merit instead of non-merit. Thus, inadvertently, the phenomenon of testocracy became a solution "disguised as a meritocracy".[24] The tests now possess the monopoly over merit; Guinier calls it "unassailable merit", which means unquestioned and undefeated merit.[25]

Talent, or merit, is an unethical, inane moral choice that singularly relies on the idea of selections. This singularity of selection further fragments into the model of selectionism. The phenomenon is so normalized that it resurrects the models of the nepotism of aristocracy as the order of the day. The tests like SATs in the US or entrance tests in India, if they do not measure the aptitude and the quality of a student's capacity to cultivate talent, then they surely act as a test of caste merit riding as a first qualifier of casteocracy. It provides the upper hand for an already upwardly mobile section of the community. The aptitude tests that are based on some mathematical calculations and vocabularies cannot define and describe students' innate capacity to work together or judge their potential to create new innovation with independent thinking. The world's problems are not only complex ones that require working together, but they also have the potential to outlaw certain traditional, dogmatic values.[26] Thus, the incorporation of traditionally repressed groups would redefine the conceptions of merit-making and merit-seeking.

The Culture of Merit

In her extensive analysis, Guinier adds cultural dynamics to the competition-oriented model of education. She lays down the reports published by College Boards and the works of scholars on minority education. Guinier advances a concept called "stereotype threat", developed by an African American social psychologist, Claude Steele, in his book *Whistling Vivaldi: How Stereotypes Affect Us and What We Can Do.*[27]

In his searing analysis, Steele shows how a particular individual from a certain background is constantly living under the threat of certain imposed stereotypes perceived as truth. How, then, are such stereotypes internalized into someone's life at an early age? Take, for example, a Dalit or a tribal being told from childhood about the negative aspects of their being—that their physical features, their mental abilities and their social behaviors are unworthy. This pressure is so apparent that the person has to now behave according to the stereotype that s/he was casted into. If s/he transcends or attempts to upend that stereotype, it is mocked or laughed down by the society that imposes the gaze of its stereotype. Thus, the person living under such a constant and palpable stereotype threat is always following the perception of others about him or her. It is in this light that having to perform under these stereotypes puts the student's *ability* to work secondary, but his incapacity to *cope* becomes a primary factor. Therefore, if a test simply evaluates student's capacity by his/her ability to work and participate in the educational process, then the stereotyped children could outperform anyone who is not subjected to such a stereotypical threat.

Taking the example of the American college admission system, Guinier emphasizes the negative impact of the perpetual stereotype threat for African American or Mexican American groups, compared to other non-white ethnic groups in America. The first, second-generation immigrants with a professional and educated class background, arrive with already-set plans for the future and know the signals and hints for making their way into the system. They do not suffer the most important hindrance that other colored groups do, which is the issue of discrimination internalized as a stereotype threat. Therefore, Indians or any other ethnic groups who come to the US to study do not have that disadvantage. In addition, they perform in a system familiar to them. Many Indians/international students who go to schools in the US have gone to better, if not the best, schools in the US. They come from the "better off" families.[28]

Guinier passionately argues that we need to make a cultural and paradigm shift from meritocratic method to a democratic one. In the former, we get undisputed position and power, whereas in democracy, we get collective action that can be challenged and altered too.

Casteocratic Merit in Lieu of Dalit Merit

Presently, we are looking at the model of achievement as something that comes with prestige and free perks. In a casteocratic society, the normalizing of caste-based professional hierarchies is retained. The structure of vertical arrangement as a model of admiration and meritocratic superiority is held sacrosanct. Thus, caste diversities in professional hierarchies might have increased, but labor superiority is still tied to the Brahminical social order with a few at the top and most at the bottom falling into the rituals of Brahmins at the top with Dalits at the bottom.[29]

The casteocratic system essentially encourages people to replicate a system of aristocracy. It was aristocrats and bureaucrats who were at the helm of the exploitative colonial government in India. They imposed all sorts of punitive measures and oppressive mechanics to torture Indians. The selected few individuals empowered themselves through competitive-based examinations. Brahmins in India were the first to advocate for getting into the oppressive system of control—the bureaucracy.[30] Thus, the elite Indian Civil Service (ICS) that was opened to Indians in effect became a gate pass for the Brahmin to become ruling class. Brahmins worked full time to replicate the models of caste-based oppression. The subalterns and other non-elites are given hopes of becoming something that is apparently ridden with elitism and exclusion. Hence, an average student coming from meager resources and limited time is forced into becoming something better than the status quo. The hopes of the social classes are invested in gaining autonomy.

During my many engagements with Indian students in the US and India, I meet many such students avoiding the anchor of social responsibility. They wander about trying to make sense of their identity and living in the consciousness of doubleness, the Du Boisian notion of "twoness" operating within oneself.[31] In 2015, a child of a Dalit income tax commissioner attended a Dalit group solidarity camp, also known as cadre camps, over two days in New Jersey. Toward the end of the two days, she expressed her wish to leave. She acknowledged that she never felt the brunt of caste and the issues that we are discussing were not part of her lived reality. Hence, she did not feel like she belonged there.

This twoness can be observed among the upper echelons of selected Dalits. This twoness is wedded with apathy toward the stigmatized past as humiliation and promises of modernity as respect. When a sudden rise in the professional scale of respect is seen, the stigmatized Dalit body needs an assurance to sustain in the newfound space of reverence. Thus, to cope with the conditions set by the system, Dalit assertion is kept minimal. It only comes out when injustice is marked glaringly and other options of compromise are overtaken. Such thin tensions are negotiated regularly. There are no set boundaries or codes of conducting business, with a marked Dalit body being in the superior position.

A Dalit government official who had gotten into a top position in his department once tried to prove to me his merit. Even though he had achieved the desired status and had cleared one of India's rigorous examinations, this official wanted to show me his grades from his education in the UK. The test-inspired merit had put the subject in permanent doubt, even though they had assailed the boundaries of merit. It was possible due to the culture of casteocracy that normalizes violence upon the autonomous mind of a thinking Dalit. "It starts at the training center. We are marked and people discuss about our status. Unknowingly that sense of insecurity is inserted" said a senior Dalit officer currently working with the Andhra Pradesh government.

This weaves into the phenomenon of elitism that is a purveyor of the testocratic sensibility. It is the same elite group that sees continuance of their heritage through the regimen of banal methods of testing and selection. The emergence of test-oriented admission criteria was proposed by a New England Brahmin, Endicott Peabody, who, in the nineteenth century, encouraged this system that aimed to elevate his rich students to gain admissions into the "Big Three"—Harvard, Yale and Princeton. It was a system that favored the breed of protestant, Anglo Saxon students and was aimed at excluding the rest. As a result, unfamiliar, arbitrary methods of testing proved desirable to these groups. The extremely complex system of gaining access to education intends to discourage subalterns. This system was created to exclude those who did not belong to the categories of their desired nobles.[32]

The question then remains—why should private institutions worry about the public good? It is because private institutions are not solely run with private money and they are not entirely private after all. It is the state that takes care of providing subsidies, offering land at a cheaper rate, bank loans, and other amenities that come from public-funded tax dollars. Therefore, the possibility to obscure the role of public good and state accountability on the part of privately funded, wealthy institutions is a trapdoor for the elites. The private educational systems, after all, are not monopolies of primary ownership of the few. It is, rather, a publicly funded charity. All the Ivy League schools are registered as non-profits.[33] This non-profit status gives them immense benefits in tax exemptions and deductions. Due to its non-profit status, Harvard was able to build an endowment from

$4.7 billion in 1990 to $40.9 billion in 2020.[34] The National Association for College Admission Counseling (NACAC) notes that colleges and universities fall into three broad categories: public schools (state schools and community colleges), private non-profit schools, and for-profit schools (career colleges, often online universities).[35]

The Collectives Over Individualized Individuals

If you ask a student what they aspire to become at a certain age, they will have differing views. Many children who are socialized in a collective environment often choose to become construction workers, nurses, teachers, social activists, or travelers.

This demonstrates the fact that the children value the basics of satisfaction of working in a team. That is why, when they build Lego houses or mud forts, they nurture the feeling of complete composure as construction worker, or nurse when nursing their sick doll, or tutoring their students in an imaginative classrooms, disciplining their students as teachers, or experiencing the marvels of the world, becoming travelers or travel writers, or becoming a social activist, who likes to imagine the world as just and fight for the rights of their younger sibling when bullied.

Currently, we are living in a world where quick degrees with adequate training to outperform in a conflicted market of exploitation of every resource at one's disposal—human, natural, technological—is rewarded the most. The executives run the world and finance and insurance companies are bailed out by the governments. This overemphasis on the neoliberal framework that goes beyond one's innate capacity to develop a moral institution called universe is losing its grip while simultaneously disregarding spiritual sensitivities.

We are rewarding and lauding the individual-oriented society. Individuals of this society enter the professional world by trying to be someone else, which comes at a cost of losing their character and developing a breed of soul-less humankind. These are the ones who are trying to rush to grab a ladder-up rather than a ladder-lateral—which would allow for the distribution of the resources and welfare of all. The ladder-up scheming is effectively taking place in the elite schools that reward the students who value a culture of competitive education, private tuition, personal tutoring, constant support and emotional intelligence. Contrastingly, the student who comes from a humble caste-class background has to work out their life problems first—family, culture, money—while at the same time trying to make it into the intimidating, social-aversive society.

In a testocratic society, there are inordinate assumptions about that the candidates' worth, which is already judged by test scores. By overlooking the candidate's environment, this method rewards the already advantaged and suppresses the disadvantaged in casteocratic assumptions of social welfare.

Thus, in the individual as well as collective forms of learning, casteocracy overtakes these measures and negatively targets the talent of Dalit students. Group collaboration is seen as a form of democratic merit that nurtures values of democracy and individual spirit. Democratic merit looks at merit from the basics of education—i.e. providing equal opportunity of access and fostering more the ability to collaborate and contribute to the society than to satisfy their personal greed. The elites, due to their models of operation, define the purpose of their education as to rule and govern— one class upon the other.

The idea that there are losers and winners is a determined factoid of the society infested with sacred values of the market. Candidates with certain skill sets are told that they are less talented because they do not fit into the model invented by IQ test prejudices. Thus, the people who failed to pass the test of being talented were not only stigmatized as failures but bossed by someone else who says they *deserve* to be a failure. This has changed over the years and it has gone more leftward and rightward. Depending on one's status in society, people have acquired their position in meritocracy.

In a meritocracy and testocracy, there is an understanding of individualism, so there is a call to move toward collectivism. In casteocracy, however, it is the collective that becomes cardinal to one's ranking. However, in this collective working, the groupings act as a base for imposing collective violence by invoking merit as a criterion of distinction. In a study edited by Malone and Bernstein that examined the impact of working together which they referred to as "Collective Intelligence", they found the importance of thinking and working together for overall success.[36] We are trained to think and work using individuated techniques, thereby limiting our complete potential. We live in a world where we are asked to solve problems, and hence, the approach to problem-solving does not need unidimensional approach. If the unidimensional approach succeeds, irrespective of its limitations, it produces similar results that have been produced for generations. This offers no fresh perspective and certainly does not cater to the larger group, which is universal in result and global in method. The male-dominated circles of decision making, planning and executing sans women have hindered progress similarly. Another research on collective intelligence found that the presence of women in the group produced positive results.[37]

The Casteocracy Index in a Diversity of Merit

Anita Woolley et al. experimented by putting together a group of the smartest people and some with diversity of smartness. The results were striking, given our perceived notion that smart people working together might produce the smartest solutions.[38] Woolley et. al.'s study instead demonstrated that collective intelligence was better rewarded if there was diversity of talent. "Talent" here refers to the groups with lower and higher grades, different genders, and different class backgrounds, among others.

Scott Page, in his well-known book *The Difference: How the Power of Diversity Creates Better Groups, Firms, Schools, and Societies*, records that diversity of groups is an important indicator; however, it will only outperform the homogenous groups.[39] This limitation indicates that groups working together might sound like a win-win game but in the groupism, this might not necessarily be true. The group might generate a competitive spirit, which could be healthy to the working environment. However, on the other hand, if one is coming from strongly xenophobic group sensibilities of ingrained prejudices, it might impose harm on the other side. This is exactly what is seen around campuses. The Rohith Vemula incident was also about the strong groupism. One group against another group was inspired by its ideology to the extent of taking the other down. The dominant groups always look to the dominated world with their insecurities, thereby creating an environment of intimidation that poses a threat to their security.

On the questions of diversity, one needs to pay attention to the cultural factors of class while promoting diversity and inclusion. The people who fight for caste-based criteria are the foot soldiers who sacrifice their lower-paying jobs for the sake of preserving policy because they are the ones who are at the threshold of disaster and thus need the most. Contrastingly, the students who come from a well-to-do background supplemented with quality education easily fit into the pre-fixed models of tests of the ruling class. Inclusion and justice are traded here with "endogamous diversity" to the admissions and selections system.

Individual and collective talent is subjective. They develop and derail on many accounts. Individual intelligence grows with collective sensibilities. Currently, society values individual merit, as opposed to working in the collective as a team. The competitiveness of merit is usually tested on individuated labor as a measurement to showcase one's spirit.

Conclusion

Testocratic merit, Guinier observes, is dogmatic and reluctant to change. Dogmatic methods of testing do not necessarily arm students with the courage to be brave and test the methods of learning, experimenting and testing beyond the traditional codes of learning. This curtails the fresh approaches the student might take with an advanced knowledge.[40]

Casteocratic merit is a socially sanctioned principle of society that will not change with a change in dogmatic values. It has to be approached through subverting models of dogmatic virtues. The dogma of self-service seems to be causing the social health of society to fester. The capacities of the universities to produce active citizens who have the larger interests of humankind at heart appears to be working against the primary missions of schools.

Individuals are taught that merit is the final epiphany. It is static and almost everything is defined under its norm. Time and again, it is proven that merit is not static and can change over time; it can be "cultivated and not merely scored".[41] It requires proper training and accurate methods of teaching. Merit in its original sense was earned by service that was applauded by the community as a recognition of one's work toward the larger good. However, this concept came to be about one's individualized, worthy entitlements. Thus, we have debates concerning merit when, in fact, the larger social good is incorporative of merit. So, if the meaning of merit can change, then why not merit itself? Tests can only showcase one's performance in three hours of an exam-oriented structure, and casteocracy only privileges dominance, elitism and accumulated, traditional arrogance.

Market-driven corporate greed is seen penetrating into the minds of the testocratic generation. We see an increase in the growing count of the global elite that maintain a global meritocratic order. There needs a stronger alliance of non-elites that would counter anti-marginalized policies propagated by the exclusionary cocky boys. The global education system and the globalized commodities of education-led talent is proving disastrous to the egalitarian ethos of education as a learning system. Initiatives like the global affirmative action alliance or international moral equity programs led by anti-casteocratic, meritocratic believers could address some of these issues.

Note

1. Harvard University, U.S.A.
2. Young, Michael (1958) *The Rise of the Meritocracy 1870–2033 An Essay on Education and Equality.* London: Thames and Hudson.
3. Markovits, Daniel (2019) *The Meritocracy Trap: How America's Foundational Myth Feeds Inequality, Dismantles the Middle Class, and Devours the Elite.* New York: Penguin Press, 2019.
4. Special Report (2006) "Meritocracy and Its Discontents," *The Economist,* October 7, www.economist.com/node/7961962
5. Lani Guinier, Lani (2015) *The Tyranny of the Meritocracy Democratizing Higher Education in America.* Boston, MA: Beacon, p. ix
6. Reeves, Richard R. (2019) "Book Review: The Meritocracy Trap By Daniel Markovits", *Financial Times,* September 24, www.ft.com/content/907a775e-d306-11e9-8d46-8def889b4137
7. Young, p. 152.
8. Young, p. 14.

9. Young, p. 154.
10. Young, Michael (2001) "Down with Meritocracy", *The Guardian*, June 28, www.theguardian.com/politics/2001/jun/29/comment
11. Ibid.
12. "UPSC Exam: How Many Apply VS How Many Clear", *BYJU's*, https://byjus.com/free-ias-prep/upsc-exam-how-many-apply-vs-how-many-clear/
13. Gupta, Akhil (2012) *Red Tape Bureaucracy, Structural Violence, and Poverty in India*. Durham, NC: Duke University Press.
14. Guinier, Lani (2015) Op. Cit., p. x
15. Guinier, Lani (2015) Op. Cit., p. 11.
16. EVR, Periyar (2016) "Why Brahmins Hate Reservation?", In K Veeramni (ed.), *Collected Works of Periyar EVR*, pp. 271–272.
17. EVR, Periyar (2016), Op. Cit.
18. Guinier, Lani (2015) Op. Cit., p. xii.
19. Guinier, Lani (2015) Op. Cit., p. x.
20. Botstein, Leon (2014) "College President: SAT Is Part Hoax, Part Fraud", *Times*, March 7, p. 17.
21. Botstein, Leon (2014) Op. Cit.
22. Joshi, Siddharth and Malghan, Deepak (2018) "Why Are There Still Such Few SCs, STs and OBCs at IIMs?", *The Wire*, January 18, https://thewire.in/caste/iim-sc-st-obc-diversity; also see, Joshi, Siddharth and Malghan, Deepak (2017) Faculty Diversity at the Indian Institutes of Management (IIMs): A Preliminary Snapshot", *IIM Bangalore Research Paper No. 539*, https://papers.ssrn.com/sol3/papers.cfm?abstract_id=2921720
23. Sharma, Kritika (2019) "Diversity Deficit in IIMs, IITs—Just 23 STs and 157 SCs in 9,640 Faculty Posts", *The Print*, February 13, https://theprint.in/india/education/diversity-deficit-in-iims-iits-just-23-sts-and-157-scs-in-9640-faculty-posts/191246/
24. Guinier, Lani (2015) Op. Cit., p. 15.
25. Guinier, Lani (2015) Op. Cit., p. 17.
26. Reynolds, Alison and Lewis, David (2017) "Teams Solve Problems Faster When They're More Cognitively Diverse", *Harvard Business Review*, March 30.
27. Steele, Claude (2011) *Whistling Vivaldi: How Stereotypes Affect Us and What We Can Do*. New York: W.W. Norton & Co.
28. Guinier, Lani (2015) Op. Cit., p. 40.
29. Yengde, Suraj (2019) *Caste Matters*. Gurgaon: Penguin Random House.
30. Anil Seal's work covers the appeal and lobbying of Brahmins for their share in the colonial government. Seal, Anil (1968) *The Emergence of Indian Nationalism: Competition and Collaboration in the Later Nineteenth Century*. Cambridge: Cambridge University Press. In addition to this, there are historical works that demonstrate the Brahmin's interest in the colonial government jobs as the chosen ones. O'Hanlon, Rosalind (1985) *Caste, Conflict and Ideology: Mahatma Jotirao Phule and Low Caste Protest in Nineteenth-Century Western India*. Cambridge: Cambridge University Press.
31. Du Bois, William Edward Burghardt (1903) *The Souls of Black Folk*. New York: Dover Publications).
32. Guinier, Lani (2015) Op. Cit., pp. 14–15.
33. TBS Staff, (2019) "For-Profit Colleges vs. Non-Profit Colleges—What's the Difference?", *The Best Schools*, July 29, https://thebestschools.org/magazine/for-profit-vs-non-profit/#:~:text=No.,of%20a%20non%2Dprofit%20institution

34. Burstein, Ellen M. and Caldera, Camille G. (2020) "Who Does Harvard's Endowment Serve?", *The Harvard Crimson*, May 27. www.thecrimson.com/article/2020/5/27/commencement-2020-endowment
35. NACAD, "For-Profit Colleges: What to Know Before You Enroll", www.nacacnet.org/news--publications/publications/for-profit-colleges-what-to-know-before-you-enroll
36. Malone, Thomas W. and Bernstein, Michael S. (2015) (eds.), *Handbook of Collective Intelligence*. Cambridge, MA: MIT Press.
37. Kim, Young Ji *et al.* (2017) "What Makes a Strong Team? Using Collective Intelligence to Predict Team Performance in League of Legends", *CSCW '17*, February 25–March 1, Portland, OR, USA ACM 978-1-4503-4335-0/17/03. http://dx.doi.org/10.1145/2998181.2998185
38. Woolley, Anita, Aggarwal, Ishani and Malone, Thomas (2015) "Collective Intelligence in Teams and Organizations", in Thomas W. Malone and Michael S. Bernstein (eds.), *Handbook of Collective Intelligence*. Cambridge, MA: MIT Press, pp. 143–168.
39. Page, Scott (2007) *The Difference: How the Power of Diversity Creates Better Groups, Firms, Schools, and Societies (New Edition)*.Princeton, NJ: Princeton University Press.
40. Guinier, Lani (2015) Op. Cit., pp. 130–131.
41. Guinier, Lani (2015) Op. Cit., p. 4.

7 Reading Foucault's *History of Madness* to Obliterate Caste in Hindu-Majority Indian Society

Rajesh Sampath[1]

Introduction

The common intuition and understanding of caste is that it is something that enforces hierarchy, social stratification, and division (Dummont, 1980) based on a pure-impure distinction and birth-based assignment of identities from which one cannot escape. In some senses, it is stranger than any hierarchy that has levels of stratification in which it is impossible to move from one level to another across generations. There is no predecessor or successor system in human societies, including intergenerational slavery through the ages, Western feudalism, or Jim Crow white-Black segregation in America, that compares with the caste system. And this dynamic of caste continues inter-generationally and has for over two millennia (Anand, 2014). A seemingly eternal order that never seems to change or die repeats itself over time. What is imperceptible to the outsider (someone not born into Hindu caste), who sees an unchanging social stratification system, is something far worse for those trapped in a system that regenerates itself silently, secretly, and invisibly. And that each caste then in a tribal way preserves its own identity precisely by denying other castes entrance into that identity. This is a hallmark feature of impenetrable social exclusion. All of this occurs in a precolonial phase to a Muslim Moghul empire, to British colonialism, and onto the postcolonial reality of India's liberal, secular, pluralistic, legal, constitutional democracy. Nevertheless, we want to open this chapter with a hypothesis; namely, that there are still lingering mysteries as to the origins of caste, its nature, and self-perpetuation that can be examined using philosophical-speculative tools. This will require turning to other contexts that philosophers of history have explored, which at face value have nothing to do with caste or the Eastern context of postcolonial, Global South India.

For example, one can ask how does a structural and phenomenological analysis of the experience of madness strictly within the confines of Western history have anything to do with the question of caste in India today,

DOI: 10.4324/9781003155065-7

let alone its pre-colonial and colonial pasts. If we can turn to Foucault's 1961 dissertation, *History of Madness* (Foucault, 2009), we can put forward a different view from the aforementioned, commonplace definitions of caste. Admittedly this is the work of philosophical inventiveness and speculation and not the empirical work of the social sciences. Our question is this: how is it that Brahmanical supremacy constantly conceals the underlying experience of madness before madness becomes an object of scientific or social scientific representation—a complex event as an 'undifferentiated experience, the undivided experience of the division' (Foucault, 2009, p. xxvii)? Moreover, caste is precisely a dividing phenomenon of label and practice breeding ever more divisions akin to the power dynamics of discourses as a 'monologue of reason about madness' (Foucault, 2009, p. xxviii). It is when the Hindu majority of the Indian subcontinent continues to justify, through its politics, religious scriptures and myths, the solidification necessary for a hereditary, birth-based, intergenerational division of divisions. And that has to become a question for philosophers of history. What is the relation of the limit, the alterity, the transcendence of history itself for us to speculate about the 'origin' of caste without retrospectively working from our historical present's assumptions of what caste is and why it persists? The erasure of the origin of caste in historical memory has to be reckoned so that caste can be erased from the historical present at work that is fashioning the future as we write these words.

Again, although not a work of empirical social science that works with facts and data, this inquiry has everything to do with the enigmas of time, history, and epochal shifts, let alone their interrelations. This will be the question we will explore in this chapter through a close deconstruction and appropriation of Foucault's text in our phenomenological exposition of the question of caste, how it is framed, how it is discussed, and what can be other to it as yet unimagined. Our aim is to apply it in a manner that can cultivate a new understanding of caste and, through the Ambedkarite quest, to discover new strategies of either resistance or mechanisms that will one day abolish caste itself—a permanent purging of caste from the basic anatomy of Hindu-majority Indian society.

One can write a book just on Foucault's 1961 Preface alone, something that the Preface of the 1972 Edition called into question (Foucault, 2009, p. xxxvii). Like that 1972 Preface, we are not trying to uncover the truth or secret of the final meaning of Foucault's first great treatise. Rather, our aim stems from an entirely other vantage point; namely, the moment and threshold of implosion within a postcolonial, Eastern, Global South, non-Abrahamic religion; namely, Hinduism. And this is something Foucault could not or would not conceive in his work; the latter is strictly on the Western (European) experience from the Middle Ages to Foucault's European present in the early 1960s. We want to critically deconstruct his text, appropriate hidden impulses, change concepts and orientations, and offer new speculations that arise from a context that requires its own 'archaeology of silence' (Foucault, 2009, p. xxviii). We are utterly mystified about the relation between the transcendental origin of caste that would be irreducible to history but also the thoroughly immanent historical contingency that caste—a human-made invention—is also something that can disappear. This is a speculative exercise about a non-original space before identity or difference is born and form relations with each other to see the other side of caste, something that caste itself, as propped up by Brahmanical supremacy and its wisdom texts of Hinduism, cannot see. It is through this revolutionary charge in search of liberation and emancipation from one of the longest standing systems of oppression in human history that we are driving the inquiry.

Caste, in many respects, defies any current Western intuitions of reason and madness (as an object of scientific reason) and therefore traditional anthropologies or sociologies of caste. Caste hides the name of something that is neither reason nor madness. Caste is the other side of social stratification as a purely material structure of culture that relies on religious myths to propel itself; rather, caste has to do with a speculative, metaphysical realm of temporality and the transmigration of souls that punish bodies in their lived states. Caste has nothing to do with culture, despite all anthropological bias. A phantom-like quality pulses within the material core of caste as a continuous dividing of divisions in social space. Ambedkar's critique (Anand, 2014) is illustrative, but admittedly, it does not go far enough in its thrust named as an 'annihilation' (Anand, 2014). As great a polymath mind, Ambedkar was in law, politics, economics, social theory, anthropology, and whatever tools from Western philosophy were available to him in his time—for example, his mentor at Columbia University, the American pragmatist John Dewey (Stroud, 2017 – https://papers.ssrn.com/sol3/papers.cfm?abstract_id=2991131)—the fact remains: Ambedkar did not live to see the philosophical developments that exploded in continental Europe from the 1960s onwards.

For us, we want to develop a series of phenomenological theories on the phantasm of Hindu myth as caste mutating a very materialist religious power in the form of an undifferentiated social body of divisions. This work of deconstruction requires the decimation of the meta-subject of domination known as the Hindutva-National structure, of which the highest prestige within caste is accorded to the religious-priestly mystification of supreme Brahmanical knowledge. Caste is a tribe-like deification elevated to a persona based on the accident of birth and symbol of false pride. From a genealogical deconstruction of these origins of caste (that caste in its own self-representation cannot include) we find interesting resemblances or analogies to what Foucault conveys in his 1961 Preface to his massive tomb—the full version of his dissertation—namely, *History of Madness* (Foucault, 2009).

Reason and madness in our modern age are now separate, and the relation between knowledge and power involves the futile quest by reason via science and policy to extract some kind of experiential truth of how 'madness' in clinical settings truly operates in its plethora and diversity. But Foucault does not want to write that accessible history of what is expressed by experts, governments, institutions, and policymakers, but rather an abyssal 'silence' (Foucault, 2009, p. xxviii). The silence has not been in articulated in the triumphant narrative of reason coming to consciousness of itself as something as difference and division itself; namely, as different from madness while according to itself a specious sovereignty to be able to diagnose and understand madness as an object of scientific reflection and beneficiary of humanitarian care.

Similarly, the neo-fascistic authoritarian personality—Hindutva RSS Nationalism (Jaffrelot, 2021, 2018)—as the uplifting of caste system has to be theorized. The manipulation of social reality by concealing myth and presenting myth as truth instead is, of course, one of the main tropes of any fascistic movement. The commodification of myth becomes the more real political reality for the sole purpose of everyday domination. But here, we have something more. We need to excavate the deep roots that allow for a system of domination to not only separate families, communities, and villages in segregated geographic space and deep into the crevices of civil society, but to plunge the whole mass of the Hindu social body in a complete merging of society and state in a phantasmagorical, diverse totalitarian whole. This is not simply the question of an external state that rules society because the state itself is encased by a much larger entity that must be theorized.

In some regards, the earlier Marx's only and unfinished reflections on political theory and political philosophy can be helpful, particularly his 1843 incomplete essay, 'Contribution to the Critique of Hegel's *Philosophy of Right*' (Tucker, 1978). There are the dialectical interactions of state, civil society, family, religion, sovereignty, democracy, politics, and bureaucracy, which the early Marx teases out. They are complex ensembles of relations within relations precisely in a mid-nineteenth century, nascent industrial-capitalist, European world that failed to undergo a complete social revolution, at least according to the early Marx (Tucker, 1978, p. 16). Similarly, caste is an imaginary complex of contorted and twisting relations that have real material affects while ideologically presenting a false reality that conceals lived oppression and alienation down to the microscopic levels. Death becomes the ultimate limit, not as endpoint of lived time, but an embodiment of a punished life, so that death is crossed out in reincarnation; and yet, the interminable nature of historical time is not circular or linear. And all of this occurs miraculously, while reproducing itself over generations in a primordial spiritual-cultural whole beneath the superficial surface of history as a series of empirical social and political changes. So that, in a democracy, a hierarchy exists which is a contradiction, while the lie of constitutional liberty and equality of all citizens regardless of background, religion, identity, etc., continues. Ideology helps conceal the contradiction as the elite at the top of the hierarchy get to define what democracy is while manipulating it for its own cultural and religious uses to monopolize a concept of national identity. One only has to turn to the U.S. context since 2017 and the Indian context since 2014 to compare similar dynamics. It would be too simple to say that white supremacy and Brahmanical supremacy emanate from single events or cause-effect relations. Something else is at work, which must be uncovered.

We can then conclude our investigation by analyzing that which allows the 'right to have and protect a caste' to embed itself. Caste burrows itself as a fundamental feature of the Indian democratic constitution; this is so, even though the latter asserts individual liberty, equality, and fraternity and freedom from discrimination on the basis of many protected categories, including caste, though, in principle, 'untouchability' itself is abolished. But eradicating discrimination on the basis of caste is not the same thing as eradicating the caste system itself, just like constitutional guarantees banning discrimination on the basis of race is not the same thing as eradicating societal, systemic, institutional, political-economic, and cultural racism. Our detour away from mainstream political-economic, sociological, and anthropological discussions of caste (Chatterji et al., 2018) needs to be justified. We will attempt to re-submerge into a philosophical arena far afield in terms of historical context and geographic location; namely, the question of madness and the history of the West as presented in Foucault's text.

Main Text

Foucault's text opens with an uncanny suspicion as he fundamentally questions all heretofore knowable reality: that everything history has taught us about the great 'progress' of modern science, jurisprudential knowledge, medicine, and policy—in contrast to prior non-modern epochs—can be thrown into question. Common, taken-for-granted assumptions about progress are as follows. Previous phases in Western history, such as the closing of the Middle Ages in the fourteenth century and the pre-modern seventeenth century, could not understand madness because science and knowledge were primitive and underdeveloped in those times. And over time, human reason improved itself, modern science based on experimentation was born, and our knowledge of both biology and behavior became more reliable; truth can be gleaned from an empirical orientation to what is observable and ready for comprehension of not just physical nature but human-created social and political systems and institutions. Reason can be critical of itself, as Kant showed us. But this narrative of progress and linear, historical time as progression is something Foucault expels at the beginning. He invites us into a space where even language and representation cannot be taken for granted at the outset of his work; namely, the sterling Preface of 1961.

Similarly, caste is a space of division but also a concealment of the origin of divisions in general. It is an origin that does not present itself unless we are trapped in the binary thinking of divisions to which the origin gave rise. We cannot be on the other side of the division, so to speak. Practically speaking, how would one imagine—as Ambedkar tried to do—Indian society without caste and therefore without the religion of Hinduism in its rootedness of caste in divinely ordained scriptures? After all, there are over 800 million practitioners of this oldest of living, continuous religions and millions of Hindus in the Indian diaspora as citizens of Western countries, for example, or other democracies around the world; for example, Indonesia. For many, there may be no inner contradiction between a feudalistic, hierarchic, birth-based system of inequality and a liberal, secular democracy that promises equality and liberty to all citizens. Leaving aside questions of interfaith dialogue and international norms of principles of non-interference in other cultures and religions embedded in states, the issue remains: why does caste exist, why does it present itself in ways to those outside it in the manners that it does, what is another history and experience that can be excavated, and moreover, what is the driving impulse of liberation and emancipation from an intractable social reality? Caste appears as a division of groupings of people that transcend class, labor, race, etc., but its conditions of possibility could arise from something else.

We need some initial propositions about caste before diving into the enormously rich and complex world known as the text that is *History of Madness* (Foucault, 2009). Caste, by nature, is an intersectionally and epistemologically complex object, in contradistinction to the intersectional analyses of class, race, ethnicity, gender, and sexuality and disability in purely Western contexts, for example. Caste is a phenomenologically complex object of 'non-existence' in the intermixture of a non-Abrahamic, polytheistic, ritually based religious culture in the South Asian-Indian context: one that blurs thresholds of what is visible and invisible to an outsider's view. Notions of 'state and state ideological apparatuses' (Althusser, 1971) are not sufficient to tackle the complexity because caste is at once material and immaterial, yet caste is also neither, since it requires the embodiment of a non-linear temporality whereby past, present, and future do not follow a simple sequence. Caste lies beyond any material-immanent or immaterial-transcendental distinctions. It is not just 'ideology as the representation of the imaginary relationship of individuals to their real conditions of existence' as the structure of the historical present (Althusser, 1971, 1970). Capitalism and the immanent critique from within its own contradictions through the growth of revolutionary consciousness means time and history are subsumed in a more complex whole (Althusser, 2015). But this structuralist, Marxist orientation requires added theoretical components before we begin this journey in to the mysteries of caste.

As crucial as it is, the legacy of Marx's notion of 'Primitive Accumulation' (Marx, 1990, p. 873) and why we need to reexamine very early twentieth century sociologies of religion (Weber, 2002; Durkheim, 1965) as responses to Marx's dialectical and historical materialism is quite revealing. Ignoring traditions of twentieth-century, Western Marxists in Germany and France is also impossible (Jay, 1984) when studying the nature of ideology and hegemony in capitalist democracies. However, even when considering those pillars of Western social theory in relation to modes of domination inherent in modern Western capitalist societies, the phenomenon of caste lies beyond the Western historical modalities of alienation, oppression, and expropriation of the human essence in the commodification of labor. It lies on some other side of history itself and therefore our presentism in historical memory, which is the colonial legacy of Western concepts in general. To reiterate, it is irreducible to Western theories of ideology and hegemony (Gramsci, 1971) when those theories are deployed to analyze Western historical and structural experiences of oppression in all realms—culture, civil society, politics, economy, and the state.

What remains unclear is the work of synthesis when bringing these Western traditions into dialogue with a figure like Ambedkar and his extensive corpus to understand caste and therefore inform a social movement and revolution to destroy it completely (Anand, 2014). Lastly, newer historical and political theoretical investigations of neo-fascism, nationalism, and right-wing authoritarianism in the heart of liberal democracies in postcolonial, Global South contexts such as India, (Jaffrelot, 2021, 2018) has a peculiar set of relations to the sociological and theoretical complexity of why 'caste' persists in neoliberal capitalism. Yet, when seen through the resources of modern continental European philosophy, we still need to get to a deeper layer of cosmic and metaphysical reality to investigate caste down to its depths. A critical attitude to this metaphysics becomes necessary precisely to unravel its contradictory logic and expose it to the threat of obsolescence when its incoherence becomes public to all.

Hence, isolating Western thinkers of the nineteenth and twentieth centuries in continental Europe—Hegel, Marx, Nietzsche, Husserl, Heidegger, Weber, Foucault, and Derrida—in contrast to robust examples of critical theory and postcolonial theory indigenous to the Global South is inadequate for the task at hand. What we need is comparative dialogue of the West and East and everything in between, utilizing the resources of poststructuralist phenomenology and deconstruction. The latter themselves grew out of and in direct response to older intellectual traditions; for example, existentialism, structuralism, Marxism, twentieth-century treatments of Hegel, and psychoanalysis (Jay, 1993).

This is a very cursory framing of the intellectual, historical context in our attempt to read Foucault's 1961 text. Beyond the twentieth-century context, however, our goal is to further expand on the philosophical complexity of caste and the search for justifications for it to be completely abolished, as was slavery in the U.S. after the Civil War. Even with that American historical context, legalized ante-bellum slavery and twentieth-century Jim Crow segregation may have disappeared in their strict epochal manifestations of the past. But other systems, which are more subtle, coercive, invidious, and invisible live and breathe in a contemporary democracy rooted in 'civil rights and liberties'; namely, the systemic, anti-Black racism of the school-to-prison pipeline (Alexander, 2012) and 'the prison-industrial complex' (James, 1998).

Today, new modalities of structural inequality and oppression are taking shape. Law, society, and political-economy have colluded in ways that are irreducible to single agents or groups that has created a new system of systemic white supremacy and Black oppression precisely within the realms of law and justice (Crenshaw, 2022). Similar attempts are underway today to see how these two different contexts, racism in the U.S., and caste from its South Asian origins, share an uncanny set of resemblances (Wilkerson, 2020). Yet even here, in this rapidly emerging context, there are outstanding philosophical presuppositions on how caste is discussed which must be deconstructed. Interestingly enough, whether it is the white-male dominated canon of Anglo-American and European philosophers of the twentieth century or the seminal work of racial minorities in America—particularly the Black Feminist tradition—we must take some precautions here not to conflate what we see as the intersectional phenomena of domination in Western society and caste, which has its roots in South Asia/Hindu-majority India.

Given this enormous backdrop, we now turn to a close reading of Foucault's text; for caste is an enigma that transcends the boundaries of society, law, political-economy, civil society, and the state. We must get to a buried set of layers that do not show up in those realms but point to the very enigma of time and history itself. The first few paragraphs of Foucault's 1961 Preface open up all these issues up front (Foucault, 2009, p. xxvii). Madness as an 'object' that appears to our modern scientific, normalizing gaze has a complex birth that Foucault tries to enter into; but it's not a single point in recorded chronological, historical time for this birth to be identified (Foucault, 2009, p. xxix). We are not talking about being-in-time altogether when time is presupposed as spatialized in some way to go back to Heidegger (1962). Caste, in a way, also conceals a birth and splits in to several domains; it is related to the death of another; it is a crossing of that death and materialization of transition, and what emerge in every birth is, rather, a rebirth and thus a duplication of all prior terms. If there are two births, there must be two deaths. The problem is that someone else's previous life is the harbinger of a future person's pain, torment, and anguish when born into the lowest caste. It is this threshold that we have to theorize with the early Foucault as a guiding inspiration.

Returning to Foucault (2009) on madness, he opens the 1961 Preface with this:

We need a history of that other trick that madness plays—that other trick through which men, in the gesture of sovereign reason that locks up their neighbor, communicate and recognize each other in the merciless language of non-madness; we identify the moment of that expulsion, before it was definitely established in the reign of truth, before it was brought back to life by the lyricism of protestation. To try to recapture, in history, this degree zero of the history of madness, when it was undifferentiated experience, the still undivided experience of the division itself. To describe, from the origin of its curve, that 'other trick' which, on either side of its movement, allows Reason and Madness to fall away, like things henceforth foreign to each other, deaf to any exchange, almost dead to each other.

It is, no doubt, an uncomfortable region. To pass through it we must renounce the comforts of terminal truths and never allow ourselves to be guided by what we might know of madness.

(p. xxvii)

We need to stay with Foucault's passage for a while. The idea is not to move too quickly to some superficial analogical juxtaposition; for example, Dalit, formerly known as 'untouchable,' impurity is to Brahmanical supremacist purity as 'Madness' in Foucault's text is to 'Reason,' at least in terms of what he is saying here in this lengthy passage (Foucault, 2009, p. xxvii). If we do go down that path, then obviously we are not dealing with Foucault's non-dialectical ingenuity in trying to think about 'madness, non-madness,' 'Madness,' and 'Reason' (Foucault, 2009, p. xxvii) precisely as those terms are brought into play on Dalit/'untouchability,' impurity, karmic sin, Brahmanical supremacy, transcendence, and purity. Trying to imagine a super-synthesis of all those terms into some higher whole that can capture a new phenomenological understanding of caste in relation to madness is tempting. Just as Foucault speaks of a renunciation of all senses, intuitions, and ideas about madness, we must do the same about 'caste.' There is no doubt a dimension of power in both realms—madness and caste—and in different cultural contexts that needs to be explicated philosophically beneath the surface level of history.

In solipsistic fashion, one can ask if in fact 'madness' exists or whether it is a social construction whose public descriptions change arbitrarily over time. And the ad hoc points 'in' time are themselves undisclosed if one needs to continue to believe in the illusion of a successive, chronological, entropic, linear historical time—i.e. years, decades, centuries, millennia. Time (and history) have to be made into questions whereby a whole other sense becomes possible (Heidegger, 1962). It is another thing to say that we necessarily have to proscribe madness as an independent reality and existence, otherwise the social body can't normalize and therefore justify the sovereignty of the state to manage and contain clinically people diagnosed as such. These positive forms of power and maximization of life and discourse utilize the arsenal of forms of knowledge (the state, law, medicine, behavioral health policy) on how to deal with the matter in the most benign ways possible. The state cannot be an anarchy of the 'mad,' even though the state conceals the anarchic nature of its continued self-justification. The state is a shell of a fabricated, imagined entity, which uses material force to protect everyone within both madness and reason, so that the former never crosses over into the latter and neither become substitutes for the other. Yet no one before Foucault really questioned this. The permeant dilation of difference in their relation becomes the a priori proof both that sovereignty exists and that sovereignty and existence are one.

It is yet another thing to say that madness is neither a construction nor an object, but a vast expanse of possibilities without geometric design. It embodies the infinite genius and wisdom of human expression breaking through confines, strictures, and regulations for language to be operable at all and for coherent sense to be manufactured; that is, to communicate realms that are real and true, yet because of the manifestation of speech or body, those on the side of 'reason' have something to fear like a threat. Reason fears its own interrogation as it interrogates everything as to their nature and laws. Without intentionality and signification and a belief in human subjects as endowed intrinsically with those gifts, the most frightening thing imaginable for reason is that neither 'madness' nor 'reason' mean anything at all. Madness becomes a transcendental horizon of why reason, through a 'trick,' gets to conceal its own form of madness, while an 'other' is produced as something external or exterior to it.

Foucault is interested not so much in the pure origin (that can be illuminated through reason alone) of this division between madness and how we understand it in our age, and the imperial solidity of modern scientific reason both contains and magnifies it. Nor is he duplicating the fascination of our late-nineteenth-century-to-the-present quest to plumb the hidden secrets of madness at the borders of other-humanly possibilities: ones that transcend all our mundane norms of what it means to be human—say, the artist or the actions of a dictator that would risk all human life on the planet with an act of war or an unchecked pandemic. Rather, he is doing something else, as he says in the opening passage. The question is what is it that is being interrogated if we can't start with any assumption of what it is, which is the primary impulse of a phenomenological exercise. And then we can try to see how this may function within the realm of caste as systemic origination of difference and valorization of difference, pure-impure distinctions which are manifold in nature, recyclable souls in new bodies constantly being born and dying in a form of temporalization (irreducible to linear, chronological historical time), and the pursuit of transcendence for a self-segregated elite purporting to represent the highest wisdom; namely, Brahmanical supremacy. If one cannot rely on reason to write the history of madness, then one cannot rely on Brahmanical ideology to explain the history, existence, and justification for caste.

Furthermore, Brahmanical consciousness would like nothing better than to transcend all human history, taken over by the West, at least since colonialism, and now the East rising that may supplant that Western suzerainty over all history. In a way, nothing (the 'untouchable') should never touch that level of transcendence of being, time, consciousness, history whose non-eschatological secret—a time without origin and end, non-origin and non-end—remains an undisclosed event. Nothing literally changes—that nothingness itself transmutes—so the Brahman as Being can hover over it without submerging into decay, defecation, and death. The Brahman floats around and past human death. That Brahmanical core, as concealed madness, gives birth to the death that is ascribed to others, who carry death literally in themselves and other expired bodies to the fire, while erasing it for itself. The fire points back like a trace to an origin of death while symbolizing the crossing, not an end.

Returning to Foucault, we can say he is concerned with a double movement of two reversals, which is not exactly 'two sides' of a single movement, say, in opposite directions. Imperceptible to the historian's eye is this invisible birth (which is not a point in chronological time) whereby, suddenly, reason became aligned with sovereignty, confinement, and punishment; but it also naturalizes as normal the perpetual medical and juridical experimentation to force us all to obey in the fetishistic pursuit of 'truth' about madness in people, groups, things (such as states), events, and individuals. A whole epoch of being was set up. Since, in the secular West and the separation of church and state, there no can longer be any equation of madness with the demonic that, say, Jesus in the Gospels casts out; hence, there must be another way to conceive and inhabit madness as it unfolds itself in ways that neither religion nor science can explain. But, in the other reversal, because of the coercive nature of modernity, we must objectify and study the mad artist and philosophical genius. Or one can think of the horrifically sadistic, sexually minded (think of the worst forms of serial killers in the twentieth century who torture and kill children while engaging in necrophilia and cannibalism) and then listen to the media, psychologists, and criminologists try to unlock the mystery of its isolated truth. Madness and the plea of insanity are then debated within the intricacies of law on whether the death penalty should be applied or spared when such individuals are caught. The point is that, even in this darkest space of evil, the interrogation of madness begins with prescribed rules on reason's side to handle the matter in a way that the law recognizes as processual, real, and valid.

Foucault is mesmerized with these discontinuous regimes of knowledge and power that shift, whereby the experience of something and its phenomenon—the mode in which it manifests—alters and there is no connection between the past and the present. One can inquire about this question itself. We can ask about why, within the space of difference and therefore a non-relation, there are two tricks, so to speak: a) convincing oneself as the duty of citizenship and the social contract that they are not mad while the sadistic power of sovereign reason experiments continuously on the boundary of madness and non-madness to structure society and accord privileges and powers; and b) the breaking of the yoke in which either the opposition or dichotomy of anything like 'Madness' and 'Reason' occurs in a perpetual cycle of misery to remind us all that we cannot depart the history that enslaves us today. Therefore, it is too simple to say that madness and reason do not recognize each other as they don't recognize themselves in themselves or in the other. This would invoke Hegel's dilemmas on the double movement of two self-consciousnesses in the master-slave dialectic (Hegel, 1977, p. 112). The excitation and frenzy of the language of law, medicine, policy, and social and behavioral psychology can only arise from the fabrication of the 'division' that is constantly instantiated. Moreover, the mysterious birth of the division is constantly being produced beneath the surface level of an historical change of epochs. Madness then appears as limitless possibility, not the jester in the medieval court or the demonic spirit in biblical antiquity. Moreover, the vast expanse that threatens to engulf everything and swallow up all of human history itself can never be named without erasing the term 'history' itself—a morally unthinkable possibility. For what is human history but the insoluble problem of human suffering, tragedy, and pain in which madness is both the manifestation of that history but perhaps a way out too.

Excavating deeper into what Foucault means by the 'degree zero of history,' 'the undifferentiated experience,' 'the still undivided experience of the division' (Foucault, 2009, p. xxvii) means a phenomenological reduction; we must cast away all of our modern, juridical-medical-legalistic-moralistic compulsions that force us to represent madness, acquire knowledge about it, extract its inner-logic, and tame what is construed as untamable. All of this can be brought to bear on the question of caste, the Brahmanical regimes of manipulation, coercion, and control on what is 'pure' and 'impure' in the heart of a human species. In principle, as a generalized universality, our humanity should thwart those distinctions from ever coming into being. The fundamental question is whether having the caste system and being human simultaneously is ever possible. It is impossible. What is this primordial drive that propels only one group in the name of metaphysical reason endowed at birth;—namely, the 'trick,' known as the Brahmin—to be the sole pursuer of transcendence through the subjection, humiliation, and destruction of others who are lowest in the system and even outside it—namely, the Dalit/'untouchable' (Anand, 2014). We search for this 'degree zero,' too, before we enter into the categories of the Dalit—formerly known as 'untouchable'—as probed to their depths in the thought and life of Ambedkar (Anand, 2014).

Let us reread Foucault's text but this time open up the space whereby caste can be understood as something other to what we think it is today; again, not to justify its existence but to erase it from existence. An 'undifferentiated experience' and the 'undivided experience of dividing' (Foucault, 2009, p. xxvii) discloses a realm whereby caste can be seen for what it truly is, and not why we are told to believe in its ritualistic, real materiality and its metaphysical truth; the latter is the self-praise Brahmins heap on the non-Abrahamic faith of Hinduism as totally other and unlike any other religious tradition in the world. And perhaps the Western world shutters in the face of this increasing globalization of Hinduism and its increasing visibility in the West, given the West's Nietzschean nihilism with its own monotheistic roots.

The state formerly known as 'untouchable,' or Dalit, bodyhood and self-consciousness seeks transcendence from the division of divisions, and therefore is akin to the 'undifferentiated experience' that is irreducible to the cold, calculating logic of the Brahmanical caste. Such transcendence leaves behind what has been un-touched, what is touchable, and what is neither-nor, neither untouchable nor touchable. The other side of this history that spans millennia is separated off by an indecipherable threshold: one that cannot be crossed if one moves today within the caste system to a time immemorial when the stormy elements were gathering together, long before the caste system came into being. What is torturous about this condition is the ideological duplication that takes place in Brahmanical discourse: that 'reincarnation' is, in fact, the supreme Truth that no other religion was able to discover, and once we accept that fact, then a universal acceptance will unfold. Moreover, this self-apprehension of Truth requires an utter supersession of the human and passage into the inhuman. The cruelty of this thinking, however, is that it still requires a designation at birth that excludes others. Imagine some elixir that descends on humanity to alleviate it from all suffering, and yet it is provided to only a few who guard it jealously. But what is guarded from the moment of conception never appears in history. Yet, even these ruminations are simplifying the nature of caste.

We still have to drill further. What we need is a theory of consciousness as a self-splitting event between the baggage of a dead previous self, the erasure of that trace of absence that is death as the cancellation of life, the forced dialogue where the two can never meet (past and present selves), and the ever-impending doom of the Brahmanical cosmo-metaphysical, but this-worldly condescension to control the entire event to disallow escape from a perpetually tortuous condition. Let us bring this proposition back to the 'undifferentiated experience, and undivided experience of the division' before 'Madness and Reason fell away from each other and became dead to each other' (Foucault, 2009, p. xxvii). This non-communicable exchange is really a 'monologue' (Foucault, 2009, p. xxviii) of Reason's supremacy over the latest concoction of what 'Madness' is supposed to be and mean.

We can line up both structures to try to interweave patterns of interrelations: both relations of identity and non-relations of differences between the philosophical ground of caste we are explicating and Foucault's quest for the 'degree zero' (Foucault, 2009, p. xxvii) of history. To repeat, Foucault inhabits a rupture whereby 'Madness' is not what appears to be to our modern, scientific-juridico-political-medical-policy calculus of benign clinical treatment and managerial care. It can never be a historical present grounded in empirical or hermeneutic reason in looking at the pre-scientific age of the experience of madness either, say, in antiquity or the Middle Ages. If something as fundamental as the relation, difference, and transcendence of 'Madness' and 'Reason as the sovereign distinction of the West's identity over the epochs can disappear, then so can caste within the Hindu societal anatomy that shapes all ritualistic reality. Hinduism does not magnify society as the transcendental pursuit of justice and mercy. On the contrary, it reduces all society to a carnival-like ritual that is jealously guarded for the observation of all outside the sacred space as spectacle, whereby the condition of exteriority is the other that must be despised; namely, the Dalit/'untouchable.' The seen and the unseen switch places; the Brahmin can never see the outside, for it is untouchable, and the Dalit is forced to see what it can never be; namely, the moment of transcendence from a circle drawn around space to which they can never enter. There is no way to touch, let alone cross, the periphery to enter the circle, and so the temporalization of the outside cannot be circular or linear. It is entirely Other.

There is always the impossibility of proving beyond any relation of identity or difference the constituted object of 'Madness' as a language and experience by that which would be other to madness; namely, reason. We don't have a phenomenologically robust way of even posing the question of time and space when we think of the signifiers 'madness,' 'reason,' their distinctions and relations. Reason is never a unified structure without boundaries; nor is it an infinite, boundary-less expanse that can predict where it began or where it is going. To invert the order of things in Foucault's response to Pascal's intriguing quote in the Preface of 1961, 'the other trick' is when those who cross over into not-being-mad don't realize that not-being itself is a form of being-mad too, and therefore something that emanates from the ground of a primordial madness. We don't want to attempt to represent the event buried in these paradoxes. It is tempting to go in to all of Hegel's dialectical paradoxes on self, consciousness, self-consciousness, and Spirit, particularly the section on 'Reason' in his *Phenomenology of Spirit* (Hegel, 1977, p. 139). But that must be deferred to a future investigation.

To come full circle about the 'other trick' means to dispense with circularity when considering how all these terms interrelate: primordial madness that encompasses the state of human nature as madness (without boundary, object, content, definition), the primordial break and therefore opaque origin (as a trace of absence) of the emergence into whatever not-being-mad means, and how an 'another trick' irreducible to all makes the break happen. Some kind of twisting and turning takes place in this 'degree zero' because Foucault launches his treatise from Pascal's paradox by stating from the outset that we need to be 'uncomfortable' (Foucault, 2009, p. xxvii) and not assume anything about reason, madness, language, power, science, and society. People may be incited to discourse about such matters, but none of that can be trusted. Otherwise, we will continue to be trapped within the historical present we find ourselves in, just like being trapped in a single universe of a multiverse we can never traverse.

Shifting over to the paradoxical structures of caste, we find more distinctions. This is when Brahmanical sovereign, pure, transcendental-metaphysical-cosmological prayer, ritual, scriptures, or 'Shrastras,' as Ambedkar says (Anand, 2014, p. 286), constitute an inescapable horizon within which falsified distinctions are constantly being promulgated; some are so horrifying when canvassing the history of human civilizations that, from birth, the outsider/Dalit/formerly 'untouchable' is forced to equate their body with death and defecation—the outer limit of human existence. We don't need to turn to either the great theories of psychoanalysis or anthropology to probe the phenomenological questions of the greatest taboos in human culture; arguably, the mystery surrounding death in each culture and religion deals differently with the question of waste, excess, and impurity. And this has nothing to do with a defense of metaphysical principles of transmigration of souls, karmic sin, and succession of bodily reincarnations (Vedas, Upanishads, Mahabarata-Bhavagad Gita) in relation to the unchangeable and immovable social stratification of caste. Ambedkar calls caste not only a 'division of labor, but a division of laborers' within each division (Anand, 2014, p. 233). So, regardless of any class measured by wealth or social plane of recognition (titles and honors), or rather within both, is a caste. There are social consequences to this, based on a pure-impure distinction in which caste prohibits many functions, such as inter-marriage and dining, social and occupational mobility, segregation in public space, particularly temples and sacred sites, and worst of all, perpetual humiliation, chastisement, and ritualistic abuse to reproduce incessantly the distinction of pure and impure. In some sense, caste is the embodiment of a prison that hides invisibly within society, politics, and economy. One would think that the substances of society are just and fair institutions that defend equality and liberty, particularly in the forms of political and civil rights, (Rawls, 2005) particularly in a secular, pluralistic, liberal, secular, legal, constitutional democracy and its underlying political economy. For Ambedkar, before and after independence, this is not the case in India and, one can say, particularly in today's Hindu-nationalist, postcolonial Global South Indian democratic culture. Perhaps, we need to deconstruct the notion of India's modern democracy, which draws from Western constitutions (English, French, and American), and ask whether a democracy is even possible in a feudalistic system like caste.

Yet we are not going to inquire into these relations between caste and democracy while trying to explicate the contents of Hinduism's metaphysical and theological principles; we must suspend them phenomenologically, as Foucault does in a genealogical deconstruction of a 'history.' Or, rather, one must consider the 'birth of history' (Foucault, 2009, p. xxix) itself, and one that does not begin a priori with an acceptance of some break between madness and the reason by which the modern, scientific, social-managerial, rational administrative, clinical-medical, and legal juridical onslaught continues to justify itself. We need to go deeper into this analogy of caste and Brahmanical supremacy, which is as dubious as the distinction of madness and reason in the history of the West.

Conclusion

Let us attempt those reflections here in closing. We want to proffer the possibility of a longer, deeper investigation into such difficult, comparative matters. One can say that 'another trick' is an inversion of Brahmanical supremacy. The trick has a function that sacralizes a prestidigitation, allowing it to-be-not-mad while concealing the emanation from madness that lies in a type of religion whose sociological category is unrecognizable. For philosophers, this means asking what religion is and posing it as a philosophical question—something that does not have any easy, empirical answers. For this sole, uncanny religion—Hinduism—is bereft of any recognizable morality of compassion, sacrifice, and acceptance of others that we find in all other major religions, and not just the Abrahamic faiths born in the Middle East and then West and now in the postcolonial era everywhere around the world. This 'trick' that allows pure-impure distinctions to manifest between

a) Bodily transcendence toward a super-sensory absolute consciousness whereby all time-eternity, motion-rest, earthly existence and some other post- life and death state of pure detachment phenomenally un-discloses itself to the birth-ordained few and
b) Embodied death and expulsion as the outer-limit which justifies primordially from a mythic-cosmic sacrifice at the threshold of the most ancient time before humans even existed and the impossibility of transforming historical time in which the basic social structure called caste refuses to disappear.

The logic of caste is lodged in another trick that allows these distinctions to take hold and promote a maddening fear of both death and excreta, whereby psychoanalysis and 'psychopathology' are inadequate when it comes to writing this history, this very historical origin of History. This concept of History as true historical, chronological time and the contents of human consciousness, language, and invention have a 'birth,' as Foucault aptly noted with regard to the history of madness and reason in the West (Foucault, 2009, p. xxix.). In other words, from within Hinduism and the sovereign metaphysical power of Brahmanical caste, we cannot write this historical-phenomenological deconstruction of caste itself. We need something other to Brahmanical wisdom and philosophical metaphysics.

So, we turn elsewhere. The critical project is one of exigent resistance, challenge, and annihilation. It is an irruption of the emancipatory moment where, perhaps, in a twilight, all reality and society can change, which was the hope of Ambedkar. Dalit/formerly known as 'untouchable' consciousness can arise in a self-consciousness that does not invert the pure-impure distinction whereby the Dalit supplants the Brahmin in a new hierarchy. Rather, independent of any Western philosophical influences and therefore any unnecessary postcolonial or subaltern critiques of that Western hegemony on Eastern structures, languages, and consciousness is a matter internal to the Dalit mind. So, this is not the work of 'postcolonial studies' either. That is neither of the West nor the East—that is what we mean by an irreducible singularity. What is invisible to the former has been buried in the latter, but no more.

This is the space of an infinite expanse and the condition of possibility of a new Being and beginning. Yet being towards this birth is like a stretching-relation that is never present in time because time itself is what is being reckoned (Heidegger, 1962, p. 425). Having said that, the philosophical treasures of the modern West still fall short in this quest for transcendence of the West (Jay, 1984, 1993) and everything it has known. Rather, an-other epoch, an-other history that is not West or East (or any difference or globalizing merger) becomes the question. It lies precisely between a secret, millennia-long stretch of time occupying the darkest, immoral crevices of a human society and defeating such as society's stranglehold on its most vulnerable populations. This is particularly acute when such a society can never permit a rewriting of its own physical and customary boundaries akin to an obstinate, falsely created 'nation-state' that refuses to relinquish its own borders, let alone others' territories that it begins to occupy in an illegal move to the aghast of all other surrounding nations. The geo-political analogy is incomplete, however compelling it may be.

In short, the theory of revolution must be linked to this enduring question from Hegel and Marx, one can say, of the nature of religion, its self-sustaining mechanisms, and its perpetuation. What is other to religion, which is not our secular, capitalist, democratic, or non-democratic/centralized modernity, say China, has yet to appear. This is not to get into issues of the place of religion in secular modernity and questions of basic rights, at least not yet. Rather, we must, like Foucault attempted for the West in his time, take a step back to leap ahead and above the now in this deeply philosophical maneuver. Nothing less is at stake than the possibility of eradicating caste once and for all.

Note

1. Brandeis University, U.S.A.

References

Alexander, M. (2012). *The new Jim Crow: Mass incarceration in the age of color-blindness.* The New Press.
Althusser, L. (1970). *Lenin and philosophy and other essays: Ideology and ideological state apparatuses* (B. Brewster, Trans.). Monthly Review Press. www.marxists.org/reference/archive/althusser/1970/ideology.htm
Althusser, L. (1971). *Lenin and philosophy and other essays* (B. Brewster, Trans.). Monthly Review Press.
Althusser, L. (2015). *Reading capital* (B. Brewster & D. Fernbach, Trans.). Verso.

Anand, S. (Ed.). (2014). *Annihilation of caste: The annotated critical edition: B.R. Ambedkar.* Verso Press.

Chatterji, A., Hansen, B., & Jaffrelot, C. (Eds.). (2018). *Majoritarian state: How Hindu nationalism is changing India.* Oxford University Press.

Crenshaw, K. (2022). *On intersectionality: Essential writings.* The New Press.

Dummont, L. (1980). *Homo Hiearchicus: The caste system and its implications.* (M. Sainsbury, L. Dumont, & B. Gulati, Trans.). University of Chicago Press.

Durkheim, E. (1965). *Elementary forms of the religious life* (J.W. Swain, Trans.). The Free Press.

Foucault, M. (2009). *History of madness* (J. Murphy & J. Khalfa, Trans.). Routledge Press.

Gramsci, A. (1971). *Selections from the prison notebooks* (Q. Hoare & G.N. Smith, Trans.). Lawrence and Wishart.

Hegel, G. W. F. (1977). *Phenomenology of spirit* (A. V. Miller, Trans.). Oxford University Press.

Heidegger, M. (1962). *Being and time* (J. MacQuarrie & E. Robinson, Eds.). Harper and Row.

Jaffrelot, C. (Ed.). (2018). *Hindu nationalism: A reader.* Permanent Black.

Jaffrelot, C. (2021). *Modi's India: Hindu nationalism and the rise of ethnic democracy* (Cynthia Schoch). Princeton University.

James, J. (Ed.). (1998). *The Angela Davis reader.* Blackwell Publishers.

Jay, M. (1984). *Marxism and totality: The adventures of a concept from Lukács to Habermas.* University of California Press.

Jay, M. (1993). *Downcast eyes: The denigration of vision in twentieth-century France.* University of California Press.

Marx, K. (1990). *Capital: vol. 1* (B. Fowkes, Trans.). Penguin Classics.

Rawls, J. (2005). *Political liberalism: Expanded edition.* Columbia University Press.

Tucker, R. (Ed.). (1978). *The Marx-Engels reader* (2nd ed.). W. W. Norton & Company.

Weber, M. (2002). *Protestant ethic and the spirit of capitalism and other writings* (P. Baehr & G. C. Wells, Trans.). Penguin Books.

Wilkerson, I. (2020). *Caste: The origins of our discontent.* Random House.

8 Epistemological Untouchability
The Deafening Silence of Indian Academics

Murzban Jal[1]

The question, "Can the subaltern speak?", which was raised once by cultural theorists, gets an immediate and furious answer: "It is not merely that the subaltern speak, but how one is to shut the mouth of the master caste elite and puppeteer—the infamous Brāhman!" While certain types of academics in India have tried to democratize the puppeteer and, many times, have brought in the subalterns in the academic "mainstream"—in the phantasmagorical academic fraternity—the specter of caste, with its disciplining apparatus of stratification and hierarchy based on the totem of purity and taboo of pollution, keeps on haunting Indian academics. There are two ways that the academic elites have managed the discipline of teaching and research: (1) open caste overlordship; and (2) silence.

This essay talks of Indian academics as "transformed feudal ideology", a transformation in the form of deceptive metamorphosis. It claims that there is not merely the silence of caste but a blindness that I call, after Freud, "hysterical blindness". This chapter further argues that caste has to be seen not only in the ambit of stratification and hierarchy, combined with a form of racism, but also as a form of racist schizophrenia where not only one cannot hear, but where the terror of what I call "silent blindness" is hurling India into intellectual backwardness from where there can be no return.

> *Na Shudray mati dadyat ("Do not impart education to the Śūdra").*
> *The Dharmashastras.*

> *Without knowledge, intelligence was lost, without intelligence morality was lost and without morality was lost all dynamism! Without dynamism money was lost and without money Śūdras sank. All this miserly was caused by lack of knowledge.*
> *Jotiba Phule, Cultivator's Whipcord*

DOI: 10.4324/9781003155065-8

It is usual to hear all those who feel moved by the deplorable condition of the Untouchables unburden themselves by uttering the cry "We must do something for the Untouchables". One seldom hears any of the persons interested in the problem saying "let us do something to change the Touchable Hindus".

B.R. Ambedkar, Untouchables or the Children of India's Ghetto

The naïve belief that all education is necessarily good, both for the individual or for society, and that it will necessarily lead to progress can be harmful as it is misplaced. Quantitatively, education can be organized to promote social justice or to retard it. History shows numerous instances where small social groups and elites have used education as a prerogative of their rule and as a tool for maintaining their hegemony and perpetuating the value upon which it has rested.

Report of the Education Commission, 1964–66

Caste and the Phantasmagoria of "Hinduism"

"Far from being ashamed of Untouchability"—so said the great social democrat B.R. Ambedkar—"the Hindus try to defend it".[2] As the opening quote alludes to, not only is there a defense of Untouchability, there is also great pride attached to it. And this defense and pride continues to this day; for this Indian form of apartheid, which began centuries back, which resisted Buddhism, Christianity, Islam and modernity, exists sometimes with cacophony and sometimes with the terror of silence. And it is this cacophony-silence combination that rules, where what results is the refusal to even recognize the caste system with its inbuilt ranking, exclusion and exploitation (forget confronting it), a refusal that is akin to what Freud called "hysterical blindness".[3]

To articulate the Indian form of hysterical blindness and the refusal to confront the terrible reality of caste, let us see how psychoanalysis understands this form of induced blindness which:

is taken as the type of a psychogenic visual disturbance. . . . For we are in a position to produce blindness of this kind experimentally if we have at our disposal someone who is susceptible to somnambulism. If we put him into deep hypnosis and suggest the idea to him that he sees nothing with one of his eyes, he will in fact behave as though he had become blind in that eye, like a hysteric who has developed a visual disturbance spontaneously. We may thus construct the mechanism of spontaneous hysterical disturbances of vision on the model of suggested hypnotic ones. In a hysteric the idea of being blind arises, not from the prompting of a hypnotist, but spontaneously—by autosuggestion, as people say; and in both cases this idea is so powerful that it turns into reality, exactly like a suggested hallucination, paralysis, etc.[4]

While Freud's analysis of hysterical blindness opens up a path for understanding the refusal to recognize and then confront caste, it must be noted that this induced blondness that led to hallucination and paralysis has a colonial hand. For it was the Orientalists, at least since William Jones and Max Müller, who had postulated a high, Sanskritized interpretation of Indian civilization with its phantasmagorical "Aryan" roots, which the upper-caste Hindu orthodox immediately internalized, a feature that would give rise to the modern nationalist consciousness, ranging from the liberal interpretation of Nehru and Gandhi to the right-wing Hindutva school of political thought where Hindus were seen a "race" (to be precise members of the "Aryan race"). Caste, was of course, absent from this high, Sanskritized interpretation. And when it did appear, as in Herbert Risley,[5] it appeared in the European idea of "race", where the upper castes were depicted as descendants of Europeans. And, since it is this very ideology of racist, xenophobic nationalism that is dominant today, it is necessary to begin our reflections with a consideration of this right-wing interpretation of Hinduism:

> The foreign races in Hindustan must either adopt Hindu culture and language, must hold to respect and hold in reverence Hindu religion, must entertain no idea but those of the glorification of the Hindu religion and lose their separate existence, to merge in the Hindu race, or may stay in the country, wholly subordinated to the Hindu nation, claiming nothing, deserving no privileges, far less any preferential treatment—not even citizen's rights.[6]

While this interpretation of national imagination is dominant today infused by the Bharatiya Janata Party (the political outfit of the Rashtriya Swayamsevak Sangh or the RSS) that consistently has been propagating the idea that India was and is basically "Hindu", this idea was also shared by the elites of the national movement from Vivekananda, A.K. Coomaraswamy and Aurobindo Ghosh to Bankim Chandra Chattopadhyay, Lalla Lajpat Rai and Gandhi. What is forgotten in this discourse is that "the notion of 'Hinduism' is itself a Western-inspired abstraction",[7] an abstraction that completely forgets caste only to hypostasize it as "Hinduism" and the "Hindu Nation". The exploitative mechanisms of the caste system would be veiled here.

What happened was the fiction of "Hinduism" that was created by the Orientalists and manufactured by the colonial British state after the 1857 anti-British uprising would seep deep into the imagination of the popular classes, the ramifications of which is being felt today with the political and cultural shift to the extreme right. Consequently, instead of caste domination and Brāhmanism, an innocent term called "Hinduism" was created. While the producers of this fiction were the British state and their ideologists, the Indian national movement would be the vehicle where this alien term was inserted into popular imagination. The question of "Hinduism" conceived as an "eternal religion" (*sanatana dharma*) was born. *Sanatana dharma* naturally erased *Chaturvarna* (the four-caste system).

While William Jones and Max Müller created their Orientalist repertoire in the eighteenth and nineteenth centuries, presently, this idea of "Hinduism" and the "Hindu nation" is supported now in India, North America and Europe by the following ideologues of "born-again Hinduism" like David Frawley (the theorist of the fiction of the "ingenious Aryan" theory who was honored in 2015 by the BJP government with the Padma Bhushan, the third highest civilian award), Francis Gautier, Koernaard Elst (close friend of L.K. Advani), Sita Ram Goel (the founder of the publishing house "Voice of India", which has been publishing the literature of Hindutva, including the works of Arun Shourie), Ram Swarup (who later joined "Voice of India") and Rajiv Malhotra (founder of "Infinite Foundation", which funds revisionist and right-wing projects both in India and abroad). Elst must be mentioned for his close connection with the BJP patriarch Advani and the ideologue and organizer of the destruction of the Babri mosque in 1992. One must note his notorious *Ram Janmabhoomi vs. Babri Masjid: A Case Study in Hindu Muslim Conflict*, which was released by Advani in 1990, two years before Advani personally supervised the destruction of the historical mosque, which led to anti-Muslim riots all over India. The manner in which the right-wing "Hindu" lobby misuses ideas like "decolonization" must be noted. For them, "decolonization" means freeing oneself from authentic, historical research mainly done by scholars like Irfan Habib and Romila Thapar. Consequently, one has to recall Elst's *Decolonizing the Hindu Mind, Who is a Hindu*, and *The Saffron Swastika: The Notion of Hindu 'Fascism'*.

The tragedy is that, in this right-wing, born-again misinterpretation of Indian society, the old genre of "Hinduism" as Gnostic philosophizing and Neo-Platonism that influenced the theosophists, Coomaraswamy, René Guénon and Gandhi is completely obliterated for a violent, fascist version of Hinduism that talks of the eternal conflict between "Hinduism" and Islam. Hinduism, for them, is indigenous, tolerant and peaceful, while Islam is of alien origin, completely intolerant and violent.

For the previously mentioned ideologues, what is important is creating an imagined "Vedic textuality", grounded in the Brāhmanical imagination, which completely erases all anti-Brāhmanical, subaltern traditions, or, when recalling non-Brāhmanical traditions, keeps this at the service of Brāhmanism. As Friedhelm Hardy said, "it would appear that there is an intrinsic connection between the "Hinduism" that is being constructed in the political arena and the "Hinduism" of academic study".[8]

What is distressing to note is that, along with the noting of this erasure of anti-Brāhmanical traditions, one must also recognize that this same Brāhmanical tradition is now operating both as the ruling ideology of the Indian state and as official state policy and practice that not only privileges upper caste Hindus, but primarily demonizes Muslims (as terrorists) and Christians (as forcibly converting gullible Hindus), along with communists, who are depicted as anti-nationals. What needs to be stated is that, well before the BJP started practicing the politics of demonization that depicted Marxism and Islam as destroying Hinduism, this imagined ideology of "violent anti-nationalist Marxism" as the enemy was propagated by the European far right. One has to recall here Andres Breivik, the butcher of Norway, who stated, in his fascist manifesto *2083—The Declaration of Independence in Europe* that the then-secular government of India led by the Congress party "relies on appeasing Muslims and, very sadly, proselytizing Christian missionaries who illegally convert low caste Hindus with lies and fear, alongside communists who want total destruction of the Hindu faith and culture".

While noting this fascist tone, let us note another view:

Hinduism was invented or constructed by European colonizers, mostly British, sometime after 1800 is false. The evidence instead suggests that a Hindu religion theologically and devotionally grounded in texts such as the *Bhagavad-Gita*, the Puranas, and philosophical commentaries on the six *dars'anas* gradually acquired a much sharper self-conscious identity through the rivalry between Muslims and Hindus in the period between 1200 and 1500, and was firmly established long before 1800. The obvious danger of this thesis is that it can be modified to provide support to a Hindu communalist argument that a self-conscious Hindu identity arose out of the violent persecution of Hindus by Muslims. In fact state-sponsored persecution was only sporadic and directed mostly at temple buildings, not people. Nonetheless, religious literature by Hindu poets such as Kabir, Ekanath, and Vidyapati (some of this quoted below) suggests that socio-religious conflict—occasionally violent conflict—did occur among people on a local level. In any case, only a recognition of the fact that much of modern Hindu identity is rooted in the history of the rivalry between Hinduism and Islam will enable us to correctly gauge the strength of communalist forces and wage a war against them.[9]

In contrast to this idea of the eternal conflict between Hinduism and Islam along with the idea that the subaltern caste, Muslims of India, ought to be called "Hindu-Muslims"[10] (an idea that is central to the RSS and the BJP), it is necessary to state that the very idea of "Hinduism" is an alien term that was created to colonize the minds of the popular classes. To understand this, let us to turn to Ambedkar, who actively resisted this imposition of an alien term, as well as resisting in transfiguring an exploitative system into terms of innocence, arguing instead for the mythical character of "Hindu society". Consider him:

The first and foremost thing that must be recognized is that Hindu society is a myth. The name Hindu is itself a foreign name. . . . Hindu society as such does not exist. It is only a collection of castes. . . . A caste has no feeling that it is affiliated to other castes except when there is a Hindu-Muslim riot. On all other occasions each caste endeavors to segregate itself and distinguish itself from other castes. . . . Indeed the ideal Hindu must be like a rat living in his own hole refusing to have contact with others. There is an utter lack among the Hindus of what the sociologists call "consciousness of kind". There is no Hindu consciousness of kind. In every Hindu the consciousness that exists is the consciousness of his caste. That is the reason why the Hindus cannot be considered to form a society or nation.[11]

For the Indian elites, and not only the orthodox and fascist section but even the liberals like Nehru and Gandhi, the question as to why an alien term was internalized was never even once raised. As Romila Thapar once said:

The imposing of a religious identity as the primary political identity is of course the contribution of colonial scholarship and policy and eventually found its way even into anti-colonial nationalism. The tragedy is that, after independence, we did not question these identities but retained them. Some historians and social scientists questioned them suggesting alternative identities, but they were attacked and described as western stooges (oddly enough), anti-national and as Marxists (thought to be the worst abuse possible)! It was not the failure of our historical imagination but the general resistance to accepting a more nuanced and accurate understanding of the past. The methods and arguments used by religious "nationalisms" in India are rooted in colonial perceptions and procedures and will flourish as long as we accept these. We haven't even excised those colonial laws that are harmful to democracy—we continue to be governed by them.[12]

While the idea presented by Thapar is true, the reader, usually not familiar with the scene of Indian history and influenced by the drama of the
"greatness of Indian civilization", would be rather perplexed by seeing
that nothing called "Hinduism" ever existed and, of course, horrified when
hearing that Hinduism is related to caste and Untouchability. This reader,
who would have been familiar with the works of Gandhi and Nehru or
even with the works of Annie Besant and the Theosophists, would have
related Hinduism with alleged spiritualism and idealism of the sages. Like
Radhakrishna, the reader would have talked of the inherent spiritualism of India, where this reader would prattle the names of Vivekananda
and Aurobindo Ghosh. The reader would then ask: "Who is the upstart
Ambedkar who links Hinduism with not only the practice of Untouchability, but also to its grotesque defense? And how dare Ambedkar argue for a
democratic culture based on radical equality by ignoring Brāhmanical traditions? Did he not know that the ancient law books prohibited the lower
castes from many activities including education? Had he not read the
Dharmashastras, quoted at the start of this chapter, which clearly states
that education must not be imparted to the toiling Śūdra servile masses?
Why was Ambedkar arguing for the complete destruction of caste society
and consequently Hinduism itself?"

Our starting point in the critique of induced blindness to the caste question is that the word "Hindu" is not something indigenous to India, it being
originally a Persian term. Evidence of this can be gathered from the studies
on the Achaemenians, Parthians and Sasanians who talk of the people on
the eastern border of the Persian Empire as "Hindus", while the Holy Book
of the ancient Iranians—the *Avesta*—calls this land *Hapt-Hindûkan.*[13]
Later, the Arabs, too, used this Persian term. Consequently, this term, as
used by West Asians, was a geo-cultural West Asian usage, a feature that
emerges in Albêrûnî. With the Mughals, *Hapt-Hindûkân* became "Hindustan". In ancient India, there were no people called the "Hindus". Instead,
one had the *"bamanshramanan"* (the Brāhmans) and the *"shramanas"*
(the Buddhists and the Jains). How an alien term got internalized such that
it now drives national policy and the imagination of the popular classes is
a matter of great concern.

The Neurotic and Psychotic Republic of Caste

One needs to recall Ambedkar once again:

Hindu society seems to me to be in need of a moral regeneration which
it is dangerous to postpone. And the question is who can determine and
control this moral regeneration? Obviously only those who have undergone an intellectual regeneration and those who are honest enough to

have the courage of their convictions born of intellectual emancipation. Judged by this standard the Hindu leaders who count are in my opinion quite unfit for this task.[14]

So then, what is the problem if there is any problem with Indian society? While somebody trained in developmental economics would say that the essential problem with India is underdevelopment, a scientific understanding on what underdevelopment is would not merely have to concentrate on the feudal-like characteristics of Indian society but the very nature of this "feudalism" itself. I have used the term "feudalism" in inverted commas, since I insist that India is constituted in the Asiatic mode of production with the hierarchical caste system (based on the totem of purity and taboo of pollution, which itself is based on a gradation system with its systematic exclusion and exploitation of the toiling masses categorized as the Śūdra and the ati- Śūdra), forming what Marx once called the "solid foundation of Oriental despotism".[15]

And, since our discussion revolves around caste, it is necessary to have a brief outline of it. To the question "What is caste?", the answer given is that caste is an enclosed, deformed and clannish class system where human relations are based on domination and servitude grafted on the totem of purity (for the upper castes) and taboo of pollution (for the subaltern castes), thereby repressing the principles of liberty, equality and fraternity. In the *Grundrisse*, Marx understood caste as groups "separated from the other, without the right of intermarriage, quite different in [degree of] privilege; each with an exclusive, irrevocable occupation".[16] Ambedkar was more contemptuous with this "close corporation"[17] that acted as "gangs" and "cliques".[18] What we have here is the ideology and unfortunate reality of this divided and violent humanity based on what Ambedkar calls "division of laborers" and the principle of "graded inequality". In fact, this dimension of an ontological division of laborers would be so intense that it would be expressed as what R.D. Laing called the "divided self".[19] And so divided would this "Indian self" be that Ambedkar hesitated in even giving the status of "nation" to India under the Hindus.[20]

While the preceding understanding could be said to be a broad outline of caste, one must also note that there is also a form of South Asian racism based on race-marked, stratified society that propagates the binaries of superiority and inferiority, master and slave, which actively promotes hatred and xenophobia.[21] Consequently, besides the first idea of caste as ranking and segregation and the denial of education and fundamental human rights, we have a second understanding, where a form of South Asian racism is also articulated. However, the strange and uncanny feature of the caste system, with its infinite rankings and gradation of castes, with its reverence and contempt, is that this system is internalized so deeply that even those suffering this brutality accept it and accept it through a strange form of mimesis that Ambedkar calls the "infection of imitation".[22]

And that is why, to the two understandings of caste, it is necessary to add a third dimension and thus link caste with a new form of mental illness that we call "neurosis-psychosis" (superseding Freud's old ideas of separation of neurosis and psychosis), where all forms of critical thinking and the development of democratic culture are totally destroyed. For Freud, neurosis indicates the "eternal return of the self-same trauma", while, by psychosis, he meant the "complete withdrawal from reality".[23] In the system of caste, the neurotic return (of caste) appears again and again, while in the psychotic dimension of caste, a complete detachment from reality is attained. Both the violence and silence that the caste system evokes suggest this neurosis-psychosis and the hysterical blindness emanating thereon, which leads to cultural and ideological hallucination and paralysis.

Let us have a look at the first instance of caste in Indian literature which appears thus:

The Brāhman was his mouth, of both his
arms was the Rājanya made.
His thighs became the Vaiśya, from his
feet the Śūdra was produced.[24]

For the uninitiated, the Brāhman is the priest, while the Rājanya, later to become the Kshatriya, refers to royalty along with the warriors, while the Vaiśya is the artisan and peasant, later to become the trader and merchant, and the Śūdra is the laboring-servile caste. While these are the basic markers of caste-stratification internal to the Brāhmanical social order, it is important to note that scholars have differed on the third and fourth castes and the role that they play within the political economy of a particular era. Also, when hierarchy, exclusion and apartheid-like structure developed is much debated from the racist colonial idea of Herbert Risley (taken over by the 1901 Census) and John Wilson to complex articulations by D.D. Kosambi, Irfan Habib, R.S Sharma, D.N. Jha and Romila Thapar. Ambedkar proposed the idea that, with the fall of Buddhism, a counterrevolution emerged and the ghost of apartheid haunted India. The most recent comer in the debate on caste is Nicholas Dirks, who, in his *Castes of Mind*, locates caste with the coming of British colonialism. For Dirks caste is a "modern invention".[25]

It must be noted that it is one class of people (the Brāhmans) who wield the entire ideological superstructure (or the "Ideological State Apparatus", to borrow Louis Althusser's term) of India. And it is not only in pre-capitalist India where this form of uncanny domination and hegemony was exercised. Even in modern India, this foundational myth is reflected.

The Brāhmans, who compromise probably 3.5 percent of the population of India, control the ideological and political apparatus like the bureaucracy, media, educational institutes, etc., along with the merchant class (the Vaiśya) who fund amply this form of Indian capitalism.

Ambedkar had understood this form of hegemony and had said that India has two enemies: Brāhmanism and capitalism.[26] For him, the Brāhmans are the "hereditary ruling class".[27] Consequently, one can understand that the Brāhmans are thus literally the "mouth" of not only Indian politics and the ideologues of neoliberal capitalism; they are the mouths of the Indian life-world itself. And "by Brāhmanism", so Ambedkar once said:

I mean the negation of the spirit of liberty, equality and fraternity. In that sense it is rampant in all classes and is not confined to the Brāhmans although they have been the originators of it".[28]

Brāhmanism is thus a Frankenstein-like fetish that has now been given life of its own and is ruling over people. Brāhmanism "pervades everywhere and . . . regulates the thoughts and deeds of all classes".[29] It is a terrible virus that is not merely destroying India, but a virus that has given birth to Indian fascism, where almost all gains under Constitutional Democracy that the Indian subalterns achieved have been destroyed. Thus, for him:

Manu (the mythical law maker, my insertion, M.J.) is not a matter of the past. It is even more than a past of the present. It is a "living past" and therefore as really present as any present can be.[30]

The tragedy is that even those who oppose or attempt to oppose the system of caste are overwhelmed by it. Thus:

Instead of abandoning Brāhmanism, they had been holding on to the spirit of it as being the ideal they ought to reach.[31]

While the psychoanalytic dimension of caste is briefly mentioned, it is necessary to locate the political economy of caste in the context of historical materialism, where the first three castes comprise various sections of the bourgeoisie and the bureaucratic state apparatus, while the last is the Indian working class. Yet, it is imperative to note that a simple reduction of the caste system into the modern class may not exactly be a scientific idea. The relation is mediated by a very complex dialectic. What happens in India is that the modern proletariat is struck by the Brāhman virus. And, because of the principle of graded inequality, the various sub-castes in the last caste also fight amongst themselves for a superior status instead of battling directly with the ruling elite. The subalterns are thus not able to achieve a proletarianized revolutionary class consciousness. All they are conscious of is of their caste status. What happens, thus, is that a form of neurosis and psychosis afflict the Indian population, where they are unable to recognize either the world or even themselves. These issues, liberal secularism has never ever recognized.

But, despite the variety of scholarly views, one thing is certain: the first three castes are the born-again castes, "*dvija*", or "twice born" (considered "clean" and "pure"), while the Śūdras, followed by the ati- Śūdras (considered "unclean" and "polluted"), were the excluded, especially excluded from education, entrance to the temple, using the common well to draw water, etc. They, in fact, were made to reside outside the main village. They became Untouchables. The Śūdras and the ati- Śūdras thus became the "Jews" and the "Negroes" of India.[32] The racism is apparent here, considering what the Nazis did to the Jews and what the White Supremacists did and yet do to the Afro-Americans. Whatever the historical genealogy of caste, "they remained (and yet remain) the Untouchables and the Outsiders,[33] having no rights; they are only to serve and submit".[34] "They are there", so Ambedkar continues, "to do or to die".[35]

To articulate education and the institutions of education in independent India and how they insist on being silent on the caste question even when basing their complete practice on caste hierarchy, it is necessary to articulate the Hindu social order and what Ambedkar calls "the place given to Untouchables therein";[36] for it is this social order that forms the essential mechanisms of how education operates even in modern democratic India. In fact, this "place" accorded to the Untouchables—later called, in legal language, "Scheduled Castes" (SCs) and, more popularly, "Dalits"—is an essential part of the social, cultural and religious ideology of the Hindus. And Hinduism, despite its reforms, continues to have this despotic system of ranking, placements and exclusion within its ideological cranium. Ambedkar knew that Hinduism in whatever form (even in its most reformed form) could not shrug off caste and its diabolic system of governance. As it continued in the economic, social, cultural and religious lifeworlds of Hinduism, it also entered the space of modern education. The only difference is that, in the village, the apartheid system was obvious; in modern education, it became subtle, silent but extremely dangerous. And it is this silence that became deafening.

It was Jotiba Phule, quoted at the start of this chapter, who, in the nineteenth century, initiated a systematic anti-Brāhmanical revolution when he created new concepts and a new way of articulating everyday politics of existence by introducing the idea of the "Bahujan", or the "multitude", reminiscent of Gramsci's idea of the "popular classes". For him, the popular classes had firstly to break free from ideological domination of Hinduism, and thus, from the "cunning" and "silly" myths created.

Ambedkar and the entire anti-caste revolutionaries took this theme forward. The main task was to break the ideological hegemony that was enslaving the toiling Dalit population. A counter-hegemony had to be created. The struggle to draft the Indian Constitution under the chairmanship of Ambedkar emerges from this radical historical negation of the Hindu social order.

While India did gain political democracy—especially after the Constitution, which Ambedkar himself, as Chairman of the Drafting Committee, scripted—where the regime of political democracy could be inserted into the Indian life-world, there was, beneath this regime of political democracy, the terrible world of social and economic inequality. This is what he had to say:

Democracy in India is only a top-dressing on an Indian soil which is essentially undemocratic.[37]

To understand both what Ambedkar was saying as well as to understand how the modern Republic of India, even after its Constitution and the heralding of political democracy, could be realized only as the unfortunate "Republic of Caste" is to understand the dominance of the caste oligarchs and how the agrarian elites could mold modern India after its own, awful image. Education, too, faced the same fate. We shall discuss this in our articulation of the educational revolution later in this chapter.

What is important to understand is that, though modernity entered India, the specter and terrible reality of caste did not vanish. This is because of the neurotic characteristic of caste that, like Freud's rendering of neurosis as the eternal recurrence of the self-same trauma, caste, too, returns. Just as the neurotic gets cured only to be hit by the trauma, the same happens to caste. It seems to vanish, only to return with vengeance.

On the eve of his resignation from the Cabinet in 1951, he asked:

What is the position of the Scheduled Castes today?[38]

His answer was:

So far as I see it is the same as before. The same old tyranny, the same old oppression, the same old discrimination which existed before exists now, and perhaps in worst form.[39]

Post-Independence, it seems, the era of British colonialism got over. But what Ambedkar called "the colonialism of the Hindus designed to exploit the Untouchables"[40] got a new life. The village republics that Gandhi celebrated got to strangle the modern Republic. Ambedkar, a fierce realist who had no place for sentimentalism and romanticism, held a contrary position on rural India and the much-celebrated village republics. For him, "sentiment must be outlawed from the domain of science and things must be judged from an objective standpoint".[41] In 1948, he noted the state of the human condition in these villages and wondered how they could have survived even in the age of modernity.[42] For him:

> these village republics have been the ruination of India. . . . What is the village but a sink of localism, a den of ignorance, narrow-mindedness and communalism?[43]

He said that he was surprised by even those who condemned provincialism and communalism would be "champions of the village".[44] There could be no Indian village without caste; thus, without Untouchability, segregation and apartheid, not to forget economic dependence on the caste oligarchs. In the villages "the Untouchables has no escape from Untouchability".[45] One thought that the Indian Constitution would govern modern India. But then, one forgot the caste oligarchs who would be hiding behind the Constitution. Ambedkar sought to expel the ideology of the village system from the Constitution. The caste oligarchs who thrived on this system smuggled it in. In every aspect of life, it was the village system based on caste and governed by the oligarch that would reign. It became the Hegelian essence (*Wesen*) of Indian society. And as the essence became the "ground of existence" of the Indian life-world.[46]

In the domain of education, too, it was the footprint of the caste oligarchs that would be found. India needed an educational revolution. What they got was the counterrevolution. Let us have a look at it.

The Counterrevolution

While independence was celebrated in 1947, despite the balkanization of India into two parts, there was also somber critique of the same, a critique that was wrapped with a warning: you may have given up one form of colonialism (the British rule), but you have not left the other one (the Hindu social order of the caste oligarchs). Ambedkar knew that, in the makings of the modern Indian state (along with the terrible Partition) stood two self-centered narcissistic leaders:

> We have on the horizon of India two great men, so big that they could be identified without being named—Gandhi and Jinnah, What sort of a history they will make may be a matter for posterity to tell. For us it is enough that they do indisputably make headlines for the Press. They hold leading strings. One leads the Hindus, the other leads the

Muslims. They are the idols and heroes of the hour. . . . It is necessary
to make some observations upon their temperaments and methods
with which they have now familiarized us. I can give only my impres-
sions of them, for what they are worth. The first thing that strikes me
is that it would be difficult to find two persons who would rival them
for their colossal egotism, to whom personal ascendency is everything
and the cause of the country a mere counter on the table. They have
made Indian politics a matter of personal feud. Consequences have no
terror for them; indeed they do not occur to them until they happen.
When they do happen they either forget the cause, or if they remember it, they overlook it with a complacency which saves them from
any remorse. They choose to stand on a pedestal of splendid isolation. They wall themselves off from their equals. They prefer to open
themselves to their inferiors. They are very unhappy at and impatient
of criticism, but are very happy to be fawned upon by flunkeys. Both
have developed a wonderful stagecraft and arrange things in such a
way that they are always in the limelight wherever they go. Each of
course claims to be supreme. If supremacy was their only claim, it
would be a small wonder. In addition to supremacy each claims infallibility for himself. Pius IX during whose sacred regime as Pope the
issue of infallibility was raging said—"Before I was Pope I believed in
Papal infallibility, now I feel it." This is exactly the attitude of the two
leaders whom Providence—may I say in his unguarded moments—
has appointed to lead us. This feeling of supremacy and infallibility is
strengthened by the Press.[47]

Ambedkar is saying this in 1943. Note how he also points out to the Press
in disseminating and popularizing the cult of personality. He goes further:

Never has the interest of country been sacrificed so senselessly for the
propagation of hero-worship. Never has hero-worship become so blind
as we see it in India today. There are, I am glad to say, honourable excep-
tions. But they are too few and their voice is never heard. Entrenched
behind the plaudits of the Press, the spirit of domination exhibited by
these two great men has transgressed all limits. By their domination
they have demoralized their followers and demoralized politics. By their
domination they have made half their followers fools and the other half
hypocrites. In establishing their supremacy they have taken the aid of
"big business" and money magnates. For the first time in our country
money is taking the field as an organized power. The question . . . (is):
Who shall rule—wealth or man? Which shall lead money or intellect?
Who shall fill public stations, educated and patriotic free men or the
feudal serfs of corporate capital?[48]

Note Ambedkar's most important question as to who will wield power in independent India. The choice was simple and stark, both, at the same time: "Who would rule money or intellect?" He knew, of course, what was going to happen. It would not be humanity and thus free Indians who would rule, but wealth monopolized by the *feudal serfs of corporate capital*. In fact, this idea of feudal serfs of corporate capital is precise to identify the character of the dominant classes who would lead India to freedom and who would continue to rule India.

While Ambedkar was scathing in his critique of the feudal overlords, a similar idea was reflected in *Report of the Education Commission (1964–66)*, quoted at the start of this chapter, which talked of the educational elites as "largely parasitical in character".[49] This extremely important (but largely ignored) Report also noted that "the present system of education (is) designed to meet the needs of the imperial administration within the limits sent by feudal and traditional society".[50] And, just as Ambedkar had argued for a radical transformation of society, this Report advocated the same:

> Tinkering with the existing situation and moving forward with faltering steps and lack of faith can make things worse than before.[51]

"What the situation calls for", so the Report said, "is action".[52] This action never came. What was perpetuated was the domination of the feudal overlords, who treated citizens as serfs, and their stubborn refusal for involving the annihilation and the transcendence of the caste system. What independent India got was political democracy grafted on the ground of social serfdom. After all, for Ambedkar:

> Hindu religion does not recognize the principle of equality of social status; on the other hand it fosters inequality by insisting upon grading people as Brāhmans, Kshatriyas, Vaiśyas and Śūdras which now stands towards one another in an ascending scale of hatred and descending scale of contempt.[53]

In a different context, the communist poet Faiz Ahmed Faiz had said this about independence (of India and Pakistan) that was crafted alongside the communal Partition of the Indian subcontinent:

> This leprous daybreak, dawn night's fangs have mangled—
> This is not that long-looked for break of day,
> Not that clear dawn in quest of which those comrades
> Set out, believing that in heaven's wide void
> Somewhere must be the stars' last halting place,

Somewhere the verge of night's slow-washing tide,
Somewhere the anchorage for the ship of heartache.[54]

Independent India, unlike the newly formed nation of Pakistan, boasted that it was formed on the basis of Constitutional Democracy, where it was not the caste overlords and religious elites who would have a say in the makings of the Constitution, but an ex-Untouchable, the legendary Ambedkar. The role of Ambedkar (as the Chairman of the Drafting Committee), in critiquing the reactionary and romantic ideas of India living in an apparent "Golden Age" in order to create a secular and democratic Constitution based on the regimes of rights, is unparallel in the history of social democracy in India. But prying out the Constitution from the lifeworld of Ambedkar's philosophical repertoire—especially his socialist version of society that he clearly outlined in his *States and Minorities*, not to forget his radical critique of caste and the Hindu social order whereby the annihilation and transcendence of caste would give birth to an authentic modernity—shifts the perspective from Ambedkar's radicalism to a form of social and political quietism, which, by and large, has reigned since independence.

And, because of this prying of Ambedkar's modernity and socialism from the Constitution, coupled with the failure of creating anti-caste, anti-capitalist organic intellectuals to lead the nation, the social structure of caste and its terrible regime of inequality remained, whereby the Indian Constitution became not so much the document of citizenship and freedom but a social contract between the elites and the subalterns. For Ambedkar, political democracy had to be accompanied by social democracy and the complete economic reorganization of society. These important issues, the political elites never wanted to address, never wanted, and thus never allowed. Ambedkar's resignation as Law Minister in 1951 was because of this precise reason.

And, because Gandhi's romantic idea of caste and the Indian village system as the model of Indian democracy prevailed over Ambedkar's radicalism (post-1951), *citizens* were in the last resort turned into *clients* by the Nehruvian welfare state. The state thus became the Big Brother always ready to shower gifts on the oppressed. That this Nehruvian Big Brother then became the Big Other (to use a term of Jacques Lacan and Slavoj Žižek), with the Hindutva counterrevolution (or political Hinduism, which transfigures the secular state into a Hindu state) unleashed by the BJP with its political victories in 2014 and 2019, must be noted. The right-wing, neo-fascist counterrevolution emerged from the basis of the failure to create an anti-feudal revolution that would end the perpetuities of caste hierarchies and segregation. While, in the traditional Hindu social order, the Untouchables were the hellish other, the neo-fascists put the Muslim population (along with all communists and a section of liberals) as an object of hate and persecution.

The selection of Shantishri Pandit, a rabid and open votary of racism and genocide against Christians, Muslims and communists who called out for the shutting of the Jamia Millia University (JMI) and St. Stephen College (both based in the capital New Delhi), as the Vice Chancellor of the prestigious Jawaharlal Nehru University (JNU) (also based in New Delhi) in February 2022, which was already under attack since at least 2016, where the bogey of anti-nationalism was unleashed on the student population, is a clear example of the fascistization of education that grew from the soil of the failure to create an anti-feudal revolution.[55] That this same learned professor propagating mass hatred and open votary of fascism was convicted in a massive corruption scam when she served at the Savatribai Phule University (SPPU) must also be noted.[56]

One must note, however, that the awful tree of fascism has not grown from its own seed, but the seed of caste hierarchies and segregation—the seed that the Nehruvian liberals refused to even acknowledge, forget confront. While Gandhi's romanticized version of the Indian village prevailed over the national imagination, little was it understood that caste would serve to discipline the Indian masses. Unlike the European revolutions since the French Revolution that openly confronted feudalism, in India, there was no anti-feudal revolution. In fact, it was the feudalists who transformed themselves into capitalists. Both democracy and fascism then grew from this form of Indic variation of the Asiatic mode of production. Marx's oriental despot would first rule India (at least since the early 1990s) as a liberal. Then, just as Dr. Jekyll became Mr. Hyde, the liberal democrat became a fascist despot.

India needed a complete break from its caste oligarchic and colonial past. For that, it needed what the socialist educationist J.P. Naik called an "educational revolution".[57] But the new elites saw that this was never done. Never did they even imagine that the education system needed an overhauling. Never did they imagine a critique of the Eurocentric colonial educational apparatus planted on the agrarian colony. Instead, the same political elites got into the business of education where these caste-oligarchic lords would not only make money, but would be involved in creating a system of hegemony by actively keeping a large part of the Indian population out of the education system. All these elites did was that they evoked the system of "reservations" for the Scheduled Castes and Scheduled Tribes by taking a miniscule number of the subalterns in the system while actively excluding the majority of the subaltern population. Even then, this evoking of the democratic system of reservation for the subaltern masses was seen not as a proactive system of social justice but as a system of charity. Gandhi's idea of charity prevailed over Ambedkar's idea of praxis for social justice. The revolutionary agency that Ambedkar espoused for the subalterns was totally and absolutely negated. Kanshi Ram—the founder of the Bahujan Samaj Party (BSP), which broke out from the traditional Ambedkarite parties, thus ridiculing the Dalit elites as stooges ("Chamchas" in his words)—was not quite off the mark.[58]

Unable to break from the Hindu social order, unable to challenge the hegemony of the caste order, Dalit politicians (post-Ambedkar) became the agent provocateurs of the caste oligarchs. While the dominance of caste oligarchy was being asserted in the nineteenth and twentieth centuries— even while accepting certain reforms in caste society, especially against Untouchability—there was a systematic counterrevolution created against the growing New Democratic Order. And this counterrevolution was institutionalized both by the orthodox Hindu Mahasabha and Gandhi (in denying the legitimate rights of Dalits, especially against Ambedkar's argument that separate electorates were needed for Dalits to break free from the domination of the elites), which was then perfected by the Nehruvian elites, which would have Dalits as mere clients and beneficiaries of an alleged benevolent state. Ambedkar's slogan—"educate, organize, agitate"—was transcended for the ideology of the magnanimous state, giving charity to the "poor and the downtrodden". What is veiled from public discourse is that Ambedkar argued for an autonomous space for the subalterns to create free and creative political praxis, instead of them being dependent on the elites. He saw, thus, the regime of separate electorates where they could find a public voice. But it was Gandhi who voraciously went against Ambedkar, going as far as to go on fast unto death that resulted in the infamous "Poona Pact". Ambedkar's radical idea was buried by Gandhi's threats of suicide.

When Ambedkar argued that Dalits must break out from the Hindu social order, Gandhi did not think that Ambedkar was breaking the unity of the Indian masses. He saw him breaking the unity of the Hindus. In fact, Gandhi appeared less as the leader of the Indian masses and more of the leader of the Hindus.[59] Ambedkar was coerced by Gandhi's emotional blackmail where the sword of threats (fast-unto-death) was raised over his head, recalling what Ambedkar once said:

Social boycott has always held over the heads of the Untouchables by the Caste Hindus a Cha-chas sword of Damocles. Only the Untouchables know what a terrible weapon it is in the hands of the Hindus.[60]

Gandhi, alongside the upper-caste Hindu reactionaries, forced Ambedkar to sign the "Poona Pact". Marx's statement "they cannot represent themselves, they must be represented"[61] should now be changed into the new statement: "they *must not* represent themselves, they *must* be represented by the caste oligarchs". And just as Louis Bonaparte came to represent the lumpenproletariat in the terrible disk of the French counterrevolution, so, in India, it was Gandhi who came as the Indian Bonaparte.

Reservations given by the elites to the subalterns and governed by the same elites would replace Ambedkar's idea of creating radical subjectivity. 24 September 1932, the date of the signing of this Pact, was also the death knell of radical Dalit politics in India. And Ambedkar both knew this and regretted this until his death. According to him, the Poona Pact was "fraught with mischief", forced onto him by "the coercive fast of Mr. Gandhi".[62] It created a system of dependency where Dalits would be perpetually dependent on the caste elites. The fact that Dalit politicians have never challenged this infamous Pact and accepted the system of charity and dependency has obviously made them stooges and agent provocateurs in the hands of the oligarchs. The master and the slave would return once again. Yet, unlike this dialectic that Hegel expounded in his *Phenomenology of Mind*, the slave in the caste system can never rebel, forget, overthrow the master.

A radical critique of this system of charity that converts citizens into clients is thus necessary. Thus, while the elites painted Ambedkar as the "author" of the Constitution, keeping silent on his program of the annihilation of caste (instead of seeing him as the Chairman of the Drafting Committee who had to go through extreme hardship to put his view of social democracy), they made sure that the Indian masses were not told that the Constituent Assembly was dominated by upper caste elites of the Congress who were clearly hostile to Ambedkar.

Here, it is important to note that, from the subaltern position, there have been critiques of not only the system of reservations (which actually squash the ideology of rebellion against injustice or as Herbert Marcuse says "pacifying rebellious desire"[63]) but also of the Constitution itself. After all, the counterrevolution in India has emerged and worked itself from within constitutional propriety. The radical critics of not merely reservations (as a humiliating signifier of charity) but also of the Constitution (that is conservative and bourgeois through and through) claim that "three quarters of the Resultant Constitution was simply the last colonial constitution, the India Act of 1935, poured into a new vessel".[64] One simply has to "dispel the illusion that the Constitution handed over by Ambedkar to the Chairman of the Constitutional Assembly carried his writ".[65]

According to this radical point of view, the system of reservations, while keeping the façade of social justice and inclusion, has been largely a handy tool for creating dependents who work for the elites. What is implied here is that the monopoly of the elites remains and that some crumbs are handed hand out from time to time (by the same monopolists in the form of the Big Brother/Big Other) to create their own Uncle Toms. However, if reservations have actually preserved the monopolist position of the caste oligarchs and not disturbed the caste-based status quo, even failed to uplift the subaltern masses, instead consecrating the caste system, silence on caste and imaging that meritocracy would help replace this system would be highly erroneous.

What free India thus got was not the annihilation of caste and the ushering in of real equality with the creation of a common school system and free and compulsory education that would usher in universal education— i.e. education of the same scientific level for all citizens where students of all social strata would sit, learn and eat together in the same schools.[66] Instead, this common schooling was never ever initiated. And it was not only the right-wing reactionaries who saw that this never took place. It was the Nehruvian elites who systematically saw that this never ever took place. Nehru's dismissal of the first communist government elected by parliament led by E.M.S. Namboodiripad in 1959 because the Communist Party of India (CPI) began a process of educational reform in Kerala is proof that even the liberals did not want the feudal status quo touched by democratic reform.

Nehru then simply forgot his so-called socialist ideals and, along with the Catholic Church, the Muslim League and the Nair Service Society the *Vimochana Samaran* (the "liberation struggle"), turned to the USA, which gave the CIA the job of unsettling and uprooting the CPI from power.[67] What the CPI intended to do was that, under Education Minister Joseph Mundassery, they intended to initiate educational reforms in Kerala, such that a democratic and corruption-free administration (especially payment of salaries to teachers) could take root. Nehru consequently became, as a contemporary commentator says, "a silent participant in the molestation of democracy."[68]

It must also be noted that, in Kerala, it was not only educational reform which was being initiated by the CPI but also land reform, which neither the big landlords nor (especially) the Church and the Nairs wanted. Nehru, for all his socialist rhetoric, stood against the communists and with the landlords and the Church, not to forget with American imperialism. Independent India became the India controlled by the landlords. And Indian modernity, likewise, became the modernity that refused to let go of its primeval caste-oligarchic past. It was Ranajit Guha who once mentioned the "vast tolerance of pre-capitalist values and institutions in Indian society".[69]

But it was not merely the tolerance of the pre-capitalist elites. It was the cruel domination of the feudal overlords and the caste elites who were incubated in the double wombs of the Indic variation of the Asiatic mode of production and colonial capitalism. The Indian educational system (like the social and political systems) has the double parentage of the caste despot and colonial capitalist state. The place of colonialism in creating these overlords has to be stressed. For these overlords were born from the cranium of the Land Settlement Act of 1793, initiated by Lord Cornwallis, that created the class of zamindars (landlords). It is these zamindars, created by the British, who became the overlords that would govern modern India. While British capital destroyed the Indian economy, converting India into an agricultural colony, the British educational system created the army of native elites who would be trained to serve imperial Britain.

Nehru turned a blind eye to the class of landlords and moneylenders who were not only seeping into the political system but controlling institutions. Like the communists, it was Ambedkar who realized the domination of the landlords and moneylenders and that breaking free from pre-capitalist India was the prerogative and prelude of any real substantial democracy in India. In this sense, he was in total disagreement with the Nehruvian intellectuals, who sought not the transcendence of religion and caste but the secularization of religion and caste, and consequently, making a secular version of Hindu religion and caste by what Dilip Menon calls the "hitch-hiking on the grand narrative of Western civilization".[70] And we all, the children of modern India, had to face the burden of this. At least until the Nehrivians led the country, "an uncompromising retreat into tradition did not seem possible".[71] What resulted was a "strategic compromise almost creating a dichotomous, schizophrenic consciousness".[72]

The ideology of the social reform movement that was manifested in the Constitution where Untouchability was outlawed but caste instrumentalized (and not annihilated) was a necessary product of this strategic compromise, which then led to a schizophrenic political consciousness. Ambedkar was well aware of this, and that is why he resigned as Law Minister. Ambedkar was a realist and thus well aware that the battle was a long one. Those who project him as a mere liberal and pragmatist who imagined that parliamentary democracy would be the solution to all the problems of India would need to understand this:

India is negotiating to have parliamentary democracy. There is great need for someone with sufficient courage to tell Indians: "Beware of parliamentary democracy, it is not the best product as it appears to be".[73]

Further, for him:

Democracy is another name for equality. Parliamentary democracy developed a passion for liberty. It never made even a nodding acquaintance with equality.[74]

Ambedkar noted an "evil" in society, an evil that had to be stopped—"all political societies get divided into two classes, the rulers and the ruled" where the "rulers are always drawn from the ruling classes".[75] But here, the ruling class would also be the ruling caste and working as if ordained by the gods to perpetually govern. When the *Rg Veda* linked (which we brought out in the first part of this chapter) the mouth of god with the Brāhman (who is depicted as representing the divine mouth), what was meant was that these Brāhmans would totally monopolize Indian ideology. The Brāhmans would be what Marx called the "oriental despots". They would also be the master ideologists and, as representing the mouth of god, would be the bearers of the Indian Ideological State Apparatus. But they would also be the writers of the primeval algorithm, where, well before the Americans discovered Artificial Intelligence, putting it in the service of global capital, turning humanity into mere robots, they would create their own panoptic system of calculation and control. For the Brāhmans, each and every individual has a well-defined and predestined place in society; a place defined by cosmic laws. There is no escape from this. For them, the annihilation of caste is merely a dream.

And when the Dalits, who were converted into lambs by Gandhi and the Nehruvian elites, screamed at the terrible injustice and atrocities committed against them, they had to be silenced. Those who accepted their fate with quiet resignation and who took doles from Big Brother/Big Other became "nationalists". Those who opposed this system of injustice and charity were declared "terrorists".

What was needed and what is needed is political education, along with the organizational abilities of the subalterns followed by mass agitation. After all, Ambedkar's words "educate, organize, agitate" could not be hollow words. Education as the philosophy of praxis was needed. For that, one had to cultivate the idea of understanding humanity as humanity.

Educational Revolution as the Cultivation of Humanity as Humanity

Education as knowledge and the philosophy of praxis has almost always been at a crossroads with education as power—complete political, economic and social power. While the process of democratic education in India in the latter part of the nineteenth century, initiated by Jotiba Phule in Maharashtra, argued for education as a process of social transformation for replacing the old feudal and colonial educational apparatus with a democratic apparatus based on equality, liberty and fraternity, the modern education system post-independence has been at the most unplanned and anarchic in form and content. If any sort of if not "planning" then at least as a sense of some sort of order was restored in the education process, then it was with the post-Nehruvian phase of globalization where education would be dictated by the dictates of the world market, where the World

Bank and the IMF would replace both reason and Phule. But this "planning" and "order" would be worse than the anarchy and un-thought policies in education in the Nehruvian era.

In a seminal essay, J.P. Naik, the doyen of Indian education, argued for what he called an "educational revolution".[76] He argued that, in 1947, an educational revolution should have followed national independence in the form of what he called the "political revolution".[77] Naik notes that even Nehru, as the first Prime Minister of independent India in 1948, said at the Educational Conference conveyed by the Ministry of Education:

> Whenever conferences were called in the past to form a plan for education in India, the tendency as a rule was to maintain the existing system with slight modifications. This must not happen now. Great changes have taken place in the country and the educational system must keep pace with them. *The entire basis of education must be revolutionized.*[78]

Yet Naik noted that "we did not make the most of this opportunity, to the detriment not only of education but of life itself".[79] He hoped that a second chance could come such that an educational revolution as a prelude to the socio-economic revolution would herald "a great adventure of national reconstruction whose objective is to abolish poverty, unemployment and ill-health and to create a new social order based on the dignity of the individual, liberty, equality, and social justice".[80]

For Naik, as for Ambedkar, education referred to the German Enlightenment sense of *die Bildung*, meaning "being cultured", where cultivation of the mind led to individual and social maturation.[81] By "cultivation of the mind" is at the same time meant cultivation of humanity as humanity, where humanity finds its lost self and where philosophy, science and aesthetics not only meet, but are synthesized.[82] By "education" is thus meant the perfection of the individual and society.

In this sense of the Enlightenment project, which, in education, was institutionalized by Wilhelm Humboldt, education meant essentially shaping the character of the individual and simultaneously shaping society at large. Education most certainly did not mean mere "training"; most certainly, not "skill development". Instead, it is moral and aesthetical awakening, where the idea of the good society is put into practice.

It could most certainly be argued that, until the early 1990s, this idea of the "good society" was prevalent at least until the advent of globalization as the official policy of the Indian state, accompanied by the rise of the Hindutva right, which not only tore down the Babri mosque, but tore modern India into warring communities. Genocide was first spoken of in the public space in independent India in the early 1990s. Now it seems to have become both state policy as well as a terrible reality.

Ambedkar argued for thinking and reason, not sentiments. For him, Gandhi stood for not only sentiments, but outdated ones. And that is why he said that Gandhi:

prefers to follow the saints. Like a conservative with his reverence for consecrated notions, he is afraid that if he once starts thinking, many ideals and institutions to which he clings will be doomed. One must sympathize with him. For every act of independent thinking puts some portion of an apparently stable world in peril. But it is equally true that dependence on saints cannot lead us to know the truth. The saints are after all only human beings, and as Lord Balfour said, "the human mind is no more a truth-finding apparatus than the snout of a pig". Insofar as he does think, to me he really appears to be prostituting his intelligence to find reasons for supporting this archaic social structure of the Hindus. He is the most influential apologist of it, and therefore the worst enemy of the Hindus.[83]

What the fascist Hindutva project had done is that it appropriated Gandhi's idea of the saint (in fact, the unthinking saint)—the saint that replaces thinking humanity. But while the Gandhian saint is non-violent merely involved in "prostituting his intelligence", this fascist saint is violent to the extreme. What Georg Lukács called "the destruction of reason"[84] has now come. Fascism, after all, means the destruction of reason and critical thinking. Both reason and critical thinking, along with the challenge to the dominant order, would become the New Untouchables in India. While capitalism would increasingly interpenetrate almost all areas of society, proletarianizing and pauperizing a large section of society, the public space would increasingly become feudal. After all, the *fuehrer* had to be totally feudal.

And it was this feudal character of Indian society that Ambedkar recognized. This feudal character would not only embrace capitalism; it would also embrace fascism. "If Hindu Raj becomes a fact", so he famously said, "it will, no doubt, be the greatest calamity for this country".[85]

Intellectual Feudalism and "Colonialism Within Colonialism"

And this "greatest calamity" has come. Hindu raj has become a terrible reality. "Hindus live in villages", so Ambedkar said, while "the Untouchables live in the Ghettos".[86] Mass education as the democratization of consciousness was needed where "the object is to free the Untouchables from the thralldom of the Hindus".[87] Education means conscientization and the breaking of the hegemony of oppression. In India, it means breaking the hegemony of the caste oligarchs and the Hindu social order.

With the advent of the British, India was being converted into an agrarian colony and being colonized by an alien and oppressive system. But India is unique in the sense that it has "colonialism within colonialism".[88] One recalls again Ambedkar's idea of the "colonialism of the Hindus designed to exploit the Untouchables".[89] It was Phule who theorized on this strange phenomenon of colonialism within colonialism, followed by Ambedkar. In his classic *Slavery*, Phule decoded the ideological mechanisms of the caste oligarchs. He said that the Brāhmans—who were basically a parasitic class living off the labor of the producing subaltern communities—with their religious Vedic education claimed to have "magical powers".[90] And it is with this ideological weapon of magic that they terrified the population. Phule mentions the story of how a Brāhman sage called "Bhrugu" kicked the god Vishnu on his chest and, instead of getting angry, Vishnu started massaging the foot of the Brāhman because he thought that the Brāhman must have hurt his foot.[91] The moral of this story is that, if even the god Vishnu could bear the kicks of the Brāhman, then "why should the Śūdras complain about the kicks, blows and the murderous assaults of the Brāhmans?"[92]

For Phule, the Brāhmans were "rascals" who ruled with their "black magic",[93] propagating "atrocious fictions" that "corrupt the minds of young children."[94] What the Brāhmans are involved in is only the creation of "dirty tricks".[95] Orientalism did not see this discourse that Phule outlined. For them (since Jones), the Brāhmans were descendants of the Europeans and of course could not be involved in the business of doing dirty tricks. In fact, it is Orientalism that refashioned Sanskrit texts for colonial governance. Phule wanted to break what Žižek in *Organs without Bodies* calls this "symbolic authority".[96]

Orientalism wanted this symbolic authority. For them, the Brāhmans were of great importance. They had to refashion Indian "tradition". This they did through the refashioning of the Sanskrit texts. Caste did not disappear for them. In fact, caste became exotic with Orientalism. *The Laws of Manu* was picked at random, first translated in a European language (in English) by William Jones in 1794. The fact that at St. Paul's Cathedral stands a statue of Jones with *The Laws of Manu* must be mentioned. Why is this book—this ultra "Brāhmanical" text—held in the hands of a European scholar and discoverer (Jones), deified outside a cathedral in London? So fascinated were the Europeans with this text that the English translation was followed by a German one published in Weimer by Johann Christian Hüttner in 1797, followed by French, Portuguese and Russian translations. The questions posed are: "Why did the Orientalists—from Jones to Max Müller, not to forget the German philosopher Friedrich Nietzsche—give such importance to *The Laws of Manu*? Why did John Duncan Martin Derrett, the esteemed Professor of Oriental Laws at the

Epistemological Untouchability 213

University of London, claim that *The Laws of Manu* "constitutes India's greatest achievement in the field of jurisdiction"?[97] Why, then, this European obsession with Manu? But most importantly, why did Herbert Risley rely on what Nicholas Dirks calls the "Brāhmanical sociology of knowledge", where he "depended almost entirely on Brāhmans and other high castes"?[98] Why did he organize "his entire understanding of caste structure and rank according to Brāhmanical indices"?[99]

To understand how colonialism re-fashioned caste, it must be mentioned that it is Herbert Risley's 1901 *Census of India*, followed by his *The People of India*, that forms the modern, administrative imagination of caste.[100] But behind this imagination was the West European idea of race. That the ideology of racism and eugenics is inherent in Risley and the makings of the Census must be mentioned. Risley, in his *The People of India*, said that there were "seven physical types" of people in India—the Turko-Iranian, Indo-Aryan, Scytho-Dravidian, Aryo-Dravadian, Monglo-Dravadian, Mongoloid and Dravadian types.[101] For him, race, and along with it what he called "the shape of the head"[102] and other physical markers defined his imagined "people of India", and along with it, the ideology of caste. And along with this is the method of physical geography.[103] "Caste", for him, meant "purity of breed"[104] and was evolved from the intermixture of the alleged invading Indo-Aryans with the Dravidian population.[105] For him:

A caste may be defined as a collection of families or groups of families bearing a common name, claiming common descent from a mythical ancestor, human or divine; professing to follow the same hereditary calling and regarded by those who are competent to give an opinion as forming a single homogenous community.[106]

Besides contrasting these alleged "caste" societies, which were understood as being fashioned according to so-called "tribal" lines, Risley opposed these to the so-called "open societies" of the West. If Risley imagined the Indian caste system according to European racist imaginary, the same could be said about his predecessor, Arthur de Gobineau (1816–1882). Take his *An Essay on the Inequality of the Human Races*, where he mentioned how aristocrats were from the "Aryan" stock and thus superior to the plebian masses.

The freedom movement needed Phule and Ambedkar for a democratic organization of scientific categories. But, sans Phule and Ambedkar and armed with the racism of the Orientalists and the romanticism of Gandhi and Nehru, the Indian educational elites never bothered to question the categories invented by the colonialists and the educational system that grew systematically from the seeds sown by the colonial masters. While Risley understood caste in terms of race and eugenics (a feature that also is echoed in Gandhi and Nehru, Savarkar and Golwalkar) for Ambedkar, besides the system of ranking, hierarchy, exploitation and segregation and ghettoization, there was also basic class analysis in his presentation:

> Really seen, there are only two castes in the world—the first, that of the rich, and the second, that of the poor.[107]

In contrast was the privileging of Brāhmanism and caste as a cultural category by Gandhi and Nehru. Consider Gandhi:

> Brāhmanism owes its unrivalled position to its self-abnegation, its inward purity, its severe austerity—all these illumined by knowledge.[108]

And:

> The Hindu has an ages-old civilization. He is essentially non-violent. His civilization has passed through the experiences that the two recent ones are still passing through. If Hinduism was ever imperialistic in the modern sense of the term, it has outlived its imperialism and has either deliberately or as a matter of course given it up. Pre-dominance of the non-violent spirit has restricted the use of arms to a small minority which must always be subordinate to a civil power highly spiritual, learned and selfless. The Hindus as a body are therefore not equipped for fighting. But not having retained their spiritual training, they have forgotten the use of an effective substitute for arms, and not knowing their use nor having an aptitude for them, they have become docile to the point of timidity or cowardice. This vice is therefore a natural excrescence of gentleness. Holding this view, I do not think that the Hindu exclusiveness, bad as it undoubtedly is, has much to do with the Hindu timidity. Hence also my disbelief in *akhadas* as a means of self-defence. I prize them for physical culture but, for self-defence, I would restore the spiritual culture. The best and most lasting self-defence is self-purification.[109]

Without doubts, Gandhi and Nehru romanticized caste and the Hindu social order of ranking. That, for them, the "race question" was central to caste as it was also for the Indian right-wing from Savarkar to Golwalkar must be mentioned as to why a truly democratic system could not evolve in India. Let us turn to Nehru's *The Discovery of India*, where the idea of race is privileged as a central category in understanding Indian civilization.[110] He says that caste was in actuality a "peaceful solution" to the conflict between the Aryan and Dravidian races[111] and that caste was a type of "joint family".[112] Further, there was nothing wrong with this system, since it was "an all-inclusive order without any common dogma and allowing the fullest latitude to each group".[113] Not only this, he also saw caste as "trade unions or craft-guilds" governed by a "strong sense of solidarity".[114] Besides this high romanticization of caste, it must also be noted that Nehru held Savarkar (the founder of the xenophobic and fascist Hindutva school of thought) in high esteem[115] and also another right-wing leader of the Hindu Mahasabha Madan Mohan Malaviya.[116]

It is clear that there is a shared code on caste and the Hindu social order between Gandhi and Nehru, on the one hand, and Savarkar and Golwalkar, on the other hand. But to understand the terrible consequences of the phantasmagoria of the "golden past" of Hindu civilization, it is necessary to look into the deep interconnection between this imagined "Hindu tradition" and Nazism. This is what I had once said:

It must be noted that the Indian fascists place at the centre of their violent ideology, the figure of the warrior-priest. But did Indian liberalism not have this image? Did not Jawaharlal Nehru and M.K. Gandhi not believe in this warrior-priest ideology? It must also be noted that it is not merely the case that the Indian fascists borrowed (and continue borrowing) from the Nazis. What is interesting to note is that the Nazis were avid readers of the *Vedas* and the *Gita*. And considering that the *Gita*, as the so-called 'Holy Book' of Hinduism, is being propelled by the RSS to be the National Book, it also implies that the Democratic Constitution is also in the process of being sidelined. It must be noted that Heinrich Himmler imagined that he was the mythical Hindu 'hero' Arjun and Hitler was Krishna, the ideologist par excellence of the caste system. For Himmler deeds of the most violent type do not harm the inner self. This he learnt from the *Gita*. Note also how Mathias Tietke the German author of *Yoga in the Third Reich: Concepts, Contrasts, Consequences* talks of how Himmler lectured on reaching the status of "Kshatriyakaste" (the military and ruling elite of ancient India) where salvation (Moksha) is realized through bloody wars. Note also that for Walter Wust—German Orientalist and Nazi ideologue who from 1937 was the President of the Research Institute of the Ahnenerbe (literally "inherited from the forefathers")—Hitler was a "Chakravartin" (Indo-Aryan world emperor). In his speech of Posener, Himmler—influenced by the spirit of *Gita* where Krishna the hero of Hindu religion instructs Arjuna to attack his kin and kill them—said that it was the duty of every associate of the SS to carry out action without pity and without considering any human relationships. In this age of mass yoga, which the contemporary Indian fascist government is promoting, it is important to note how yoga enthusiasts like the German Indologist and SS Capt. Jakob Wilhelm Hauer influenced the Nazis on the Aryan theory of racial superiority. The Nazi order according to Himmler was conceived as a spiritual order—a spirituality that led to the consciousness of the superman—willing to kill without looking at the consequences, killing of relatives and family members not excluded. He demanded that one has to detach oneself from such concepts as "good" and "evil." Moksha is this fascist going beyond good and evil. Without this understanding, it is impossible to understand the rise of Indian fascism. Why do we say this? We say this because the Indian bourgeois democratic revolution has not been accomplished and can never be accomplished. In this sense the very idea of the bourgeois democratic revolution could be a myth. This is because the bourgeoisie were incapable of being revolutionary anymore. In India the bourgeoisie (especially the bania capitalists, the Kshatriya kulaks and upper caste ideologues, along with the political kulaks and the bureaucracy) carried caste within its economic base and ideological cranium.[117]

After noting the relation between the imagined "Hindu tradition" and Nazism, let us turn now to Gandhi in 1921 writing in *Young India*:

I call myself a Sanatani Hindu because

1. I believe in the Vedas, the Upanishads, the Puranas and all that goes by the name of Hindu scriptures, and therefore in avtars and re-birth,
2. In believe in Varnashrama Dharma in a sense in my opinion strictly Vedic, but not in its present and crude sense,
3. I believe in protecting of cows in its much larger sense than the popular,
4. I do not disbelieve in idol-worship.[118]

And:

The beauty of the caste system is that it does not base itself upon distinctions of wealth possessions. . . . Caste is but an extension of the principle of the family. Both are governed by blood and heredity. . . . The spirit behind caste is not one of arrogant superiority; it is the classification of different systems of self-culture. It is the best possible adjustment of social stability and progress.[119]

And also:

Brāhmanism owes its unrivalled position to its self-abnegation, its inward purity, its severe austerity—all these illumined by knowledge.[120]

And for those who imagine that Gandhi was for the oppressed, one must recall his words: "The Śūdra is a person without moral education, without sense, and without knowledge"[121] and "the caste system has saved Hinduism from disintegration".[122] In fact, Gandhi explicitly agreed with the Old Hindu Order on the prohibition of education for the peasant masses. To understand the fine nuances of Hinduism and the scriptures, so Gandhi said, "one must have a well-cultivated moral sensibility, and experience in the practice of their truths".[123] Clearly for him, the servile masses had no "well-cultivated moral sensibility". Gandhi's three symbolic monkeys, with their respective eyes, ears and mouths shut, were constituted to act as an ideological signifier not to recognize the caste apartheid system. See no evil, hear no evil, and speak no evil actually meant, *silent blindness and dumbness*. In Gandhi's ideology, what is meant is *just shut up and carry the burden of apartheid on your shoulders*.

If this is Gandhi's ideology of the prohibition of knowledge for the masses with a corresponding contempt for the masses, then why was an imagined Gandhi created by the Nehruvian elites—a creation that the fascists have also internalized? Let us look at Gandhi once more:

One of my correspondents suggests that we should abolish the caste [system] but adopt the class system of Europe—meaning thereby I suppose that the idea of heredity in caste should be rejected. I am inclined to think that the law of heredity is an eternal law and any attempt to alter the law must lead us, as it has before led, to utter confusion. I can see very great use in considering Brāhman to be always a Brāhman through his life. If he does not behave himself as a Brāhman, he will naturally cease to command the respect that is due to the real Brāhman.[124]

What the educational elites since independence did was not question the open defense of the caste system by its own alleged "father of the nation". What they were silent and blind to was the dehumanization present in Indian society and the transfiguration and romanticization of this dehumanization. His views on Muslims and Islam were also not all that progressive:

The Mussulman being generally in a minority has as a class developed into a bully . . . (where) thirteen thousand years of imperialistic expansion has made the Mussulmans fighters as a body. They are therefore aggressive. Bullying is the natural excrescence of an aggressive spirit.[125]

Modern India was bequeathed by the most irrational imagination. When urbanization took place, this was again re-imagined according to caste lines. The Untouchable of the village was "settled" in slums and each slum divided on caste lines. What Ambedkar called "division of laborers" and "graded inequality" were born again in urban, capitalist India.

In education, too, this same pattern followed. And that is why it is extremely important to note that, in actuality, the modern Indian political state (like the earlier colonial state) was at best a patronizing state, where it was not democracy and teacher-student relation that were cultivated. Instead, the relation that was established was that of patron and client. The teacher would be the patron and the students would become mere clients. What is not remembered is that, in this patron-client nexus, both the Indian political state as well as the education system started reproducing extreme social divisions based on primordial identities. Students as clients could exist only when there would be divisions of such magnitude, divisions that one could call, after Ambedkar, "enclosures".[126] These "enclosures" would create so-called students of "merit" and others who cannot achieve that level. Segregation, especially educational segregation, thus came in naturally in India that was devoid of its anti-feudal, anti-caste revolution. The Indian education system since independence, instead of creating the letter and spirit of *education as democracy*, created and recreated hierarchies. These are silent hierarchies. But the cries of these hierarchies do speak out.

Hierarchies are then continually being manufactured. But then, this "manufacturing" of caste starts from primary school level, where children enter the education system with the stamp of caste marked on their foreheads. It is thus not mere university education that is in crisis, not only education per se, but society itself that is in a terminal state of crisis. *The education revolution thus needs to create a comprehensive system from KG to PG.* We have forgotten the idea of common schools. We have also forgotten that real national bonding will start from the common schools. We start at KG level in an extremely uneven manner—excellent schools for the rich and next to nothing for the poor. Have, for instance, educationists ever seriously though how to annihilate caste and with it the annihilation of hierarchies and poverty that accompanies caste?

Naik, in his *Equality, Quality and Quantity. The Elusive Triangle*, talks of the feudal lords of the eighteenth and nineteenth centuries, with their dependents and supporters.[127] He also noted how Indian feudalism had no systematic, formal education sector;[128] that people were socialized in the caste or class where they belonged;[129] that only a "small class which lived a parasitic life had leisure and access to formal education and to the great cultural traditions of the society".[130] And lastly, Naik notes that besides a deeply hierarchical caste society with its pains and penalties was the ideology that was consumed by the subaltern masses, which made people accept this "with quite resignation".[131]

This feudalism was and is yet the crux of the issue. The question is: "Does the modern education system even refer to this? Can this Indian form of modernity really point to the pulse of the problem such that coherent and workable answers can be given?" Obviously, the answer had to be and today also has to be an Indian subaltern answer. The solution cannot be a hyper-capitalist mode borrowed from the Brits and the Yanks. The understanding of the Indic variation of the Asiatic mode of production and how colonial Britain created an "Indian feudalism" and "colonialism within colonialism" must be understood. Otherwise, one will be building castles on quicksand.

It was Tagore who had said that "the imposing tower of misery which today rests on the heart of India has its sole foundation in the absence of education".[132] Now, we have misery, combined with the fascist phantasmagoria of total genocide. The fact that this fascist phantasmagoria stands on the hierarchical and schizophrenic caste system must be recognized. An alternative must be seen, an alternative that cannot be a liberal democrat answer.

The answer has to be a humanist one:

> The *rich* human being is simultaneously the human being *in need of* a totality of human manifestations of life—the human in whom his own realization exists as an inner necessity, as *need*. Not only wealth, but likewise the *poverty* of humanity—under the assumption of socialism—receives in equal measure a *human* and therefore social significance. Poverty is the passive bond which causes the human being to experience the need of the greatest wealth—the *other* human being. The domination of the objective being in me, the sensuous outburst of my life activity, is *passion* which thus becomes here the *activity* of my being.[133]

The educational revolution required a de-feudalization of society and education. But most importantly, it required a humanization of society. It also required a decolonization of education and knowledge. Phule and Ambedkar were badly needed in the educational curriculum. Unfortunately, this process was never even started. In fact, it would be the feudal lords and the colonial elites who would soon control education, both private and public. The educational revolution that Naik refers to is at the same time democratization and humanization of education of society and humanity. But for this, the democratization and humanization had to be necessary. Education, for Naik, was a national mission. It could neither be a profession nor a business.

Reflecting on the Three Ideas of Education and Science

Let us see these multiple understandings of the social sciences internationally and how they operate in India. The first form follows the Weberian logic, where science is understood as vocation. Now we know that Max Weber in his celebrated 1919 essay "Science as Vocation" (*Wissenschaft als Beruf*) had drawn out the etiology of how science as a vocation is seen in what he calls a "material sense of the term", where employability is the main theme of this endeavor of science.[134] For Weber, the main question is: "What is the prospect of a graduate student who is resolved to dedicate himself professionally to science in university life?" Specialization, atomization and the compartmentalization of the sciences are the leitmotivs of this idea of science as vocation. This theme of science as vocation was a theme of the use of the sciences in the history of capitalism, probably until 1945 in Europe and North America and until the 1990s in India. The end of the Second Imperialist World War ended this theme of science as vocation in Europe and North America for a new theme of science as business and science solely in the service of big business. The collapse of the Soviet bloc of nations and the unhindered growth of neo-liberal capitalism has now transformed this understanding of science as vocation into the understanding of science as big business.

This third idea of science as revolutionary endeavor is basically a Marxist idea, but it is an idea that was also a part of the foundation of educational philosophy in newly independent India that talked of beginning a Revolution with a Revolution.[135] Now, this idea of education in India as a revolutionary endeavor in the first moments of India's independence was against both the ideas of education as vocation and education as business. Now, this theme of Revolution with a Revolution is basically an idea that emerged in the French Revolution, a theme that Slavoj Žižek keeps central to his philosophical discourse.[136] Science is not something innocent, nor is it a commodity that can be bought in the global market. *Science is fundamentally revolutionary in essence.*

However, with the advent of neo-liberalism in the world economy, the role of the sciences has totally changed. Science as vocation and business will now be subservient to the authoritarian forces that are scripting their politics of the Hindu Nation, where the subalterns are told to forget their subaltern position and unite in fighting Muslims. Unfortunately, studies in authoritarianism and fascism in India in particular and Asia in general have not taken center stage in the academic imagination. One could point to Jairus Banaji's work on authoritarianism and fascism that has raised the issue of the rise of authoritarianism and fascism in India.[137] However, the finer details in the Asiatic mode of production and the role of caste hegemony have not been brought out in his works. In a way, then, one can say that even critical social sciences of some sort that did not take the idea of the Asiatic mode of production and caste seriously are struck by the specter of Eurocentric discourses. The main point is, then, to look into an alternative discourse of the social sciences in India.

In 2006, Syed Farid Alatas published his *Alternative Discourses in the Asian Social Sciences: Responses to Eurocentrism*, where he argued for an alternative model that is neither caught up in abstract particularism (the natavist discourses) nor in abstract universalism (Eurocentrism). What Alatas claims is that Western imperialism has systematically created what he calls the "captive mind", where the sciences in non-Western countries are subservient to the interests of imperialism.[138] In this sense, by and large, the social sciences in not only India but in Asia as a whole are, by and large, under the grip of what we know as the "imperialism of categories".[139] According to this line of thinking, one has academic imperialism that is predicated on economic and political imperialism. What the elites of the Third World have done is that they have formed a politics and policy of what Alatas calls "intellectual dependence" on the capitalist elites and corporate institutions of the First World.[140]

The counterpoint to this is the decolonization of the education that thinkers like Paulo Freire, Frantz Fanon and Pierre Bourdeieu talked of. In this sense, we are directly in opposition to the old Weberian thesis of science as vocation and the neo-liberal ideology of science as big business. What one does is that one directly confronts educational and scientific orthodoxy.

Intellectual Dependency and Hyper-Capitalism

For those arguing for a total revamping of the educational system, post-independence, this overhauling seemed only to be a mirage. Naik (as we noted earlier) pointed out to the caste oligarchs as the New Sovereigns who took power in 1947 (the New Sovereign that I call, after Pierre Bourdieu, "the naked emperors of the university"[141]), and while Naik implicitly pointed out the question of academic feudalism, unfortunately, this very important point has gone almost unnoticed by scholars. India, like many totalitarian societies (despite the outward appearance of democracy) was and is governed by the oligarchs who were accountable to no one. Even today, academic institutions are governed on caste lines, where, instead of scientific investigation and the sharing of knowledge, it is caste loyalties and caste nexuses that govern Indian academics. The fact that India has gone from what Ambedkar called a "Republic of Untouchability" to a "Republic of Caste" has to be noted.[142] And the fault lies not merely with the traditional elites and the caste oligarchs whose worldview is feudal through and though. It is also the Indian form of modernity that grew from colonial capitalism, combined with Constitutional Democracy, that institutionalized caste.

Not once was it thought of the relation between the class of landlords created by British colonialism and the consequent class of native elites created by colonialism who would soon become the educational elites in independent India. Not only was Ambedkar kept merely as footnote, to be used when wanted, even the idea of anti-colonial, non-formal education was largely ignored by the Nehruvian elites. It was the same with the case of Tagore and his experiments with education. His creation—Santiniketan—became part of the bureaucratic educational system.

Not once was it thought that the structures of modern education grew from the wombs of the caste oligarchs and the colonialists. Not once was it thought that the three modern Indian universities—Bombay, Madras and Calcutta—were established in 1857, when India was involved in a bloody revolution against British rule. Not once was it thought that "education", for the British, meant ideological control of the Indian masses for the recreation of capital via the agrarian colony established by the British. Colonial ideology in education meant not so much "reform" that the Brits boasted of through their phantasmagoria of the "civilizing mission of the white man", but the imposition of the feudal-serf relation from political economy to educational practice.

Thus, a thorough critique of academic feudalism and the pertinent issues raised in the nineteenth century by educationists who talked of the population being "captive in mental slavery"[143] would have to be understood. Since education is considered as a national mission from thinkers a diverse as Phule and Ambedkar to Tagore, and since the creation of a just and egalitarian society was also their motto, the question of making scientific temper matter and the highlighting of the importance of Indian educationists for transforming and humanizing education in the twenty-first century has to be highlighted.

What need to be recognized is that policy makers and the political elites, right from the time of independence, made promises that they would never be able to keep. Maulana Azad, in the "Chairman's Address, 25th Meeting of the CABE" (1958), lamented that education was ignored when the first draft of the plan was made, and only that which brought in "quick returns" had priority for the government. It was since independence that commodity production and its logic had guided every sphere of life, education included. Free and compulsory education, the motto that seemed to have been etched in the cranium of the freedom movement, was to be swallowed by Monsieur Capital and Quick Returns, Inc.

It is not merely the case where appearances and the deeper structure of society do not coincide. It is the case where false appearances are created that veil social reality. And they veil it what Prabhat Patnaik calls, after Nicholas Kaldor, as "stylized facts".[144] In fact, it is these stylized facts that stand as the essence of policies of Third World countries, especially in the present era of liberalization and globalization. What the globalized system does is that it now argues for the "tickle down effect" along with "liberali-zation with a human face".[145]

And so, if, in the pre-globalized era, what stood out was obvious feudal-ism lying hidden under the rhetoric of socialism, in the era of globaliza-tion, the mantras of hyper-individualization, merit and competition stand out. Since the 1990s, there has been an explosion of private educational institutions from primary schools to hyper-modern universities. But then, it was never the case that, in the pre-globalized era, private educational institutions were not promoted. One merely has to see the educational institutions running since at least the 1960s, and one will see the hands of politicians as the founders and chancellors of these institutions. One merely mentions the D.Y. Patil chain of institutions (run by the Congress-man D.Y. Patil) and the Bharatiya Vidyapeet Deemed University (run by the family of the late Congress leader Patangrao Kadam).

It is in this concrete situation that one sees policy formulations and the so-called rhetoric of overhauling of the educational system. But then, what is not said is that such policies that do not recognize the real social and economic basis of society and the control of educational institutes create only a "dithering higher education policy", where practice and policy do not go hand in hand.[146] In practice, one sees the withdrawal of the state from public-funded institutes and the active promotion of privatization and market-friendly practices like competition, ranking, self-financing and market loans.[147]

Now, while the system of reservations for the educationally marginal-ized communities was introduced—via section 46 of the Directive Principle of the Indian Constitution—there is also now mention that it is capitalism that will emancipate the Dalits, where "development for all" (the slogan of the BJP since 2014) would efface caste inequalities, segregation and ghet-toization. Since at least 2013, certain Dalit intellectuals have been arguing for what they call "Dalit capitalism," where Dalits as entrepreneurs would establish real equality and dignity.[148] What is meant by this argument is that the system of social justice as espoused in the Indian Constitution is passé and that capitalism would provide equality and dignity to the Dalits.

In my *Why We are not Hindus*, this is what I had said:

> that 'Dalit capitalism' is a commodity needed by the big bourgeoisie especially the Tatas and the Godrejs to produce the spare parts of these global magnates. But this 'Dalit capitalism' is also as a spectacle. Chan-dra Bhan Prasad (one of the ideologues of 'Dalit capitalism') also for-gets that the Tatas and the Godrejs do not belong to the clan of the varna fetish worshipers, but belong to a faith that has been diametri-cally opposed to caste and Brahmanism for well over two and a half millennia. Thus whilst equality (albeit only formal equality) is possible

for faiths other that Hinduism, it is impossible for Hinduism to accept any form of equality. Yet the proponents of 'Dalit capitalism' like the proponents of 'Islamic capitalism' (many who are friends of Narendra Modi) forget that capitalism both sweeps the remnants of pre-capitalist societies, as well as re-imagines and re-builds these primordial social formations. Therefore Rosa Luxemburg's argument that there can be no neat picture of capitalism devoid of pre-capitalism and that capitalism needs pre-capitalist societies for the realization of surplus value is of great importance.[149]

I also had said that:

'Dalit capitalism' (as a) a form of phantasmagorical version of capitalism is pure fiction, a fiction devoid of the bloody history of primitive accumulation, devoid of what we know since David Harvey as 'accumulation through dispossession'. Remember that for this form of neo-liberal sponsored fiction, we now do not talk of 'victimhood', we 'don't ask for doles, reservations, favours . . . (and) complains'. Instead of the struggle of the oppressed, a struggle that is between master and slave—rather lordship and bondage—(a struggle as in Hegel's *Phenomenology of Mind* where lordship is bound to be overthrown), the oppressed are seen as Chandra Bhan Prasad claims, to have 'risen on their own'. The struggle of the oppressed has 'outlived its potential and power', as the ex-Maoist, turned neo-liberal (Chandra Bhan Prasad) claims. That this neo-liberal narrative echoes the narrative that India is the subordinate partner of American imperialism should be stressed. That Dalit capitalism is made up of small and medium enterprises based largely on family labour, and subservient to the needs of big capital also should not be forgotten.[150]

After noting this new turn in Dalit politics that argues for capitalism in the era of late imperialism in permanent crisis, one returns to the idea of stylized facts. Would the vision of multi-disciplinary institutes that the BJP government proposes to establish be able to serve the interests of the popular classes of India? Would these privatized institutions aid the removal of caste hierarchy and the accompanying economic and cultural poverty? To understand this, one must locate the principal contradiction in education—excellent research and teaching in some educational institutions along with anarchy, academic feudalism and the now increasing growth of capitalist educational institutions. We state this as an extension in the contradiction in the nature of the Indian state and governance; namely, the contradiction between Constitutional Democracy and political feudalism.

After all, it was Ambedkar who has said:

On 26 January 1950, we are going to enter into a life of contradictions. In politics we will have equality and in social and economic life we will have inequality. In politics we will be recognizing the principle of one man one vote and one vote one value. In our social and economic life, we shall, by reason of our social and economic structure, continue to deny the principle of one man one value. How long shall we continue to live this life of contradictions? How long shall we continue to deny equality in our social and economic life? If we continue to deny it for long, we will do so only by putting our political democracy in peril. We must remove this contradiction at the earliest possible moment or else those who suffer from inequality will blow up the structure of political democracy which this Assembly has to laboriously built up.[151]

Of course, this contradiction was never recognized, forget overcome. And even after the entrance of global capitalism since the early 1990s, when India officially followed the policies of neo-liberal capitalism, the feudal organization built around caste ordering of society and the consequent stratification never ended. *It was merely reorganized.* Even today, in each of the states of the Indian Republic, educational institutions privately run are of the upper-caste elites who are necessarily members of the dominant political parties (be it the Congress, the BJP or any regional parties). There are no Dalit-run educational institutions to date in India.

To talk thus of education, especially education policy, one needs to talk of this essential feudalism of the caste oligarchs in governance. Despite some excellent institutes in the education sector, India is, by and large, governed by a type of feudalism where knowledge is restricted by the educational elites. In this respect, we need to enlarge Jean-Paul Sartre's ideas of colonial and native elites that he espoused in his *Colonialism and Neocolonialism* to educational elites.[152]

By and large, the single biggest problem in education is political interference, and despite the best teachers, researchers and scientists, and despite the *Radhakrishna Report* and the *Report of the Education Commission. 1964–66*, it is not the idea of education as the common good that reflects the dreams of a free country which is dominant, but academic feudalism. In fact, there are three fundamental problems that one locates: (1) academic feudalism; (2) anarchy in the education sector governed by market forces, combined with the anarchy in planning and policy; and (3) being yet in the shadow of colonialism and the education system that free Indians inherited from the British. In this sense, a true decolonization, democratization and humanization of education were never started. Education, by and large, remained feudal and colonized. Feudalism had thus to be its necessary part.

The dire need of the educational revolution was completely forgotten. While the Nehruvian elites had said that "the entire basis of education must be revolutionized", the deed and the will to perform the deed was totally missing that lead to the missing of the historical opportunity to transform education for the public good. And that is why it is important to recall Naik once again:

> We did not make the most of this opportunity, to the detriment, not only of education but of life itself.[153]

It is ironic that India has a large number of higher education institutions in the world, comparable to China and the USA.[154] However, the Gross Enrollment Rate is a mere 10 percent. There is a clear divide between the number of educational institutions and the intake of the student population. Besides, the quality of education institutions is also unevenly distributed. While some universities and institutions are of high quality—the IITs and IIMs, and some central and private universities—the quality in the majority of educational institutes leaves much to be desired.

One must note that, in the Shanghai World Rankings and the Times Global Rankings, only a few Indian institutes are mentioned as top ranking. While policy documentation is an extremely easy affair, even rigorous theorization, forget implementation of an effective policy that can transform India truly into a democratic society has never been done. What neo-liberal intervention in Indian education has done is created what Michel Foucault calls "governmentality". But the main concern is to search for an alternative to the hyper-capitalist model of education that is now being offered that will reduce students from "acquirers of knowledge" to "customers of knowledge".

What neo-liberalism does is involves both stylized facts and rhetoric. Consequently, the rhetoric of transforming the educational sector that the BJP champions via their *National Education Policy* (2020) is based on a complete capitalist transformation, where "productivity" and "merit" (as defined by the elites and which is subservient to the global market) would solely qualify. But this form of *educational transformation* is completely different from *educational revolution*. This is the most important question, a question that remains completely veiled. Overhauling and revolution are completely two different concepts. Revolution implies a complete destruction of the old economic, social and political order. Revolution implies subalterns, workers and peasants destroying feudalism and capitalism. Revolutions, after all, are always "from below". The "overhauling" that the BJP advocates not only advocates the neo-liberal market and the authoritarian state guiding education, but it also means the complete negation of the ideas of Phule and Ambedkar. "Overhauling" would thus turn out to be a neo-liberal catastrophe akin to the "shock doctrine" (that Naomi Klein articulates in her 2007 classic *The Shock Doctrine. The Rise of Disaster Capitalism*), where only the ability to pay for education would carry the writ.

Thus, this neo-liberal form of capitalism does not remove the classical model of caste-hierarchy. In fact, what Ambedkar called "the Indian village . . . (as) the ideal form of social organization"[155] would remain at the core of the neo-liberal model. And, with the BJP in power, this model of the village with its hierarchies would create New Untouchables. By and large, the leftists would turn out to be the New Untouchables. The hounding of leftists from universities has been institutionalized at least since the 2016 incident at the JNU, when the BJP claimed that the communists are anti-nationals celebrating the balkanization of India.

"Destiny is ruthless",[156] so Naik had said. He had not anticipated fascism. That is why he was charged by a certain form of optimism. Destiny, so he said, "generally gives *one* chance for survival and we are unfortunate to have had *two*". We "missed the first. Can we dare miss the second?"[157] Do we, then, miss what Žižek, after Lenin, calls the *Augenblick* ("the unique chance of revolution")[158] and follow the reformist and Menshevik line of Revolution *without* the Revolution—maybe like Stalin, Zinoviev and Kamenev fear the revolution—and try best to sabotage it? Do we strive for a "decaffeinated revolution", a "revolution that does not smell like a revolution", a Revolution *without* a Revolution?[159]

Most certainly, we missed the first chance when independence had to be accompanied by at least an anti-feudal revolution. Nehru did not allow this. Like the reformists, he imagined that evolution could transform the feudal lord into, if not his brand of socialism, then at least human beings. But then, feudalism, and most certainly of the Indian caste-oligarchic type, would never be humanistic.

With educational institutions under attack, with democracy in India on the back foot, one can most certainly say that the inability to create a revolution in education has been the central tragedy of the education system in India. Yet, it must be stated that one has to be an optimist. One needs a "second chance", "a very rare occurrence in life", where the revolution in ideas has now to precede and accompany a socio-economic revolution in life.[160] And for this, the very idea of education and science has to be transformed and revolutionized.

Education as *Bildung*, Education as Repression

And, to transform and revolutionize education, the very idea of what "education" means has to be clearly and scientifically clarified. The problem, however, is that one starts with the word "education" without locating its very meaning and essence. Consequently, only schooling and higher education is taken as education, or at best, the removal of illiteracy. Schooling and the learning process become the fundamental axis for this mundane idea of education. That education is basically related to the idea of philosophy as the search for wisdom—philosophers are the friends of wisdom—and thus involved with the cultivation of the mind is almost completely forgotten by those theorizing and practicing education today.

A fundamental important point has to be noted—education is not mere training, but something much deeper that deals with humanity as a whole. We locate education in the project of the Enlightenment of *die Bildung*, where individual maturation, along with the development of the spirit of humanity as humanity, is kept central to educational discourse. According to Humboldt, who was instrumental in ushering in this idea:

> Education [*Bildung*], truth and virtue must be disseminated to such an extent that the concept of mankind takes on a great and dignified form in each individual. However, this shall be achieved personally by each individual, who must absorb the great mass of material offered to him by the world around him and by his inner existence, using all the possibilities of his receptiveness; he must then reshape that material with all the energies of his own activity and appropriate it to himself so as to create an interaction between his own personality and nature in a most general, active and harmonious form.[161]

As cultivation, as *die Bildung*, education deals with the synthesis of philosophy, science and aesthetics. It is philosophical and asks the classical questions: "What is truth?", "What is ethical?" and "What is beautiful?". But fundamental to these questions is the question: "What is humanity and where is humanity heading?", which culminates in the last question: "What is free humanity and can this be possible?". Wisdom, knowledge, virtue, truth-seeking and the culture and cultivation to realize these are fundamental ideas in education. Since we are relating education with cultivation and thus broadening the horizon of culture, we are also bringing in different ideas of culture. These are:

1. Culture as a "whole way of life" and "common resource of meaning" (to borrow expressions of Raymond Williams). Here, one also includes mindsets, sets of values, the realm of literature and the arts (the so-called "high culture"), also spelled out as "refinement".
2. Culture as *die Bildung*, a theme derived from the European Enlightenment, most clearly in Hegel's *Phenomenology of Mind*. Ambedkar evokes this in his *What the Congress and Gandhi Done to the Untouchables*. Culture here is meant as cultivating human sensibilities and the

acquisition of the knowledge of the true, the good and the beautiful. Along with these ideas is intrinsically tied the question of human freedom. Thus, when one talks of culture, one does not move to one's gun in horrible fright.[162] Here, culture as cultivating humanity is not mere petty bourgeois cultivating, but is the cultivating of the desire for revolution. *Rebellion is then related to this idea of culture.*

3. The regression of culture from *die Bildung* to the emergence of the culture industry—where "shiny white teeth and freedom from body odors and emotions" (as Max Horkheimer and Theodor Adorno pointed out)[163] matter more than humanity. In fact, it is shiny, white teeth and even more shiny, white skin that matter the most when culture as *Bildung* moves into the state of regression. In this mode of regression, one also moves into the state of repression that Freud placed at the center of his scientific study. In this domain of culture as culture industry, one also negates the old bourgeois idea of "high culture" as the Concert Hall idea of culture or even the Museum Definition of Culture, where culture is understood as the collections of exotic objects. Culture is here commoditized, where the complete destruction of critical thinking and consequently the misuse and abuse of reason is placed at its epicenter. *The use of reason then becomes the abuse of reason.*

4. Culture as cultural nationalism. One now moves from the site of culture as commodity to culture as racial and theological supremacy. The "spectaclization of culture" (that we borrow from Walter Benjamin)[164] and the production of what we call after Fredric Jameson as the "hysterical sublime"[165] become the two important motifs of cultural nationalism. Its leitmotiv is the devaluation of the idea of culture as resistance. Cultural nationalism is the epitome of the post-Enlightenment project, where psychosis and mass hysteria replace the use of reason.

"Knowledge as Capital" or "Capitalism and the End of Knowledge"?

Cultural nationalism of the fascist variety has come, and come riding on the backs of neo-liberal capital. This singular dominance of finance as dictating education in not only constituted in terms of funding higher education but the very reorganization of it. The earlier idea of education was the idea of education as state responsibility and public good. The new neo-liberal idea—education is treated as private good—also heralds the idea of knowledge as capital. While the idea of knowledge as capital has taken prominence since the Organization for Economic Corporation and Development's (OECD) 1996 *The Knowledge-based Economy* and the 1998 World Development Report *Knowledge for Development*, what one has not been understood is "the general idea of neo-liberalization . . . (is) the restoration of class power and, in particular, the restoration of class power to a very privileged elite".[166]

While the argument of the preceding two (Organization for Economic Corporation and Development and World Development Report) and also the Draft Foreign Educational Institutional Bill is that reform (meaning the financialization and hyper-privatization of education) is necessary in the education sector to bring in efficiency, the argument against this is that it would only lead to the lowering of both efficiency and equity.[167] Consequently, it would be financial houses that would be determining research to be done and the courses to be taught in colleges and universities. Clearly, change is seen from the Welfare State as the sovereign representing people's interests to the state, giving way to financial corporate houses and then itself becoming a Corporate State, not to forget the Warfare State. In this sense, the state has not distanced itself from the sphere of the economy, but the nature of the state itself has changed from Welfare to Warfare State.

Bureaucratic rationality gives way to what is now called "busnocratic rationality".[168] And in order to understand this, one moves from the sociology of Max Weber and Michel Foucault to James Marshall. What we get from this hyper-capitalism is the following:

1. The creation of the self-interest of the individual independent of the larger national group and the conquest creation of the culture of hyper-individualism.
2. The celebration of free-market economics, which includes the abolition of subsidies to higher education.
3. Distrust in welfare-governmental power and commitment to laissez-faire ideology, where the global market is seen as running the world with its so-called "invisible hand".[169]

Consequently, the classical liberal idea of private interest motivating individuals is transformed into a new form of governmentality, a new form of political reason as a form of disciplining society itself.[170] "Private interest" would never want to talk of the social. Caste would continue to be veiled. Its violence, meanwhile, would continue.

Education institutions would then be not so much places to discover knowledge and become forms of learning, but panoptic systems to discipline students to be fit for the global market. It is ironic that neo-liberalism, in the Friedrich Hayek-inspired sense that was constructed to promote freedom, would create a system to destroy this very freedom. What one experiences is a dialectic within the neo-liberal education system thrust on the unwilling Indian population, where, instead of moving forward to create a better system, it would actually be devouring itself.

Busnopower, as neo-liberal educational pedagogy, talks of "choices" available to students, and through "choices", deals with the "will to choosing" educational curriculum.[171] But this "will to choose" that neo-liberal capitalism promotes is irrational, as Jacques Lacan mentioned. This alleged "free" choice is actually *forced choice*. The choice is: "*Your money or your life!*".[172]

Meanwhile, the double-bound colonialism—colonialism within colonialism—continues. The Brāhmans first came to discipline Indian society and created their macabre caste algorithm. Then the Brits came to help their Brāhmanical brothers. They extended their "civilizing mission", creating an agrarian colony for British capital, where "the bones of weavers were bleaching the plains of India".[173]

The fact that the Warfare State has replaced the Welfare State in India, at least since 2014, when the policies of Hindutva are thrust onto the masses, the bones of the weavers continue to bleach the plains of India. After all, as it well known:

If money, according to Augier, 'comes into the world with a congenital blood-stain on one cheek', capital comes dripping from head to foot, from every pore, with blood and dirt.[174]

And it is the subalterns who are made to face the brunt of this. Gandhi turned them into lambs, calling them "Harijans" ("children of God") despite his holding to the view that they had no morals. Now, the subalterns have once again come. And they are no lambs. They see that the Constitution that they prided on in being stamped with fascist jackboots.

This time, when they scream, the caste algorithm will come crashing down. It is then that humanity as humanity would be able to speak in its own voice, the voice of revolution. After all, as two philosophers said in the late 1840s, that it is "not criticism but revolution (that) is the driving force of history".[175]

Note

1. Indian Council of Social Science Research, New Delhi, India.
2. Ambedkar, Bhimrao Ramji (1989) "Untouchables or the Children of India's Ghetto and Other Essays", in *Dr. Babasaheb Ambedkar. Writings and Speeches*, Vol. 5. Mumbai: Education Department, Government of Maharashtra, p. 9.
3. Freud, Sigmund (1993) "The Psychoanalytic View of the Psychogenic Disturbance of Vision", in *The Penguins Freud Library, Vol. 10, On Psychopathology. Inhibitions, Symptoms and Anxiety and Other Works*. London: Penguin Books, p. 107.
4. Freud, Sigmund (1993) Op. Cit.
5. Risley, Herbert (1903) *Census of India*. Calcutta: Office of the Superintendent of Government, Printing, India and Risley, Herbert (1908) *The People of India*. Calcutta: Thacker, Spink and Co.

6. Golwalkar, M. S. (2006) "We or Our Nation Defined", in Shamsul Islam (ed.), *Golwalkar's We Our Nation Defined. A Critique with the Full Text of the Book*. New Delhi: Pharos Media, p. 47.
7. King, Richard (2008) *Orientalism and the Myth of Modern Hinduis*m. New Delhi: Critical Quest, p. 14.
8. Hardy, Friedhelm (1995) "A Radical Reassessment of the Vedic Heritage-The *Acaryahrdayam* with Its Wider Implications", in Vasudha Dalamia and Heinrich von Stieitencron (eds.), *Representing Hinduism: The Construction of Religious Traditions and National Identity*. New Delhi: Sage Publication, p. 48.
9. Lorenzen, David (1999) "Who Invented Hinduism?", *Comparative Studies in Society and History*, Vol. 41, No. 4, October, p. 631.
10. Lorenzen, David (1999) Op. Cit., p. 636.
11. Ambedkar, Bhimrao Ramji (2008) "Annihilation of Caste", in Valerian Rodrigues (ed.), *The Essential Writings of B.R. Ambedkar*. New Delhi: Oxford University Press, p. 267.
12. Swamy, Praveen (2014) Interview of Romila Thapar, "Ideas of History", *The Hindu*, April 5.
13. See the Zoroastrian (2002) *Pahlavi Vendidâd* (Zand=Î Jvît-Dêv=Dât), transliteration and translation by B. T. Anklesaria. Mumbai: K. R. Cama Oriental Institute, p. 12.
14. Ambedkar, Bhimrao Ramji (2008) "Reply to the Mahatma", in Valerian Rodrigues (ed.), *The Essential Writings of B.R. Ambedkar*. New Delhi: Oxford University Press.
15. Marx, Karl (1976) "The British Rule in India", in *On Colonialism*. Moscow: Progress Publishers, p. 40.
16. Marx, Karl (1974) *Grundrisse*, trans. Martin Nicholaus. Harmondsworth: Penguin Books, p. 478.
17. Ambedkar, Bhimrao Ramji (2008) "Annihilation of Caste", Op. Cit. p. 272.
18. Ambedkar, Bhimrao Ramji (2008) "Annihilation of Caste", Op. Cit. p. 268.
19. See Laing, R. D. (1990) *The Divided Self. An Existential Study in Sanity and Madness*. London: Penguin Books.
20. See his "Annihilation of Caste", p. 267; Ambedkar, Bhimrao, Ramji (1990) "Pakistan or the Partition of India", in *Dr. Babasaheb Ambedkar. Writings and Speeches*, Vol. 8 (Mumbai: Education Department, Government of Maharashtra, pp. 29–30; "On the Adoption of the Constitution", in Das Bhagwan (2010) (ed.), *Thus Spoke Ambedkar, Vol. 1. A Stake in the Nation*. New Delhi: Navayana, p. 220.
21. See Pinto, Ambrose (2002) "Caste Discrimination and UN", *Economic & Political Weekly*, September 28, who while writing on the August-September 2001 United Nations World Conference on Racism where he argues that caste-based atrocities is akin to race-based thus allowing international bodies to intervene in Third World countries says that:

> Members of the International Dalit Solidarity Network, Ambedkar Centre for Peace and Justice in Canada and others have warmly welcomed this important new development in the international human rights arena. Shigeyuki Kumisaka of the Buraku Liberation League declared that 'this General Recommendation will serve to encourage and empower three million Burakumin in Japan, as well as 260 million people suffering from caste-based and similar forms of discrimination in India and other countries in south Asia and Africa people who have long been forgotten, and on whose situation little light has ever been thrown'. According to Paul Divakar, the convener

of National Campaign on Dalit Human Rights, India 'the flood gates are now being flung open for addressing caste based discrimination at the United Nations. This will pressurize the government in India to take the issue of enforcement more seriously'.

22. Ambedkar, Bhimrao Ramji (2008) "Castes in India", in Valerian Rodrigues (ed.), *The Essential Writings of B.R. Ambedkar.* New Delhi: Oxford University Press, p. 257.

23. See Freud, Sigmund (1993) "Neurosis and Psychosis" and "Loss of Reality in Neurosis and Psychosis", in *The Penguin Freud Library, Vol. 10, On Psychopathology. Inhibitions, Symptoms and Anxiety and Other Works.* London: Penguin Books, pp. 213–226.

24. This is the passage from the (1992) *Rg Veda, Sacred Writings. Hinduism,* trans. Ralf T. F. Griffith. New York: Quality Paperback Books, p. 603, where this first reference to castes in Indian society emerges.

25. Dirks, Nicholas (2001) *Caste of Mind. Colonialism and the Making of Modern India.* Princeton, NJ: Princeton University Press, pp. 3–18.

26. See Ambedkar, Bhimrao Ramji (2010) "Capitalism, Labour and Brahmanism", in Bhagwan Das (ed.), *Thus Spoke Ambedkar. A Stake in the Nation,* Vol. 1. New Delhi: Navayana, p. 50.

27. Ambedkar, Bhimrao Ramji (2010) "The Failures of Parliamentary Democracy", in Bhagwan Das (ed.), *Thus Spoke Ambedkar. A Stake in the Nation,* Vol. 1. New Delhi: Navayana, p. 48.

28. Ambedkar, Bhimrao Ramji (2010) "Capitalism, Labour and Brāhmanism", Op. Cit., p. 51.

29. Ambedkar, Bhimrao Ramji (2010) "Capitalism, Labour and Brāhmanism", Op. Cit.

30. Ambedkar, Bhimrao Ramji (1993) "Manu and the Shudras", in *Dr Babasaheb Ambedkar. Writing and Speeches,* Vol. 12. Bombay: Education Department, Government of Maharashtra, p 719.

31. Ambedkar, Bhimrao Ramji (2010) "On the Justice Party of Madras", in Bhagwan Das (ed.), *Thus Spoke Ambedkar, Vol. 1. A Stake in the Nation.* New Delhi: Navayana, 2010, p. 106.

32. For the comparison of the Jews and Afro-Americans with the Untouchables see Ambedkar, Bhimrao Ramji (1989) "Untouchables or the Children of India's Ghetto and Other Essays", Op. Cit. pp. 3–5, pp. 12–14.

33. Ambedkar says that the Untouchables are constituted "outside the Hindu fold". Ambedkar, Bhimrao Ramji (1989) "Untouchables or the Children of India's Ghetto and Other Essays", Op. Cit., pp. 26, 27.

34. Ambedkar, Bhimrao Ramji (1989) "Untouchables or the Children of India's Ghetto and Other Essays", Op. Cit., p. 26.

35. Ambedkar, Bhimrao Ramji (1989) "Untouchables or the Children of India's Ghetto and Other Essays", Op. Cit.

36. Ambedkar, Bhimrao Ramji (1990) "Untouchables or the Children of India's Ghetto and Other Essays", in *Dr. Babasaheb Ambedkar. Writings and Speeches,* Vol. 5. Mumbai: Education Department, Government of Maharashtra, p. 19.

37. Ambedkar, Bhimrao Ramji (2010) "On the Draft Constitution", in Bhagwan Das (ed.), *Thus Spoke Ambedkar, Vol. 1. A Stake in the Nation.* New Delhi: Navayana, p. 175.

38. Ambedkar, Bhimrao Ramji (2010) "On the Eve of Resigning from the Cabinet", in Bhagwan Das (ed.), *Thus Spoke Ambedkar, Vol. 1. A Stake in the Nation.* New Delhi: Navayana, p. 124.

39. Ambedkar, Bhimrao Ramji (2010) "On the Eve of Resigning from the Cabinet", Op. Cit.
40. Ambedkar, Bhimrao Ramji (1989) "Untouchables or the Children of India's Ghetto", Op. Cit., p. 26.
41. Ambedkar, Bhimrao Ramji (2008) "Castes in India", Op. Cit., p. 262.
42. Ambedkar, Bhimrao Ramji (2010) "On the Draft Constitution", Op. Cit. p. 176.
43. Ambedkar, Bhimrao Ramji (2010) "On the Draft Constitution", Op. Cit.
44. Ambedkar, Bhimrao Ramji (2010) "On the Draft Constitution", Op. Cit.
45. Ambedkar, Bhimrao Ramji (1989) "States and Minorities", in *Dr Babasaheb Ambedkar Writings and Speeches*, Vol. 1, Bombay: Education Department, Government of Maharashtra, p. 425.
46. The idea of essence (*Wesen*) as the "ground of existence" is taken from the second part of Hegel's *Science of Logic*.
47. Ambedkar, Bhimrao Ramji (1989) "Ranade, Gandhi and Jinnah", in *Dr Babasaheb Ambedkar Writings and Speeches*, Vol. 1. Bombay: Education Department, Government of Maharashtra, pp. 226–227.
48. Ambedkar, Bhimrao Ramji (1989) "Ranade, Gandhi and Jinnah", Op. Cit. p. 227.
49. (1966) *Report of the Education Commission. 1964–66. Education and National Development*. New Delhi: Government of India, p. 11.
50. (1966) *Report of the Education Commission* Op. Cit., p. 7.
51. (1966) *Report of the Education Commission* Op. Cit., p. VIII.
52. (1966) *Report of the Education Commission* Op. Cit., p. IV.
53. Ambedkar, Bhimrao Ramji (2016) "What Congress and Gandhi Have Done to the Untouchables. Mr. Gandhi and the Emancipation of the Untouchables", in *Dr B.R. Ambedkar. Writings and Speeches*, Vol. 9. Mumbai: Dr Babasaheb Ambedkar Source Material Publication Committee, p. 109.
54. See Faiz, Ahmad (2000) "Subh-e-Azadi" (Freedom's Dawn), in V.G. Kiernan (ed.), *Poems by Faiz*. Delhi: Oxford University Press, p. 402. Also see Guha, Ramchandra (2012) *India after Gandhi. The History of the World's Largest Democracy*. London: Picador, p. 30.
55. See Shukla, Priyam (2022) "Tukde-Tukde, Jihadi, Khalistani: Popular Tweets from JNU's New Vice-Chancellor Shantishree Pandit", *Outlook*, February 15; Mahaprashasta, Ajay Ashirwad (2022) "On Twitter, New JNU VC Has Supported Genocide Calls, Attacked Students, Farmers", *The Wire*, February 7.
56. "UoP Shielding Indicted Former ISC Director", (2011) *The Times of India*, August 5.
57. See Naik, J.P. (1978) "To Begin a Revolution with a Revolution", in *The Social Context of Education. Essays in Honour of Professor J.P. Naik*. New Delhi: Allied Publishers Ltd., p. 1. See also (1966) *Report of the Education Commission. 1964–66. Education and National Development*. New Delhi: Government of India, p. 7.
58. See Jodhka, Surinder (2021) "Kanshi Ram and the Making of Dalit Political Agency. Leadership Legacies and the Politics of *Hissedari*", *Economic & Political Weekly*, Vol. 56, No. 3, 16 January.
59. See Dutt, R. Palme (2008) *India Today*. Bombay: Popular Publishing House, p. 471.
60. Ambedkar, Bhimrao Ramji (1989) "States and Minorities", Op. Cit. p. 416.
61. Marx, Karl (1975) "The Eighteenth Brumaire of Louis Bonaparte", in *Marx. Engels. Selected Works*. Moscow: Progress Publishers, p. 171.
62. Ambedkar, Bhimrao Ramji (1989) "States and Minorities", Op. Cit. p. 432.

63. Marcuse, Herbert (1968) *Negations. Essays in Critical Theory*, trans. Jeremy J. Shapiro. London: Alen Lane, The Penguin Press, p. 121.
64. Teltumbde, Anand (2018) *Republic of Caste. Thinking Equality in the Time of Neoliberal Hindutva*. New Delhi: Navayana, p. 24.
65. Teltumbde, Anand (2018) *Republic of Caste*. Op. Cit.
66. Free and compulsory education until the age of 14, as espoused originally in section 45 of the Directive Principles of the Constitution is noted in the *Report of the Education Commission. 1964–1966*, p. XIII. The fact that not only would this idea never be practiced, but the fact that it would be watered down must also be mentioned. Theory and practice in the Indian public world are always split.
67. See Moynihan, Daniel Patrick and Weaver, Suzanne (1980) *A Dangerous Place*. Berkeley, CA: Berkeley Publishing Group, p. 41. Daniel Patrick Moynihan later became American ambassador to India. Quite recently T.J.S. George wrote on this alleged "liberation struggle" of the landlords, capitalists and imperialist USA. It was Indira Gandhi who took on the responsibility of destabilizing the communist government at the behest of Nehru. It was her husband, Feroze Gandhi, who told her that "she had joined hands with the "caste monsters" in the state to undo a democratic election. You are bullying the people. You are a fascist". George, T.J.S. (2019) "Using State Powers to Crush Democracy: Congress Did It Then, BJP Now", *The New Indian Express*, August 18.
68. George, T.J.S. (2019) "Using State Powers to Crush Democracy: Congress Did it Then, BJP Now. Op. Cit., p. 7.
69. Guha, Ranajit (1988) *Dominance without Hegemony: History and Power in Colonial India*. New Delhi: Oxford University Press, p. 5. Also see Menon, Dilip M. (2011) *The Blindness of Insight. Essays on Caste in Modern India*. New Delhi: Vavayana, p. 75.
70. Menon, Dilip M. (2011) *The Blindness of Insight*. Op. Cit., p. 110.
71. Menon, Dilip M. (2011) *The Blindness of Insight*. Op. Cit.
72. Menon, Dilip M. (2011) *The Blindness of Insight*. Op. Cit.
73. Ambedkar, Bhimrao Ramji (2010) "The Failures of Parliamentary Democracy", Op Cit., p. 46.
74. Ambedkar, Bhimrao Ramji (2010) "The Failures of Parliamentary Democracy", Op Cit., p. 48.
75. Ambedkar, Bhimrao Ramji (2010) "The Failures of Parliamentary Democracy", Op Cit.
76. J.P. Naik, (1978) "To Begin a Revolution with a Revolution", in A.B. Shah, *The Social Context of Education*. New Delhi: Allied Publishers, p. 1, (1978), *Education for our People. A Policy Frame for the Development of Education* (1978–87). New Delhi: Allied Publishers, p. 1. Also see *Report of the Education Commission, 1964–66. Education & National Development*. New Delhi, Government of India, 1966), pp. 4–5.
77. Naik, J.P. (1978) "To Begin a Revolution with a Revolution", Op. Cit., p. 1.
78. Naik, J.P. (1978) "To Begin a Revolution with a Revolution", Op. Cit.
79. Naik, J.P. (1978) "To Begin a Revolution with a Revolution", Op. Cit.
80. Naik, J.P. (1978) "To Begin a Revolution with a Revolution", Op. Cit.
81. Ambedkar, Bhimrao, Ramji, "What Congress and Gandhi have Done to the Untouchables. Mr. Gandhi and the Emancipation of the Untouchables", Op. Cit., p. 270.
82. "Mind" here does not mean individualistic thinking in the Anglo-Saxon sense of the term, but more in the Hegelian sense of the *Geist*, or the spirit in ferment.
83. Ambedkar, Bhimrao Ramji (2008) "Annihilation of Caste", Op. Cit. p. 318.

84. See Lukács Georg (2016) *Destruction of Reason*, trans. Peter Palmer. Delhi: Aakar Books.
85. Ambedkar, Bhimrao Ramji (1990) "Pakistan or the Partition of India", in *Dr. Babasaheb Ambedkar. Writings and Speeches*, Vol. 8. Mumbai: Education Department, Government of Maharashtra, p. 358.
86. Ambedkar, Bhimrao Ramji (1989) "States and Minorities", Op. Cit., p. 425.
87. Ambedkar, Bhimrao Ramji (1989) "States and Minorities", Op. Cit.
88. Gavaskar, Mahesh (2007) "Colonialism within Colonialism", in S.M. Michael (ed.), *Dalits in Modern India. Visions and Values*. New Delhi: SAGE.
89. Ambedkar, Bhimrao Ramji (1989) "Untouchables or the Children of India's Ghetto and Other Essays", Op. Cit., p. 26.
90. Phule, Jotiba (2010) "Slavery", in G.P. Deshpande (ed.), *The Writings of Jotiba Phule*. New Delhi: LeftWord, p. 71.
91. Phule, Jotiba (2010) "Slavery", Op. Cit.
92. Phule, Jotiba (2010) "Slavery", Op. Cit.
93. Phule, Jotiba (2010) "Slavery", Op. Cit.
94. Phule, Jotiba (2010) "Slavery", Op. Cit., p. 73.
95. Phule, Jotiba (2010) "Slavery", Op. Cit., p. 72.
96. Žižek, Slavoj (2012) *Organs without Bodies*. London and New York: Routledge, p. 4.
97. See Derrett, John Duncan Martin (1975) *Manuśāstravivarana*. Wiesbaden: Brill.
98. Dirks, Nicholas (2001) *Castes of Mind*. Op. Cit., p. 218.
99. Dirks, Nicholas (2001) *Castes of Mind*. Op. Cit.
100. Risley, Herbert (1908) *Census of India*. Op. Cit. also (1908) *The People of India*. Calcutta: Thacker, Spink and Co.
101. Risley, Herbert (1908) *The People of India*, Op. Cit., pp. 31–47.
102. Risley, Herbert (1908) *The People of India*, Op. Cit., p. 26.
103. Risley, Herbert (1908) *The People of India*, Op. Cit., p. 50.
104. Risley, Herbert (1908) *The People of India*, Op. Cit., p. 66.
105. Risley, Herbert (1908) *The People of India*, Op. Cit., pp. 53–54.
106. Risley, Herbert (1908) *The People of India*, Op. Cit., p. 67.
107. Quoted in Omvedt, Gail (1994) *Dalits and the Democratic Revolution. Dr Ambedkar and the Dalit Movement in Colonial India*. New Delhi: SAGE Publication, p. 197; Also Jaferlot, Christophe (2005) *Dr Ambedkar and Untouchability. Analyzing and Fighting Caste*. Delhi: Permanent Black, p. 78.
108. Gandhi, M.K. (2011) "The Congress and After", *Young India*, January 5, 1922, in *What is Hinduism?* New Delhi: National Book Trust, p. 15.
109. Gandhi, M.K. (1924) "What May Hindus Do?", *Young India*, June 19, pp. 21–22.
110. Nehru, Jawaharlal (1946) *The Discovery of India*. London: Meridian Press, pp. 60–62.
111. Nehru, Jawaharlal (1946) *The Discovery of India*, Op. Cit.
112. Nehru, Jawaharlal (1946) *The Discovery of India*, Op. Cit., pp. 206–212.
113. Nehru, Jawaharlal (1946) *The Discovery of India*, Op. Cit., p. 207.
114. Nehru, Jawaharlal (1946) *The Discovery of India*, Op. Cit.
115. Nehru, Jawaharlal (1946) *The Discovery of India*, Op. Cit., p. 273.
116. Nehru, Jawaharlal (2001) *An Autobiography*. New Delhi: Oxford University Press, p. 459.
117. See Jal, Murzban (2018) *In the Name of Marx*. Delhi: Aakar Books, pp. 52–53.

118. Gandhi, M.K. (2011) "Hinduism", *Young India*, October 6, 1921, in *What Is Hinduism?* New Delhi: National Book Trust, p. 6. See also Dutt, R. Palme (2008) *India Today*, Op. Cit., p. 471.
119. Gandhi, M.K. (1966) "Caste Versus Class", *Young India*, December 29, 1920, in *Collected Works of Mahatma Gandhi*, Vol. 22. Ahmedabad: The Publication Division, Ministry of Information and Broadcasting, Government of India, pp. 154–155.
120. Gandhi, M.K. (2011) "The Congress and After", Op. Cit. p. 15.
121. Gandhi, M.K. (2017) *The Bhagavad Gita*. Mumbai: Jaico Publishing House, p. 3.
122. Gandhi, M.K. (1966) "The Caste System", (1920) in *Collected Works of Mahatma Gandhi*, Vol. 19. Ahmedabad: The Publication Division, Ministry of Information and Broadcasting, Government of India, p. 83. See also Anderson, Perry (2012) *The Indian Ideology*. Gurgaon: Three Essays Collective, p. 37, n. 40.
123. Gandhi, M.K. (2017) *The Bhagavad Gita*, Op. Cit., p. 3.
124. Gandhi, M.K. (1966) "The Caste System", Op. Cit., p. 84.
125. Gandhi, M.K. (1924) "What May Hindus Do?", Op. Cit., p. 21.
126. Ambedkar, Bhimrao Ramji (2008) "Castes in India", Op. Cit., p. 253.
127. Naik, J.P. (1975) *Equality, Quality and Quantity. The Elusive Triangle*. Pune: Indian Institute of Education, p. 1.
128. Naik, J.P. (1975) *Equality, Quality and Quantity*. Op. Cit., p. 2.
129. Naik, J.P. (1975) *Equality, Quality and Quantity*. Op. Cit.
130. Naik, J.P. (1975) *Equality, Quality and Quantity*. Op. Cit., p. 3.
131. Naik, J.P. (1975) *Equality, Quality and Quantity*. Op. Cit.
132. Quoted in Dreze, Jean and Sen, Amartya (2013) *An Uncertain Glory. India and Its Contradictions*. London: Allen Lane, p. 107.
133. Marx, Karl (1982) *Economic and Philosophic Manuscripts of 1844*. Moscow: Progress Publishers, p. 99.
134. Weber, Max (1922) 'Science as a Vocation', 'Wissenschaftals Beruf,' from *Gesammlte Aufsaetze zur Wissenschaftslehre*. Tubingen, pp. 524–55. Originally delivered as a speech at Munich University, 1918. Published in 1919 by Duncker & Humblodt, Munich.
135. Naik, J.P. (1978) "To Begin a Revolution with a Revolution", Op. Cit., pp. 1–13.
136. See Žižek, Slavoj (2007) "Introduction. Robespierre, or, 'Divine violence' of Terror", in Maximilien Robespierre (ed.), *Virtue and Terror*. London: Verso, op. XII.
137. See Banaji, Jairus (2013) (ed.), *Fascism. Essays on Europe and India*. Gurgaon: Three Essays Collective. Also see Zachariah, Benjamin (2014) "A Voluntary *Gleichschaltung*? Perspectives for India Towards a Non-Eurocentric Understanding of Fascism", *The Journal of Transcultural Studies*, Vol. 5, No. 2; and Pavoe, Federico (2019) *Fascism in Asia: A Comparative Analysis*, Department of Political Science, Luiss University, Rome.
138. Alatas, Syed Farid (2006) *Alternative Discourses in Asian Social Science. Responses to Eurocentrism*. New Delhi: SAGE Publications, pp. 47–50. See also his father Alatas, Syed Hussein (1972) "The Captive Mind in Development Studies", *International Social Science Journal*, Vol. 34, No. 1; also Alatas, Syed Hussein (2000) "Intellectual Imperialism: Definition, Traits and Problems", *Southeast Asian Journal of Social Science*, Vol. 28, No. 1; and Alatas, Syed Hussein (1977) *The Myth of the Lazy Native: A Study of Malays,*

Filipinos and Javanese from the Sixteenth to the Twentieth Century and Its Functions in the Ideology of Colonial Capitalism. London: Frank Cass.

139. See Nandy, Ashis (2010) "History's Forgotten Doubles", in *The Romance of the State and the Fate of Dissent in the Tropics.* New Delhi: Oxford University Press, p. 94.
140. Alatas, Syed Farid (2006) *Alternative Discourses in Asian Social Science.* Op. Cit., p. 25.
141. Bourdieu, Pierre (2008) "The Naked Emperors of the University", in *Political Interventions. Social Science and Political Action*, trans. David Fernbach. New Delhi: Navayana, pp. 147–155.
142. For the idea of the "Republic of Untouchability" see Ambedkar, Bhimrao Ramji, (1989) "Untouchables or the Children of India's Ghetto and Other Essays", Op. Cit.; and for the idea of the "Republic of Caste" see Teltumbde, Anand (2018) *Republic of Caste.* Op. Cit.
143. Phule, Jotiba (2020) "Slavery", Op. Cit., p. 45.
144. See Patnaik, Prabha (2012) *Re-envisioning Socialism.* New Delhi: Tulika Books, p. 112.
145. Patnaik, Prabha (2012) *Re-envisioning Socialism*, Op. Cit.
146. Bhushan, Sudanshu (2019) "A Dithering Higher Education Policy", *Economic and Political Weekly*, Vol. LIV, No 24, June 15.
147. Bhushan, Sudanshu (2019) "A Dithering Higher Education Policy", Op. Cit., p. 12.
148. See Prasad, Chandra Ban (2013) "Capitalism Is Changing Caste Much Faster Than Any Human Being. Dalits Should Look at Capitalism as a Crusader against Caste", *Indian Express*, June 11.
149. See Jal, Murzban (2018) *Why We Are Not Hindus.* Delhi: Aakar Books, p. 117.
150. Jal, Murzban (2018) *Why We Are Not Hindus.* Op. Cit., pp. 116–117.
151. Ambedkar, Bhimrao Ramji (2010) "On the Adoption of the Constitution", Op. Cit., p. 219.
152. See Sartre, Jean-Paul (2007) *Colonialism and Neocolonialism.* London and New York: Routledge.
153. Naik, J.P. (1978) "To Begin a Revolution with a Revolution". Op. Cit.
154. Paul, Samuel (2014) "Internationalization of Education", in J.B.G. Tilak (ed.), *Higher Education in India. In Search of Equality, Quality and Quantity.* Hyderabad: Orient Blackswan, pp. 449–460. Paul however says that India has "the largest number of higher educational institutes . . . well above those of the US and China", p. 453.
155. Ambedkar, Bhimrao Ramji (1989) "The Untouchables", Op. Cit., p. 19.
156. Naik, J.P. (1978) "To Begin a Revolution with a Revolution", Op. Cit., p. 2.
157. Naik, J.P. (1978) "To Begin a Revolution with a Revolution". Op. Cit.
158. See his "Repeating Lenin", in Lacan.com.
159. See Žižek, Slavoj "Introduction. Robespierre, Op. Cit., p. XII.
160. Naik, J.P. (1978) "To Begin a Revolution with a Revolution" Op. Cit.
161. von Humbold, Wilhelm (2012) "Theory of *Bildung*", in Ian Westbury, Stefan Hopmann, and Kurt Riquarts (eds.), *Teaching as a Reflective Practice: The German Didaktik Tradition.* London: Routledge.
162. One is making a parody on the infamous statement by the Nazi Minister of Propaganda, Josef Goebbels, who said: "When I hear the word culture I reach for my gun". See Žižek, Slavoj (2007) "Tolerance as Ideological Category", *Critical Inquiry*, Autumn.

163. Horkheimer, Max and Adorno, Theodor (1972) *Dialectic of Enlightenment*, trans. John Cumming. New York: Herder and Herder, p. 167.
164. Walter Benjamin, Walter (1979) "The Work of Art in the Age of Mechanical Reproduction", in *Illuminations*, trans. Harry Zohn. Glasgow: Fontana/Collins, p. 249.
165. Jameson, Fredric (1991) *Postmodernism or the Cultural Logic of Late Capitalism*. London: Verso, p. 14.
166. Harvey, David (2007) "Neo-liberalism and the City", *Studies in Social Justice*, Vol. 1, No. 1, Winter, p. 13.
167. See Chattopadhyay, Saumen (2010) "An Elitist and Flawed Approach towards Higher Education", *Economic & Political Weekly*, Vol. XIV, No. 18.
168. This is James Marshall's term. See Maureen Ford, '"Willed" to Choose: Education Power and Busno-power', in A. Neimann (ed.), in *Philosophy of Education. 1995. Proceedings of the Philosophy of Education Society* (Champagne: Philosophy of Education Society, 1995).
169. See Olssen, Mark and. Peters, Michael A. (2005) "Neoliberalism, Higher Education and the Knowledge Economy: From the Free Market to Knowledge Capitalism", *Journal of Education Policy*, Vol. 20, No. 3, pp. 314–315.
170. Ibid. Also see Foucault, Michel (1991) "Governmentality", in G. Burchell, C. Gordon and P. Miller (eds.), *The Foucault Effect: Studies in Governmentality*. Chicago, IL: University of Chicago Press.
171. Marshall, James (1999) "The Mode of Information and Education. Insights on Critical Theory from Michel Foucault", in Thomas S. Popkewitz and Lynn Fendler (eds.), *Changing Terrain of Knowledge and Politics*. London and New York: Routledge, p. 165.
172. Lacan, Jacques (1978) *The Four Fundamental Concepts of Psychoanalysis*, trans. Alan Sheridan. London: Penguin Books, p. 212.
173. This is a quote of Lord Benedict. See, Dutt, R. Palme *India Today* Op. Cit., p. 82.
174. Marx, Karl (1983) *Capital*, Vol. I, trans. Samuel Moore and Edward Aveling. Moscow: Progress Publishers, p. 711.
175. Marx, Karl and Engels, Frederick (1976) *The German Ideology*. Moscow: Progress Publishers, p. 61.

9 Critical and Caring Pedagogies

Habermas and Ambedkar at the Intersections of Caste and Gender[1]

Kanchana Mahadevan[2]

> Education should encourage the new young to ask the teacher, one new question a day.
>
> —(Ambedkar 2014g, p. 378)

State education commissions in post-colonial India replaced the British civilisational mission with postcolonial welfare nationalism. In tandem with these goals, policy focused on equitable access to scientific and technological vocational skills needed for employment. These institutional measures culminated in the enforcement of the Right of Children to Free and Compulsory Education Act or Right to Education Act (RTE) in 2009, making education a fundamental right. Thus, those without socio-economic privileges have been gradually accessing educational institutions.

These gains notwithstanding, communicative gaps across divides of caste, gender and class have widened. As Dewey notes, and as alluded to in the opening quote from Ambedkar, communication is integral to "creative democracy" in which new solidarities of egalitarianism can be constructed through heightened dialogue between social groups, as well as between groups and individuals. The relationship between the individual and the group, as well as between groups becomes integral to inclusiveness. Thus, autonomy is related to solidarity, following Habermas. Yet, critique becomes a necessary condition for such communication to materialise, for which the curriculum has to enable a Habermasian critique of hegemonic ideologies of caste and gender. But, unlike Habermas's abstract critique of the system world, the critique of caste and patriarchy would have to be both contextual and substantive. This requires a pedagogical space that scrutinises knowledge systems developed through privileges of caste, class, gender, tribe (and others). Jyotiba Phule articulated such a substantive notion of critique as *Trutiya Ratna*, or the "third eye", as the first step in his version of the pedagogy of the oppressed. Sharmila Rege and Shailaja Paik have empirically documented how such critique forms

DOI: 10.4324/9781003155065-9

the basis of contemporary Dalit-feminist pedagogical practice. Ambedkar developed Phule into a full-blown critique of segregation as the dominant Brahmanical concept and practice impeding egalitarianism. He suggests a Deweyan mode of communication across barriers of caste and gender in Indian society to forge alternate, egalitarian solidarities of community. This resonates with Habermas as well. For both Ambedkar and Habermas, such communities can be ushered in through the agency of the underprivileged via critique and communities that blur the line between the social and the political.

Communicative solidarities cannot be achieved through critique alone; they require simultaneous affective practices of care. However, extending the insights of critics such as Olena Hankivsky, caring practices are enmeshed in relations of power, compelling those from vulnerable castes, especially women, to perform exploitative caring practices. Further, the British civilizing mission sustained itself in India through care. Hence, care poses questions of equity: How can one decolonise care both externally, from imperialist knowledge production, and internally, from Brahminism, both of which are patriarchal? Would the privileged pedagogically adopt the caring practices of the underprivileged to initiate non-exploitative communities? This chapter examines prospects for pedagogies of critical care and caring critiques through Ambedkar's notion of critique as embedded in care. It argues that he offers a richer notion of critique in relation to Habermas, given his appropriation of the Buddhist notion of *karuna* (compassion). The latter can respond to critiques of care by engaging with care at the intersection of caste and gender.

I Right to Education and the Persistent Inaccessibility to Education

The "colonial encounter" (Devy 2017) with the British in India since the 18th century had dismantled the earlier educational systems to create "cultural amnesia" towards Indian knowledge systems; however, as Devy himself notes, one cannot simply foist the prevailing ills on the imperialistic designs of the British (Devy 2017, p. 15). Devy cites Ambedkar's analysis of the crisis to show how discrimination against the oppressed castes, tribes and women was institutionalised by traditional knowledge systems. The divisions and fractures become evident in their being inadequately represented in institutions. He notes how pre-British India had two knowledge frameworks, the hegemonic Brahminical canon to which a privileged few had access.

Access to education has been the most difficult problem in India. This is especially troubling because the marginalised sections of India are vast and have sedimented structures (Devy 2017, p. 47). Accessibility of education reflects a society that is egalitarian and democratic; while the struggle to gain access to education reflects the struggle for democratising society. In this context, the Right to Education Act, enacted in the Parliament in 2009[3] (and becoming effective in 2010), has been pathbreaking. For it enunciates free education as a right following the 86th Amendment to the Indian Constitution in 2002, under Article 21A in an endeavour to remedy the long-standing struggle of large sections of Indians to gain access to education. Education has become a fundamental right in India almost a hundred years after Gopal Krishna Gokhale introduced a resolution for free and compulsory education to the Imperial Legislative Assembly in 1910, followed by a bill in 1911 (Mondal 2017; Mehendale 2018). Gokhale's bill was rejected; for it would prevent the easy availability of cheap agricultural labour; moreover, those with financial resources did not want to pay additional tax for free education. Gokhale was inspired by Sir Sayajirao Gaikwad, who introduced such education in the princely state of Baroda. Before Gokhale, activists like Jyotiba Phule, Savitribai Phule and Pherozeshah Mehta pioneered free and compulsory mass education. The Phules started the first school for girls in 1848. Nationalistic-minded Indians made a case for such education against the backdrop of England, having introduced free and compulsory schooling in 1870. However, these efforts gave rise to a widespread social interest and demand for free and compulsory education. Ambedkar's work focused on the need to give access to education to the disempowered sections of society (Ambedkar 2019). Even the colonial government felt it necessary to offer access to education through periodic legislations that paralleled the ban on children working in industry. Endeavours to make education accessible continued through the decades after Indian independence. The various commissions in post-independent India for education, women, scheduled castes, scheduled tribes, women and minorities have not managed to effectively change either the lack of access or the lack of memory of those from the margins (Devy 49). Despite all the legal efforts, the All India Survey for Higher Education in India reveals the following dismal figures for students from socially vulnerable sections in institutions of higher learning for the year 2019–20: 14.7% Scheduled Castes, 5.6% Scheduled Tribes, 37% Other Backward Castes, 5.5% Muslims and 2.3% Other Minority Communities (AISHE 2020). It terms women's enrollment in public educational institutions as the lowest. School enrollment figures in the seventh survey conducted in 2002 reflect how imbalances at the primary school level get translated to those at the higher education levels: 21.07% Scheduled Castes, 9.37% Scheduled Tribes and 15.46% Educationally Backward Minority Community (NCERT 2006).

Yet a change was ushered in; education as a fundamental right was made official after the 86th Amendment to the Constitution of India. The 2009

RTE Act mandating free and compulsory education under Article 21(A) of the Indian Constitution also underlines the duties of the state, family, school and teachers in this regard.[4] Moreover, it also makes non-minority schools, along with the government and the parents of children, responsible for such education that was seen as a right for the child. The Act is also "childcentric" in many ways. The RTE has ushered in the ideal of education as every child's fundamental right and thereby introduced a new way to look at education. Hence, although the age for entry is prescribed as six, it explicitly notes the need for "early childhood care" for those below this age. Hence, the Act states that "local authorities" should make arrangements for pre-schooling and for preparing those from age three for elementary education. The RTE also makes it clear that children will not be denied admission for want of a document certifying age or held back in classes. It prohibits unethical practices such as capitation fees and screening procedures at the time of admission. It states that "No child shall be subjected to physical punishment or mental harassment". Moreover, it is committed to "making the child free of free, trauma and anxiety and helping the child express views freely". It "ensures that the child belonging to weaker section and disadvantaged group" is not discriminated against simply on the basis of caste, class, gender and religion. It is especially significant because it makes it mandatory for all privately funded schools to reserve 25% of their seats for children from the socially and economically vulnerable groups in the neighbourhood.

Although the RTE had equitable access to education as its central goal, its implementation has been bleak as only 9.54% schools had moved towards its ideals in 2017 (Dhankar 2019).[5] The inadequacy of financial sources for fulfilling the obligations for inclusive education is an oft-cited reason. Even the modest figure of allocating 6% of the GDP for schooling has not materialised (India Today 2021). The economic responsibility is undertaken by government bodies such as Sarva Shikshan Abhyan,[6] which has been seeing a decline of funds. Moreover, there is scant information regarding the number and status of students from marginalised communities who have gained admission through RTE, both in public and private schools. Educationists observe that the RTE has led to an increase in enrolment over the years[7] and even improvement in infrastructure; however, it has not improved in terms of students from underprivileged backgrounds staying back to acquire quality education for self and community development. The latter requires having sufficient numbers of teachers mentoring students to prevent dropouts (India Today 2021).[8] It also needs institutions that do not discriminate against students or subject them to violence. Statistics divulge how those from vulnerable groups struggle to stay in an educational system, even after entering it. For instance, in 2014–15, the dropout rates were as follows: boys, 17.6%; girls, 16.9%;

scheduled castes, over 19%; scheduled tribes, over 24% (Dejaeghere and Arur 2020, p. 2). As Paik, Dejaeghere and Arur note, such figures show the need for adopting an intersectional approach that takes gender, along-side caste, class and social disadvantages to understand the difficulties of students who drop out. Dropout rates indicate the absence of support that such students receive in the educational process. They routinely face discrimination and violence in schools and institutions, which are often even physically beyond their reach (Dejaeghere and Arur 2020, p. 3; Paik 2014; Lahariya 2018).

The obstacles to realising the goals of inclusive education specified in the RTE are financial constraints, commodification of education and social stratification (Arora and Rai 2020; India Today 2021). Those from afflu-ent backgrounds prefer to send their students to expensive private schools, rather than public educational institutes. This is because they prefer a gated school-going community. Given social stratification along the lines of caste, class and gender, the vulnerable have no access to commodified education in private schools. As analysts observe, the very idea of a common neigh-bourhood school as a "common resource" (India Today 2021) was sug-gested so that children from diverse caste, class and gendered groups could mingle and be interdependent, regardless of their social position. However, such a free attitude to children from diverse backgrounds intermingling with one another is held in great suspicion in "graded" social contexts such as the Indian context. Indeed, the RTE does not foreground a com-mon school that would allow students from multifarious backgrounds to intermingle (India Today 2021). Yet the Education Commission under Dr. Kothari (1964–66) had made this recommendation years ago, while sug-gesting that free and fair, equitable education be accessible to all (India Today 2021).

The social fences of caste and gender (among other vulnerabilities) in accessing education are encapsulated in the predicament of Ekalavya, a character in the *Mahabharata*, an epic about warring brothers.[9] The episode on Ekalavya, a prince from the forest-dwelling, disempowered Nishada tribe,[10] narrates his wish to learn archery from a renowned teacher, Dro-nacharya. However, Drona refused to teach Ekalavya, in whom he did see potential and talent; Drona did not want his favourite talented pupil from the dominant Kshatriya caste, Arjuna, to be overtaken. Ekalavya returned to the forest and created a clay image of Drona, which he worshipped as his teacher as he practiced his archery. He excelled in his skills to eventu-ally be discovered by Arjuna and his brothers, to whom he proclaimed that he was Drona's disciple. On learning about Ekalavya's abilities from a jeal-ous Arjuna, Drona extracted a price from Ekalavya for being his teacher, whereby Ekalavya sacrificed his right-hand thumb. Ekalavya readily gave his thumb, but realised that he had lost his earlier deftness in handling arms; as a result, Arjuna's position in the art and craft of warfare remained unvanquished. This story reveals how social diremptions violate students, such as Ekalavya, from unprivileged backgrounds, subjecting them to the dominant social order. It also conveys the extent of authoritarianism in the figure of a teacher, whose reverence is also the reverence of the wall of casteist prejudice that hinders the student from getting the deserved recognition.

Pedagogic situations are enmeshed in social contexts, whereby they can influence and be influenced by society. As Ambedkar notes, "It will be granted that each kind of association, as it is an educative environment, exercises a formative influence on the active dispositions of its members. Consequently, what one is as a person is what one is as associated with others" (Ambedkar 2014c, 251). Given the social character of individuals, they are not primary sovereign units constituting society (Ambedkar 2014b, 2014c; Dewey 1957; Habermas 1989/90). Rather their individuality is linked to, but not reducible to the social horizons with opportunities for or impediments to self-development. Ambedkar cites Dewey, who notes that the relationship between individuals and society reveals that one cannot emphasise the givenness of either the individual or society (Dewey 1957, pp. 194–197). Neither is an instrument of the other, but their coevality implies that each contributes to creating and nurturing the other. Individual moral development is related to social change and transformation and vice versa (Dewey 1957, p. 196). Thus, social organisations and institutions directed towards human welfare are environments for achieving individuals. Individuality is a process of "achievements" comprising "initiative, inventiveness, varied resourcefulness, assumption of responsibility in choice of belief and conduct" (Dewey 1957, p. 194). Further such a perspective on self-hood as a work in progress is linked to social change as a way of cultivating, vitalising and tending individuals (1957, pp. 196–197). The social contexts are assessed through their "educative effect: with reference to the type of individuals they foster" (1957, p. 196). The individual cannot be essentialised into one idea, it rather refers to varieties of actions, tendencies and abilities that occur through the social as associated life (Dewey 1957, p. 200). Similarly, the social refers to diverse notions such as voluntary associations, tribes, villages, urban cities and even transnational co-operations (Dewey 1957, p. 200).

Given this relationship between the individual and society, the ability to chalk the course of one's life at the individual level is also connected with shaping the larger social order. Individual and collective self-determination accompany one another in the struggle for freedom.[11] As Habermas notes, freedom from external tyrannical forces and freedom from within to pursue a project or action are corelated in a democracy (1996, pp. 84–104). The relationship between individual rights and democracy implies that each is necessary in fostering and sustaining the other. Hence, private and public or political autonomy are, for Habermas, "co-original" (Habermas 1996, 104). Thus, freedom at the individual level is linked to its facilitation and intersubjective recognition at the political legal level; however, the process of dialogue and deliberation connects the private and public dimensions of freedom (Habermas 1996, p. 104).[12] The capacity to discourse and debate reinforces individual freedom in a larger culture of freedom. Habermas draws upon the women's movement to argue that, at the personal level, women can freely pursue their projects only if the public sphere does not discriminate against them and also enables their active participation. All of this, in turn, requires vigorous communicative contestations of taken-for-granted gender roles, assumed to be fallible and changing, in which both men and women participate (1996, pp. 425–426).

The social domain lends itself to pedagogy, both literally, in offering schools, and also metaphorically, in creating an environment for development. Thus, individuals who are situated in society can grow and develop only if the barriers to communication are removed. This, in turn, requires a critique of impediments to social interaction. Social critique occurs from a commitment to the regulative ideal of the normative force of inclusive social communication; the aspiration for realising social communication—however inadequate—motivates such communication. The obstacles to Ekalavya's self-development are rooted in the structural discrimination based on the hierarchies of caste and gender. The latter dither social communication and spill into an educational system, segregating learners from each other and their teachers. In the Indian context, the segregation of caste and gender are reflected in what Habermas has termed as a technical civilisation's separation between theory and praxis through the division between "social engineers and inmates of institutions" (1973, p. 282). Critique of fractured social relations is a step towards creating inclusive communicative cultures of education.

II Critiquing Caste, Peregrinating Towards Communicative Pedagogies

Contemporary reiterations of Ekalavya's story have often been mentioned by Dalit writers who reimagine the possibilities of Ekalavya as a figure of resistance (Doniger 2014, pp. 554–555). They critique Ekalavya's sacrifice, as the following verse from Shashikant Hingonekar's poem reveals:

"If you had kept your thumb
history would have happened
somewhat differently.
But . . . you gave your thumb

and history also
became theirs"
(Doniger 2014, p. 554)

Similarly, Tryambak Sapkale's poem implores

"O Ekalavya,
You ideal disciple!
Give me the finger you cut off;
That will be my fulcrum."
(Doniger 2014, p. 554)

But all contemporary writers do not critique or reject the figure Ekalavya, who represents learners from disadvantaged backgrounds, as Doniger claims (2014, p. 555), although they do critique and reject the Hindu caste order via Ekalavya. There are poets who have reimagined Ekalavya's sacrifice as motivating them to work towards getting an education, as the following words by the poet Waman Nimbalkar reveal: "I am conscious of my resolve,/the worth of the blood of Ekalavya's finger" (Doniger 2014, p. 554). Dalit writers have also reimagined Ekalavya's story in alternate ways that encourage self-development without depending on teachers. The following poem, *Sabak* ("Lesson"), by Surekha Ratan Bhagat, reveals that present day Ekalavyas do not gullibly depend on teachers, such as Dronacharya, who extract their freedom and talent as sacrificial fees. Indeed, *Sabak*[13] reveals that they develop themselves through a critical distance from social hierarchies.

"He fondled the chisel,
Each chisel stroke
Shapes a song into being.
He'd found that out all right!
So that he could lay his hands on the chisel
He managed to learn everything—
No Dronacharya for him!
Unlike Ekalavya
This Ekalavya was his own guru.
That was when they stopped
Exacting the fee from the disciple.
The way Dronacharya did."

This poem focuses on the modern Ekalavya's ability to comprehend his talent and develop it as an independent seeker without the "blessings"— however imaginary—of a guru. Following Ambedkar, he questions "old habits, ideas, practices" (2014g, p. 378) to thereby distance himself from the flawed teachers in myths and traditions. Consequently, Ekalavya critiques the barriers of caste because of which he does not simply hand over the "fee" of his thumb to his guru. Rather, he wields his chisel to critique the barriers to learning while cultivating his own skills and creating art. In ridding Ekalavya of the presence of Drona, the poem gestures towards opportunities for self-development and creativity. He becomes his own light in the spirit of Ambedkar (2014g, p. 382). Yet, foisting off the iron grip of teachers such as Drona is not a one-off psychological act exclusively dependent on individual resilience. Ekalavya was not tyrannised so much for his individual talent as for his membership in a stigmatised social group. Ambedkar points out how groups are guarded carefully with a heightened sense of patriotic "group belonging"[14]; each group competes with others due to "interests of its own" (Ambedkar 2014b, p. 52).[15] Ekalavya's plight is the outcome of such "anti-social spirit" (Ambedkar 2014b, pp. 51–52) that isolates clans from each other by mobilising them to patrol their possessions and skills without sharing them with those from other groups.[16] Hindrances to socialisation that obstruct individual growth of the Ekalavyas in education have to be critiqued both as freedom from oppressive social relations and the freedom to self-development.

Rathod's *Sabak* shows how social inheritance needs to be selectively transmitted to the new generations through critique and reconstruction (Ambedkar 2014b, p. 79). Citing his teacher, Dewey, Ambedkar notes that "what is trivial, with dead wood from the past, and with what is positively perverse" (Ibid, p. 79) cannot be handed down, as it hinders freedom and growth. Critique enables opening up emancipatory social relations by diagnosing the norms, institutions and practices responsible for crisis to explore possibilities for unrestricted and free social relations (Cordero 2014, p. 498). Like the 20th-century Ekalavya in *Sabak*, girls from underprivileged caste backgrounds strived hard to develop themselves, despite the hindrances to mass education. Urmila Pawar and Meenakshi Moon note that it was possible for those from socially vulnerable castes to get an education only after the British arrived in India (2008, pp. 73–81). They note how "untouchables" received employment in the British military and did diverse jobs; Ambedkar's father himself served in the army. Pawar and Moon document various efforts made during the late 19th and early 20th centuries to establish free schools for girls from underprivileged castes. They note that teachers with caste privilege would often refuse to work in such schools, which had teachers from the Muslim and Christian communities. Scholarships, reading rooms, debating associations and hostels were initiated as means of motivating these students (Pawar and Moon 2014 [2008], p. 77). Princely rulers, such as Sayajirao Gaikwad from Baroda and Shahu Maharaj from Kohlapur, took deep interest in their education.

Under such crushing circumstances, girls from underprivileged caste backgrounds did manage to get an education, with immense effort, through their critical powers.

Critique has been integral to the practices of Dalit pedagogies as Paik (2014, pp. 146–186)[17] and Rege (2021) have documented. Paik observes how, since the 19th century, with the efforts of Jyotiba Phule, Savitribai Phule and their student Muktabai Salve, a critique of several layers of discrimination that include caste, class and gender faced by Dalit women was articulated as the first step towards creating educational institutions for them.[18] She notes how Phule and Salve describe the specific ways caste intersected with gender to exclude Dalit women from the ambit of education (2014, pp. 150–151). Their critiques revealed how Brahminism practiced hypocrisy by projecting the goal of education but denying it to underprivileged castes and women. Moreover, women from privileged castes did not care to include those without caste capital in their accounts of women's emancipation. With Ambedkar's raising of social consciousness, since the 1920s, more Dalit women entered the domain of education (a space that tied together politics and society) as agents (Paik 2014, pp. 158–172). Paik delineates how women such as Chandrikabai Ramteke, Jaibai Chaudhari, Sulochanabai Dongre, Ratibai Naik, Lakmibai Puranik, Radhabai Kamble, Parbatabai Meshram and many others pioneered Dalit women's activism in the socio-political domain (Paik 2014, pp. 172–180).[19] She documents their participation in the public sphere, with a focus on dignity, self-respect and equal rights for underprivileged women to create educative spaces and opportunities for learning for Dalit girls, in particular. Kannabiran notes how Dalit women's agency combines the affirmation of a distinct identity with that of the collective (2006) to reach out to other spheres in society. Rege gives a detailed account of Dalit critical pedagogy in recent contexts, with efforts undertaken by girls from underprivileged castes critically engaging with the educational system (2021). Velaskar describes the agency that Dalit women acquired through building egalitarian communities as they educated them themselves (2012, pp. 257–264).

Critique, which etymologically belongs to the Greek *kritikos* (to make judgements) and *krinein* (to distinguish), as well as the Latin *criticus* (to judge or censor), is not simply fault finding. It is, rather, a mode of comprehending the manner in which the assumptions and ideologies of social domination have become a part of everyday practices, both for the oppressed and for the oppressor. Habermas does not think of individuals as deluded by irrationality in upholding dominating social relations that inhibit them. According to him, social domination is maintained through institutionalisation, giving it a tone of legitimacy to mask its instrumentalism (Habermas 1989, pp. 106–107, 1974, p. 8; Ortega-Esquembre 2015, p. 4). For Habermas, the perspectives of instrumentalism and intersubjective communication are linked to interests, the former to control and the latter to emancipation (1974, p. 8). Instrumentalism does not problematise the ethical or practical aspects of social relations; it only aims at exercising technical control over possible sources of social conflicts. In the classical version of Ekalavya's story, the notions of sacrifice and reverence for the teacher as an omniscient guru are used to maintain social domination. Ekalavya willingly hands over his thumb as an act of sacrifice because of the highest esteem in which he held his guru. Although Doniger considers the Ekalavya story to focus more on the devotion of a disciple to a teacher, rather than the inequality of the Nishada tribes (Doniger 2014, p. 549), it clearly depicts how a teacher from a privileged caste treats a person from the underprivileged caste. Hence, it is not simply about an abstract teacher-student relationship, but one that is entangled in hierarchies of caste and tribe. Notions of sacrifice and guru reverence have been instrumental in maintaining the power of the teacher in classical Indian educational system.[20] Such ideological notions of guru reverence and sacrifice have also sustained the telos of graded inequality of caste in Indian society by keeping those without privilege from classrooms, as the Ekalavya story shows.

Ambedkar stressed critique as an integral part of the educational process (2003b, 2003e, 2003f). As Rege observes, he put forth a pedagogy of dissent and learning, rather than just teaching and learning (Rege 93). Indeed, critique is a prerequisite to embark on a learning programme. It is on such a note that Ambedkar critiqued the University of Bombay's bill in 1927 as being exceedingly oriented towards examination (Ambedkar 2014e; Rege 93). Such an orientation did not give those from vulnerable backgrounds the chance to excel in education; besides, it stifled thought in its emphasis on rote learning. The latter was a part of Brahminical pedagogy that kept out most Indians. Instead, an education that encourages critical thinking would not just regurgitate the given, but would indeed question it. For him, educational institutions and universities were spaces for creation of knowledge and not simply administrative centers for providing one-way skills to train skills (Ambedkar 2003e, p. 471). Ambedkar pre-empts Habermas's critique of systematically distorted communication in upholding that critique at the pedagogical level would both prevent the teacher from becoming the central pillar of education and also examine the role of unequal power structures in the production of knowledge. Ambedkar's critique of hegemonic epistemologies for preventing communication from occurring between the different sections of society is both a critique of dominant social understanding of knowledge and also that of dominant social practices inhibiting interaction. He upheld that there is a close relationship between community and educational spaces, whereby the community's progress can be judged by its institutional composition (2003d).

Although individuals, in their social capacity, inhabit classes (Ambedkar 2014a, p. 15), which could be economic, intellectual or even social and allow for mobility,[21] in India the rigidity of caste permeates class. "A caste is an enclosed class" (Ambedkar 2014a, p. 15) or constitute "a graded system of sovereignties, high and low" (Ambedkar 2014b, p. 72) prevalent in India. The class enclosure is enforced through rigid customs that prevent classes from interacting with each other and creating "an unnatural institution" (Ambedkar 2014a, p. 15) of caste. Castes divide human beings into communities that occupy a "graded order one above the other in social status" (Ambedkar 2014b, p. 72). Caste prevents communities from engaging in common activities that allow for empathetic bonds with one another (Ibid, p. 51). Yet class and caste are very closely related as "next door neighbours and it is only a span that separates the two" (2014a, p. 15). Further, those who are from underprivileged castes are poor and experience the inequality of gender more acutely. Hence, there are several degrees of discrimination experienced by women from the oppressed castes. The disparities of caste, religion and gender afflicting the social context in India requires that their intersections have to be explored in the quest for accessible education. For there is a specific way in which social communication is inhibited because of the dominance of caste. "Hindu society" Ambedkar observes, "is like a tower, each floor of which is allocated to one caste. The point worth remembering is that this tower has no staircase" (2020). Further, excommunication also served to maintain the rigid borders of caste. Caste is characterised through spatial and temporal metaphors such as "lower" and "higher", "forward" and "backward" (175). Jaaware describes the social world of caste as one of "segmented sociabilities"[22] (Jaaware 2019, p. 180) depicting a "relation of nonrelation" (Jaaware 2019, p. 180) whereby one can interact with members of castes and clans without impacting them or being affected by them.

Ambedkar also argues that caste is sustained through patriarchal controls over women. For caste emerged through the proscription of marrying across social units with the consequence of confining those who were born within it. "*The superposition of endogamy on exogamy means the creation of caste*" (Ambedkar 2014a, p. 9), an artificial separation as exogamy prevailed as a norm since ancient times. Women have been the focus on maintaining the homogeneity of caste, as it is by controlling their sexuality that caste barriers are maintained (Manjrekar 2021, p. 13). Ambedkar argues that endogamy demands an equal proportion of women and men as "marriageable units" (2014a, p. 10) within a given caste. However, this can never be realised in the real world, as both men and women would have to be born and die at the same time! Often women outlive their husbands and men outlive wives, whereby there is a danger of their marrying outside their group and having children who defy caste boundaries. Hence, caste structures focus on "repairing the disparity" (2014a, p. 10) between men and women through strategies that manage the "surplus" (2014a, p. 10) men and women. In the process, Ambedkar observes men's power over women is multiplied by containing them within the caste with humiliating practices of *sati* and widowhood (2014a, p. 11). Men are treated with more concern, as they are invested with value; their being confined to celibacy on the widower is one way of maintaining parity in the numbers between men and women. However, this would not serve the purpose of endogamous caste preservation as they need to be playing an active role in the life of caste. Hence, the "surplus man" (2014a, p. 12), in order to be bound to the group, are made to marry a young girl. Thus, gender regimes reflect casteism, while caste, in turn, perpetuates women's oppression.

The rise of caste, according to Ambedkar, cannot be attributed to religious sanction in Hindu scriptural Dharmashastras alone (although it has been maintained through such sanction over the years). Nor can one attribute responsibility for caste to any single group or individual, given its all-pervasiveness (2014a, pp. 16–17). The various races—Aryan, Dravidian, Mongolian, Scythian—that came together in ancient India had cultural unity and formed cohesive groups (2014a, pp. 6–9).[23] The various groups over a period of time evolved hierarchically through enclosed structuring by caste. Caste can etymologically be traced to the Spanish/Portuguese *casta*, or lineage, which, in turn, is derived from the Latin *castus* meaning pure (Kannabiran 2006; Hiwrale 2020, pp. 79–80). Kannabiran observes that the meaning became more specific in the 18th century, where the various castes, or *jatis* (3,000 or so at that time), were divided into the four-tiered group of *varnas*. The Brahmins, or the priests, the Kshatriyas, or the military group, and Vaishyas, or the merchants, were considered *dvija*, or twice born, in the sense of having the purity of being initiated into Hindusim (Kannabiran 2006). The Shudras, or the laborers, were all classes to begin with, with some degree of mobility (Ambedkar 2014a, p. 18). However, with the fifth tier of Panchama/Untouchables primarily engaged in public conservancy work, the Shudras were kept away as unclean (Kannabiran 2006). The priests cut themselves off from the other classes to become a self-contained caste. The other classes, such as the Vaishyas and Shudras, splintered further; while the Kshatriyas divided themselves into administrators and soldiers. The non-Brahminical classes also adopted caste identities through imitation, since Brahmins enjoyed social prestige. Those who were closer to the Brahmins—Kshatriyas and Vaishyas—adopted practices of Sati, enforced widowhood and marriage of young girls to old men (2014a, p. 20). Those who were more distant from Brahmins retained one or two among these. Thus, the gatekeeping of Brahmins, which initiated caste, had a derivative character in other castes. Moreover, across all castes, there was excommunication if caste barriers were broken. Thus, the process of intensification of caste identity was one in which "there is a double line of answer: *Some closed the door: Others found it closed against them*" (Ambedkar 2014a, p. 18). Thus, the Brahmins, while creating patterns of caste-based behaviour for themselves, also gave rise to castes in other social classes. Ambedkar has argued how prohibition of marriages across diverse social groups has led to segregated, patriarchal communities with strong caste identities in India.

Ambedkar's critical look at the Indian social order via the lens of caste and gender, thus, reveals an all-pervasive presence of exploitative social stratifications that stifle the very notion of society to the point of being what Ambedkar terms as "anti-social" (2014b, p. 51). Given the domination of caste in the domain of the social in India, there are no shared activities in which everyone participates without fear (Ambedkar 2014b, p. 51; Jaaware 2019, pp. 170–189; Stroud 2020). Ambedkar observes that, although "society" connotes the ideals of public welfare–empathy—they are absent in the Indian social order (2003g, pp. 518–519). Social interaction is curtailed on grounds of caste and also gender, making women unfree. The Hindi/Marathi word *samaj* can be translated as "society" or even as Hindu religious association (Merriam Webster). But, as Jaaware points out, the two are not unequivocally the same, as *samaj* also means clan, caste, community and the like in Marathi (Jaaware 2019, p. 170). He notes how "society", in its ancient Roman roots, originates in the Latin *socius*, or companionship, which *samaj* misses out on. Further, the clans and communities of *samaj* are not just segregated from one another, whereby each community has an internal association. Rather, Jaaware notes that it is segmented, since the various *samaj*(s) form an ascending order, whereby "There is an intimate cut: We interact with but will not relate to that other *samaj*. The members of that *samaj* are not from ours" (Jaaware 2019, p. 170). Thus, the simultaneous, "parallel" (Ambedkar 2014b, p. 51) activities within such hierarchical social units, separated from one, are not associated activities. Those performing manual labour, care work, public cleanliness or those who lived in forests were all dismissed as people from the lower rung of the caste hierarchy, subject to norms of pollution and discrimination (Ambedkar 2014g, p. 379). They are also prevented from undertaking economic activities for mobility outside the sphere in which they are circumscribed. The division of Hindu social groups into the touchables and the untouchables (Ambedkar 2014c, p. 550) inhibits communication and individual freedom. It is precisely this syndrome that is reflected in the inadequacy of shared school spaces in India, hindering inclusive education. It is unlike a society with shared activities that are related to one another based on communication; society "continues to exist by communication and in communication" (Ambedkar 2014b, p. 51). Such communication cannot occur merely through groups being in physical proximity with one another; it rather requires psycho-logical connection on grounds of "beliefs, aspirations and knowledge" (Ambedkar 2014b) One has to "resocialise" earlier forms of "segmented sociabilities" through endosmosis (Ambedkar 2014c, p. 249). As Mukherjee notes, endosmosis is not about communicating with each other at the individual level alone; it is rather about individuals communicating by representing their group identities or about groups communicating with each other (2009, p. 355).

Ambedkar's critique of society reveals the extent to which it is fractured by the divisiveness of caste. His critique also discloses alternate ways of thinking about society without social ostracisation, so that educational ideals such as the RTE can be realised. His is not a "weak"[24] critique that upholds norms internal to its social framework.[25] Rather, Ambedkar espouses a "strong" critique with commitment to universal norms from which social orders are assessed. Yet, this strong critique does not occur from an external position to that of society. There is a problem of paternalism in such a critique, where the figure outside the domain of society exercises authoritarian control over society. However, strong critique does not have to be transcendent or authoritarian as Ortega-Esquembre notes. It can also be "reconstructive" in the sense of bringing out the normative aspirations of a society from within and also exposing the failure to live up to such aspirations (Ortega-Esquembre 2015, p. 2).[26] Critique attempts to identify the relationships of dominance that are implicit in what Habermas terms as a "systematically distorted communication" (1974, p. 9). Ambedkar's critique exposes the implicit distortions in communication as an outcome of caste. His critique has similarities with genealogical critiques in exposing the roots of so-called legitimate social norms in forces of control; however, it differs in being committed to norms aspiring to a better society.[27] Ortega-Esquembre interprets Habermas's ideology critique as rooted in the lifeworld of everyday practices whose communicative assumptions he reconstructs as normative (Habermas 1974, p. 9, 1989, p. 107).[28] It is, thus, not a strong constructive-externalist critique that transcends the horizons of a given society (Ortega-Esquembre 2015, p. 2). Ambedkar's critique can similarly be comprehended as a reconstructive way of describing and deconstructing the operations of the phenomenon of caste, while at the same time enabling a space for social communication. Reconstructive critique does not transcend its contexts (Stroud 2020, p. 182) but rather endeavours to articulate the ideals underlying contextual practices. It is rooted in reconstructing the normativity of social communication that is assumed in everyday practices. In reconstructing practices which have roots in the past, one does not reject or accept them completely; rather, reconstruction is rooted in the experiences of everyday practices without assuming them to be ideal.[29]

Ambedkar is committed to an ideal society that sustains and creates several avenues through which critiques, innovations and changes circulate. It divulges that free-flowing communication of diverse interests in its diverse parts take place in part to all other parts. It encourages free and fearless association that is not controlled by baggage from the past. Democracy, according to Ambedkar, is not merely a political mode of organising society. It is especially also "primarily a mode of associated living, of conjoint communicated experience. It is essentially an attitude of respect and reverence towards fellowmen" (Ambedkar 2014b).[30] Education impacts social democracy and vice versa in cultivating what Ambedkar regards as the "*habit* of interacting with others and solving problems in concert with one's peers" (Stroud 2020, p. 181). Thus, communication via the use of language is central to social democracy which will also impact the classroom. Language is oriented towards thinking and speaking to the other to reach an understanding about a matter at hand. Moreover, such a process is also critical, as several points of view are taken into consideration while doing this. Speakers subject each other's and their own claims to scrutiny and validity by giving reasons. Following Habermas, one can distinguish four types of validity claims in a sentence raised in dialogue with another. These include comprehensibility, truth, appropriateness and sincerity of the speaker (Habermas 1974, pp. 17–19). Ambedkar's commitment to language is evident in his view that democracy should hear out all those who have something to say on an issue that impacts them (2003a, p. 169). Thus, diversity of points of view with their attendant disagreements becomes an integral part of democracy. Indeed, according to Ambedkar, democracy needs more than one opinion so that it generates debate and discussion. An autocracy that wants obedience has only one voice. It is in this spirit that Ambedkar engaged with Gandhi, by giving reasons for his critiques (Ambedkar 2014b, pp. 86–96). Gandhi had interpreted Ambedkar's critique of caste from his own perspective, where he endorsed the *varna* system of four broad categories that are not necessarily hereditary in order to distinguish them from caste. However, Ambedkar engaged with this interpretation to show that it was a misunderstanding of what he meant. He also appealed to Gandhi to introspect, as what he preaches under the *varna* system is in fact caste (Ambedkar 2014b,). He took up each of Gandhi's claims and followed them through counter claims to make his point of view. Gandhi also undertook a similar path in his correspondence with Ambedkar (Gandhi-Ambedkar 1932–1945). Rather than inflict a point of view on others, Ambedkar focusses on dialogue as a mode of comprehending it critically (Ambedkar 2003c). Thus, communication—particularly with those who do not agree—is a way of moving across social barriers.

The Habermasian model of communication has similarities with Ambedkar's. Following Ortega-Esquembre, Habermas's account of communication is about at least two individuals who collaborate with one another to critique and interpret a common problem that could be from their a norm in the social world, an expression in the subjective world or a fact in the objective world (Ortega-Esquembre 2015, p. 5; Habermas 1996, p. 4). Both individuals are enmeshed in a common frame of reference or taken for granted assumptions, which Habermas, following Husserl, terms as the "lifeworld". The latter is constituted through culture (science, law, morality, art), society (practices and associations) and personality (competencies for self-expression). Participants in the lifeworld renew it through processes of interaction that underlie cultural transmission, social integration and self-development. All of this requires communication, as these aspects are removed—in a piecemeal way, of course—from traditional understandings and consensus to be discussed when they become problematised as a question. The common problem that they try to critically interpret is an aspect of the lifeworld itself that is called into question. Habermas attempts to reconstruct the implicit rationality—namely, a "communicative" (Habermas 1996, p. 4) one—that underlies the everyday practices of speech in interacting with others. Thus, the dialogue has to be pursued without constraint, while there should be readiness to be criticised, accept the responsibilities that result from dialogue and even take it forward (Habermas 1996, p. 4). Habermas observes that he does not offer a normative blue print for an ideal social life. Instead, he aims at "reconstructing the network of discourses that, aimed at forming opinions and preparing decisions . . . the matrix from which democratic authority emerges" (Habermas 1996, p. 5). Reflection on segments of cultures, practices and identities in the lifeworld has resulted in greater personal individualism and pluralism in collective life (Habermas 1996, p. 97). Yet, such reflectiveness is accompanied by the reflexivity underlying the norms of linguistic interaction to foster a critical perspective that can be a mirror to one's own self and community (Habermas 1996, p. 97).

Ambedkar regards democracy and communication as closely related, whereby one implies the other. The representation of diverse opinions and people are integral to a democratic education and society (Ambedkar 2014c, p. 247). Habermas similarly argues for a close relationship communication and democracy.[31] Hence, creating the space for social democracy also opens up possibilities for communicative education that is grounded in critique. But critique alone is not adequate to create possible pedagogies of communication. One needs to also bring in the affective dimension as the latter would show.

III Caring to Learn from the Disempowered

The link between individuals and society reveals that an increasing individuation occurs with deeper social immersiveness comprising interdependencies and interactions (Ambedkar 2014b, p. 57; Habermas 1989/90, p. 46). As Habermas puts it, "the person forms an inner center only to the extent to which she simultaneously externalises herself in communicatively produced interpersonal relationships" (Habermas 1989/90, p. 46). Individual identities do not exist in a vacuum, given their embeddedness in larger social networks; they are, consequently, vulnerable to wider group dynamics. As Ambedkar argues, individuals have to inhabit social communities with "aims, beliefs, aspirations, knowledge, a common understanding" as "like-minded" (2014c, pp. 248–249). Hence, the identities and integrities of individuals cannot be upheld or developed without their cultural, social and personal worlds. Interpersonal bonds and interfaces of mutual recognition, initiated and sustained through communication, establish the individual in larger processes of socialisation. Being "like-minded", for Ambedkar in the context of his critique of caste, is having the capacity to share, rather than being homogeneous. Thus, "Like-mindedness is essential for a harmonious life, social or political and, as has just been shown, it depends upon the extent of communication, participation or endosmosis" (Ambedkar 2014c, p. 249). Both, Ambedkar and Habermas underscore the "double aspect" (Habermas 1989/90, p. 46) of the intersubjective dimension and individual cohesiveness; the well-being of both the self and group are interwoven; they have to be developed together by the members of the association. This also leads to a greater responsibility for engaging with those from vulnerable social groups kept out of social interaction due to structural barriers like caste, class, gender and tribe, among others. The "inviolability of socialized individuals" (Habermas 1989/90, p. 47) demands that individuals have an equal right to self-determination, but this, in turn, mandates relationships of mutual recognition among individuals in the larger group (to which the socialised individual belongs).

Ambedkar's critique of the unequal relations between social groups divided by barriers such as caste and gender discloses how mutual recognition requires more than mobility in the economic sense. Such mobility cannot necessarily overcome the chasms of "segmented sociabilities" (Jaaware 2019, p. 182); Ambedkar's autobiography reveals how, despite having an economic status, he was discriminated against because of his caste (1993). He describes, for instance, how his caste identity never affected him when he went for higher studies to Europe and America. However, on returning back to India, he had to impersonate to get an accommodation, as no one was ready to rent to a person who was considered "untouchable" (Ambedkar 1993, pp. 673–678, p. 690). Similarly, he had great difficulty accessing drinking water, which he often had to forego while working in an office, because he was not allowed touch common water. On the same note, Ambedkar narrates how he was prohibited from sitting on common chairs in government offices (Ambedkar 1993, pp. 690–691). Thus, regardless of his economic status, Ambedkar was stigmatised because of his caste identity. Hence, Ambedkar argues that education alone—without addressing social caste barriers—cannot remove caste; the Brahmins who discriminate are educated (2003g, p. 522). In his autobiography, Ambedkar cites the instance of a teacher from the "untouchable" caste who lost his wife and newborn baby because they were denied medical attention by an educated doctor (1993, p. 687). Yet, if education is acquired by those, such as Ekalavya, who are socially marginalised, it can remove the barriers of caste and gender (Ambedkar 2003g, pp. 522–523). For what Ambedkar terms as "resocialization" (2014c, p. 249) to occur, one needs to traverse, following Jaaware, "planes and vertices" of the divided units (Jaaware 2019, pp. 182–189) by crossing towards unknown territories of alterity (Jaaware 2019, p. 182). An engagement with alterity through receptiveness is the basis for fraternity[32] or solidarity.

Isolation between groups—the absence of "like-mindedness" among them—is the basis of social conflict (Ambedkar 2014c, p. 249). Ambedkar terms fraternity as a "new like-mindedness" (2014c, p. 249) that brings together the interests of all groups through communication between groups that leads to "resocialization" (Ambedkar 2014c, p. 249). Habermas, similarly, defines solidarity as "the welfare of consociates who are intimately linked in an intersubjectively shared form of life" (1989/90, p. 47). Groups have to establish bonds of equal recognition with one another to establish such "shared" forms of coexistence transcending their local "concrete lifeworlds" (Habermas 1989/90, p. 48). Ambedkar and Habermas consider communication to be rooted in the context of specific lifeworlds that can also critique it as playing a significant role in establishing bonds through critique of isolationist practices. To develop a nonpartisan perspective, there has to be an unrestricted freedom for all individuals to participate in a discussion relevant to them. However, there has to also be an empathy for those in situations other than one's own, situations without privilege for intimate bonds between individuals and groups, as well as between groups. Yet is empathy derived from solidarity, which is established through rational, argumentative discourse, as Habermas thinks (1989/90, p. 49)? To traverse the gaps of divided groups, one has to establish relationships of what Jaaware terms as "welcoming hospitality" (p. 183), where both privilege and it's lack are undone. As Jaaware notes, although the segments are different from each other, their separating/connecting vertices are grounded in the notion of those who are different. This will make it possible, following Jaaware, to think of society as an ideal oriented towards the future. Ambedkar's "like-mindedness", Habermas's "solidarity" and Jaaware's "welcoming hospitality" cannot be achieved only through dialogue via argumentative discourse. Solidarity relationships require the empathetic dimension of caring for and caring with, whereby empathy and care are two inextricable aspects of the same process.

For an empathetic pedagogy of receptiveness, both at the social and educational levels, the teacher would have to cease being authoritarian and become empathetic. It is not enough for the student to become self-reliant. Indeed, as the relationship between individual autonomy and social relations reveal, students such as Ekalavya can freely develop themselves only if the larger world is also freed from the shackles of social hierarchy. A detour to another telling of Ekalavya's story—this time in the Jain tradition from the 16th century—can illuminate other possibilities for Dronacharya's relationship with Ekalavya and Ekalavya's self-development.[33] In the Jain version, Ekalavya is named Bhimala and he is from the Bhil tribe. He establishes himself as an accomplished archer through inspiration and dedication to Dronacharya's mud statue. However, on discovering the skills of a humble forest dweller which are better than his, the Kshatriya Arjuna demands his thumb out of jealousy, to which Bhimala accedes. Dronacharya condemns Arjuna as a cheat and hands over the power of being the best archer to Bhimala by using his middle finger and forefinger. This story opens up the possibilities for Ekalavya/Bhimala developing alternate skills through their disabled physical and social conditions when Dronacharya has *karuna* (compassion) and *maitri* (fellow feeling). Like Bhimala in the 16th century Jain version, Rathod's 20th century Ekalavya in the poem *Sabak* (Zelliot and Deo 1994, pp. 50–51) works around the various obstacles that surround him to get an education. However, the teacher is discarded as inherently authoritarian. But then, can one not envision a teacher with empathy? As Doniger notes, even in the original version of the Mahabharata, where this story first appears, Dronacharya's demand for a fee—without even having taught Ekalavya directly—is regarded as " 'terrible' *daruna*" (Doniger 2014, p. 549), whose words demanding such a sacrifice from Ekalavya are described as "terrible" (Doniger 2014, p. 548) and "cruel" (Ganguli 2005, p. CXXXIV). Thus, Dronacharya's act is regarded as problematic and other versions as the Jain open up alternate possibilities with "compassion", or *karuna*, as the opposite of "terrible", or *daruna*.

Majumdar's novel *The Middle Finger* (2022) adds to the retelling of the Ekalavya myth with a focus on the relationship between the teacher and student while examining how the student develops, despite the teacher's initial lack of responsiveness. It is the story of a professor of English and a poet from an upper-class and -caste, private University in Delhi, Megha has a relationship of openness with her wealthy students, despite her frustration with their pretentiousness. It also depicts Megha's own relationship with her professor, Simon from the US, who was visiting India. She questions Simon about the lack of mentoring of global students in the US universities, who have to often go elsewhere for jobs. The novel examines how learning occurs as much within the confines of a classroom as in larger social interaction by presenting the multiple worlds that Megha interacts with, including those without privilege. But it is just that Megha does not know much about those without privilege, nor does she care to, as her interface with Poonam, a tribal convert to Christianity from the state of Jharkhand, reveals. Poonam is Megha's house help. Poonam is interested in her large book collection and keen to learn English from Megha. Yet, Megha dissuades her, saying that she is "not good at the kind of teaching you need" (2022, p. 129). Poonam is well aware that their social distance is what inhibits Megha from teaching her; "She did not teach girls like me" (2022, p. 129). After attending a session on Megha's poetry, Poonam starts borrowing her books and "learnt from her words" (2022, p. 128). She learned in her own way, like the Jain Bhimala and Rathod's Ekalavya about "Love for the stories shared among newcomers" (2022, p. 128). Poonam starts writing on her with Megha as her inspiration and, like Ekalavya, she also attributes her learning to Megha, who is surprised, as she never consciously taught her. In a telling line, Poonam retorts that Megha would naturally think so because "What do you know about me *didi?*" (2022, p. 184). This line opens up the entire problem of teachers from privileged backgrounds failing to empathise with students who do not have such privilege. The novel then focuses on Megha acquiring empathy towards Poonam, like the Jain Dronacharya to Bhimala.[34] Acquisition of empathy and care towards learners—in formal and informal contexts—from underprivileged backgrounds to learn from them requires that the teacher unlearns taken-for-granted privileges. The Jain Bhimala redefined archery practice under severe obstacles through his forefinger and middle finger.

Would it be possible to learn a different way of practicing archery from Bhimala? Moreover, to also comprehend the inequalities that underlie such a practice that comes from social privileges in which the teacher participates? Such learning requires self-criticism that acknowledges the privileges in social location. It also demands that routine assumptions about knowledge that take the teacher as supreme be unlearnt. The standard assumption underlying the inclusiveness of those from the margins in educational systems is that they have to learn what the privileged mainstream has to offer. The manner in which the latter have violated the likes of Ekalavya/Bhimala is never foregrounded. Indeed, the memory of Ekalavya's/Bhimala's thumb reveals that the oppressed have learnt other ways of cultivating themselves, through their injuries; inclusiveness requires that this be included in the curriculum. As Devy (2017) notes, "If we continue to insist that they must learn what we have to teach them, they will not fare well. But is it not likely that we try to learn from them? Is it not possible that the entire society is seen as a vast university, very community in it an open treasurer of knowledge, as if collectively they were a vast reference library, and the institution of learning a co-curator, a co-supervisor of that knowledge?" (Devy, 2017, p. 50). Devy suggests going beyond institutional divisions of disciplines to remember variegated knowledge traditions—often transmitted orally—of the non-canonical, non-Brahmanical people that has been forgotten due to domination at the internal and external levels (p. 50). Hence, the entry of hitherto marginalised people in educational institutions should offer new grounds for creating new knowledge systems and new pedagogies and reinforce forgotten oral and written knowledges of people. Devy reminds us of how people from marginalised communities are repositories of ecological wisdom. The severity of the climate crisis and the extent to which our sciences have been steeped in anthropocentrism shows the transformative possibilities of such wisdom. Gadgil and Guha illustrate how a modern, industrialised entity such as the West Coast Paper Mill in the forests of Northern Karnataka had a very limited perspective, even to the commercialisation of nature, as it could not achieve a good growth of bamboo culms (1995, pp. 140–141). This was because the thorny branch cover at the base would be removed, exposing the fresh shoots to attacks by monkeys and cattle. The local forest community was well aware of the dangers posed by the removal of the thorny cover. Yet the paper mill's forest department never engaged with the local communities to learn from them about ecology.[35] During the colonial period, the British tried to develop monocultural plantations of teak, while independent India attempted to do so with eucalyptus; both instances show the attempt to possess forests for commercial gain without heeding the wisdom of ordinary communities that practised plant diversity (Gadgil and Guha 1995, p. 141).

Such receptiveness to knowledges from the vulnerable requires caring teachers. Care in education does not merely mean care in the virtue sense of the term, in the sense of doing their duties conscientiously for the students from the point of view of what they think is correct for the students. Such a focus on how the students ought to be and what they do to do is based on the teacher's image of what the student ought to be. The teacher thinks of herself or himself as possessing some "hard won" (Noddings 2005) qualities in an individual capacity and thinks of education as imparting such individualism to students. In *The Middle Finger*, Megha is critical of teachers in universities like Princeton who try to shape their students into "little Xerox copies . . . the greatest narcissism" (Majumdar 2022, p. 149).

While talking to her own teacher, Simon in India, Megha realises his own narcissism in appreciating her undertaking a job in India, simply because it was his dream as well (Majumdar 2022, p. 150). This entirely misses the point. As Nel Noddings notes, care is about being open and receptive, where one gives oneself rather than inflict one's own image upon others. Care situates the individual in a larger social fabric, whose material and experiential dimensions are integral to personhood. The caregiver/care-receiver relationship underlies the process of being individuated as a separate being. Care is a relationship, not simply a virtue acquired, following Noddings (1999). Hence, teachers have to care for, in the relational sense of the term, by establishing a relationship of "attentive love" (Noddings 2005). There is a special kind of attention of the caregiver, an "engrossment" (Noddings 2005) that is open and receptive to the care-receiver. In a care relation, giver and receiver do not have identical feelings but then do share with each other, despite their differences. Being engrossed, attentive and respective require respect (Noddings 2002b, pp. 85–89, 2005). One can also add sympathy to this, making it a part of the activity of care. However, a sympathetic disposition also initiates, encourages and supports the practice of care as its foundation. Both as the source and part of caring practice, sympathy is natural and spontaneous for Noddings. However, she also acknowledges, following Hume, that sympathy is not a simple given; it has to be cultivated.[36]

Yet, an attempt to relate sympathy with care has to contend with the possibility of sympathy mutating into an authoritarianism that foregrounds the patronage of the giver rather than highlighting the giver's privilege as rooted in the destitution of the reception of sympathy. Rai and Narayan have argued how European civilisation claimed to be superior not through gratuitous violence but through sympathy towards its colonies.[37] Sympathy could homogenise if the feelings of the self and other are put on the plane of cohesive familiarity. As Rai argues, it could also lead to objectifying those with whom one sympathises. Thus, if a person sympathises with another because she or he has a similar feeling, the sympathiser is privileged as someone in whose image the sympathised is constructed.[38] As an alternative to such imperialisms that retain the lessons of care, Hankivsky suggests that care adopt the route of intersectionality (2014). She argues that it can expose power hierarchies and Eurocentric knowledges to highlight diversity in geographic locations that takes the global South into consideration (pp. 255–262). One could extend this insight by noting, with Ambedkar, that critique is the first step to resisting authoritarianism, even that of sympathy. As Ambedkar notes, one has to critique the internal barriers, such as those of caste, class, tribe and gender, as well as external colonialism, while being open to all (Ambedkar 1957, pp. 204–205). Moreover, following Ambedkar, sympathy cannot be a stand-alone notion; it would have to be accompanied by other dimensions that underscore relations of solidarity. Ambedkar observes that just *karuna* or compassion or sympathy is inadequate for being ethical for precisely this reason. He suggests that it has to be accompanied by the ecological spirit of love and fellowship with all living beings, or *maitri* (1957, pp. 211–214). Ambedkar narrates how *karuna* can become violent without such fellowship by citing a story in which a seemingly sympathetic and compassionate woman lost her cool when her maid did not do as she dictated. Thus, as Paik notes, Ambedkar's vision of education philosophically highlights the relationship of mutual interdependence between knowledge (*vidya*), understanding (*pradnya*), compassion (*karuna*), values and conduct (*sheel*), friendship (*maitri*) and equality (*samata*); each of these would add inclusive and democratic, pedagogic content, making it possible for those from vulnerable backgrounds to develop themselves.[39] Ambedkar points out that mere learning will be inadequate without larger understanding; this is well-evident in casteist forms of education (1957, pp. 210–212). Understanding also has to be rooted in affects and larger web of values and fellowship.

Care theory, similarly, has the resources for decolonising a relationship of patronage. It reverses the individualism of taken-for-granted notions of subjectivity rooted in liberalism. Care regards dependency as an everyday feature of human life rather than an affliction. Following Noddings, care is not simply a case of "caring-about", where the person cared for is an object of concern or sympathy. Rather, the phenomenon of care also includes the aspect of "caring for" (Noddings 2002a, p. 19). In the latter, the caregiver undertakes responsibility to comprehend the needs of the dependent, who, in turn, responds through approvals, denials, modifications and debates. As Noddings notes, rather than a cognitive control over the receiver through knowledge, the attentiveness in care requires sensitivity and supportiveness towards its recipient (Noddings 2002a, p. 16). Further, as the giver connects to the receiver, the latter's responses encourage the giver to act in specific ways. The phenomenon of care reveals that the care-receiver is not a passive recipient of altruistic feeling. The person who is cared for has to acknowledge the relation and respond to it appropriately (Noddings 2005). In what Noddings terms as the flow of energy in care, an egalitarian bond between the care giver and receiver is established. Thus, an active collaboration between the receiver and the giver transforms the former's condition of vulnerability. Noddings's phenomenology of care, thus, questions the interference in the notion of "teacher knows best" (2005). Such a caring "encounter" does not establish a permanent but a temporary and finite relationship. It is not simply the outcome of spontaneous sympathy; rather, caring encounters result from cultivating sympathy through literary works, for instance. The engagement with the varied histories of Ekalavya is a step in such a direction of bringing together what Kannabiran terms as histories of both oppressions and resistances (2006).

Empathy and care, as articulated by Ambedkar and Noddings—which Habermas briefly gestures towards—is a mode of "Traversal . . . opens up the realm of freedom" (Jaaware 2019, p. 184). It acknowledges dependencies on sociabilities that are different, such as Ekalavya's/Bhimala's. It is a refusal to abide by the dictate of segregation that prevents those who are different from entering a given sociability, such as a well, a temple, a school. It is, thus, a freedom from constraint so that the door that was closed "was pushed inward and opened" (Jaaware 2019, p. 185). It is also a freedom to shift one's social location to sociabilities that are unknown and unpredictable; that will allow for creativity (Jaaware 2019, pp. 187–189). Critique and care in pedagogical practices enables questioning social barriers, while, at the same time, establishing relationships of openness between teachers and learners that go beyond formal education to a whole cultural landscape.

Notes

1. Gratitude to João M. Paraskeva for motivation, suggestions and oceanic patience. Many thanks to Narayan Gadade, Biraj Mehta and Ayush Srivastav for their interest and comments. However, any drawbacks that might limit this chapter are entirely due to me.
2. University of Mumbai, India.
3. Henceforth RTE.
4. The details are derived from the Right to Education Act, 2009.
5. Dhankar cites Disha Nawani in support of his empirical claims.
6. This policy of education for all at the primary level was enacted in 2001, and free education at the secondary level was enacted in 2009 under Rashtriya Madhyamik Shiksha Abhayan (Dejaeghere & Arur 2020, p. 3).
7. See Dejaeghere and Arur 2020, p. 2 and Lahariya 2018 for an account of the improving enrolment rates.
8. This is based on the inputs from a Senior Education Specialist at Child Fund India, Aekta Chanda (India Today 2021).
9. This narration of Ekalavya is derived from section CXXXIV of Kisari Mohan Ganguli's translation of the Vyasa's *Mahabharata* (Ganguli 2005) and Doniger 2014, pp. 547–550. Ganguli's 19th-century translation of the *Mahabharata* was the first in English. The epic *Mahabharata*'s life and its relationship to the Indian imagination stretches back to over 2,000 years. Much of it is said to have been composed from 400 BC to 200 CE (Doniger 2020). Oral traditions of narration and storytelling have added to it during its long history. Given its long period and complex history of composition and reception, the idea of Vyasa as the *Mahabharata*'s author is nominalistic. The *Mahabharata* is a mixture of myths and history, narrated Hindu philosophical themes such as *dharma* (moral law) and *karma* (human action). It also has devotional components.
10. Nishadas are forest-dwelling tribes (Ambedkar 2014f, p. 224; Doniger 2014, p. 547). They are called Adivasis, or original inhabitants; they are, at times, in the most vulnerable of the caste group or then even outside the fold of the

caste (Doniger 2014, p. 547). Forest-dwelling tribes have been at the periphery of Indian social orders both physically and culturally, as Doniger notes. In the case of the Nishada tribe, Doniger notes that they did follow Hindu norms, but the caste-based Hindu social order did not acknowledge them (Doniger 2014, p. 548). Ambedkar notes that the Manusmirti—a text upholding the caste system—refers to the Nishadas as children of "Brahmin males and Shudra females" (2014f, p. 224).

11. As Susen (2017, p. 45) puts it, "the self-determination of individuals is pointless if not granted by collectives, just as the self-determination of collectives is worthless if not supported by individuals".
12. Habermas notes that the "addresses of law are simultaneously authors of their rights" (1996, p. 104), which is, of course, based on Kant's "kingdom of ends".
13. This poem is from Zelliot and Deo, pp. 50–51.
14. This is a quote from Mukherjee 2009, p. 355.
15. Mukherjee's (2009) analysis of Ambedkar is culled in another context.
16. Also see Stroud 2020, pp. 186–87.
17. Also see Paik 2016, 2021, 2022 for detailed accounts of the struggle on the part of Dalit women to acquire an education.
18. Phule's play from Paik and Rege. Phule used the term *Stree-purush* to accentuate the equality between women and men (Paik 2014, p. 152).
19. Pawar and Moon give a detailed account of Dalit women's struggles in the public sphere in their own words (2014 (2008), pp. 201–347).
20. T.M. Krishna, the Carnatic vocalist, shows how the power structurally favours the guru, or the teacher, who is, therefore, in a position to exploit the disciple, or *shishya*, in the classical Indian arts that follow such a methodology (Krishna 2021, pp. 98–101). Rather than romanticise this problematic bond, he suggests that the guru's position be dismantled so that the *shishya*'s freedom is opened.
21. Unlike the Soviet Marxists of his time, Ambedkar does not think of class as a primarily economic category.
22. He objects to using the notion of hierarchy.
23. Ambedkar had presented his argument for the centrality of endogamy in caste in 1916 and published it in 1917 (2014a).
24. The distinction between "weak"/internal, "strong"/external, "reconstructive" and "genealogical" critiques is derived from Ortega-Esquembre's discussion of Axel Honneth (2015, pp. 2–3).
25. Such weak critique is upheld by pragmatists and communitarians (Ortega-Esquembre, p. 3).
26. See Stroud 2020 for an interpretation of Ambedkar as reconstructing everyday practices.
27. Following Nietzsche and Foucault (Ortega-Esquembre 2015, p. 3).
28. As Ortega-Esquembre notes, Habermas has articulated his critical theory in diverse ways through cognitive interests, universal pragmatics or even the ideal speech situation (2015, pp. 6–7).
29. See Stroud 2020, pp. 182–185, for an account of Ambedkar as reconstructing democracy in the Indian context as an Indian pragmatist.
30. Ambedkar's epigraph to his *Annihilation of Caste* (2014b) contains this vision of an ideal society.
31. Ambedkar reveals shades of Dewey, but then also his own independent thought methodology for thinking about democratic communication via argumentation. One cannot think of Ambedkar as circumscribed by Dewey. In this is respect, again, Habermas is similar to Ambedkar. Habermas is also similar to Ambedkar

in engaging with Dewey. He notes that Dewey is "a democratic thinker" (2006, p. 135) who is "egalitarian through and through" (2006, p. 135). He appreciates Dewey's focus on everyday practices and rejection of the "spectator model of knowledge" (Habermas 2006, p. 133) in spelling out the cognitive domain. Yet, there is a need as Habermas notes to supplement Dewey with Mead's adopting the perspective of the other in social interaction (2006, p. 134) so that the egalitarianism in knowledge is realised. See Fleming for an analysis of the role of education in democracy from a Habermasian perspective (2020).

32. Ambedkar uses the term "fraternity".
33. See Doniger 2014, 550–552. I am indebted to the epigraph in Majumdar's novel (2022) for drawing my attention to Doniger's Jain version. Also see Krishnan 2022 for a discussion of the novel in this context.
34. Majumdar observes that he rewrote the Ekalavya story in such a way that "Drona eventually sides with Ekalavya and abandons Arjun, and does so with a humane and vulnerable kind of love. Wendy Doniger describes a medieval Jain myth where it is Arjun who cheats Ekalavya of his thumb, and when Drona comes to know about it, he accuses Arjun of deception and blesses that a Bhil warrior will be able to shoot arrows using just their index and middle finger. But there is a utopia here" (Gupta 2022).
35. Gadgil and Guha note that they, too, did not do so until they embarked on a detailed investigation on the site (Gadgil and Guha 1995, p. 141).
36. "The approbation of moral qualities most certainly is not derived from reason, or any comparison of ideas; but proceeds entirely from a moral taste, and from certain sentiments of pleasure or disgust, which *arise upon the contemplation and view* of particular qualities". Noddings invokes the preceding passage from Hume's *Treatise* as a foundation for her account of care (Noddings 2002a, p. 24). For a more detailed account of sympathy, see Annette Baier's account (Baier and Waldow 2008, pp. 63–64). Yet, the problem with Baier is that she upholds sympathy to establish feelings of familiarity, while the whole point of receptiveness is to feel the unfamiliar, especially in the context of societies stratified by caste and gender.
37. See Rai (2002) and Narayan (1995) for the detailed arguments. Also see Hankivsky, pp. 254–255. For an engagement with Rai's and Narayan's positions in the light of patronising strand in Western culture, see Mahadevan 2014, pp. 131–133.
38. Hume himself has emphasised nearness in his account of sympathy. There is a danger of reproducing this dimension if one is uncritically rooted in Hume.
39. Paik 2022 cites Ambedkar writing in *Janata* on December 17, 1955. Also see Velaskar 2012 for an account of Ambedkar's pedagogy that took women and men as equals, without attributing a primarily domestic role to women in the manner of other nationalist discourses (pp. 249–257).

References

AISHE (All India Survey on Higher Education). 2020. Accessed on March 8, 2022. www.education.gov.in/sites/upload_files/mhrd/files/statistics-new/aishe_eng.pdf
Ambedkar, B.R. 1957. *The Buddha and His Dhamma*. Bombay: Siddharth Publications.
Ambedkar, B.R. 1993. "Waiting for a Visa," in Vasant Moon, ed., *Dr Babasaheb Ambedkar: Writings and Speeches*, vol. 12, 661–691. Bombay: Education Department, Government of Maharashtra.

Ambedkar, B.R. 2003a. "Democracy Must Give Respectful Hearing to All Who Are worth Listening to," in Hari Narke, N.G. Kamble, M.L. Kasare, and Ashok Godghate, eds., *Dr Babasaheb Ambedkar: Writings and Speeches*, vol. 17, Part III, 168–169. New Delhi: Dr. Ambedkar Foundation, Government of India.

Ambedkar, B.R. 2003b. "Educate, Agitate, Organize, Have Faith and Lose No Hope," in Hari Narke, N.G. Kamble, M.L. Kasare, and Ashok Godghate, eds., *Dr Babasaheb Ambedkar: Writings and Speeches*, vol. 17, Part III, 273–283. New Delhi: Dr. Ambedkar Foundation, Government of India.

Ambedkar, B.R. 2003c. "The Minority Must Always Be Won Over. It Must Never Be Dictated To," in Hari Narke, N.G. Kamble, M.L. Kasare, and Ashok Godghate, eds., *Dr Babasaheb Ambedkar: Writings and Speeches*, vol, 17, Part III, 374–383. New Delhi: Dr. Ambedkar Foundation, Government of India.

Ambedkar, B.R. 2003d. "Progress of a Community Always Depends Upon Education," in Hari Narke, N.G. Kamble, M.L. Kasare, and Ashok Godghate, eds., *Dr Babasaheb Ambedkar: Writings and Speeches*, vol. 17, Part III, 395. New Delhi: Dr. Ambedkar Foundation, Government of India.

Ambedkar, B.R. 2003e. "Recognise University Education to Meet the Requirements of the Modern World," in Hari Narke, N.G. Kamble, M.L. Kasare, and Ashok Godghate, eds., *Dr Babasaheb Ambedkar: Writings and Speeches*, vol. 17, Part III, 471. New Delhi: Dr. Ambedkar Foundation, Government of India.

Ambedkar, B.R. 2003f. "Knowledge Is the Foundation of Man's Life," in Hari Narke, N.G. Kamble, M.L. Kasare, and Ashok Godghate, eds., *Dr Babasaheb Ambedkar: Writings and Speeches*, vol. 17, Part III, 487. New Delhi: Dr. Ambedkar Foundation, Government of India.

Ambedkar, B.R. 2003g. "Prospects of Democracy in India," in Hari Narke, N.G. Kamble, M.L. Kasare, and Ashok Godghate, eds., *Dr Babasaheb Ambedkar: Writings and Speeches*, vol. 17, Part III, 519–523. New Delhi: Dr. Ambedkar Foundation, Government of India.

Ambedkar, B.R. 2014a (1979). "Castes in India," in Vasant Moon, ed., *Dr Babasaheb Ambedkar: Writings and Speeches*, vol. 1, 3–22. New Delhi: Dr. Ambedkar Foundation, Government of India.

Ambedkar, B.R. 2014b (1979). "Annihilation of Caste," in Vasant Moon, ed., *Dr Babasaheb Ambedkar: Writings and Speeches*, vol. 1, 23–96. New Delhi: Dr. Ambedkar Foundation, Government of India.

Ambedkar, B.R. 2014c (1979). "Evidence before the Southborough Committee," in Vasant Moon, ed., *Dr Babasaheb Ambedkar: Writings and Speeches*, vol. 1, 243–278. New Delhi: Dr. Ambedkar Foundation, Government of India.

Ambedkar, B.R. 2014d (1982). "On Grants for Education," in Hari Narke and Vasant Moon, eds., *Dr Babasaheb Ambedkar: Writings and Speeches*, vol. 2, 29–44. New Delhi: Dr. Ambedkar Foundation, Government of India.

Ambedkar, B.R. 2014e (1982). "On the Bombay University Amendment Bill:1," in Hari Narke and Vasant Moon, eds., *Dr Babasaheb Ambedkar: Writings and Speeches*, vol. 2, 45. New Delhi: Dr. Ambedkar Foundation, Government of India.

Ambedkar, B.R. 2014f (1987). "Riddles in Hinduism: An Exposition to Enlighten the Masses," in Ram Meghe, Chandrika Keniya et al., eds., *Dr Babasaheb Ambedkar: Writings and Speeches*, vol. 4. New Delhi: Dr. Ambedkar Foundation, Government of India.

Ambedkar, B.R. 2014g (2003). "Be Your Own Light!," in Hari Narke, N.G. Kamble, M.L. Kasare, and Ashok Godghate, eds., *Dr Babasaheb Ambedkar: Writings and Speeches*, vol. 17, Part I, 378–382. New Delhi: Dr. Ambedkar Foundation, Government of India.

Ambedkar, B.R. 2019 (1979). "Knowledge is Power in Every Field of Life," in Hari Narke, N.G. Kamble, M.L. Kasare, and Ashok Godghate, eds., *Dr Babasaheb Ambedkar: Writings and Speeches*, vol. 17, Part II, 72. New Delhi: Dr. Ambedkar Foundation, Government of India.

Ambedkar, B.R. 2020 (1920). "In a Tower without a Staircase: An Extract from the Inaugural Issue of B.R. Ambedkar's Journal *Mooknayak*," trans. Sheoraj Singh Bechain and Tapan Basu. *The Hindu*, February 1, 2020. Accessed on March 4, 2022. www.thehindu.com/books/in-a-tower-without-a-staircase-an-extract-from-the-inaugural-issue-of-br-ambedkars-journal-mooknayak/article 30700662.ece

Arora, Nipun and Shivkrit Rai. 2020. "India's Right to Education Is Failing in Reality," *The Leaflet*, September 7, 2020. Accessed on March 1, 2022. www.theleaflet.in/indias-right-to-education-is-a-failing-in-reality/

Baier, Annette and Anik Waldow. 2008. "A Conversation between Annette Baier and Anik Waldow about Hume's Account of Sympathy," *Hume Studies* 34 (1): 61–87.

Cordero, Rodrigo. 2014. "Crisis and Critique in Jürgen Habermas's Social Theory," *European Journal of Social Theory* 17 (4): 497–515.

Dejaeghere, Joan and Aditi Ashok Arur. 2020. "How Schooling Is Creating Social Changes for Lowered-Caste Girls in Rural India," *Gender & Society* 20 (10): 1–25.

Devy, Ganesh. 2017. *The Crisis Within: On Knowledge and Education in India*. New Delhi: Aleph.

Dewey, John. 1957. *Reconstruction in Philosophy*. Boston, MA: Beacon.

Dhankar, Rohit. 2019. "National Education Policy: Why Education in India Failed to Make the Grade," *EPW Engage*. www.epw.in/node/154698/pdf

Dhankar, Rohit. 2020. "A Practitioner's Take on Philosophy of Education," in Prakash Iyer, ed., *Conceptualising Education and Related Issues: Proceedings of International Conferences on Philosophy of Education (2013–17)*, vol. 1, 19–38. Bengaluru & Margao: Azim Premji University & Common Teal Publishing.

Doniger, Wendy. 2014. "The History of Ekalavya," in her '*On Hinduism*', 517–555. Oxford: Oxford University Press.

Doniger, Wendy. 2020. "Mahabharata," *Encyclopedia Britannica*. Accessed on March 27, 2022. www.britannica.com/topic/Mahabharata.

Fleming, Ted. 2020. "Jürgen Habermas (1929–): The Importance of Higher Education for Democracy," in Ronald Barnett and Amanda Fulford, eds., *Philosophers on the University: Reconsidering Higher Education*, 191–203. Cham: Springer Nature Switzerland AG.

Gadgil, Madhav and Ramchandra Guha. 1995. *Ecology and Equity: The Use and Abuse of Nature in Contemporary India*. London & New York: Routledge.

Gandhi-Ambedkar. 1932–1945. "Gandhi-Ambedkar Correspondence," in *Mahatma Gandhi's Writings, Philosophy, Audio, Video and Photographs*. Mumbai: Bombay Sarvodaya Mandal & Gandhi Research Foundation. www.mkgandhi.org/Selected%20Letters/amb-gandhi%20corr.htm

Ganguli, Kisari Mohan (trans). 2005. *The Mahabharata of Krishna-Dwaipayana Vyasa, Volume 1 Books 1, 2, and 3*. The Project Gutenberg E-book. Accessed on March 3, 2022. www.gutenberg.org/files/15474/15474-h/15474-h.htm#link 2H_4_0135

Gupta, Ruchira. 2022. "Author Saikat Majumdar on the Makings of His Book 'The Middle Finger'," *Telegraph India*. Accessed on March 10, 2022. www.telegraphindia.com/my-kolkata/people/author-saikat-majumdar-on-the-makings-of-his-book-the-middle-finger/cid/1849967

Habermas, Jürgen. 1974. *Theory and Practice*. Boston, MA: Beacon.

Habermas, Jürgen. 1989. *Towards a Rational Society*. Boston, MA: Beacon.

Habermas, Jürgen. 1989/90. "Justice and Solidarity: On the Discussion Concerning 'Stage 6'," *Philosophical Forum* XXI (1–2): 32–59.

Habermas, Jürgen. 1996. *Between Facts and Norms: Contributions to a Discourse Theory of Law and Democracy*. Cambridge, MA: MIT Press.

Habermas, Jürgen. 2006. *Time of Transitions*. Cambridge and Malden, MA: Polity Press.

Habermas, Jürgen and Michaël Foessel. 2015. "Critique and Communication: Philosophy's Missions, A Conversation with Jürgen Habermas," *Eurozone*. Accessed on March 6, 2022. www.eurozine.com/critique-and-communication-philosophys-missions/

Hankivsky, Olena. 2014. "Rethinking Care Ethics: On the Promise and Potential of an Intersectional Analysis," *The American Political Science Review* 108 (2): 252–264.

Hiwrale, Anup. 2020. "Caste: Understanding the Nuances from Ambedkar's Expositions," *Journal of Social Inclusion Studies* 6 (1): 78–96.

India Today Web Desk. 2021. "Right to Education Act: Significance, Guarantees, Gaps and Reforms," December 1, 2021. Accessed on March 1, 2022. www.indiatoday.in/education-today/gk-current-affairs/story/right-to-education-act-significance-guarantees-gaps-and-reforms-1883012-2021-12-01

Jaaware, Aniket. 2019. *Practicing Caste: On Touching and Not Touching*. Hyderabad: Orient Blackswan.

Kannabiran, Kalpana. 2006. "A Cartography of Resistance: The National Federation of Dalit Women," in Nira Yuval-Davis, Kalpana Kannabiran and Ulrike Vieten, eds., *Situating Contemporary Politics of Belonging*. London: Sage. Accessed on March 20, 2022. www.academia.edu/6253602/A_Cartography_of_Resistance

Krishna, T.M. 2021. *The Spirit of Inquiry: Notes of Dissent, Selected Writings of T.M. Krishna*. Gurugram: Penguin Random House, India.

Krishnan, Yamini. 2022. "Writing Fiction Is Becoming Other People along with Many Invented Selves of One's Own," Interview with Saikat Majumdar, *The Scroll*, February 12, 2022. Accessed on February 15, 2022. https://scroll.in/article/1017046/writing-fiction-is-becoming-other-people-along-with-many-invented-selves-of-ones-own

Lahariya, Khabar. 2018. "Education Is a Distant Dream for Some Children," *The Wire*, April 25, 2018. https://thewire.in/caste/dalit-history-month-education-is-a-distant-dream-for-some-children

Mahadevan, Kanchana. 2014. *Between Femininity and Feminism: Colonial and Postcolonial Perspectives on Care*. New Delhi: D.K. Printworld and Indian Council of Philosophical Research.

Majumdar, Saikat. 2022. *The Middle Finger*. New Delhi: Simon & Shuster India.

Manjrekar, Nandini. 2021. "Introduction," in *Gender and Education in India: A Reader*, 1–27. London and New York: Routledge.

Mehendale, Archana. 2018. "Compulsion to Educate," in Krishna Kumar, ed., *Routledge Handbook of Education in India: Debates, Practices, and Policies*. London and New York: Routledge.

Mondal, Ajit. 2017. "Free and Compulsory Primary Education in India Under the British Raj: A Tale of an Unfulfilled Dream," *SAGE Open* 7 (3): 1–12.

Mukherjee, Arun. 2009. "B. R. Ambedkar, John Dewey, and the Meaning of Democracy," *New Literary History* 40 (2): 345–370.

Narayan, Uma. 1995. "Colonialism and Its Others: Considerations on Rights and Care Discourses," *Hypatia* 10 (2): 133–140.

National Council of Educational Research and Training NCERT 7th Survey. 2006. Accessed on March 8, 2022. https://ncert.nic.in/pdf/programmes/7thSurvey%20Reports/Enrolment_in_school.pdf

Noddings, Nel. 1999. "Caring and Competence," in G. Griffen, ed., *The Education of Teachers*, 205–220. Chicago, IL: National Society of Education.

Noddings, Nel. 2002a. *Starting at Home: Caring and Social Policy*. Berkeley, CA and Los Angeles, CA: University of California Press.

Noddings, Nel. 2002b. *Educating Moral People: A Caring Alternative to Character Education*. New York and London: Teacher's College Press.

Noddings, Nel. 2005. "Caring in Education," *The Encyclopedia of Informal Education*. www.infed.org/biblio/noddings_caring_in_education.htm

Ortega-Esquembre, César. 2015. "Social Pathologies and Ideologies in Light of Jürgen Habermas: A New Interpretation of the Thesis of Colonisation," *Humanities and Social Science Communications* 7: 72. Accessed on March 3, 2022. https://doi.org/10.1057/s41599-020-00563-2

Paik, Shailaja. 2014. *Dalit Women's Education in Modern India: Double Discrimination*. London and New York: Routledge.

Paik, Shailaja. 2016. "Education and Exclusion of Dalits: A History of Hurt and Humiliation," *The Wire*, May 14, 2016. Accessed on February 5, 2022. https://thewire.in/education/education-and-exclusion-of-dalits-a-history-of-hurt-and-humiliation

Paik, Shailaja. 2021. "Chhadi Lage Chham Chham, Vidya Yeyi Gham Gham (The Harder the Stick Beats, the Faster the Flow of Knowledge): Dalit Women's Struggle for Education," in Nandini Manjrekar, ed., *Gender and Education in India: A Reader*, 248–265. London and New York: Routledge.

Paik, Shailaja. 2022. "What Dalit People Taught Us About Education and Why We Must Commit to It," *The Wire*, February 1. Accessed on February 25, 2022. https://thewire.in/caste/what-dalit-people-taught-us-about-education-and-why-we-must-commit-to-it

Pawar, Urmila and Meenakshi Moon. 2014 (2008). *We Also Made History: Women in the Ambedkarite Movement*. New Delhi: Zubaan Books.

Rai, Amit S. 2002. *Rule of Sympathy: Sentiment, Race and Power 1750-1850*. New York: Palgrave Macmillan.

Rege, Sharmila. 2021. "Education as Trutiya Ratna: Towards Phule-Ambedkerite Feminist Pedagogical Practice," in Nandini Manjrekar, ed., *Gender and Education in India: A Reader*, 275–295. London and New York: Routledge.

Right to Education Act. 2009. Accessed on January 4, 2022. www.education.gov. in/hi/sites/upload_files/mhrd/files/upload_document/rte.pdf

"Samaj." Merriam-Webster.com Dictionary, Merriam-Webster. Accessed on March 28, 2022. www.merriam-webster.com/dictionary/Samaj

Stroud, Scott R. 2020. "Communication, Justice, and Reconstruction: Ambedkar as an Indian Pragmatist," in Aakash Singh Rathore, ed., *B.R. Ambedkar: The Quest for Justice*, vol. 1, 175–195. New Delhi: Oxford University Press.

Susen, Simon. 2017. "*Jürgen Habermas:* Between Democratic Deliberation and Deliberative Democracy," in Ruth Wodak and Bernhard Forchtner, eds., *The Routledge Handbook of Language and Politics*, 43–66. Routledge. Accessed on March 15, 2022. www.routledgehandbooks.com/doi/10.4324/9781315183718.ch3

Velaskar, Padma. 2012. "Education for Liberation: Ambedkar's Thought and Dalit Women's Perspectives," *Contemporary Education Dialogue* 9 (2): 245–271.

Zelliot, Eleanor and Veena Deo. 1994. "Dalit Literature—Twenty-Five Years of Protest? Of Progress?," *Journal of South Asian Literature* 29 (2): 41–37.

10 Contextualizing the Emergence of Dalit Studies in Indian Academia

Gaurav J. Pathania[1] and K. Kalyani[2]

Introduction

The beginning of the 21st century witnessed the emergence of Dalit[3] Studies in Indian academia. However, Dalit writers from India had already been researching and writing about caste-based struggles, including caste discrimination, oppression, "untouchability," poverty, and resisting Brahmanical hegemony. Following the foundational writings on caste by Jyotirao Phule and then Dr. B. R. Ambedkar (from 1920–1956), multiple scholars internationally have contributed to a vast scholarship on various aspects of caste in Indian society and documented various forms of discrimination in different institutional settings, making caste an interdisciplinary and multilingual field in the humanities and social sciences.[4] This wide spectrum of disciplines heavily emphasizes Dr. Ambedkar's writings on caste—thus establishing Ambedkar's ideas—and serves as the basis of Dalit literature, more recently referred to as Dalit Studies. Today, there is a range of global scholars who are known as Dalit scholars.[5] Therefore, the words "Dalit" and "caste" have gained global recognition. They are less stigmatized and more assimilated than in the last century.

This chapter sets broadly two aims: first, it surveys the emergence and practice of Dalit Studies within academia through a critical engagement with curriculum structures that exist within pedagogic discourses. Secondly, the chapter explores different kinds of academic writings that have prevailed within Dalit discourse by looking into their composition, engagement with the curriculum, and pedagogic practices. Through ethnographic accounts with 20 Dalit scholars, the chapter explores the meanings of the emergence of Dalit Studies that have imbued within curriculum practices.[6] Dalit Studies emerged from Dalit, anti-caste movements; however, socially and politically these movements are not homogenous and occurred in different time periods and in different parts of the country. Therefore, we have broadly defined specific moments of Dalit movements that gave rise to three waves of Dalit Studies. Conceptually, the chapter understands the

DOI: 10.4324/9781003155065-10

emergence of Dalit Studies—its curriculum and academic practices—as the form of "civil repair" (Alexander, 2006). Using cultural sociologist Jeffrey Alexander's framework, we conclude the chapter with the argument that, similar to Women's and Gender Studies and Black Studies, Dalit Studies has as its larger social goal a "civil repair" that needs to be understood by those who are part of it, irrespective of their caste membership (and identity).

Methodology

We engaged with academic practitioners, writers, and institution-builders who are pioneers in the making of the Dalit discourse in Indian academia using cyber/digital ethnographic accounts. Cyber ethnography has developed as a significant methodological tool with the emergence of cyberspace. Hine (2000) has argued that the use of cyberspace provides symmetry to research and an access to multi-sited ethnographic research. In her discussion of the Internet as a "cultural artifact," she argues that it allows for an unconstrained access and interaction (Hine, 2000, p. 19). Doing ethnography of the academicians and writers of Dalit Studies has enabled us to understand the different nuanced aspects of Dalit writing, its definition, and emergence. The ethnographic accounts of pedagogic practitioners reflect upon what Dalit Studies means, what are its parameters, and how it has been perceived within mainstream discourse. Using the Internet as a space for doing ethnography was an enabling experience due to constraints in access to different spaces during COVID-19. We conducted 20 open-ended interviews with academic practitioners and writers among Dalits. The purpose of in-depth interactions with them was to explore their own experiences of curriculum practices. The interviews also addressed their personal life-narratives of being Dalit-Bahujan[7] and the kinds of interventions they have made within Dalit discourse and in establishing Dalit Studies. Our research constantly tracked the respondents' work, writings, and activism over a period of time.

Background

First Wave of Dalit Studies

The first wave of Dalit Studies began with a Literary Movement that can be traced from Savitribai and Jyotiba Phule's writings, which paved the way for Ambedkar's efforts to annihilate caste. Along with his large body of academic research on caste, Ambedkar approached the masses through his newspapers, such as *Mooknayak* (1920), *Bahishkrut Bharat* (1927), *Janata* (1930), and *Prabuddha Bharat* (1956). Through these platforms, he connected the 'untouchables' and built a mass movement for human rights, such as accessing public water-ponds and the right to access any religious place (i.e., the Kalaram temple entry movement). Along with Ambedkar's ideas, his newspapers carried the anti-caste poetry of *Marathi Bhakti* poets. *Mooknayak* brought a collective consciousness to lower-caste communities and highlighted the limitations of the binary of Brahmin and non-Brahmin categories.[8] Through his anti-caste writings and activism, Ambedkar continued his struggle for social justice for people referred to as untouchables.

With the independence of India in 1947, Ambedkar became India's first Law Minister and was given the responsibility of writing the constitution. In the constitution, he abolished untouchability and caste practices. For the first time, untouchables and other lower castes were given the right to equality and the right to live a dignified life. Ambedkar's writings generated a new wave of anti-caste consciousness. After Ambedkar's sudden death in 1956, his writings became the inspirational text for millions of those who remained at the margins of society and had been treated as subhuman (or "subaltern") for thousands of years. This marks the end of the first wave of Dalit Studies that saw a burgeoning body of literature. However, it was limited to the Maharashtra region in the beginning yet gradually spread throughout the country.

Second Wave of Dalit Studies

After the implementation of the constitution, over the next 20 years, a generation of Dalits gained entry into higher education, especially in the western region of Maharashtra, and they were inspired by the struggle and success of Ambedkar and his slogan: "Educate, Agitate and Organize." In the southern part of India, anti-caste writings were already available due to the efforts of Ramaswamy Periyar, Iyothee Thass, and many other social reformers. In the state of Andhra Pradesh, many Telugu scholars started writing to bring anti-caste consciousness. In Maharashtra, the Dalit literary movement like Little Magazine Movement was inspiring radical Dalit youth movements. A section of university radical youth formed the Dalit Panthers and opted for radical strategies. Later, many of the founding members wrote their autobiographies, which added a new dimension to Dalit literature. Later, Ambedkar's writings were compiled by the Maharashtra government and published in different volumes. Subsequently, in the northern part of India, Kanshi Ram emerged as a Dalit-Bahujan icon with the formation of the first independent Dalit political party (Bahujan Samaj Party). Kanshi Ram successfully conveyed his theory of *Bahujan (Unity/ Rule of Majority)* by publishing newspapers and other printed materials that provided a direct critique to the prevailing Hindu caste hegemony.

From 1960 to 1990, a saga of anti-caste literature was published in the forms of novels and autobiographies.[9] These writings were not part of Indian academia because, until the late 1990s, there was almost no presence of active Dalit voices in academia. Gradually, by the 1990s, many educated Dalits started writing their autobiographies. Dalits who were part of higher education (mainly first-generation students) started using the term "Dalit Literature"; and by the end of 1990s, the term was well-established in Indian academia. Ambedkar's persona as *Babasaheb* in the socio-political arena became larger than life in India, as well as a world-class scholar in the social sciences. With hundreds of weekly and monthly magazines, along with an abundance of talks and seminars on Ambedkar and caste, Dalits influenced the political and literary spaces of academics,[10] and the word "Dalit" became part of academic language, curriculum, and discourse. Many Dalit professors have been actively engaged with the content of these magazines as writers and as part of their editorial committees.

Third Wave of Dalit Studies

The 21st century brought new debates and directions for Dalit scholars. The World Conference against Racism, Xenophobia and Related Intolerance in Durban (2001) opened up new frameworks among global scholars. Some scholars have compared caste with the racial struggles of Black groups in South Africa and the U.S. and examined how Black writings inspired Dalit literature.[11] Such comparisons subsequently gave rise to internal contradictions among Dalit intellectuals in academia. Scholars have disagreements on the precise definitions of Dalit, Dalit Studies,[12] and Dalit Literature.

Dalit literature, as a literary movement, brought structural changes that gradually affected academic teachings and research practices. The establishment of institutions such as the Indian Institute for Dalit Studies (IIDS) outside the university system, with the vision of creating a "socially inclusive society, economy, politics, governance and development,"[13] is one of many successful examples. In the past 15 years, IIDS has produced a large data set on the socio-economic and educational conditions of Dalits; and, through its primary research, created a discourse on the situation of the socially marginalized. With its collaborations with global scholars, the organization has also launched several journals, books, and working papers. IIDS created a special unit on *Dalit Literature and Arts* and established the journals *Dalit Asmita* (in Hindi) and *Journal for Social Inclusion Studies* (in English). All have gained accolades for their contributions to the area of social discrimination studies.

Through global alliances, the Dalit community has created spaces for the emergence of public debates and conferences, study groups, and seminars that enable the discursive engagement with Dalit Studies. Through the efforts of Dalit intellectuals and activists, there are now 32 Centers for the Study of Social Exclusion and Inclusive Policy established all over India. A global alliance through education and curriculum structure has been recently seen at universities like Brandeis University,[14] Columbia University,[15] University of Massachusetts-Amherst, University of California-Berkeley, University of Pennsylvania, and The New School, where courses on caste have been introduced.[16]

Concurrently, with the rise of the Internet and social media, anti-caste art, music, and literature among mostly university youth added to the collective consciousness of campus life. Such consciousness is also reflected in campus activism and larger student politics.[17] In the past decade, we have witnessed the "edutainment"[18] phenomenon on many Indian campuses, where Dalit activists have created forms of anti-caste art, music, and songs as more complex and serve a curricular function as an "on-and-off school site where learning can and indeed does take place" (Ibhrahim, 2009, p. 245). Anti-caste hip-hop[19] is a new narrative that has the potential to shift the pre-existing "cultural-codes" of music in academia and motivates historically marginalized students to deconstruct given socio-political and literary structures. Such efforts shape the relationship between students and self-identification. Their music-of-resistance is "creating a contested space" in the existing popular forms of music. The emergence of musical forms like "Tathagata Buddha songs, Bhimgeet have given them new meanings and a sense of dignity" (Kalyani, 2020, p. 60). The nature of this music and art reveals as well as heals the historical wounds of the caste system.

Defining Dalit Literature

Who is Dalit and how did Dalit literature emerge as a field of inquiry? There has been no consensus among scholars regarding the exact time period of the emergence of Dalit Studies.[20] While some consider it as old as anti-caste consciousness developed since the emergence of Buddha, many others have considered its emergence from the anti-caste movement led by Ambedkar, particularly in modern India. Many trace it with the writings of Bhakti Saints, such as Kabir and Raidas, who criticized caste systems and promoted equality in their poetry. A section of scholars tracks the origin of Dalit literature from Gautam Buddha's time and they believe that Amedkarism cannot be completed without Buddhism. The writings of Ambedkar draw from Buddhist literature as well. Buddhist writings and literature have also been part of the popular writings that have helped generate Buddhist ideology and anti-caste consciousness. However, some scholars have distanced from Buddhist literature to consider it as Dalit literature.

According to Rajender Budgujar: *"Buddhist literature talks about equality and love; but it is not Dalit literature, because Buddha was a Kshtriya king. The primary condition to define Dalit literature is that it should be writer by those who have lived experience of being Dalit."*
A Hindi literature scholar, Ram Chandra[21] (Jawaharlal Nehru University), traces Dalit writings particularly from the emancipation of Dr. Ambedkar's conversion from 1956 onwards. He has argued that merely having an anti-caste consciousness doesn't make literature "Dalit" literature; rather, the writings of Dalit literature must be located in the historical trajectory[22] and in the legacy led by Ambedkar. He also believes that Dalit literature in North India became popular with the emergence of Bahujan Samaj Party—a political party formed by a Dalit icon Kanshi Ram that eventually grew into a national party. Therefore, as stated by Chandar, "The inclusion of Babasaheb in national discourse happened only when Bahujan Samaj Party (BSP) paved its way into Indian politics." No doubt, political power paves the way for institutional changes. The emergence of BSP as a movement has inspired many activists to write anti-caste literature. Another anti-caste scholar, Vivek Kumar, argues that the genesis of Dalit literature can be rooted in Maharashtra's Dalit movement of the 1960s; however, from late 1970s onward, it flourished in Northern India. Sushila Takhbhore argues that the emergence of Dalit Studies can be closely linked with the Dalit movement, beginning with the writings of Ambedkar. With a social movement like the Dalit Panthers in Maharashtra, Dalit literature got a major boost and acclamation. She says, "वाह नहीं, आह का साहित्य है दलित साहित्य" ("Dalit literature and Dalit writings is not about gaining popularity and immediate acclamation; rather it is about accounting pain and anguish that Dalit face in their life").
A scholar of Hindi literature, Sheoraj Singh Bechain considers the emergence of Dalit discourse important to claim a dignified recognition of the work done on and by Dalits. He says "Prior to the emergence of Dalit discourse, the writings or theses on Dalit were straightly rejected. No one would even recognize what Dalit meant." The emergence of Dalit discourse is significant to the extent that it enabled a dignified recognition of Dalit writings within academic practice.

Contributions of Dalit Literature in Mainstream Academia

Dalit literature has brought a paradigmatic shift in the ways in which subaltern studies were conventionally understood within the academic practices. Historian Yagati Chinna Rao says that a shift toward Dalit Studies was made possible only because of the debates that had emerged after the Durban conference. The Durban conference raised important concerns about the mechanisms to deal with issues of racism and racial discrimination. Even though the issue of "caste discrimination" was considered to be an "internal matter" of India, the conference did successfully raise the issue of caste discrimination at an international platform. Within academic discourse, this recognition of caste discrimination was an important moment for the beginning of Dalit discursive practices.

One of the major milestones in Dalit discourse was taken up by Sukhadeo Thorat, who, under his chairmanship of University Grants Commission, granted the institutional setup of the Center for the Study of Social Discrimination and Exclusion for a systematic engagement with Dalit discourse. Another major milestone in caste discourse was started with the establishment of Ambedkar Chairs in social science schools of all the centrally funded universities. The goal was to develop the "Dalit perspective," according to Vivek Kumar, who is currently heading the chair in JNU, which was first established in 1995 under the chairmanship of Nandu Ram, a sociologist who contributed five volumes of *Encyclopedia of Scheduled Castes in India.*

Within curriculum practices, Dalit Studies has gained center-stage only in the post-Durban conference wave, when the issue of caste was globally discussed along with the race question. Today, within Indian universities, Dalit Studies has become embedded in the study of literature or part of a full-fledged course structure. This, according to Chinna Rao,[23] translated into the establishment of Centers for Discrimination Studies and Exclusion in all the centrally (federal) funded institutions:

> Overall, Center for Discrimination Studies and Exclusion, JNU, has been remarkable in terms of not only engaging with the anti-caste discourse, but also critically engaging with the disciplinary limitations/failure to engage with the caste question. The interdisciplinary approach has further ensured that the question of discrimination and social justice is engaged holistically within discursive practices. Thus, the CSDE center in JNU has been an important discursive moment that has engaged with Dalit questions at epistemological level.

Gradually, public as well as private universities have included caste discourses in their syllabi. Recently, Azim Premji University started an animation series to present the biography of Savitribai Phule.[24] In Ambedkar University, Delhi, and in Jamia Millia Islamia, there is a significant number of Ambedkar's writings, along with other Dalit literary writings, included in syllabi. Along with many other Dalit autobiographies, the Hindi Department of Lucknow University has included Tulsi Ram's *Murdahiyya* in their syllabi. Chinna Rao also reflected from his personal experience and pointed out: "I was happy to see the presence of Dalit Panel in Indian History

Congress, which was initiated only after there was a constant engagement with Dalit questions, particularly towards the early 21st century."[25]

The curriculum practices have acknowledged Dalit writings only in parts. The writings of Ramchandra, Sheoraj Singh Bechain, Sushila Takhbhore, Anita Bharti, Mohandass Namishray, Rajat Rani "Meenu," and many others have been sparsely included within curriculum structures. For instance, Sheoraj Singh Bechain's autobiographical work like *Mera Bachpan mere kandho par*[26] is part of the Department of English, Delhi University, curriculum.[27]

Dalit Studies Approach to Critical Knowledge: Challenging Feminism

Dalit feminist scholars have highlighted "contradictions in schooling in that curricula and school cultures reproduce Brahmanical values" (Arur and DeJaeghere, 2019: 505). The education of Dalit-*bahujan* girls is further compromised because of the intersectionality of caste and gender oppression. Extending the argument of Paik, Arur has argued that the Dalit-*bahujan* epistemologies are often compromised by the existing dominant "Brahminical-white ideologies of superiority" (ibid: 497). Even within feminist discourse, the Dalit-*bahujan* epistemology is guarded by "Brahman" women, who somehow fail to capture the nuances of caste and intersectionality.

There is scant evidence that Marxists ever challenged the religious and ritualized hegemony of Hindu myths that rule the education system. For example, a significant number of educational institutions in India have a statue of Saraswati, the Hindu Goddess of Education (*Vidya ki Devi*), on their premises. As a matter of fact, women in Indian history were never given education until the British brought new rules to give equal education to everyone.[28] The question was first raised by social scientist, activist, and public intellectual Kancha Ilaiah, who defined the term "Dalit-*bahujan*" and sought to bring all socially marginalized castes together (Scheduled Caste, Scheduled Tribes, and Other Backward Classes). Ilaiah argued that "in a country where women were never allowed to get education, it was a conspiracy to create women as a goddess of education and worship them, but in reality, they were the most vulnerable section of society" (Ilaiah, 1996, p. 170). His criticism led to a fresh debate on academic practices; in many educational institutions, the goddess of education was boycotted. This logic became part of critical knowledge. Dalit literature therefore produces such anti-caste knowledge that challenges the mythical knowledge sanctioned by religious texts (Pathania, 2016). Inspired by anti-caste thoughts, the Dalit literary movement was a radical response to the Brahmanical knowledge production (Ingole, 2020). Thus, the consciousness of Dalit women has been an important dimension of Dalit writings that needs to be elevated. The emergence of Dalit women's writings within curriculum practices emerged only close to the 1990s. These writings include autobiographical[29] works of Kambale (2009); Takbhore (2011, 2015); Pawar (2003); Pawar & Moon (2008). Their narratives challenged mainstream feminism led by upper-caste women. Anita Bharti,[30] another leading Dalit writer and activist, argues that, while the reception of her work was hugely popular in the public sphere, there was a hesitation of acceptance of her work within the academic sphere. Her work brought critiques of Dalit men who have been constantly ignorant of Dalit women's perspectives or their writings:

> The Dalit women's aesthetics and politics failed to get appreciation from the upper-caste feminist. The feminists were also willing to accept the intersection of Dalit women that were emerging through some of their writings.

Furthermore, the emergence of Dalit Studies has been an enabling experience for Dalit women, in particular. Bharti expresses that Dalit literature has given her public visibility and recognition. For Dalit women, "writing was a way of self-expression and demolishing conventional roles ascribed to women. Also, finding a position of acclamation in society was made possible only when Dalit women started conversations about their own selves and experiences." In other words, literature has been an important tool for self-expression of both Dalit men and women about their lived experiences.

Why and How Dalit Literature is Different than Mainstream Literature

In the 1990s, when a popular Dalit autobiography, *"Joothan"* ("Leftover Food"), was included in a university syllabus, it faced much criticism by upper-caste academicians. They defined it as the literature of the underclass, which is full of verbal abuses and absurd language. ["ये तो गाली-गलौच का साहित्य है।."] The language of Dalit literature cannot escape the experiences of violence and oppression. In fact, every writing that has captured the pain of Dalit experiences can be a treatise of Dalit literature. Presenting a world that is considered dirty, filthy, and foul is the strength of Dalit literature. It represents everyday language and culture. Rajendra Budgujar[31] opines that "To know Indian society better, one must understand the Dalit literature."[32] The politics of Dalit writings is discussed by K. Satyanarayana, wherein he has argued that such writings are produced by writers who have rejected their ascribed identity and have instead asserted their Dalit character with a sense of "self-worth and dignity" (Satyanarayana, 2017: 21).

The response to the polemic about Dalit literature is worded by Sushila Takhbhore as "Dalit literature is not about pure aesthetics, but pain and anguish" [वाह नहीं, आह का साहित्य है दलित साहित्य]. The uniqueness of Dalit literature is also discussed by Limbale in which discussion he says, "Dalit literature is not pleasure-giving literature (and) . . . it cannot be based on principles of aestheticist literature" (Limbale, 2004: 116). Sushila Tankbhore takes a critical note on upper-caste writings on Dalits: "In Nagarjuna's novels, the Dalit, as a protagonist, is cleaning and lifting shoes of the upper caste. His sister is raped. He died miserably in the end. This is the way Dalit is made a hero in upper caste writings. Similar phenomena exist with Mushi Premchand's writing." Takhbhore discusses the absence of an active Dalit subject with credible agency in upper-caste writings. This argument was also reflected in the interview with Chauthi Ram Yadav, who argues that, even though the essence of Dalit and Marxist writings have been focused toward egalitarianism, Marxist literature has failed to put the Dalit subject at the center of its ideological debate. Marxist literature and magazines might have brought up special sections on Dalit issues; however, this became possible only because of the Dalit literature that emerged at an "unprecedented level, thereby pressurizing upper-caste dominated academia to take up Dalit issues."[33] He further argues that Dalit literature has "de-classed" itself to produce literature. He says, "Dalit writers have produced literature that is above and beyond class structure. They have meaningfully ascertained their narratives in such writings which previously were missing."

Taking a bottom-up approach, Rajender Budgujar, who has been exploring Dalit issues in local folk of Haryana, stated that Dalit writing is not just about Dalits; it covers a wider spectrum of issues and makes people realize their selfhood and their love for the nation. Dalits face upper-caste atrocities, humiliation, and stigma throughout their lives but still overcome the struggle to live with dignity. The kind of social resilience Dalits have shown the strength to achieve successful careers.

Ideology, Experience, and Everyday Resistance

The success stories of women graduates and teachers in academia are remarkable. Being trebly deprived, Dalit women have to go through every day and every night struggles, dealing with caste outside and patriarchy at home. In her interview, a leading Dalit women writer who has an inspiring life trajectory, explains the life-world of Dalit women: *After cooking, cleaning and taking care of the kids and husband, I was able to write more than two dozen books about caste. Night is the only time a Dalit women's writer can get.* ["दलित लेखिकाएँ दफ़्तर के काम के बाद घर का भी सारा काम करती है और उनका लेखन रात को ही हो पाता है।"- सुशीला टाँकभोरे."] The lived-experiences of Dalit writers are reflected in their writings. Even at an individual level, we found that most of the Dalit writers have faced oppressive and patriarchal circumstances in their homes. For example, during the interview with two female writers from completely different age groups, we found they had similar strategies to fight for their education. What we find common among Dalit women's experience is their struggle within; their resistance to their own family patriarchy.

A young scholar, Priyanka Sonkar, who teaches at Banaras Hindu University, shares her struggle in claiming her space within academic writing. Her struggle began as early as her school days, where she would often feel the sense of exclusion in her peer group. Even to study away from her own hometown, she had to revolt against her own family members. She recalled that eventually, when she got space to write, she published herself in popular magazines like *Hans*. One of the Dalit women recounts, "When my parents didn't allow me to go to another city for higher education, I sat on hunger strike for 3 days and finally they agreed." An established Dalit writer, Anita Bharti, faces similar struggles within her family. Such examples show a strong resilience among Dalit women for their quest to acquire education by maintaining a personal and intellectual balance while dealing with everyday realities of patriarchal and casteist society.

A lifetime activist in Marxist movements, scholar Chauthi Ram Yadav stopped referring to himself as Marxist after the realization that Marxists have been ignoring the contribution of Dr. Ambedkar. During his interview, he said, "Ambedkar or Ambedkarism never existed in progressive Marxist literature," which reflects the gap within the progressive discourse to accept Ambedkar's thoughts and ideas of social justice. Yadav has argued that the difference between Marxist ideology and Ambedkarism is not as much as it is artificially created. Both Marxism and Ambedkarism have imagined a worldview in which equality can exist; however, the Hindi literary development has failed to acknowledge the writings by Dalit writers. This is a paradox in the practice of Marxism within academic discourse; it has created an exclusivist worldview of knowledge. Thus, according to Yadav, while the ideological difference between Marxism and Ambedkarism fetches the common meeting ground, such coherence is not seen in practicing Marxist writers. Somewhere, they have failed to take cognizance of Dalit writers, reducing them and their writings to the periphery. As a matter of fact, the most vibrant campus of India, which is famous as a Marxist school, had not made any effort to include Ambedkar in its social science curriculum until the late 1990s. In this sense, with the arrival of Dalit literature started a process of ideological churning in campuses like JNU, and, as we see in the present scenario, Ambedkar has emerged as the most prominent figure in academia. Ambedkar and Dalit literature are also the best examples of interdisciplinary studies.

Like Yadav, many Dalits and OBCs professors had been part of Marxist movements in their initial years and later turned to Ambedkarism and started boycotting the Brahmanical practices that exist in the form of Marxism in Indian academia. D. R. Nagaraj, in a cultural critique, establishes that Dalit literature is "an expression of Ambedkarite cultural politics" (Nagaraj, 2010: 87) and this politics is inspired by Western ideas of civil rights, equal opportunities, social justice, mobility, and cultural protests literature of decultured Dalits and contributed to the broader Indian literary traditions. Nagaraj's classification of Dalit literary culture as part of Indian culture obscures the "cultural conflict and the literary assertion engendered by Dalit writers." In the name of Indian culture, Nagaraj is arguing for the inclusion of Dalit culture in continuity with Hindu culture.[34] Nagaraj believes that Ambedkarite Dalit literature is presented as a literature of self-pity and anger. On the other hand, Baburao Bagul, another Marathi Dalit critic, believes that Dalit literature invented new modes of writings, presented experiences that were never written before, and thus offers a new perspective to modern Indian literary history. Thus, Dalit writings have been instrumental in bringing out the untold Dalit narratives and Dalit consciousness. Limbale (2004) has argued that Dalit literature written by Dalits has created its own standards of aesthetics and it has stood against "cultural dictatorship" of pre-existing literary standards.

Discussion

The evolution of Dalit literature in Indian academia has undergone a remarkable journey. It was not merely an inclusion of caste or discrimination issues, but scholars (mentioned before in their statements) have debated that the existing academic and casteist practices are not going to change until one inculcates the anti-caste ideas and practices in academics. As our chapter shows, Dalit students are bringing anti-caste consciousness to campus life in arts, music, and hip-hop. Thus, there is embedded consciousness to add to the existing literary practices, thereby enriching its diverse meanings. Dalit students are making the entire campus life of a university more diverse. Moving beyond the simple inclusion of Dalit-inspired literature (the "add and stir" approach[35]), the subsequent focus on Dalit literature in academia provides a hope of social change, despite facing and challenging the most stratified, unequal and unfair age-old structures that exist in Indian academia in the name of "merit." It will breach the binary of "civil" and "uncivil." As Alexander reminds us, the discourse of civil society can be as oppressive as liberating, legitimating not only inclusion but exclusion (Alexander, 2006: 4). Therefore, if an anti-caste consciousness is not at the heart of Dalit literature, then mere inclusion of it in academia would be meaningless.[36]

A central point that emerges from our discussions with scholars (interviewees) is that the aim of Dalit literature is to establish an anti-caste discourse in academia. This goes in contrast with mainstream discourse that talks about caste but does not provide any tools to annihilate it. For example, the existing discourse of the subaltern discourse (Guha and Spivak, 1998) discussed the need for engaging with "subalterns" in terms of understanding their inequitable access to resources, and unequal and subordinated position in the social structure. Still (2015) has, however, discussed the gaps in subaltern perspectives. She argues that the subaltern perspective has failed to have an empirical and ethnographic account of Dalit lives per se. Dalit Studies, on the one hand, has engaged with "Dalit" as an active subject by repositioning a Dalit "self" at the center of their subject matter. Within Dalit discourse, this repositioning is often done through autobiographical writings, ethnographic accounts, and through critical engagement with historical absences of Dalit life-worlds. The emergence of a Dalit perspective through Dalit Studies has been an enabling experience for Dalits, who have been otherwise historically relegated to the margins. Dalit literature, on the other hand, challenges the reader to be conscious about their privileges and then get rid of them.

The chapter attempts to present various sides of the arguments around the definition, ambiguities, and contestation around Dalit Studies and Dalit literature. Despite its ambiguities, Dalit literature has brought national and international scholars together on one platform. Dalit literature deconstructs the narrow definition of nation and includes the global histories of racism and exclusion. For example, in the past few years, Dalit scholars and activists have made a strong connection with other historically marginalized groups—Black individuals in the U.S., the Roma tribe in Europe, and Burakumins[37] in Japan. With globalization, the scope of Dalit literature has expanded from India to the West.[38] In the past few years, a new generation of Dalits are writing their memoirs and autobiographies to inspire the aspiring Dalits in India who see education as the only means of emancipation from caste. Many young Dalit scholars studying abroad, engaging, and debating caste issues are making more alliances within and outside academia.

Largely, there is an impact on courses in Ethnic Studies, Africana Studies, Black Studies, History, Anthropology, Postcolonial Studies, and Literary Studies that get closely associated with Dalit Studies. Courses that emphasize innovative methodological and theoretical approaches will find Dalit histories useful, especially for graduate students. A range of scholars who compared caste with race have taken their methodologies from critical race scholarship.

The writings of Dalit literature have explored the possibilities in which Dalit lives are embedded. The history of violence and oppression becomes an obvious extension of Dalit's lived experience in the form of patriarchy and caste violence. However, these experiential realities are not the entire worldview of Dalit writings per se. Many of these literatures have also captured the elements of resistance and acknowledgment of their cultural practices. Such literature is part of the "civil repair" that counters the humiliation and violence embedded in historical and present realities. In Alexander's words, "It is a matter of cultural struggle, of social movement, of demands for incorporation, of broken and reconstructed dialogue, of reconfiguring institutional life" (Alexander, 2006: 34–35). With the rise of South Asian diaspora in the deveopled countries, the caste is beoming a global phenomenon and so does anti-caste movement. (Pathania 2023).

Conclusion

Our chapter aimed to explore the emergence, scope, and meanings of Dalit Studies in academia. Dalit Studies refers to an engagement with Dalit cultural and critical knowledge production. Furthermore, the chapter has also looked into the dynamics of critical knowledge production and its engagement with the existing discursive practices. It is in this context that one might look at the Dalit's critique of subalterns and Marxism and the emergence of Dalit feminism.

The Dalit literature in academia has emerged like an iceberg in the ocean of academia. What we see currently in the name of Dalit literature in Indian academia is just the beginning of something larger. In this chapter, we highlighted that Dalit literature is not limited to writing memoirs, novels, or poetry; rather, its reach is much wider; it's appearing in the form of art, visual art, music, hip-hop, motivational literature, new festivals to counter the dominant festivals, online scholarly exchange of ideas, and global alliances among scholars, anti-caste conferences in academic spaces. Even a suicide note becomes part of the literary resistance. For instance, Rohith Vemula left his suicide note not just as his last words, but his letter also included the worldview through which he established the contestation between what he aspired to and the social impediments that exist to those aspirations. He wrote, "The value of a man was reduced to his immediate identity and nearest possibility . . . My birth is my fatal accident. Know that I am happier dead than being alive." As a scholar, his suicide note would always serve as a reminder to the "civil society" of academia. In the words of Alexander, "New, more civil narratives must be created, stories that allow the weak and the powerful, the victims and their persecutors, to switch moral places" (Alexander, 2006).

Dalit literature, with its global outreach in the 21st century, has been changing the intellectual climate of academia and influencing the discourses on discrimination and making the exclusion-inclusion debate more subtle. By producing global scholars and public intellectuals, it also questions the myth of merit and challenges the phenomenology of the (academic) spaces and (caste) realities that, until recently, only upper-caste hegemony had been defining. The Dalit literary movement provided a new perspective to look at the caste realities of Indian society, which is "Ambedkar'ite Perspective" (Kumar, 2014). Therefore, according to him, it would be wise to call it "Dalit Perspective" rather than "Dalit Studies." However, the experiences of Black Studies and Women's Studies in the U.S. and U.K. inform us that perspective not only reflects one's epistemic position but eventually critically interrogates the disciplinary perspective and finally determines truth.

Taking inspiration from Black Studies and Women's Studies, Dalit Studies needs to be developed as a discipline in academia. Beyond its conventional and essentialized meaning of narrativizing pain, atrocity, or illiteracy, there is a dire need for methodological engagement with Dalit Studies that may add other social categories, such as Dalit-*bahujan*, Dalit literature, and Dalit perspective that can add to the epistemology of Dalit Studies. Dalit literature opens up the window of civil dialogue, as well as a worldview that has been alien to the upper-caste life-world. It offers a dialectical notion of narrative that calls into question the role of upper/dominant castes in perpetuating caste hierarchies. It connects to global communities of struggle that provide healing and social justice.

Notes

1. Eastern Mennonite University, U.S.A.
2. Azim Premji University, Bangalore, India.
3. The term "Dalit" literally translates as oppressed, broken, crushed, downtrodden, or untouchable in the language Marathi, first used by Jyotirao Phule (1827–1890). In the 1970s, following the legacy of Black Panthers, the Dalit Panther Movement in the Maharashtra region gave "Dalit" a radical new meaning of self-identification, signifying oppositional consciousness.
4. By "Dalit Studies," we refer to the scholarly work exploring caste discrimination. Some of the recent research in this area across disciplines include:

   • History (Dirks (2001), Jangam (2017), Mohan (add), Pandey (2013), Pandian (2008), A. Rao (2008, 2009), Skaria (2014); Y. Rao (2003, 2011); Thorat & Kumar (2009)
   • Economy [A. Deshpande (2013), Prakash (2015), Thorat (2007, 2009), S. Thorat, Mosse (2015, 2018), Throat & Neuman (2009), G. Shah(2011)];
   • Society & Development [Waghmore (2013), N. Ram (2007), Paswan & Jaideva (2002), Zelliot (1996); Simon & Thorat (2020)];
   • Education [Deshpande (2013), Nambissan (2020), Paik (2014), Pathania (2018b, 2020, 2018a), A. Shah (2018), Subramaniam (2015), Wankhede (2020), Zene (2011)];
   • Health [Acharya (2017), Barooah (2018), Jadhav & Mosse (2016), Nayar (2007)];
   • Culture [R. Ram (2008), Narayana (2006), Omvedt (1995, 2011), Kalyani (2020, 2022), Natrajan (2012), Pathania (2020), Yadav (2018)];

- Religion [Judge (2018), Juergenmeyer (1998), R. Ram (2008), Viswanath (2015)];
- Philosophy [Dhanda (2019), Guru & Sarukkai (2012), Rathore (2021), Sampath (2019), Zene (2011)];
- Politics and Movement [Gorringe (2016, 1018), Jaffrelot (2003), V. Kumar (2014a), Gundimeda (2015), Gupta (2005), Omvedt (1995), Pai (2002), Pathania (2020), Pawar & Moon (2008), Rodrigues (2002), Rinker (2018), Shah (2011)];
- Gender [Arya & Rathore (2019), Brueck (2016), Chakravarti (1993), Rege (2006, 2008), Sachidanand (Add), Velayudha (2018), Paik (2014), Guru & Geetha (2000)];
- Art & Aesthetic [Alone (2017), Barak & Satyanarayan and Thiara (2019) Kalyani (2022), Unnamati (2019), Savarkar (2014), Samos (2021)]; and
- Literature (Bechain (2019), Brueck (2017), Bagul (1992), Byapari (2018), Chauhan (2014), Dutt (2018), Gidla (2017), Maitreya (2019), J. Pawar, V (2017). Pawar (2003), Rajkumar (2010), Ravikumar & Azhagarasan (2012), Rawat (2013), Rawat & Satyanarayan (2016)), Sharma (2006), Satyanarayana (2017), Tharakam (2020), V. Thorat & Badtya (2008), Valmiki (2003), Wankhede (2020), Yengde (2019)].

5. Dalit Studies in the U.S. started with a course facilitated by Gyanendra Pandey at Emory University. Pandey's course aimed to understand Dalit history along the lines of African American history. Subsequently, Dalit Studies within the curriculum was also started at the University of Washington, University of Texas-Austin, and University of Oregon. The world's first journal, titled Caste, was started by Brandeis University (which also added caste to its anti-discriminatory policies).
6. More than 50 books from Dalit writers are now part of mainstream academia. These books are primarily in Hindi, Telugu, or Marathi. Some of the popular Dalit autobiographies, such as *Joothan, Mera Bachpan Mere Kandhon Par*, and a few more were translated into English and now are taught in different institutions.
7. *Bahujan* means majority. The Dalit-Bahujan term was given by Kancha Ilaiah to unite all lower castes.
8. According to Pol (2020), *Mooknayak* argued that, although the binary had substantial political value, it nonetheless glossed over the internal contradictions within the non-Brahmin community.
9. Some of the early engagements with Dalit writings can be traced back to works taken up through small magazines and writings of Baburao Bagul, Mohan Dass Namishray, Prabhakar Mande, Chandrika Prasad Jigyasu, and many others. Writing memoirs has been a crucial part of any literature. In the U.S., life-writing has undergone a series of mutations since the early 1970s, when participants in the student protest culture began to publish their autobiographies, memoirs, and other personal histories (Halliwell and Witham 2018: 98). Nevertheless, Dalit Studies have developed "new epistemologies, bringing articulations and ideas from the margins to the center of writings on history, leading to debates around caste that have transformed notions of politics itself" (Velayudhan, 2018, p. 107).
10. Dangle has understood Dalit literature "not simply as literature . . . but something that is associated with a movement to bring change" (Dangle, 1994, p. vii-viii). Limbale, too, has considered that Dalit literature has Dalit consciousness and is connected to struggles against the caste system (Limbale, 2004: 32).
11. Black Lives Matter activists have used memories of the decade to challenge methods that have come to symbolize its approach to racial justice (Halliwell and Witham, 2018: 98).

12. Rawat and Satyanarayan edited the volume *Dalit Studies* (2016) that discusses the emergence of Dalit Studies as a new, emerging field in South Asia in the 1990s.
13. IIDS is an independent research institute, established in 2003 and recognized by the Indian Council for Social Science Research, Delhi. [www.dalitStudies.org.in/]
14. In collaboration with IIDS and Boston Study Group, the Heller School of Brandeis initiated the first conference on "The Unfinished Legacy of Dr. Ambedkar."
15. With the initiative of Anupama Rao, Columbia Global Centers hold annual discussions on Ambedkar's writings. [https://globalcenters.columbia.edu/content/mumbai-bhimrao-ramji-ambedkar]
16. Columbia University's Center for the Study of Social Difference has engaged with the caste question. Similarly, the Julien Studley Graduate Program in International Affairs, The New School, has started a course titled "Politics of Equity and Dignity: Rethinking Caste Globally" under Ashok Gurung. Brandeis University created the Heller School, which has also taken up the question of social justice. Caste is taught in the history department at University of Massachusetts, Amherst.
17. Musical and literary practices of resistance have emerged among the youth in recent times. A new, alternative cultural space is emerging through different groups like Casteless Collective by Pa Ranjith, Kabir Kala Manch, started by performers like Sheetal Sathe, and Youth for Buddhist India, started by the late Shanti Swaroop Baudh. The literature by young Dalit Scholars and writers is also something worth mentioning. Yogesh Maitraye has published his poetry collections *Blues From Bhim Nagar, Flowers on the grave of caste*. A young poet and Bahujan activist Balgangadhar "Baghi" came out with a collection of poems titled "Akash Nila Hai," to mention a few.
18. See Watkins (2005): 241.
19. The first Dalit hip-hop performer, Sumeet Samos (2018) is from JNU, New Delhi. Tarannum Baudh (2017), Ginni Mahi (2016), and many others are known for their cultural performances. Similarly, *Bhim-Drum* was established by Sarah Cobbler Chamar in Osmania University in 2012. Rajkumar at Delhi University has started groups like *Mission Pay Back to Society* that brings together Dalit-Bahujan students together at the university level for cultural and educational events.
20. A group of scholars consider autobiographies as the primary source of Dalit literature. Hazari's *An Untouchable: Autobiography of an Indian Outcaste* is the first autobiography of Independent India. Some scholars go farther back in history and consider Banarsidas' *Ardhakathanaka*, published in 1641 in Hindi, a major source.
21. He teaches Dalit literature at the Center for Indian Languages at Jawaharlal Nehru University, New Delhi. His works include *Premchand Aur Dalit Vimarsh ke Prahna, Omprakash Valmiki ki Rachnadhamita aur Dalit Sahitya*, and *Dalit Stree ka Chetna Itihas*.
22. Baburao Bagul (1992) has also discussed the genesis of Dalit literature in the "humanist legacy" as propounded by Buddha, Christ, Christ, Phule, and Ambedkar, as well as the influence of Western Enlightenment.
23. Yagati Chinna Rao published a volume on *Dalit Studies* in 2003.
24. *Savitribai: Journey of a Trailblazer*, 2014. An Azim Premji University Publication: Bangalore. https://azimpremjiuniversity.edu.in/SitePages/resources-books-published-savitri-bai.aspx accessed 7th December, 2020.

25. Chinna Rao has discussed the important contribution of having a "Dalit panel" at Indian History Congress. Tracing the trajectory of discussions on Dalit history within History discourse, one of the foremost discussions was done at a special panel on "The History and Historiography of Dalits" in 2010 held at IHC, 70th session. It involved the engagement of academics like Sabyasachi Bhattacharya, Priyadarshani Vajishri, K.N. Panikkar, S.K. Thorat, Amiya Bagchi, Raj Sekhar, and Arun (Rao, 2011: 323).
26. The autobiography gained popularity in academia; and in 2018, the Oxford University Press translated it into English with the title *My Childhood on My Shoulders.*
27. Similarly, his works, including *Uttar Sadi ke Hindi Upanayaso mai Dalit Vimarsh* and *Upanyas Sahitya mai Dalit Samasya aur Samadhan* were part of the Allahabad University syllabus. Works of Dalit women writers like Rajat Rani 'Meenu' *Hindi Dalit Katha Sahitya, Awdharnayai aur Vidhaye* are part of a post-graduate syllabus of Allahabad University.
28. The much-quoted education of Gargi and Maitryee, from ancient India, is based on an unequal premise. Access to education was still limited to upper-caste women; that, too, in a limited way (also see Chand and Karre, 2019).
29. Raj Kumar argues that, before Indian independence, Dalits had no rights to education; therefore, "it must be kept in mind that the autobiographies written by Dalits cannot be evaluated by the norms set by the educated upper caste men and women" (Kumar, 2020, p. 47). Mani and Sardar (2010) find "*Mang Maharachya Dukhvisayi*" (About the grief of the Mangs and Mahars) written by an 11-year-old girl, Mukta, published in 1855 in *Dyanodaya*, an Ahmednagar-based journal. The essay openly boycotted the Brahminic culture and Hindu religion, who degraded the lower caste and oppressed them.
30. Interviewed on 11th October, 2020. She is serving as the chair of *Dalit Lekhak Sangh,* New Delhi.
31. Along with dozens of books, he recently published a volume *Chhapkataiyaa* (2020) that deals with the upper-caste plagiarism of the folk songs that were written by lower-caste artists.
32. Interviewed on November 8, 2020.
33. Chauthi Ram Yadav interview dated November 19, 2020.
34. Acc. to Nagaraj, "Dalit literature in the sphere of Indian culture. In order to bring out the liberatory function of Dalit literature, there is a need to develop "a new aesthetics" for "Indian culture as a whole" (Nagaraj, 2010: 195).
35. Bowles and Klein (1983)
36. An anti-caste scholar, Suryakant Waghmore (2013) argues that caste played a seminal role in the creating the hegemony of civil society. Dalits with their anti-caste and anti-Brahmin movements revitalized and transformed the concept of civil society.
37. Burakumin is a historically segregrated community in Japan which faces similary kind of untouchability that Dalits face in India.
38. The Pulitzer Prize winning American journalist, Isabel Wilkerson's latest book on *Caste: The Origin of our Discontent* compared race and caste. In the end, she shares a story about a Brahmin who one day ripped off his own sacred thread and said, "it was a poisonous snake around my neck, and its toxic venom was getting inside of me" (Wilkerson, 2020: 364). New research on caste and education (Paik, 2014; Pathania and Tierney, 2018, 2020, V. Kumar, 2016) proves that Indian academia still carries that sacred thread but it's unconscious of it. The contribution of Dalit literature is to make them conscious about this poisonous, sacred thread.

References

Acharya, Sanghamitra. (2017). "Social Identities and Perceptions about Health-Care Services: Provisioning by and for the Dalits in India." *Social Identities*, 24 (1), 1–12.

Alexander, Jeffery C. (2006). *The Civil Sphere*. New York: Oxford University Press.

Alone, Y. S. (2017). "Caste Life Narratives, Visual Representation, and Protected Ignorance." *Biography*, 40 (1), 140–169.

Arur, Aditi, and John Dejaeghere. (2019). "Decolonizing Life Skills for Girls for Brahmanical India: A Dalit Bahujan Perspective." *Gender and Education*, 31 (4), 409–507. https://doi.org/10.1080/09540253.2019.1594707

Arya, Sunaina, and Aakash S. Rathore (eds.). (2019). *Dalit Feminism Theory: A Reader*. New York: Routledge.

Bagul, Baburao. (1992). Dalit Literature Is But Human Literature. In Arjun Dangle (ed.), *Poisoned Bread: Translations from Modern Marathi Dalit Literature*. Hyderabad: Orient Longman.

Barak, Judith Misrahi, K. Satyanarayana, and Nicole Thiara (eds.). (2019). *Dalit Text: Aesthetics and Politics Re-imagined*. London: Routledge.

Barooah, Vani Kant. (2018). *Health and Well-Being in India: A Quantitative Analysis of Inequality in Outcomes and Opportunities*. London: Palgrave Macmillan.

Baudh, Tarannum, Samyak Baudh Sammelan. (2017). National News Media, Nov. 13. www.youtube.com/watch?v=LpAcstyVjEw

Bechain, Sheoraj Singh. (2019). *My Childhood on My Shoulders*. Oxford University Press.

Bowles, Gloria, and Renate Duellli Klein. (1983). *Theories of Women's Studies*. New York: Routledge & Kegan Paul Inc.

Brueck, Laura R. (2014). *Writing Resistance: The Rhetorical Imagination of Hindi Dalit Literature*. New York: Columbia University Press.

Brueck, Laura R. (2017). "Narrating Dalit Womanhood and the Aesthetics of Autobiography." *The Journal of Commonwealth Literature*, 54 (1), 25–37.

Budgujar, Rajender. (2020). *Chhapkattiya*. Delhi: Siddhartha Books.

Byapari, Manoranjan. (2018). Interrogating My Chandal Life: An Autobiography of a Dalit, trans. Sipra Mukherjee, New Delhi: Sage.

Chand, Deep, and Sailu Karre. (2019). "Equal Opportunity in Education: A Perspective from Below." *Contemporary Voice of Dalit*, 11 (1), 56–61.

Chander, Ram. (2013). *Dalit Stree Chetna ka Itihas aur Dr. Ambedkar*. Varshiki [Hindi].

Chauhan, Suraj Pal. (2014). *Woh Din Zaroor Ayega*. New Delhi: Hindi Book Centre.

Dangle, Arjun. (1994). *Poisoned Bread: Translations from Modern Marathi Dalit Literature*. Mumbai: Orient Black Swan.

Deshpande, Ashwini. (2013). Social Justice Through Affirmative Action in India: An Assessment. In J. Wicks-Lim and R. Pollin (eds.), *Capitalism on Trial: Explorations in the Tradition of Thomas E. Weisskopf* (pp. 266–285). Northampton: Edward Elgar.

Deshpande, Satish. (2013). "Caste and Castelessness: Towards a Biography of the "General Category"." *Economic and Political Weekly*, 48 (15), 32–39.

Dhanda, Meena. (2019). Philosophical Foundations of Anti-Casteism. Proceedings from the Aristotelian Society (accessed January 13, 2020).

Dirks, Nicholas B. (2001). *Castes of Mind: Colonialism and the Making of Modern India*. Princeton, NJ: Princeton University Press.

Dutt, Yashica. (2018). *Coming Out as Dalit*. Delhi: Aleph Book Company.

Gangadhar, Bal. (2017). *Aakash Nila Hai*. New Delhi: Samayak Prakashan.

Geetha, V. (2016). 'A Part Apart': Dr. Ambedkar's Indictment of Hindu Social Order. In K. Kannabiran (ed.), *Violence Studies*. New Delhi: Oxford University Press.

Gidla, Sujatha. (2017). *Ants among Elephants: An Untouchable Family and the Making of Modern India*. Delhi: HarperCollins India.

Gorringe, Hugo. (2016). "Drumming Out Oppression, or Drumming It in? Identity, Culture and Contention in Dalit Politics." *Contributions to Indian Sociology*, 50 (1), 1–26.

Gorringe, Hugo. (2018). Ambedkar Icons: Whys and Wherefores. In S. Yengde and A. Teltumbde (eds.), *The Radical in Ambedkar: Critical Reflections* (pp. 328–339). Gurgaon: Penguin Random House India.

Guha, Ranjit and Gayatri Spivak. (1998). *Selected Subaltern Studies*, New York: Oxford University Press.

Gundimeda, Sambaiah. (2015). *Dalit Politics in Contemporary India*. Routledge.

Gupta, Dipankar. (2005). "Caste and Politics: Identity over System." *Annual Review of Anthropology*, 34 (1), 409–427..

Guru, Gopal. (1995). "Dalit Women Talk Differently." *Economic and Political Weekly*, 30 (41/42), 2548–2550.

Guru, Gopal. (2002). "How Egalitarian Are the Social Sciences in India?" *Economic and Political Weekly*, 37 (50), 5003–5009.

Guru, Gopal. (2012). Experience, Space and Justice. In G. Guru and S. Sarukkai (eds.), *The Cracked Mirror: An Indian Debate on Experience and Theory*. Delhi: Oxford University Press.

Guru, Gopal, and V. Geetha. (2000). "New Phase of Dalit-Bahujan Intellectual Activity." *Economic and Political Weekly*, 35 (3), 130–134.

Halliwell, Martin, and Nick Witham. (2018). *Reframing 1968*. Edinburgh: Edinburgh University Press.

Hine, Christine. (2000). *Virtual Ethnography*. SAGE.

Ibhrahim, Awad. (2009). Taking Hip-Hop to a Whole Nother Level: *Metissage*, Affect and Pedagogy in a Global Hip-Hop Nation. In H. Samy Alim, Awad Ibhrahim, and Altastair Pennycook (eds.), *Global Linguistic Flows: Hip-Hop Cultures, Youth Identities, and Politics of Language* (pp. 231–48). New York: Routledge.

Ilaiah, Kanch. (2004). *Buffalo Nationalism: A Critique of Spiritual Fascism*. Kolkata: Samya Publication.

Ilaiah, Kancha. (1996). *Why I am Not a Hindu: A Shudra Critique of Hindutva Philosophy, Culture, and Political Economy*. Calcutta: Samya Publication.

Ingole, Prashant. (2020). "Intersecting Dalit and Cultural Studies: De-Brahmanising the Disciplinary Space." *Caste: A Global Journal on Social Exclusion*, 1 (2), 91–106.

Jadhav, S., Mosse, D., & Dostaler, N. (2016). Minds of caste–Discrimination and its affects. *Anthropology Today*, 32 (1), 1–2.

Jaffrelot, Christophe. (2003). India's Silent Revolution: The Rise of the Low Caste in North Indian Politics. Ranikhet: Permanent Black.
Jain, Sumeet, and Sushrut Jadhav. (2008). "A Cultural Critic of Community Psychiatry in India." *International Journal of Health Services*, 38 (3), 561–584.
Jangam, Chinaiah. (2017). *Dalits and the Making of Modern India*. Delhi: Oxford University Press.
Jigyasu, Chandrika Prasad. (2016). *Granthawali* (Compiled by Kanwal Bharti). Kanpur: Aman Prakashan.
Jodhka, Surinder S. (2012). *Caste: Oxford Indian Short Introduction*. Delhi: Oxford University Press.
Judge, Paramjit S. (2014). "Existence, Identity and Beyond: Tracing the Contours of Dalit Literature in Punjabi." *Economic and Political Weekly*, 49 (29), 209–216.
Juergensmeyer, Mark. (1988). Religious Rebels in Punjab: The Social Vision of Untouchables. Delhi: Ajanta Publication [reprinted by Navayana].
Kalyani, K. (2020). "Tathagata Buddha Songs: Buddhism as Religion and Cultural-Resistance among Dalit Singers of Uttar Pradesh." *Caste: A Global Journal on Social Exclusion*, 1 (2), 51–62.
Kalyani, K. (2022). Resistance in Popular Visuals and Iconography: A Study of Dalit–Bahujan Calendar Art in North India. *Journal of Social Inclusion Studies*, 8 (1), 64–85.
Kumar, Vivek. (2014a). *Caste and Democracy: A Perspective from Below*. Delhi: Gyan Publishing House.
Kumar, Vivek. (2014b). "How Egalitarian Is Indian Sociology." *Economic and Political Weekly*, LI (25), pp. 33–39.
Kumar, Vivek. (2017). Exclusion of Dailt Issues in Social Sciences. In Govardhan Wankhede and Ivan Reid (eds.), *Accessing Higher Education: Footprints of Marginalized Groups*. Delhi: Aakar.
Limbale, Sharankumar. (2004). *Towards an aesthetic of Dalit Literature: Histories, Controversies and Considerations* (Translated from Marathi by Alok Mukherjee). New Delhi: Orient Blackswan.
Maitreya, Yogesh. (2019). *Flowers on the Grave of Caste*. Pune: Panthers' Paw Publications.
Mahi, Ginni. (2016). Fan Baba Saheb Di. New Punjabi Shabad, February 6, www.youtube.com/watch?v=H5XzHJBNyoI
Mani, Braj Ranjan. (trans.). (2010). The Revolt of a Dalit Girl: An Essay by A Student of Phules' School. In Braj Ranjan Mani and Pamela Sardar (eds.), *A Forgotten Liberator: The Life and Struggles of Savitribai Phule* (pp. 70–75). New Delhi: Mountain Peak.
Meenu, Rajat Rani. (2012). *Hum Kon Hai*. New Delhi: Vani Prakashan.
Mosse, David. (2015). Class, Caste and the Reproduction of Privilege. *Anthropology of This Century*, 14. (accessed September 24, 2019).
Mosse, David. (2018). "Caste and Development: Contemporary Perspectives on a Structure of Discrimination and Advantage." *World Development*, 110, 422–436.
Nagaraj, D. R. (ed.). (2010). *The Flaming Feet and Other Essays*. New York: Seagull Books.

Nambissan, Geetha B. (2020). "Caste and the Politics of Early Public Schooling: Dalit Struggle for an Equitable Education." *Contemporary Education Dialogue*, 17 (2), 126–154.

Namishray, Mohan Dass. (2003). *Caste and Race: Comparative Study of BR Ambedkar and Martin Luther King*. Rawat: Delhi.

Natrajan, Balmurli. (2012). *The Culturalization of Caste in India: Identity and Inequality in a Multicultural Age*. Abingdon: Routledge.

Navaria, Ajay. (2013). *Unclaimed Terrain: Stories by Ajay Navaria*. Trans.by Laura Brueck, Delhi: Navayana.

Nayar, K. R. (2007). "Social Exclusion, Caste & Health: A Review Based on the Social Determinants Frame-Work." *Indian Journal of Medical Research*, 126, 355–363.

Omvedt, Gail. (1995). Dalit Visions: The Anti-Caste Movement and the Construction of an Indian Identity. New Delhi: Orient Longman.

Omvedt, Gail. (2011). Cultural Revolt in a Colonial Society: The Non-Brahman Movement in Western India. New Delhi: Manohar.

Pai, Sudha. (2002). Dalit Assertion and the Unified Democratic Revolution: The Bahujan Samaj Party in Uttar Pradesh. SAGE.

Paik, Shailaja. (2014). Dalit Women's Education in Modern India: Double Discrimination. New York: Routledge.

Pandey, Gyandera. (2013). A History of Prejudice: Race, Caste and Difference in India and the United States. New York: Cambridge University Press.

Pandian, M.S.S. (2018). Writing Ordinary Lives, *Economic and Political Weekly*, 43 (38), 34–40.

Pathania, Gaurav J. (2016). "Food Politics and Counter-Hegemonic Assertion among Marginalized Students at Indian Universities," *South Asia Research*, 36 (2), 261–277.

Pathania, Gaurav J. (2018a). The University as a Site of Resistance: Identity and Student Politics. New Delhi: Oxford University Press.

Pathania, Gaurav J. (2020). "Cultural Politics of Historically Marginalized Students in Indian Universities." *Critical Times*, 3 (3), 534–550.

Pathania, Gaurav J. (2023). Caste Should not be Part of the 'American Dream' Boston Globe. February 17. https://www.bostonglobe.com/2023/02/17/opinion/caste-should-not-be-part-american-dream/

Pathania, Gaurav J. and William G. Tierney. (2018). Ethnography of Caste and Class at an Indian University: Creating Capital. *Tertiary Education and Management*, 24 (3), 221–231.

Paswan, Sanjay and Paramanshi Jaideva. (2002). *Encyclopedia of Dalits in India: Emancipation and Empowerment*, New Delhi: Kalpaz Publication.

Pawar, J. V. (2017). *Dalit Panthers*. New Delhi: Forward Press Books.

Pawar, Urmila. (2003). *The Weave of My Life: A Dalit Woman's Memoirs*. Kolkata: Stree Publication.

Pawar, Urmila and Meenakshi Moon. (2008). *We Make History: Women in the Ambedkarite Movement*. New Delhi: Zubaan.

Pol, Prabodhan. 2020. 100 Years of Mooknayak, Ambedakr's First Newspaper that Changed the the Dalit Politics Forever, *The Wire*, Jan. 31.

294   *Gaurav J. Pathania and K. Kalyani*

Prakash, Aseem. (2015). *Dalit Capital: State, Markets and Civil Society in Urban India*. New Delhi: Routledge India.

Ram, Nandu. (2007). *Encyclopedia of Scheduled Castes in India*. Delhi: Gyan Publishing House.

Ram, Ronki. (2004). "Untouchability in India with a Difference: Ad Dharm, Dalit Assertion and Caste Conflicts in Punjab." *Asian Survey*, 44 (6), 895–912.

Ram, Ronki. (2008). "Ravidass Deras and Social Protest: Making Sense of Dalit Consciousness in Punjab (India)." *The Journal of Asian Studies*, 67 (4), 1341–1364.

Rathore, Aakash (ed). (2021). *B. R Ambedkar: The Quest for Justice*. New Delhi: Oxford University Press.

Rao, A. (2008). Who Is the Dalit? The Emergence of a New Political Subject. In M. Bhagwan and A. Feldhaus (eds.), *Claiming Power from Below: Dalits and Subaltern Question in India*. Delhi: Oxford University Press.

Rao, Anupama. (2009). *The Caste Question: Dalits and the Politics of Modern India*. Berkeley, CA: University of California Press.

Rao, Yagati C. (2003). *Dalit Studies: A Bibliographical Handbook*. New Delhi: Kanishka Publishers.

Rao, Yagati C. (2011). *The Past of the Outcaste: Readings in Dalit History*. New Delhi: Orient Blackswan.

Ravikumar, D. and Azhagarasan, R. (2012). *The Oxford Anthology of Tamil Dalit Writings*. Delhi: Oxford University Press.

Rawat, Ramnaryan and K. Satyanarayana. (2016). *Dalit Studies*. Durham: Duke University Press.

Rawat, Ramnarayan S. (2013). "Occupation, Dignity, and Space: The Rise of Dalit Studies." *History Compass*, 11 (12), 1059–1067.

Rege, S. (2006). *Writing Caste, Writing Gender: Reading Dalit Women's Testimonies*. New Delhi: Zubaan.

Rege, S. (2008). "Interrogating the thesis of 'irrational deification.'" *Economic & Political Weekly*, 43 (7), 16–20.

Rinker, Jeremy. (2018). *Identity, Rights, and Awareness: Anti-Caste Activism in India and the Awakening of Justice through Discursive Practices*, Lanham, MD: Lexington Books.

Rodrigues, Valerian (ed.). (2002). *The Essential Writings of B R Ambedkar*. New Delhi: Oxford University Press.

Samos, Sumit. (2021). *Affairs of Caste: A Young Diary*. Pune: Panthers' Paw Publication.

Sampath, Rajesh. (2019). "The Dissolution of the Social Contract into the Unfathomable Perpetuity of Caste: Questions of Nature, the State, Inequality, and Sovereignty in Hobbes, Hegel, and Ambedkar." *Symposion: Theoretical and Applied Inquiries in Philosophy and the Social Sciences*, 6 (2), 195–217.

Satyanarayana, K. (2017). "The Political and Aesthetic Significance of Contemporary Dalit Literature." *The Journal of Commonwealth Literature*, 54 (1), 9–24.

Satyanarayana, K. (2017). "The Political and Aesthetic Significance of Contemporary Dalit Literature." *The Journal of Commonwealth Literature*, 54 (1), 9–24.

Shah, Alpa, Jens Lerche, Richard Axelby, Dalel Benbabaali, Brendan Donegan, Jayaseelan Raj, and Vikramaditya Thakur. (2018). *Ground Down by Growth: Tribe, Caste, Class and Inequality in 21st Century India.* London: Pluto Press.

Shah, Ghanshyam. (2011). *Social Movements in India.* New Delhi: SAGE.

Sharma, Pradeep K. (2006). *Dalit Politics and Literature.* Delhi: Shipra Publications.

Simon, Laurence and S. Thorat. (2020). "Why a Journal on Caste?" *CASTE: A Global Journal on Social Exclusion*, 1 (1).

Singh, Roja (2019). *Spotted Goddesses: Dalit Women's Agency-narratives on Caste and Gender Violence.* New Delhi: Zubaan.

Skaria, Ajay. (2014). 'Can the Dalit Articulate a Universal Position?': The Intellectual, the Social, and the Writing of History. *Social History*, 39 (3), 340–358.

Soundararajan, Thenmozhi (2022). *The Trauma of Caste: A Dalit Feminist Meditation on Survivorship, Healing and Abolition.* Berkeley: North Atlantic Books.

Still, Clarinda. (2015). Comparing Race and Caste. *Anthropology of This Century*, 12 January. (accessed January 10, 2020).

Subramanian, Ajantha. (2015). "Making Merit: The Indian Institutes of Technology and the Social Life of Caste." *Comparative Studies in Society and History*, 57 (2), 291–322.

Sukumar, N. (2013). Quota's Children: The Perils of Getting Educated. In Satish Deshpande and Usha Zacharias (eds.), *Beyond Inclusion: The Practice of Equal Access in Indian Higher Education.* India: Routledge.

Takhbhore, Sushila. (2011). *Shikanje ka Dard.* New Delhi: Vani Prakashan.

Takhbhore, Sushila. (2015). *Hashiye ka Vimarsh.* New Delhi: Neha Prakashan.

Thorat, Sukhadeo. (2009). *Dalits in India: Search for a Common Destiny.* New Delhi: SAGE.

Tharakam, Bojja. (2020). *Caste and Class.* Hyderabad: The Shared Mirror.

Thorat, Sukhadeo and Paul Attewell. (2007). "The Legacy of Social Exclusion." *Economic and Political Weekly*, 42 (41), 4141–4145.

Thorat, Sukhadeo and Narendra Kumar. (2009). *B.R. Ambedkar: Perspectives on Social Exclusion and Inclusive Policies.* New Delhi: Oxford University Press.

Throat, Sukhadeo and Katherine S. Neuman. (2009). *Blocked by Caste: Economic Discrimination in Modern India.* New Delhi: Oxford University Press.

Thorat, Vimal and Suraj Badtya. (2008). *Bhartiya Dalit Sahitya ka Virodhi Swar*, 1st edition, Delhi: Rawat.

Unnamati, Syama Sundar. (2019). *No Laughing Matter: The Ambedkar Cartoons, 1932–1956.* New Delhi: Navayana Publication.

Valmiki, Om Prakash. (2003). *Joothan* (Translated by Arun Prabha Mukherjee). New York: Columbia University Press.

Vishwanath, Rupa. (2015). *The Pariah Problem: Caste, Religion and the Social in Modern India.* New York: Columbia University Press.

Waghmore, Suryakant. (2013). *Civility against Caste, Dalit Politics and Citizenship in Western India.* New Delhi: SAGE.

Wankhede, Govardhan. (2020). *My Life: The Journey of a Dalit Sociologist.* New Delhi: Aakar.

Wilkerson, Isabel. (2020). *Caste: The Origins of Our Discontent.* New York: Random House

Yadav, Chauthi Ram. (2018). *Lok aur Ved Amne Samne*. Delhi: New Books.
Yengde, Suraj. (2019). *Caste Matters*. Delhi: Penguin Random House Pvt. Limited.
Zelliot, Eleanor. (1996). *From Untouchable to Dalit: Essays on the Ambedkar Movement*. Delhi: Manohar.
Zene, C. (2011). Self-consciousness of the Dalits as "subalterns": Reflections on Gramsci in South Asia. *Rethinking Marxism*, 23 (1), 83–99.

Websites

Caste Survey in the United States, 2018. New York: Equality Labs. www.equality labs.org

Other References

Center for Dalit Studies, Hyderabad http://cdsindia.org/about-us/
Dalit Asmita (दलित अस्मिता) (Professor Vimal Thorat). www.dalitStudies.org.in/dalit-asmita.php
Dalit Camera, Ravichandran www.youtube.com/user/kadhirnilavan
Dalit Dastak (दलित दस्तक) (Ashok Das)
Indian Institute for Dalit Studies (IIDS) website www.dalitStudies.org.in
Journal of Dalit Studies, Nepal https://dignityinitiatives.org/publication/dalit-Studies-journal/
Minds of Caste www.mindsofcaste.org
National Commission for Dalits & Human Rights website www.ncdhr.org.in
Samata Foundation https://samatafoundation.org

11 Economic Reservation as Caste and Cultural Power

Posing Challenges to Representation, Equality and Diversity in Kerala, India

K. V. Syamprasad[1]

Introduction

Culture and power are the most common themes that appear in Bourdieu's (1973, 1977, 1984; Bourdieu and Passeron, 1990) work. As I wrote in 2019, Bourdieu explored cultural reproduction in its relationship between the exchange of capital and power in different forms, symbolic capital, cultural capital and economic capital. Bourdieu developed these concepts by extending or revising Marx's (1867, 1967, 1973) economic capital and power. For Bourdieu, the ruling class cannot simply maintain their power, unlike Marx explored, by simply holding or exchanging economic capital: commodity-money-commodity or money-commodity-money (see p. 9). Bourdieu's definition of cultural capital never remained static, and it has undergone transformation from time to time. Lately, he discussed cultural capital in three forms: embodied, objectified and institutionalised. Also, he introduced another concept—habitus—as embodied cultural capital playing a predominant role in reproduction of culture and power. Bourdieu (1984, p. 170) writes

> Habitus is neither a result of free will, nor determined by structures, but created by a kind of interplay between the two over time: dispositions that are both shaped by past events and structures, and that shape current practices and structures and also, importantly, that condition our very perceptions of these.
>
> (Bourdieu, 1984, p. 170)

On the one hand, habitus could be the outcome of various cultural practices; on the other hand, habitus could reproduce that cultural practice in new forms. It refers to "a subjective but not individual system of internalised structures, schemes of perception, conception, and action common to all members of the same group or class" (Bourdieu, 1977, p. 86). These internalised structures and schemes of perception influence

DOI: 10.4324/9781003155065-11

individuals' worldviews and such worldviews themselves contribute to the development of new structures. Bourdieu considers habitus a structuring structure and a structured structure. So, both processes cannot be separated from one another: reproduction of habitus by cultural practices or the reproduction of cultural practices by habitus is not a deliberate act. In other words, habitus is a socially conditioned mindset which is reproduced unconsciously through common experiences of people, with its own unique practices, and this habitus could itself reproduce or reinforce these practices in return: "Having internalised the 'habitus' of a social structure, people are inclined to certain cultural practices such as food habits, clothing, forms of knowledge; and once they have adopted such practices they tend to reproduce them historically a potential to transmit a new form of 'habitus' to the next generation" (Syamprasad, 2019, p. 60, p. 61). Habitus gradually imposes socially conditioned beliefs as 'facts' onto the people for the sake of the interests of the dominant people in the caste system, which could be constructed as good, bad or stigmatised; examples include perceptions about physical strength, beauty and ugliness, which are relative and socially constructed. The Indian caste system has been known for reproducing inequality and exclusion; and it also justifies different forms of inequality and exclusion, such as occupational hierarchy, mobility, untouchability with the habitual dispositions of the principle of karma. People's roles and responsibilities are determined by their nature of birth (Syamprasad, 2019). This chapter focuses on the role of habitus in reproduction of culture and power as a way of extending the key findings of my previous work—"Merit and caste as cultural capital: Justifying affirmative action for the underprivileged in Kerala, India"—that offers a critique of the anti-affirmative action propaganda to unpack the veil of merit in relation to people's ability to reproduce cultural capital, power and their caste privileges. Differently from my previous work (2019), this chapter is a critique of economic policies of affirmative action in Kerala, India by exploring the extent to which such policies reproduce the upper-caste culture and power in the public sector and how people justify such economic policies with their internalised caste habitus.

The reservation system, or quota system, in India had its origin in the affirmative action across the world for any classes that are under-represented in education, employment and parliamentary politics (Kedia, 2015). Globally, affirmative action programmes are meant to represent the historically excluded groups, minorities, women, and vulnerable groups in many countries, including USA, South Africa, Brazil and India (Lloyd, 2015). Since 'affirmative action' is generally known as 'reservation policy' in India, this chapter makes use of both terms interchangeably. Diversity is the cardinal feature of the Indian social system, which has different religions, minorities, languages, races, regions and so on. People are more likely to be excluded or underrepresented due to their ascribed caste or religious identities. In order to minimise these conditions, Ambedkar (1987) included provisions of quotas for these communities in Education, Employment and Electoral politics under the Article 16 (14) of Indian constitution. Like many states in India, Kerala has a robust quota system for Dalits (Scheduled Castes), Adivasis (Scheduled Tribes) and Other Backward Classes (OBCs) that covers admission to higher education, entry to government jobs, entry to local, state and parliament electoral bodies. In addition, 50% quotas have been allocated for women in the local governing bodies since the early 1990s. Nevertheless, lower-caste occupants are still underrepresented in these spheres, even after 70 years (Sudesh, 2017), and there is no accurate data available in the public domain in relation to representation of each community in the public sector employment, which seemed to be hidden by the dominant political parties. Importantly, the current caste reservation policies have become increasingly controversial, and they rarely receive public support (Syamprasad, 2019). The call for economic reservation has dominated the political and public spheres in Kerala for many years. Importantly, the left parties in Kerala argue that state should consider class criteria along with caste criteria for reservation to be comprehensive. The Kerala government has made several amendments to the caste reservation policies, influenced by Marx's theory of economic determinism. Recently, the left government in Kerala has allocated 10% quotas to forward castes that are economically backward seeking employment in Devaswam Board Temples (News minute, 2020) by making the claim that the party does not oppose caste reservation completely, as long as the economic criteria is there, following the 103rd amendment of the Indian constitution by the central government (Narayan, 2021). Interestingly, this reservation is projected as a reservation for the economically backward or an economic reservation for the general category. This general category includes the upper caste, or the privileged communities. This is not an economic reservation because people that are already receiving caste reservation are not eligible. However, left intellectuals wish to call this a reservation for the economically backward instead of making it clearly "economically backward upper caste", which is constitutionally unfair. So, this chapter first seeks to unpack the fallacy of economic determinism for understanding the diverse Indian social structure, determined by the caste system in relation to base and super structure. Second, it goes on to explore the extent to which economic determinism forms habitual dispositions to marginalise caste and caste reservation. Third, it addresses the extent to which economic reservation reproduces the dominant culture and power in education, employment and the electoral bodies in Kerala.

Understanding Caste as Base and Superstructure

Class inequality is a growing concern across the world, including in India (D'Costa, 2016), in relation to the commercialisation of education and commodification of knowledge (Gurukkal, 2008). Many people in Kerala predominantly seek employment in the public sector because private sector jobs rarely guarantee job security, income protection or welfare (Rasheed and Wilson, 2015). Due to competition, many applicants can be easily knocked out of the entrance examination conducted by Kerala Public Service examination for securing government jobs. As I previously wrote (2019), the quota system allows candidates belonging to the underprivileged communities secure employment, as long as they meet all essential criteria required. Again, affirmative action ensures equality and diversity by ensuring the representation of the underprivileged castes in government jobs, in education and in electoral bodies across India. However, the Indian left parties frequently argue that economic factors should also be incorporated into the reservation criteria by considering class as the major determinant of inequality. On the other hand, the advocates (Deshpande, 2013; Nigam, 2000) of affirmative action refute such claims because class inequality can be dealt with through welfare measures and class is not the only determinant of social inequality in India. The ancient caste system that continues to exist in modern forms is the root cause of social inequality in India (Syamprasad, 2019). What brings inequality in India—caste or class—has been a growing debate between the Marxists and the Ambedkarists in India since its independence. According to Marx (1867/1967, p. 1), social structure is made up of both the base and superstructure:

In the social production of their existence, humans inevitably enter into definite relations, which are independent of their will, namely relations of production appropriate to any stage in the development of their material forces of production. The totality of these relations of production constitutes the economic structure of society, the real foundation, on which arises a legal and political superstructure and to which correspond definite forms of social consciousness.

'Economic structure' refers to the base where the working class forms relationships of domination and exploitation against the capitalists. Profit is the motivational factor for the capitalists, and they need to maintain such a relationship of exploitation for the sake of profit; that determines the parts of the superstructure such as ideology, religion, ethics, morality and so on. However, neo-Marxist and non-Marxist scholars have challenged these arguments because it is hard to say economy is the major determinant of the Indian social structure. Marx was predominantly interested in the structural conditions of society. Contrastingly, Gramsci's (1988) focus was on the role of superstructures because for him, economy is the determinant in the last instance only. Similarly, people's beliefs and cultural practices could trigger the origin of new economic infrastructure (Laclau and Mouffe, 2001; Mouffe, 2014), which is evident from Weber's work (2003): Protestant ethics and the spirit of capitalism in Europe, for example. Weber illustrates that economic development of people was predominantly triggered by Protestant values revolving around hard work, savings and profit. In order to please the will of God, the Protestants were motivated to work hard, to build up savings and thus to be competitive against the Catholics. These cultural practices led to the development of European capitalism. Furthermore, this was a revolutionary movement by the Protestants against conventional religious sanctions on hard work and wealth acquisition; historically, gaps between the rich and poor were justified on the belief that rich people are God's favourite; consequently, the rich were considered more virtuous than the poor. The Protestant movements challenged these beliefs and motivated everyone to work hard, spend less, build savings and accumulate profit so that everyone can be rich. Weber's findings illustrate that cultural practices can influence the base as well as the superstructure, unlike Marx. Similarly, Marx's theory of economic determinism becomes problematic when considering the relation between base and superstructure and the evolution of modes of production in different stages in different countries, as Rodney (2012, p. 9) states:

> The explanation is very complex, but in general terms the main differences between feudal Europe and feudal China lay in the superstructure—i.e. in the body of beliefs, motivations and socio-political institutions which derived from the material base but in turn affected it. In China, religious, educational and bureaucratic qualifications were of utmost importance, and government was in the hands of state officials rather than being run by the landlords on their own feudal estates.

Marx's theory of social evolution is not universally stable, even in Europe, due to culture as a determinant factor for economic and social change. Economic determinist theory requires adaptation in line with the complex nature and function of superstructure in many parts of world. For Weber, both base and superstructures are reciprocal, but neither of them could become ruling forces of society. These findings regarding the role of superstructure could negate the arguments in favour of class reservation in general, as well as similar protective measures in favour of the non-creamy layer of upper-caste Brahmins, Nairs and Varmas in Kerala. All these communities are privileged due to their access to non-economic forms of capital—symbolic, social and cultural—regardless of their class

positions. Sources of capital for these communities include their historical privileges (Bourdieu and Passeron, 1990), including priesthood, royalty, political power and over-representation in the public sector, which
is a source of empowerment for the poor, privileged communities, unlike
the poor, underprivileged communities. Unfortunately, the left parties rec-
ommend affirmative action for the poor, privileged communities, in particular, but not the poor in general; thus, they contradict themselves with
their economically deterministic view. For a detailed consideration of this
argument, a few more things need to be discussed in relation to base and
superstructure.

India has a complex social system, made up of caste, that continues
to oppress and marginalise the underprivileged communities. As Gupta
(1981) illustrates, Indian Marxists tend to place caste in the superstructure due to its association with Hinduism. The proponents of economic
criteria for affirmative action must answer some complex questions
revolving around the location of caste: Does caste belong to the base
or the superstructure? Can caste be annihilated by class? Can they both
co-exist by contributing to higher or lower social status for people in the
social stratification? Can caste be solely located in the superstructure?
Let us examine these questions in relation to the history of working-class
movements in Kerala. Karshaka Thozhilali Union (Agriculture Workers' Union), Karshaka Sangham (Agriculture Workers' Group), Coir
Thozhilali Union (Rope Makers' Union): All members of the Agriculture
Workers' Union belonged to the Dalit community (SC); all members of
the Agriculture Workers' Group belonged to the Nair community; and
all members of the Rope Makers' Union belonged to the Ezhava community. Why do these organisations represent members of a specific caste
or community? Why do they not represent a cross-section of the population, regardless of people's caste identity? This shows that caste cannot
be fully transformed into a modern class in the Indian context, unlike
Marx (1973) outlined: evolution from the primitive, feudal to a capitalist
mode of production.

Historically, the members of these organisations were indeed compelled
to choose such occupations due to their ascribed caste identity. They were
not involved in such occupations out of their choice, but choices were
imposed onto them by the caste system. So, differently from the classical
Marxists, class relations in the base were formed according to the caste
identity of workers in India. Moreover, caste is capable of determining both
the base and the superstructure, and thus, capable of reproducing unequal
distribution of social, cultural, economic and symbolic capital. A person's
social status is determined by their ability to inherit or exchange capital
from one another. The merit of each occupation, formation of occupation
and the reproduction of occupation were all determined by caste norms.

Nevertheless, Indian Marxists overlook this complex relation between caste and base and superstructure as Teltumde (2016, p. 34) writes:

> The cause of the dichotomy between the caste and the class struggle in Indian was the misunderstanding of Karl Marx's understanding of base and super structure. Ambedkar, in fact, demonstrated over and over again that the struggle against caste could be organically unified with the class struggle.

As a consequence, left intellectuals in Kerala have taken the reductionist perspective on caste as a mere component of the religious superstructure, and some of them have categorically rejected the idea of caste reservation. Let us examine the former member of the communist party in Kerala, K. Venu, who recollects a public speech delivered by a veteran communist leader in a YouTube video:

> Look at that restaurant, the son of this restaurant owner is entitled to reservation benefits, but the son of the chef in the restaurant is not entitled to reservation. This is injustice!

While criticising the veteran communist leader, Venu further recollects that the audience was excited by this leader's speech and gave him a standing ovation. Indeed, the owner of that restaurant belonged to a backward caste and the chef belonged to a Brahmin caste. These constructed 'facts' obfuscate reality and enable the privileged to safeguard their vested interests. Such constructed facts or habitualised dispositions need to be analysed contextually and critically to get the privileged exposed. Otherwise, such habitual dispositions would continue to reinforce relations of under-representation, and thus relations of exclusion and inequality. Poverty of the chef and the wealth of the restaurant owner are attempts to construct and disseminate habitus in favour of economic reservation because they obfuscate the caste identity of both individuals in the comparison. Consequently, they also obfuscate the privileges ascribed by the Brahmin chef in relation to his inherited cultural, symbolic and social capital; on the other hand, the restaurant owner only has access to economic capital, but he may lack symbolic and cultural capital and thus social capital. This complex reality is distorted by the habituation of dispositions, of the communist leader, reflecting the hidden agenda of forward caste reservation.

Classical Marxists also think that the collapse of capitalism will lead to the annihilation of religion, as well as caste, and resolve all forms of inequality, and they rarely admit transformation within capitalism, unlike Weber illustrated. Besides, they rarely admit that religion continues to influence people in the form of cultural practices, even after the collapse of the supremacy of the church in many parts of Europe. Additionally, many capitalist countries have adopted socialist principles and welfare practices without being fully transformed into a socialist state: Cuba or China. For example, social justice measures in the form of free health care, free education, and child benefits in Britain and Germany demonstrate that capitalism can be transformed by socialist and radical intervention for people's welfare from time to time. However, classical Marxists rarely problematise such contradictions between the theory and practices of economic determinism.

Furthermore, in India, as a socio-economic and cultural system, caste continues to reproduce inequality and all forms of discrimination. However, this complex reality is distorted by economic determinist ideologies and is overlooked by the left intellectuals and politicians in Kerala. Therefore, many left intellectuals oppose the idea of affirmative action; some of them favour the idea of economic reservation; and some of them argue that economic factors need to be considered along with caste as the criteria for affirmative action. By doing so, they overlook the fundamental principles of affirmative action: equality, diversity and representation. Of course, poverty can be a criterion, which should be historically, socially and culturally determined by the superstructural forces, not merely by the relations of production in the base. However, economic reservation policies in Kerala only include the lower income groups belonging to the upper-caste candidates that are already overrepresented. The principle of representation is jeopardised by economic criteria. Furthermore, they consider affirmative action as a poverty-eradication strategy, forming a fallacy at theoretical and at policy levels.

Economic Determinism as Habitual Dispositions: Marginalisation of Caste and Caste Reservation

Classical Marxists are interested in the analysis of the repressive state; but they are not keen to discuss social justice until the oppressive state is fully collapsed. Contrastingly, Ambedkar was the champion of state socialism and the welfare state (Sarkar, 2013; Khan, 2020). Ambedkar's (1987) primary aim was to transform the state democratically with constitutional amendments in favour of Dalits, backward classes and minorities. It was on these grounds that he put forward the basic policies of reservation by drawing on the principles of affirmative action across the world. But, the economic views of the left putting affirmative action at risk have gained hold in Kerala's public sphere, causing hindrance to social justice for the underprivileged communities.

Being influenced by economic determinism, left intellectuals claim that capitalism has widened the gap between the rich and power in all the castes; however, reservation enabled the lower castes to improve their economic status. It is quite common that the economic status of each citizen, including the lower castes, naturally follows the economic progress of the country as a whole. However, people believe that reservation eradicates their poverty or improves economic status. 'Reservation as economic development' veils the lived realities of the lower-caste OBCs. Reservation is meant to attack caste monopoly in the public sector by ensuring the representation of the backward classes, as outlined in the Article 14 of the Indian constitution, but not just to eradicate poverty (Jeenger, 2022).

Historically, the majority of the OBCs could only take lower-income, manual jobs due to caste taboos. However, during the early half of the 20th century, the caste system seemed to lose its hold as a result of reformative movements and modern interventions (Bijukumar, 2019; Devika, 2010; Frank and Chasin, 1992). Members of the Ezhava community abandoned their traditional occupation of toddy tapping and they were benefited from local trade, self-employment and entrepreneurship (Osella and Osella, 2000). Similarly, the traditional artisans evolved from local, working-class men to middle class traders with surplus production and mechanisation at an early age (Maruthur, 2014), although these middle-class traders got wiped off the map by the giant traders with the advent of globalisation towards the end of the 20th century (Varghese, 2003). A lot of factors together predominantly contributed to the economic progress of the lower-caste OBCs apart from the monetary benefits that they received from reservation. Therefore, 'reservation as economic progress' is the outcome of habitus putting affirmative action at risk, as discussed earlier. Consequently, people rarely unpack that complex historical reality. Nor do they transform the habitus of economic reservation or develop critical awareness.

Some left leaders claim that their leaders are aware of the importance of raising caste issues along with class. Again, they still follow the orthodox view of 'class as base' and 'caste as superstructure'—although they seem to claim themselves as reformers of economic determinism. This is a struggle of modernity, as outlined by Aditya Nigam (2000), because the privileged upper caste wanted themselves to be casteless or revolutionary with conflicting policies of social justice:

We have seen in the last two decades, but more specifically since the anti-Mandal agitation, how the entire upper caste discourse, by speaking the language of 'merit', 'efficiency' and even 'class' and 'economic deprivation', successfully repressed the category of caste. The unspeak ability of caste, I will argue, however, was not simply a matter of the casteism of the upper castes; it was also a result of the modernist discomfort with non-secular and 'retro- grade' categories that really provided the overarching rationale within which the discourse of the upper castes took shape.

(p. 4256)

Many activists, including rationalists and left intellectuals, were compelled to annihilate caste at any cost; people who raise class issues are considered secularists or casteless; on the other hand, people who raise issues of caste injustice and support caste reservation are considered propagators of caste. These made a layman not talk about caste or related injustice, misrepresentation of the underprivileged in the public sector bodies or any matter in relation to caste reservation. Consequently, raising such issues became inherently humiliating for the general population. These, in turn, reproduce the 'habitus' positioning caste in the superstructure while dismissing its role in the base, which is a matter of existence for the Marxists, as well as the left parties in Kerala and elsewhere in India. Although Sathishpande and Nigam consider class analysis as the veil of caste, they overlook how it reproduces anti-reservation habitus.

Economic Reservation as Habitual Dispositions and Power: Cultural Reproduction in the Public Sector

Marx emphasised the supremacy of the ruling class at the base in relation to economic power that flows from the capitalist to the bourgeoisie. For Marx (1867: p. 1), capital's starting point is with the circulation of commodities in two different forms: commodity-money-commodity (C-M-C) band money-commodity-money (M-C-M):

> The simplest form of the circulation of commodities is C-M-C, the transformation of commodities into money, and the change of the money back again into commodities; or selling in order to buy. But alongside of this form we find another specifically different form: M-C-M, the transformation of money into commodities, and the change of commodities back again into money; or buying in order to sell. Money that circulates in the latter manner is thereby transformed into, becomes capital, and is already potentially capital.

Marx discusses how the ruling class reproduces economic power by circulating money and commodity from one another and by accumulating profit out of this circulation. Bourdieu notices that such exchange cannot simply be limited to money as economic capital or commodity. Furthermore, other forms of capital are also exchanged, in addition to economic capital, or economic capital can be converted into non-economic capital and vice versa, so as non-economic forms of power, there are social capital, cultural capital and symbolic capital. Many scholars (Kisida et al., 2014; Keskiner, 2015; Jaeger and Breen, 2016) discuss the role of cultural capital and family habitus in differential talents of students belonging to different social classes, underprivileged communities or immigrants, drawing on Bourdieu. These findings are significant in regard to the upward mobility of migrant families across the world (Louie, 2012; Zhou, 2005). Children may also acquire cultural capital outside the family context; for example, via peers or schools (Bisin and Verdier, 2011; Kisida et al., 2014). Bourdieu raises many critical questions in relation to students' confidence levels regarding their potential to inherit cultural capital along with symbolic and social capital (Syamprasad, 2019).

Historically, the Indian caste system created a field in which different forms of capital can be produced and exchanged in favour of the privileged castes. Consequently, these communities have become the bargaining forces in various fields such as schools, colleges, public sector organisations and electoral bodies; and they have been overrepresenting these bodies since their inception with their inherited cultural and symbolic capital. Furthermore, the upper-caste people were able to reproduce their dominant culture and practices in these bodies during their official interactions, although many Marxist scholars believe that the decline of caste is inevitable with development of capitalism. Jodhka (2016, p. 229) writes:

Caste continues to matter in many different ways, and most importantly as an important aspect of social and economic inequality, as a reality that shapes opportunity structures, status differences and cultural values in contemporary India.

Additionally, upper caste symbols have colonised the public spaces, posing threats to cultural diversity. Drawing on Coomaraswami's (1909) work, Panikkar (2008) argues that the character of Indian culture is associated with historical evolution. Although Coomara swami overemphasised the cultural cause, he presented two interrelated things: culture as defining feature of nationalism; and secondly, culture as plural and secular. The definition of culture could be related to religious identity: that was reinforced during the rise of Indian nationalism. In other words, culture appeared as a tool for disseminating communalism for the sake of electoral politics too. Panikkar (2008, pp. 9–10) further writes:

The tendency to locate oneself in terms of religious belonging in public life was present even in the early colonial period. Many communal ideologues in the past had harped on the cultural differences between the Hindus and Muslims or -on the cultural superiority of the Hindus.

This was articulated by the division between '*sreshta*' (which means 'divine' or 'pure') and '*mlecha*' (which means 'barbaric' or 'uncivilised'). Panikkar argues that the division between *mlecha* and *shrestha* emerged as a political project to dismiss the Gandhian thoughts of Hindu-Muslim unity. These are habitual formations for excluding identities other than the upper-caste identity, particularly those of the Muslim minorities. However, Panikkar overlooks how Kerala's perception about this cultural division is being habitually reproduced over time; nor does he articulate the reproduction in the public sector bodies in relation to affirmative action or cultural representation of the underprivileged and the minorities.

Attempts to define culture in terms of religion in the public sphere has become much stronger in Kerala nowadays, which is an under-researched topic, too, in lighting the Hindu traditional lamp during official inaugurations and different upper-caste dress codes, such as 'Kasavu mundu' and 'Kasvu sari' on the occasion of public ceremonies. All these symbols are portrayed as representations of Kerala culture, or secular culture, rather than upper-caste Brahminical culture. Attempts to embed minority Muslim culture or attempts to challenge the majority religious practices in the public sphere are considered communal, which is evident from a recent controversy that occurred in Kerala in relation to lighting the traditional lamp (Jayaraj, 2015).

In short, overrepresentation of upper-caste individuals in these bodies led to the overrepresentation of upper-caste cultural symbols, too, by marginalising the culture of the lower caste, by marginalising the culture of the minorities and, thus, by marginalising the culture of the underrepresented. In other words, public sector institutions became a private space for the reproduction of the dominant, upper-caste culture. On the other hand, the lower caste and the minority are unable to transform their own unique culture or symbols as a common form of cultural capital, and hence, they are culturally and socially excluded from Kerala's public sphere. Unfortunately, the disparity between the majority and the minority and the disparity between the upper caste and lower caste in accessing, exchanging or reproducing cultural capital or cultural power seems to be constantly ignored by the habitual dispositions of economic criteria.

A dominant culture cannot merely exist by reproduction; it has to resist diversity, pluralism, inclusion, and affirmative action because it is part of the cultural domination project of the upper caste. Therefore, it has to marginalise any practices which are detached from, or harmful to, Brahmanism. As a result, opportunities for the marginalised would be limited in the culturally dominant public sector, which is Brahminical, no matter how wealthy the marginalised are. Schools, colleges, bureaucracy and the legislature are generally considered the sub-sections of society. The opponents of affirmative action must consider to what extent these sub-sections represent the cultural diversity of society as a whole. All of these different institutions are cultural sub-sections of the dominant, privileged communities. Affirmative action for the poor, forward caste could only reinforce this cultural power because they are already overrepresented in these institutions and could meet the vested interests of the upper caste. Although such challenges cannot be completely overcome, the integrated, participatory reservation programs could make inclusive spaces within the culturally dominant public sector. As evident from Ambedkar, the ultimate goal of affirmative action is to transform the unequal power structure. However, left parties claim that people in Kerala have a strong desire for the lower-income, upper-caste groups to become the beneficiaries of affirmative action. Representation of these culturally and symbolically rich groups could only lead to cultural monopoly of the upper caste because these measures rarely create a diverse space. In other words, affirmative action for representation means cultural representation too.

Marxists intellectuals and activists in Kerala overlook the internal revisions of economic determinist theory, and they rarely develop constructive theories or make critical interventions against the reproduction of caste and cultural power. Ambedkar called for untouchable castes to organise themselves to counter the dominant, Brahminical culture through education and reasoning. Unlike Bourdieu, Ambedkar deemphasises the oppressive nature of education. On the other hand, Bourdieu does not offer any alternative measures or policy reforms to transform the unequal relations of social, culture or symbolic power.

Representation of microscopic groups in education, employment and electoral bodies could lead to cultural pluralism, which is the essence of affirmative action for maintaining the equilibrium in relation to representation and diversity and equal distribution of power. These ideas seemed to influence many Latin American countries like Brazil as they have adopted reservation policies for blacks, indigenous people and people with special disability needs (dos Santos and Queiroz, 2010, Medeiros et al., 2017) to ensure they are represented numerically and culturally.

The economic perspectives gained a strong hold during the 1990s only when other backward castes became the beneficiaries of reservation policies at the national level. These communities, including minority Muslims, and the lower caste, including Ezhavas, Vishwakarmas and so on, were considered strangers in the public sector organisations that are overrepresented by the dominant Hindu communities. Of course, the dominant Hindu community seemed to be embarrassed of the OBC representation and inclusion of their unique culture as susceptible to the dominant caste and cultural power. Furthermore, they must also be worried about the possibilities for cultural assimilation and redistribution of caste and cultural power in these public sector bodies where the OBCs have been misrepresented or marginalised historically. So, the dominant caste and culture have to resist such assimilation at any cost for their existence. Excluding the higher-income groups of OBCs but including the lower-income groups of the privileged communities have been considered revolutionary reforms of affirmative action by the left intellectuals and rationalists in India; these measures could prevent the subaltern culture from being assimilated into the dominant culture to a great extent. Calls for economic reservation cannot simply be considered a matter of concern in relation to poverty or participation of power; on the contrary, it is a matter of concern in relation to cultural assimilation too. People in Kerala's public sphere have predominantly held an anti-caste reservation habitus. Surprisingly, even its beneficiaries are not exceptional, thanks to dominant cultural ideas that shape their habitus and their habitus that reproduces dominant cultural ideas too.

Historically, the Kerala state has been well known for having a radical and culturally diverse society (Haseena, 2015). In fact, the radicalisation of civil society began in the second half of the 19th century. It was the result of long struggles by various social groups and sections—youth, students, women, farmers, etc. Public campaigns, protest marches, public-spirited media, etc., radicalised and activated the civil society of Kerala. The anti-caste struggles led by lower-caste people, anti-feudal, anti-imperial struggles of the Malabar tenants, various community reform movements, rationalist movements, anti-British struggles first waged by petty chieftains and their bonds of loyalties, and later by broader sections of the people, democratised the civil society. However, these socio-cultural conditions have seemed to decline since the Modi era in 2013. Cultural fascism in the form of Hindutwa seems to reinforce individuals' habitus: legal prohibition of cow slaughter, homicide for eating beef, anti-immigration policies targeting Muslims. Lower caste communities rarely acknowledge the contributions of their own community leaders such as Ayyankali, Sri Narayana Guru and Poykayil Appachan. On the contrary, they consider the dominant cultural practices legitimate: '*poonool*', 'elephant procession', '*nettippattam*' have taken over the local cultural practices. These conditions also made the privileged seek legitimacy from the underprivileged in favour of economic criteria. Economic determinism thus became a habitus of OBCs in Kerala.

Conclusion

To conclude, educational, bureaucratic and legislative organisations have become the guardians of habitus, reproducing the dominant caste and cultural power of the objectified state (Bourdieu, 1973, 1984, 1986); the cultural capital of Dalits, Advasis and ethnic minorities need to be protected and integrated into these public-sector bodies to make these organisations diverse and create equal opportunities for the underprivileged. However, transformation of these social and cultural spaces will be inherently difficult, as Gillespi (2019) explored. Consequently, lower-caste people rarely develop critical knowledge about representation of their own unique culture and their own worldview of affirmative action in these bodies. Contrastingly, they passively acknowledge the supremacy of the upper-caste culture and its worldview and actively take part in its reproduction. Educational, bureaucratic and legislative bodies have been historically considered the ideological apparatuses of the state. Importantly, they have been managed by the privileged communities in Kerala and have thus become private cultural spaces for the privileged, rather than public, which must be inclusive and diverse regardless of caste, class or gender. However, these organisations can be transformed or reconstructed for the welfare of the nation, as well as the underprivileged. Therefore, affirmative action theory needs be redefined to ensure the cultural representation of the underprivileged, including the Dalits, Adivasis and Muslim minorities beyond simple numerical representation. Robust reservation policies could ensure the cultural representation of the underprivileged in the public sector organisations and, thus, keep such organisations diverse and inclusive. Caste has become a powerful tool in the superstructure for determining social inequality, unlike the classical Marxists explored. So, caste reservation is the only alternative to ensure equal opportunities for people and representation of people who are socially and culturally marginalised.

As stated earlier, caste reservation is a safeguarding measure for representation, inclusion and diversity in favour of different caste and minority groups. Nevertheless, caste reservation policies also need to be safeguarded against reactionary steps by the left parties in Kerala, India. Left parties' slogans—'reservation for economic empowerment' and 'economic criteria for reservation'—hold reality upside down and jeopardise the fundamental principles of affirmative action by its habitual production and dissemination of knowledge. This habitus needs to be broken down and transformed by critical intervention of the state, as well as by the underprivileged.

Note

1. Southampton City College, U.K.

References

Ambedkar, B. R. (1987). The Hindu social order—its essential features. In V. Moon (Ed.), *Dr. Babasaheb Ambedkar's Writings and Speeches* (Vol. 3). Education Department, Mumbai.

Bijukumar, V. (2019). Radicalised civil society and protracted political actions in Kerala (India): A socio-political narrative. *Asian Ethnicity, 20*(4), 503–521. https://doi.org/10.1080/14631369.2019.1601005

Bisin, A., & Verdier, T. (2011). The economics of cultural transmission and socialization. In J. Benhabib, A. Bisin, & M. O. Jackson (Eds.), *Handbook of social economics*, 1(n.k) (pp. 339–416), Elsevier B.V. https://doi.org/10.1016/B978-0-444-53187-2.00009-7

Bourdieu, P. (1973). Cultural reproduction and social reproduction. In R. Brown (Ed.), *Knowledge, education and cultural change: Papers in the sociology of education*. Tavistock Publications Limited.

Bourdieu, P. (1977). *Outline of a theory of practice* (Vol. 16). Cambridge University Press.

Bourdieu, P. (1984). *Distinction: A social critique of the judgement of taste*. Routledge & Kegan Paul.

Bourdieu, P. (1986). The forms of capital. In J. Richardson (Ed.), *Handbook of theory of and research for the sociology of education* (pp. 241–258). Greenwood. http://home.iitk.ac.in/~amman/soc748/bourdieu_forms_of_capital.pdf

Bourdieu, P., & Passeron, J. (1990). *Reproduction in education, society and culture*. Sheffield: Region Centre for Science and Technology. London: Sage Publications.

Coomaraswami, A. K. (1909). *Essays in national idealism*. Archeological survey of India. Available from: https://indianculture.gov.in/rarebooks/essays-national-idealism-1

D'Costa, A. P. (2016). Compressed capitalism, globalisation and the fate of Indian development. In S. Venkateswar & S. Bandyopadhyay (Eds.), *Globalisation and the challenges of development in contemporary India. Dynamics of Asian Development* (pp. 19–39). Springer. https://doi.org/10.1007/978-981-10-0454-4_2

Deshpande, S. (2013). Caste and castelessness: Towards a biography of the general category. *Economic and Political Weekly, XLVIII*(15), 32–39.

Devika, J. (2010). Egalitarian developmentalism, communist mobilization, and the question of caste in Kerala State, India. *The Journal of Asian Studies, 69*(3), 799–820. https://doi.org/10.1017/S0021911810001506

dos Santos, J. T., & Queiroz, D. M. (2010). Affirmative action and higher education in Brazil. In P. Peterson, E. Baker, & B. McGaw (Eds.), *International encyclopedia of education* (pp. 760–766). Elsevier.

Franke, R. W., & Chasin, B. H. (1992). Kerala State, India: Radical reform as development. *International Journal of Health Services, 22*(1), 139–156. https://doi.org/10.2190/HMXD-PNQF-2X2L-C8TR

Gillespi, L. (2019). *Pierre Bourdieu: Habitus*. https://criticallegalthinking.com/2019/08/06/pierre-bourdieu-habitus/

Gramsci, A. (1988). *A gramsci reader: Selected writings*. Lawrence and Wishart.

Gupta, D. (1981). Caste, infrastructure and superstructure: A critique. *Economic and Political Weekly, 16*(51), 2093–2104.

Gurukkal, R. (2008). Rethinking social science methodology in the context of globalization. *IJSAS, 1*(1), 1–15. https://www.pondiuni.edu.in/files/publications/IJSAS/ijsas15062011_1.pdf.

Haseena, V. A. (2015). The cultural diversity of Kerala and the intensity of the domestic migrant Labourers to Kerala. *Journal of Culture, Society and Development, 10*, 62–66.

Jaeger, M. M. and Breen, R. (2016). A dynamic model of cultural reproduction. *American Journal of Sociology, 121*(4), 1079–1115.

Jayaraj, V. R. (2015). *To light the lamp or not: Muslim league trying to burn off confusion.* www.dailypioneer.com/2015/india/to-light-the-lamp-or-not-muslim-league-trying-to-burn-off-confusion.html

Jeenger, K. (2022). *Reservation is about adequate representation, not poverty eradication: The idea behind reservation was always to disavow caste-monopoly in the public sector.* https://thewire.in/law/supreme-court-bench-reservation

Jodhka, S. S. (2016). Ascriptive hierarchies: Caste and its reproduction in contemporary India. *Current Sociology Monograph, 64*(2), 228–243. https://journals.sagepub.com/doi/pdf/10.1177/0011392115614784

Kedia, B. (2015). Affirmative action in India and US: A challenge to reservation policy in India. *International Journal of Law and Legal Jurisprudence Studies, 2*(1).

Keskiner, E. (2015). Is it merit or cultural capital? The role of parents during early tracking in Amsterdam and Strasbourg among descendants of immigrants from Turkey. *Journal of Comparative Migration Studies, 3*(2), 1–19.

Khan, B. A. (2020). *The relevance of Ambedkar's idea of 'state socialism' during COVID-19.* https://indianculturalforum.in/2020/04/17/the-relevance-of-ambedkars-idea-of-state-socialism-during-covid-19/

Kisida, B., Greene, J. P., & Bowen, D. H. (2014). Creating cultural consumers: The dynamics of cultural capital acquisition. *Sociology of Education, 87*(4), 281–295.

Laclau, E. and Mouffe, C. (2001). *Hegemony and socialist strategy: Towards a radical democratic politics.* Verso.

Lloyd, M. (2015). *A decade of affirmative action in Brazil: Lessons for the global debate.* https://doi.org/10.1108/S1479-358X20150000011011

Louie, V. (2012). *Keeping the immigrant bargain: The costs and rewards of success in America.* Russell Sage.

Maruthur, S. M. (2014). Skill in a globalized world: Migrant workers in the gold jewelry-making industry in Kerala, India. *WorkingUSA, 17*(3), 323–338. https://doi.org/10.1163/17434580-01703002

Marx, K. (1867). *The general formulation of capital, capital, Volume One.* www.marxists.org/archive/marx/works/1867-c1/ch04.htm

Marx, K. (1967). *Capital: A critique of political economy (vol. 1): A critical analysis of capitalist production* (S. Moore & E. Aveling, trans.). International Publishers (Original work published 1867). www.marxists.org/archive/marx/works/1859/critique-pol-economy/preface.htm

Marx, K. (1973). *Karl Marx on society and social change: With selections by Friedrich Engels.* University of Chicago Press.

Medeiros, H. A. V., Neto, R. D. & Catani, A. M. (2017). Educational democracy in graduate education: Public policies and affirmative action. *Journal of Critical Education Policy Studies, 15*(1), 252–274. www.jceps.com/wp-content/uploads/2017/03/15-1–12.pdf

Mouffe, C. (2014). *Gramsci and Marxist theory.* Routledge.

Narayan, M. S. (2021). Economically backward reservation: A paradigm shift in public policy. *Journal of Management, 18*(1), 2582–4821.

News minute. (2020). *Kerala approves 10% reservation for economically weaker sections in general category.* www.thenewsminute.com/article/kerala-approves-10-reservation-economically-weaker-sections-general-category-135910

Nigam, A. (2000). Secularism, modernity, nation: Epistemology of the dalit critique. *Economic and Political Weekly, 35*(48), 4256–4268.

Osella, F., & Osella, C. (2000). *Social mobility in Kerala: Modernity and identity in Kerala.* Pluto Press.

Panikkar, K. N. (2008). General presidents address: Culture as site of struggle. *Indian History Congress, 69,* 1–18.

Rasheed, R., & Wilson, P. R. (2015). Over educaiton and the influence of job attributes: A study conducted in the city of Kochi. *Gurgaon, 14*(2), 145–165.

Rodney, W. (2012). *How Europe underdeveloped Africa.* Pambazuka Press.

Sarkar, B. (2013). Dr. B.R. Ambedkar's theory of state socialism. *International Research Journal of Social Sciences, 2*(8), 38–41. www.isca.in/IJSS/Archive/v2/i8/6.ISCA-IRJSS-2013-113.pdf

Sudesh, M. R. (2017). Samvarnathile Pinnakka chinthakal. *Pachakkuthira Weekly.* May 2017, pp 34–42.

Syamprasad, K. V. (2019). Caste and merit as cultural capital: Justifying affirmative action for the underprivileged in Kerala, India. *The Journal for Critical Education Policy Studies, 17*(3), 50–81.

Teltumde, A. (2016). Dichotomisation of caste and class. *Economic and Political Weekly, 51*(47), 34–38.

Varghese, G. K. (2003). Globalisation traumas and new social imaginary: Visvakarma community of Kerala. *Economic and Political Weekly, 38*(45), 4794–4802.

Weber, M. (2003). *The protestant ethic and the spirit of capitalism.* Dover Publications.

Zhou, M. (2005). Ethnicity as social capital: Community-based institutions and embedded networks of social relations. In G. C. Loury, T. Moodood, & S. Teles (Eds.), *Ethnicity, social mobility and public policy in the US and UK.* Cambridge University Press.

Index

absurdity 7, 21
Abu-Lughod, Janet 19, 20
abyssal: divide 27, 56; intellectuals 55; line 10, 25, 27; non-, 57, 61, 62; post 61; reason 26, 52; science 172; theory 55; thinking 44, 79
Acharya, Sanghamitra 286
Ahmad, Aijaz 15, 22, 45, 46, 47, 48
Alatas, Syed Farid 221
Alexander, Jeffery 273, 283, 285
Alexander, Michelle 176
Al-l-Ahmad, Jalal 53, 60
Althusser, Louis 126, 174, 175, 196
Ambedkarite 52, 141, 148, 170, 205, 270, 293
Ambedkar, Bhimrao Ramji ix, 1, 2, 5, 9, 10, 11, 12, 14, 15, 16, 17, 18, 19, 22, 23, 25, 26, 29, 30, 31, 32, 35, 37, 39, 40, 48, 49, 50, 51, 52, 54, 57, 60, 63, 64, 65, 67, 68, 69, 71, 72, 73, 74, 75, 78, 79, 80, 82, 84, 98, 100, 101, 102, 103, 105, 108, 111, 115, 120, 124, 126, 131, 140, 141, 142, 144, 145, 147, 148, 170, 171, 174, 175, 181, 183, 184, 185, 189, 193, 194, 195, 196, 197, 198, 199, 200, 201, 203, 204, 205, 206, 208, 209, 211, 212, 213, 214, 217, 218, 221, 222, 225, 226, 227, 228, 231, 240, 241, 242, 245, 247, 248, 249, 250, 251, 252, 253, 254, 255, 256, 257, 258, 259, 262, 264, 265, 266, 269, 271, 272, 273, 274, 275, 276, 277, 278, 282, 283, 287, 288, 290, 299, 303, 304, 309
Amin, Samir 64, 65
Anand, S. 184

Anderson, Perry 45, 48, 49, 52
Angotti, Thomas 64
annihilation 4, 16, 18, 49, 51, 70, 125, 171, 185, 202, 203, 209, 218, 265, 303
anti-black racism 176
anti-casteism 63
anti-caste xv, xvi, 18, 25, 30, 32, 40, 41, 49, 56, 57, 66, 67, 137, 139, 140, 141, 142, 148, 156, 199, 203, 218, 272, 274, 275, 277, 278, 279, 283, 285; consciousness 67, 278; critique 137; discourse 284; intellectuals 25; reform 156; struggle 32; thought 145; untouchability 116
anti-colonial 8, 11, 25, 37, 282
anti-Muslim 191
anti-slavery 144
Appadurai, Arjun 43, 65
Apple, Michael 2, 4
Arabs 88, 194
Archeology 40, 54, 63, 66
Arora, N. & Shivkrit, R. 244
Arur, Aditi and John Dejaeghere 244, 279

Baier, A. & Anik, W. 266
Baker, Bernadette 65
Balais 84
Banaji, Jairus 137, 220
Banerjee-Dube, Ishita 15
Basu, Swaraj 15, 32, 44
Bechain, Sheoraj Singh 277, 279
Beckert, Sven 136
Benjamin, Walter 229
Bernal, Martin 41
Béteille, André 11, 28, 33, 36, 38

Bildung 210, 227, 228, 229, 238
Black, Edwin 4
black(s) xiv, 25, 43, 45, 109, 110,
    112, 212, 275, 309; emancipation
    35; intellectuals 6; lives matter 287;
    panthers 40; segregation 169; studies
    27, 286; and whites 7, 36, 38, 39,
    40, 43, 47, 48, 54, 169
border(s) 37, 98, 99, 106, 179, 186,
    194, 251
Botstein, Leon 158
Bourdieu, Pierre, & Passeron, Jean
    Claude 302
Bourdieu, Pierre 8, 13, 47, 67, 221,
    297, 298, 306, 307, 309, 310
Brahmin 10, 012, 35, 37, 43, 49, 60,
    64, 93, 94, 122, 131, 157, 181, 182,
    185, 252, 253, 258, 274, 287, 301,
    303
Brahmin body 122
Brahminhood 42, 115, 118
Brahminical canon 241
Brahminical culture 289, 303, 308,
    309
Brahminical mind 125
Brahminical pedagogy 250
Brahminical social order 161
Brahminical white ideology 279
Brahminism 102, 241, 249
Brahmin males 265
Bressey, Caroline 6
Brown, Kavin 37, 64
Buddhism 11, 30, 102, 117, 145, 189,
    196, 276
Budha 88, 276, 277
Burkholder, Zoë 6

Cabral, Amilcar 64
Caliban reason 30, 45, 55
Camus, Albert 21
canon 56, 59, 147, 176
capital 13, 66, 144, 147, 153, 208,
    209, 222, 224, 229, 297,
    302, 306; colonial 148; corporate
    12, 20, 202; cultural 67, 298, 308;
    political 4; social 29, 30, 307
capitalism 17, 21, 63, 136, 137, 144, 175,
    197, 207, 211, 223, 224, 225, 227,
    229, 230, 301, 303, 307
caste 1, 2, 6, 8, 10, 12, 14, 16, 17,
    22, 25, 28, 31, 32, 36, 37, 40, 44,
    48, 53, 58, 60, 63, 64, 65, 69, 88,
    91, 93, 95, 96, 97, 98, 99, 101,
    102, 103, 104, 105, 109, 119, 120,
    121, 122, 134, 135, 136, 138, 140,
    144, 147, 148, 152, 153, 157, 158,
    159, 160, 161, 165, 169, 170, 171,
    175, 176, 177, 178, 179, 181, 182,
    184, 186, 189, 190, 191, 196, 197,
    200, 202, 203, 208, 209, 212, 213,
    214, 215, 218, 223, 224, 225, 227,
    230, 231, 240, 241, 243, 246, 247,
    248, 249, 250, 251, 252, 254, 255,
    257, 258, 259, 262, 272, 273, 276,
    278, 279, 281, 283, 284, 285, 287,
    288, 298, 302, 303, 306, 307, 309,
    311; algorithm 231; annihilation
    51, 207; capital 249; coloniality
    23, 24; Dalits 310; dominant 158,
    310; ethics 146; exploitation 145;
    habitus 155; hegemony 205, 211,
    220; hierarchy 40, 42, 98, 100,
    224, 227, 253; Hindus 84, 190;
    ideologies 216; intermarriage 123;
    lower 274; oligarchs 206, 207, 212,
    221, 222; republic of 199, 235,
    238; reservation 299, 304; schedule
    26, 198, 242, 244; segregation 18;
    statuses 104; struggle 13, 19, 30,
    118; subaltern 193; system xiii,
    17, 20, 30, 34, 35, 38, 42, 43, 45,
    46, 49, 52, 54, 86, 92, 93, 94, 98,
    100, 101, 106, 108, 109, 172, 173,
    195, 202, 217, 219, 289, 298, 300,
    302, 305, 307; underprivileged 156;
    upper 115, 121, 124, 128, 129, 130,
    131, 143, 280, 286, 308
casteism xv, 9, 63, 125, 252, 305
casteocracy 57, 66, 152, 156, 162,
    164, 166
Catholics 39, 87, 301
CCC*theorist* 61–65
Cesaire, Aimé 64
Chakravarti, Uma 27
Chattopadhyay, Saumen 239
Chitty, Clyde 3
Christianity 30, 189, 260
civility 154
class xiii, xiv, 1, 2, 5, 6, 7, 8, 9, 11,
    12, 14, 17, 19, 20, 23, 25, 27, 28,
    29, 31, 32, 33, 34, 35, 36, 38, 41,
    42, 43, 44, 45, 51, 52, 54, 56, 57,

58, 63, 65, 67, 82, 85, 86, 87, 91,
93, 98, 99, 100, 101, 103, 104,
105, 106, 108, 134, 137, 139, 143,
144, 146, 151, 152, 153, 156, 157,
159, 160, 163, 164, 165, 174, 184,
191, 193, 194, 195, 196, 197, 198,
202, 208, 209, 212, 214, 216,
217, 218, 221, 224, 227, 228, 230,
240, 249, 251, 252, 257, 259, 275,
281, 298, 299, 300, 301, 302, 303,
304, 308, 311; backward 26, 279;
emancipation 141; middle xv, 140;
ruling 161, 297; social 37, 154;
under 30, 280; upper 3, 58; working
142, 143
cognitive 19, 24, 44, 263; justice 65
co-habitus xv, 59, 62; radical 59
colonialism 17, 20, 21, 22, 23, 169,
196, 199, 200, 207, 211, 212, 213,
219, 221, 222, 225, 262
coloniality 8, 13, 14, 20, 21, 22, 23,
26, 31; of being 26, 27; of being 26,
27; of caste 24, 25, 56; of gender 27;
of knowledge 26, 27; of labor 26,
27; of power 26, 27; power matrix
14, 63
Commitia Centuriata 89
Commonsense 4, 26
communal 50, 87, 88, 90, 157, 202,
308
communalism 192, 200, 307
consciencism 64
Coomaraswamy, Ananda 191
counter-dominant 18, 28, 38, 44, 59,
63, 309
counter-hegemonic 1, 14, 27, 30,
32, 33, 53, 54, 55, 57, 59, 62,
65, 199
Couto, Mia 39
Crenshaw, Kimberlé 176
critical caste studies 59
critical curriculum river xiv, 15, 55
critical theory 37, 38
critical thinking 196, 211, 250
curriculum 4, 5, 7, 8, 20, 21, 45, 53,
54, 58, 59, 63, 64, 65, 158, 172,
219, 231, 240, 261, 273, 275, 276,
279, 280, 282, 287; epistemicide
xvi, 2; imparity 9, 47; involution
9, 65; isonomia 58; mechanotics;
occidentosis 64; reversive

epistemicide 27, 56; theory 55, 59;
theorycide 65
Čvorović, Jelena 20

Dabashi, Hamid 19, 46
Dalit 10, 21, 22, 32, 33, 36, 40, 41,
42, 43, 45, 49, 56, 57, 58, 60, 65,
66, 67, 98, 99, 100, 102, 106, 107,
108, 109, 110, 112, 113, 115, 116,
120, 126, 127, 129, 131, 133, 134,
135, 136, 137, 139, 140, 142, 143,
144, 145, 146, 148, 149, 158, 160,
162, 164, 212, 223, 224, 232, 272,
274, 276, 277, 278, 280, 282, 284,
286, 288; activism 140; aesthetics
66; capitalism 224; educational
theory i; elites 205; emancipation
19; identity 25; intellectual 11, 35,
97; liberation 17, 18; Marxism
147; merit 161; panthers 40, 145;
pedagogies 249; reason 25, 64;
Sahitya 134, 147; heory 37; utopia
144; writing/writers 246, 247
Davenport, Charles & Laughlin, Harry
3, 4
Davis, Allison 1, 29, 38, 70
Davis, Allison; Gardner, Burleigh, &
Gardner, Mary 69
De Certeau, Michel 24
decoloniality 61
decolonizing 62, 191
De-Gandhian Gandhi 65
degree zero 60, 177, 181, 182, 183
de-iconizing 65
de-linking 18, 38, 47, 59, 61–63
de-monumentalize 64
derivative 59, 61, 252
Derrida, Jacques 8, 175
Deshpande, Satish 140, 300
deterritorialize 38
Devy, Ganesh 241, 242, 261
Dewey, John xiv, 16, 55, 97, 171, 240,
241, 245, 248, 265
Dhale, Raja 144, 145, 147, 149
Dhamankar, Vasant 145
Dhanda, Meena 20, 34, 36, 37, 42, 63
Dhankar, Rohit 243, 264
Dhasal, Namdeo 133, 134, 137, 145,
148, 149
Diop, Cheikh Anta 25
Dirks, Nicholas 1, 20, 29, 196, 213

Disempowered 242, 244, 257
division of labor 10, 14, 16, 18, 22,
    31, 184
division of laborer 10, 14, 16, 26, 27,
    31, 65, 138, 195, 217, 252
dominant: Brahmanical concept 241,
    279; caste 21, 158, 159, 244, 308,
    310; classes 202; culture 109;
    curriculum theory 59; Eurocentric 2,
    18, 38, 44, 53, 63; theory 17
Doniger, Wendy 247, 250, 259, 265
Douglass, Frederick 1, 6
DuBois, William, E. B. 1, 5, 6, 38
Dumont, Louis 9, 10, 29, 36, 38, 114,
    115, 120, 121
Duncan, John & Derrett, Martin 212
Durkheim, Émile 175
Dussel, Enrique 20, 25, 64
Dutt, R. Palme 110, 234, 237, 239,
    291
Dvija 198, 252

Eagleton, Terry 57, 50, 68
economic interpretation: of history 89,
    90; of Indian society 190, 191
economic reform 16, 90, 91
education xiii, xiv, xv, 3, 8, 12, 18,
    21, 27, 28, 33, 41, 53–57, 65, 67,
    69, 143, 152, 154, 156, 157, 160,
    162–166, 168, 189, 194, 195, 198,
    199, 200, 202, 204, 207, 210–213,
    217–223, 224–227, 229, 230, 240,
    241, 242, 244, 247, 248, 249, 250,
    251, 253, 254–256, 258, 259, 261,
    263, 264, 274–276, 279, 282, 284,
    299, 300, 301, 309, 310
Ellsworth, Elizabeth 58
Empire 8, 20, 28, 31, 88; British 136;
    Muslim 37, 88; Persian 194
empire 88, 169
empowered 140, 141, 282
empowerment 302, 311
enslavement 45
epistemicidal 38, 39, 55, 56; canon 56;
    divide 27; nature xv, 2, 5, 28, 57,
    63; reason 23, 24; sin 2
epistemicide 23, 27, 48, 56
epistemic nature 57
epistemological: blindness 14;
    cleansing 21; colors 2, 48; despotism
    27, 44; hemisphere 46, 58; matrix

21, 34, 37, 53, 59; revolution 16;
    rivers xiv, 61, 63; untouchability xv,
    66, 188; yarn 2, 55, 64
epistemologies from the South xiv,
    15–19, 48, 56, 57, 59, 62, 64, 65
ethnic 4, 22, 47, 160; studies 284
ethnicity xiv, 5, 8, 23, 42, 47, 63, 174
Eugenic xiv, xv, 1–7, 12–19, 21, 22,
    24, 29, 30, 34, 41, 44, 47, 52, 53,
    55, 56, 58, 60, 62, 63, 70, 72, 94,
    95, 213
Eurocentric i, 1, 8, 14, 18, 22, 27, 28,
    32, 35, 37–39, 44–48, 54, 55–58,
    63–65, 204, 220, 262
Eurocentrism 8, 20, 221

Faiz, Ahmad Faiz 202
Fannon, Frantz 25, 221
fascism 24, 191, 197, 204, 216, 220,
    310
Fleming, Ted 266
Foucault, Michele 180
Fraser, Nancy 64
Freudian hysterical blindness 1, 58, 66
Freud, Sigmund 12, 13, 188–190, 196,
    199, 229
functionalist 25, 57

Gadgil, Madhav & Ramchandra Guha
    261, 266
Galeano, Eduardo 20, 25
Galton, Francis xiv, 2–4
Gandhi, Mahatma 13, 16, 48–52, 65,
    119, 125, 190, 191, 193, 194, 199,
    200, 203–206, 209, 211–217, 228,
    231, 255, 308
Gavaskar Mahesh 236
genderism 12
gender xiv, xv, 2, 5, 12, 20, 23, 27, 28,
    35, 38, 47, 49, 52, 53, 56, 58, 63,
    69, 107, 144, 146, 151, 165, 174,
    240, 241, 243, 244, 246, 249, 251,
    253, 257, 258, 262, 266, 273, 283,
    311
generation of utopia xiv
genocide 34, 204, 210, 219
Gil, José 8
Glissant, Edouard 44
globalization 21, 22, 55, 181, 209,
    222, 284

Global North 24, 28, 34, 42, 58–59, 61, 64
Global South xv, 24, 32, 37, 42, 59, 61, 169, 170, 175, 262
Goody, Jack 44, 65
Gramsci, Antonio 62, 65, 175, 198, 301
Greek 112, 153, 249
Grosfoguel, Ramon 23
Guha, Ranajit 207, 234, 235, 261, 284
Guinier, Lani 152, 155, 158, 159, 161, 165
Gunder Frank, Andre 44
Gupta, Akhil 167
Gupta, Dipankar 302
Gupta, Ruchira 269
Guru, Gopal 310

Habermas, Jürgen 67, 240, 241, 245, 246, 249, 250, 254, 255, 256, 257, 258, 259, 264, 265
habitus 8, 13, 21, 67, 155, 297, 298, 303, 305–307, 310, 311
Han, Byung Chul 14, 44
Hankivsky, Olena 241, 262
Harootunian, Harry 137
Harvey, David 21, 224
Havingusrt, Robert 1, 29, 70
Hazareesingh, Sandip 136
Hegel, Georg Wilhelm Friedrich 172, 176, 180, 183, 186, 200, 206, 224, 228, 234, 235
hegemonic 1, 14, 17, 22, 23, 24, 27, 30, 32, 44, 53–55, 57, 59, 62, 65, 146, 240, 241, 250
hegemony 14, 24, 104, 134, 175, 176, 177, 185, 186, 189, 196, 197, 199, 204, 205, 211, 220, 272, 274, 279, 286, 289
Heidegger, Martin 177, 178, 186
Herrnstein, Charles & Murray, Richard 41
heterotopia 65
Hindu 61, 95, 308
Hinduism 9, 10, 13, 18, 22, 27, 49, 50, 51, 58, 62, 98, 106, 131, 170, 174, 184, 189, 190–194, 198, 203, 214, 215, 217, 271
Hindus 9, 12, 18, 37, 50, 51, 58, 61, 64, 82, 83, 84–86, 95, 102, 120, 129, 131, 141, 174, 189, 190,

192–195, 199, 200, 205, 211, 212, 214, 223, 307
Hindutva 18, 22, 24, 27, 30, 50, 58, 58, 62, 64, 65, 171, 172, 190, 191, 203, 210, 211, 215, 231
Hindutva reasoning 64
Hiwrale, Anup 252
Hobsbawm, Eric 126
Holmes, S. J. 7
Horkheimer, Max 229
human rights 274, 296
Hursh, David xiv, xv, 21, 69
Husserl, Edmund 175, 256
hysterical blindness 1, 13, 27, 66, 189, 190, 196

identical 18, 44
Immerwahr, D. 1, 29
impurity 5, 10, 64, 115, 117, 177, 184
indigenoustude malaise 57
International Congress of Eugenics 5
Ireland 39, 87
itinerant curriculum theory (ICT) i, 38, 56–58, 60–64

Jaaware, Aniket 134, 135, 146, 251, 253
Jaeger, Mads Meier & Breen, Richard 307
Jaffrelot, Christophe 36, 37, 172, 175, 287
Jal, Murzban 1, 12, 13, 27, 53, 55, 58, 60, 62, 66, 69, 188
Jameson, Frederic 45, 46, 47, 229
Jay, Martin 186
Jeenger, Kailash 305
Jha, Vivekananda 114
Jodhka, Surinder 234, 307

Kalotas 84
Kapoor, Shivani xiii, 8, 9
Karatani, Kojin 57
Kedia, Bineet 298
Keskiner, Elif 307
Khan, Badre Alam 304
Khare, R. S. 129
King, Helen Dean 4
King Jr. Martin Luther 40
knowledge: critical 279, 285, 311; ecology of 17, 18, 56, 62, 261;

emancipation 60; just 45; matrix of 23

Lacan, Jacques 203, 231
Laclau, Eernet & Mouffe, Chantal 301
liberty 17, 80, 88, 90, 173, 174, 184, 195, 197, 208–210
Lorde, Audre 64
Lorenzen, David 232
Lowe, Roy 3
Lumpen proletariat 30, 146, 206

MacKenzie, Donald 3, 70
madness 48, 66, 169, 170, 172, 174, 176, 178, 180, 182, 184, 232
Mahadevan, Kanchana 16, 55, 58, 67, 69, 240
Maitreye, Yogesh 288
Maldonado-Torres, Nelson 20, 23, 24, 69
Malone, Thomas & Bernstein, Michael 164
Manjrekar, Nandini 251
Marathi modernism 134, 147
Marcuse, Herbert 206
Mariategui, José Carlos 25
Markovits, Daniel 152
Marshall, J. 230
Marxism 18, 30, 135, 136, 140, 141, 142, 147, 176, 192, 282, 285
Marxists 32, 127, 175, 193, 279, 282, 300, 302, 303, 304, 306, 309, 311
Marx, Karl & Engels, Friedrich 33, 146, 239
Marx, Karl 27, 30, 31, 32, 86, 139, 144, 145, 146, 172, 175, 186, 195, 204, 205, 209, 220, 297, 299, 301
Mbembe, Achille 25
McCarthy, Cameron 2
Mehendale, Archana 242
Memmi, Albert 25
Menon, Dilip 208
Merit 21, 25, 66, 151, 152–162, 165–167, 218, 223, 226, 283, 286, 295, 298, 305
meritocracy 16, 21, 66, 122, 153–155, 164, 207
meritocratic 66, 152, 154, 161, 166
Mignolo, Walter 2, 11, 14, 20, 22, 26, 63

modern 2, 15, 21, 62, 95, 106, 108, 116, 121, 124, 129, 134–136, 139, 142, 146, 161, 172, 173, 175, 176, 178, 180–182, 184, 186, 189, 190, 192, 195, 196–200, 203, 207–210, 213, 214, 218, 221–223, 247, 261, 276, 283, 300, 302, 305; colonialist capitalist system 22, 23; empire 28; reason 48
modernity 8, 20, 28, 63, 116, 136, 161, 180, 186, 189, 199, 200, 203, 207, 218, 221, 305
Momentist 58
monumentalism 28, 44, 45
Moré, R. B. & Moré, Satyendra 141, 143, 148
Morgan, Thomas 5
Mosse, David 20, 42
Mouffe, Chantal 301
Moynihan, Daniel Patrick & Weaver, Suzanne 235
Mukherjee, Arun 265
Mukherjee, Ramkrishna 34
Murugkar, Lata 145
Muslim 49, 61, 107, 112, 169, 191–193, 203, 204, 207, 217, 220, 242, 248, 307–311, 313
Myrdal, Gunnar 1, 36, 38, 39

Naik, J. P. 204, 210, 218, 219, 226, 227, 234–238
Namishray, Mohan Dass 279, 287
Nandy, Ashis 238
Narayan, Badri 299
Narayan, Uma 262
National Congress 21, 82, 83, 145, 157, 192, 206, 225, 228, 279, 289
Natrajan, Balmurlil 18, 24, 32, 34, 42, 58
Nehru, Jawaharlal 16, 22, 131, 190, 193, 194, 204, 207, 208, 213, 214, 226, 227, 235, 277, 288
Nehruvian 203–210, 217, 222, 226
neo-fascism 175
neoliberal 8, 21, 22, 24, 175, 197; capital 231
New England Brahmins 162
Nietzsche, Friedrich 175, 181, 212
Nigam, Aditya 300, 305, 306
Nkrumah, Kwame 25, 64

Noddings, Nel 261, 262, 263, 264, 266
non-abyssal 58, 60, 61, 62
non-Brahminical 116, 241, 252, 274
non-canonical 241
non-derivative xv, 1, 2, 38, 56, 59, 62

Olssen, Mark & Peters, Michael 239
Omvedt, Gail 15, 17–19, 49, 58, 149, 236
oppressed 14, 19, 22, 30, 37, 41, 43, 44, 54, 67, 108, 153, 159, 203, 216, 224, 240, 241, 249, 251, 260, 286
oppressor 22, 25, 43, 108, 109, 249
Osborne, Henry 3
Osella, Filippo & Osella, Caroline 305
otherness 45, 46
outcaste 142

Paik, Shailaja 240
Pandey, Gyandera 287
Paraskeva, João, M. xiii, xiv, xv, 1, 8, 9, 20, 22, 27, 34, 35, 37, 38, 42, 54, 57, 64, 65, 264
Patels 84
Pathania, Gaurav & Kalyani, K. 57, 67, 69, 272
Pathania, Gaurav, J. 18, 20
Patnaik, Prabhat 222
Patwaris 84
Pawar, J. V. 287
Pawar, Urmila 248, 280, 287
Periyar, Erode Venkatappa Ramasamy 16–19, 156, 157, 274
Phule, Jyotirao Govindrao 15, 17–19, 156, 157, 274
Plato 2
Plebians 88, 89, 90
political 6, 8, 10, 11, 18, 20–22, 30, 38, 39, 44, 53, 59, 63, 65, 69, 87, 90, 105, 114, 115, 124, 125, 131, 134, 140–142, 144, 145, 148, 157, 172–176, 182, 184, 186, 187, 190, 191–193, 196, 199, 202–204, 207–210, 216, 218, 221, 222, 225, 230, 232, 234, 238, 239, 241, 245, 246, 249, 255, 257, 269, 274–277, 287, 299, 300–302, 308, 312–314; capital 4; economy 2, 13, 16, 29, 42, 59, 136, 176, 184, 196; power 86, 302; reason 230; reform 82, 83, 85,

88, 92; superstructure 300; theory 99, 172, 175
polluted 11, 119, 198
Poona Act 49, 50, 83, 150, 205, 206, 260
Popkewitz, Thomas 48, 55
Portuguese 98, 110, 153, 212
Proletariat 33, 91, 137, 197
Prosperous reason 14, 30, 48, 55, 64
puritanism 88
purity 4, 5, 9, 10, 35, 39, 42, 43, 64, 93, 94, 98, 100, 101, 104, 117–120, 121, 123, 130, 177, 184, 188, 195, 214, 216, 252

Quijano, Anibal 14, 20, 22, 25, 26, 63

race xiii–xvi, 1–10, 14, 20, 23, 25–28, 30–45, 47, 53–59, 63, 65, 67, 69, 71–81, 84, 91–93, 95, 100, 110–113, 134, 142, 147, 156, 173, 174, 177, 182, 183, 190, 195, 211, 213, 214, 231, 262, 270, 273, 277, 284, 287, 293
racism xv, 12, 39, 41, 47–49, 66, 109, 112, 173, 176, 188, 195, 198, 204, 213, 222, 275, 278, 284
radical co-presence 56, 59, 60
Rajputs 84, 93
Rancière, Jacques 38, 142
Rao, Anupama 25, 26, 30–33, 57, 62, 64, 133
Rawls, John 184
reform xiv, 13, 16, 46, 51–92, 106, 140, 156, 198, 205, 207, 222, 227, 230, 305; political 310; revolutionary 309; social 6, 65, 208, 274
Rege, Sharmila 67, 240, 249, 250, 265, 287
reservations 33, 34, 45, 67, 70, 118, 119, 128, 129, 157, 204, 206, 207, 223, 224, 252, 297–300, 310
Reversive epistemicide 27, 56
revolution 16, 28, 31, 70, 88, 91, 92, 145, 149, 154, 171, 172, 175, 186, 198, 199, 200, 203–206, 209, 210, 216, 218–220, 222, 226, 227, 229, 231, 234–239, 301, 305, 310
Reynolds, Alison & Lewis, David 167
Risley, Herbert 10, 37, 101, 190, 196, 213

Rodney, Walter 301
Rome 87, 88, 89, 107, 108
Roy, Arundhati 13, 21, 22, 26, 49, 56, 70

Samos, Sumit 200
Sampath, Rajesh 12, 26, 27, 31, 47, 48, 52, 58, 60, 63, 66, 66, 69, 169
Sanskritized 190
Santos, Boaventura de Sousa xiv, xv, xvi, 2, 8, 10, 11, 14–20, 26–28, 30, 32, 35, 37–39, 45, 48, 52–64, 69
Sathe, Annabhau 137, 143, 144
Satyashodh 137, 139
Scheduled Castes 11, 21, 25, 26, 140, 157, 159, 198, 199, 204, 242, 299
Schedule Tribes 204, 242, 244, 299
Seal, Anil 167
segregation xv, 2, 7, 10–13, 14, 18–21, 32, 33, 38, 40, 41, 46–49, 140, 148, 169, 176, 199, 200, 203, 204, 214, 218, 223, 241, 245, 264
Sekar, Bandyopadhyay 27
Selden, Steven xiv, xvi, 1, 4, 5
Senart, Émile 10, 37, 99, 101
Senghor, Leopold 25
sexuality 49, 63, 151, 174
Shukla, Priyam 234
slavery xiii, 6–7, 17, 20, 28, 30, 34, 35, 40, 41, 46, 47, 106–109, 150, 169, 176, 212, 222
Smith, James 6
socialism 20, 23, 91, 92, 219, 223, 227, 304
socialists 16, 82, 89, 90, 91, 92, 144, 148, 149
sociological 18, 56, 101, 114, 116, 119, 123, 131, 145, 173, 176, 185; absence 8; lab 58
Srinivas, M. N. 13, 17–19, 21, 33
state 4, 6, 21, 24, 63, 91, 112, 153, 162, 163, 172, 175, 176, 186, 190–192, 207, 210, 218, 223, 226, 231, 240, 243, 299, 304, 310, 314; ideological apparatuses 196, 197, 209; socialist 203, 304
Steele, Claude 160
Stroud, Scott 171, 253–255, 265
Śūdras 10
Sumner, Charles 6, 7, 38
Susen, Simon 265

Swamy, Praveen 232
Syamprasad, K.V. 13, 21, 23, 32, 67, 297, 299, 307

talent 25, 66, 151, 152, 154, 155, 158, 159, 164, 165, 166, 244, 247, 248, 307
Teltumbde, Anand 8, 11–15, 18, 19, 24–33, 40, 43, 52, 58, 60, 64, 65, 68, 69, 72, 98, 235, 238
testocracy 21, 153, 155, 156, 157, 158, 159, 164, 165, 166, 283
tests xiv, 4, 66, 151, 154, 157
theorycide 65
thingification 21
Tilak, J.B.G. 51, 83
translation 37; intercultural 52; theory of 38, 56, 58–60
tribal 24, 47, 160, 169, 213, 260; identities 104; wars 102

untouchable xv, 11–12, 15, 16, 17, 19–200, 25, 31, 35, 39, 41–43, 50, 56, 60, 62, 83–85, 94, 102, 105, 106, 108, 111, 112, 115, 116, 120, 121, 123–125, 127, 128–132, 177, 179, 181–183, 189, 203, 205, 211, 212, 217, 227, 231, 233, 235, 248, 252, 253, 257, 258, 274, 286, 309

Varghese, George 305
Varna 10, 11, 36, 48–50, 98–101, 104–106, 110, 127, 191, 216, 223, 252, 255
Velaskar, Padma 249, 266
violence 243, 244, 262, 280, 285
Visvanathan, Shiv 65
Von Humboldt, Wilhelm 201, 228

Wacquant, Loïc 1, 29, 45, 46, 47, 48, 52
Warner, Loyd & Davis, Allison 29
Warner, Loyd 1, 29, 36, 38
Weber, Max 13, 175, 220, 230, 301, 303
Weis, Lois 2
Western: intellectuals 35; modernity 20, 54; reason 14, 52
Western Eurocentric 8, 14, 62
Westernization 13
White xv, 3, 4, 7, 36, 38, 39, 40, 42–45, 54, 74, 81, 109, 112, 160,

173, 176, 189, 198, 222, 229, 279; reason 42, 44; supremacy 173, 176, 198
Wilkerson, Isabel xiii, xv, 1, 29, 34, 39, 40, 41, 45, 47, 52, 289
Williams, Chancellor 41
Williams, Raymond 228
Wright, Erik Olin 28, 30

Yengde, Suraj 18, 20, 21, 30, 42, 56, 65, 66, 69
Yengde, Suraj & Teltumbde, Anand 52
Young, Michael 152, 153, 154, 155

Zachariah, Benjamin 237
Zhopadi 145
Zhou, Min 307
Žižek, Slavoj 19, 45, 203, 220

9780367725105